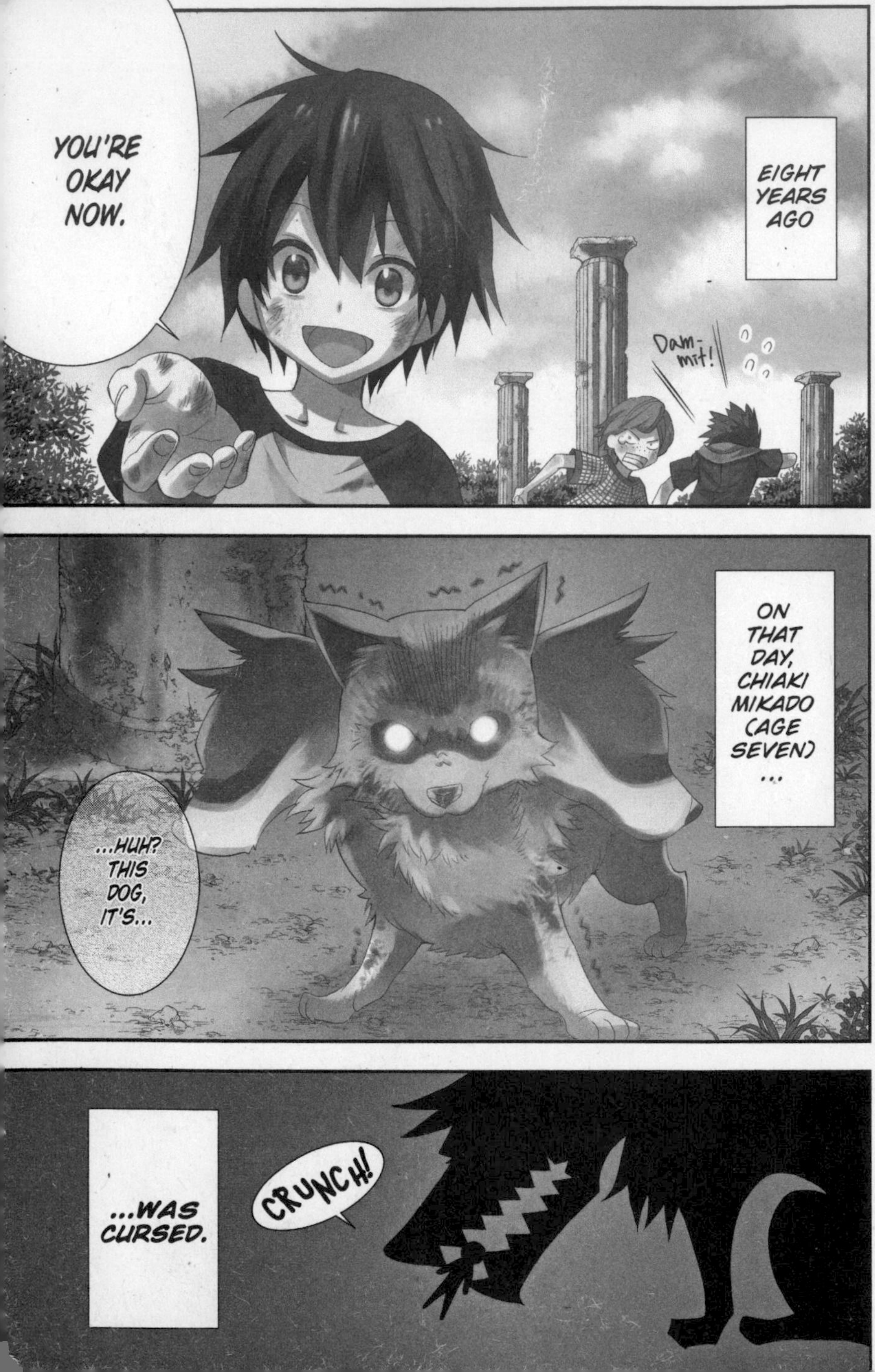
EIGHT YEARS AGO
Dam-mit!
YOU'RE OKAY NOW.
ON THAT DAY, CHIAKI MIKADO (AGE SEVEN)...
...HUH? THIS DOG, IT'S...
CRUNCH!
...WAS CURSED.

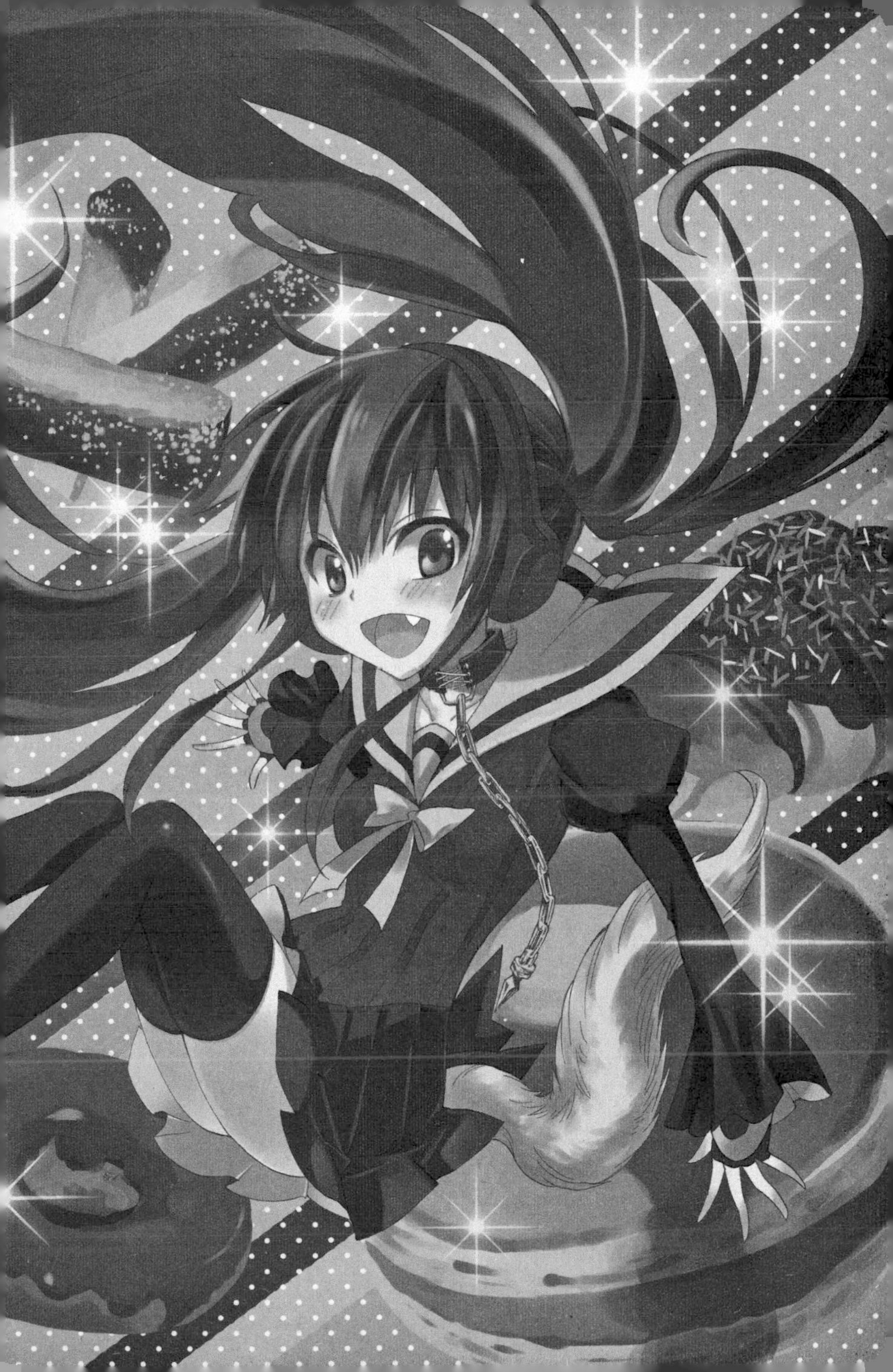

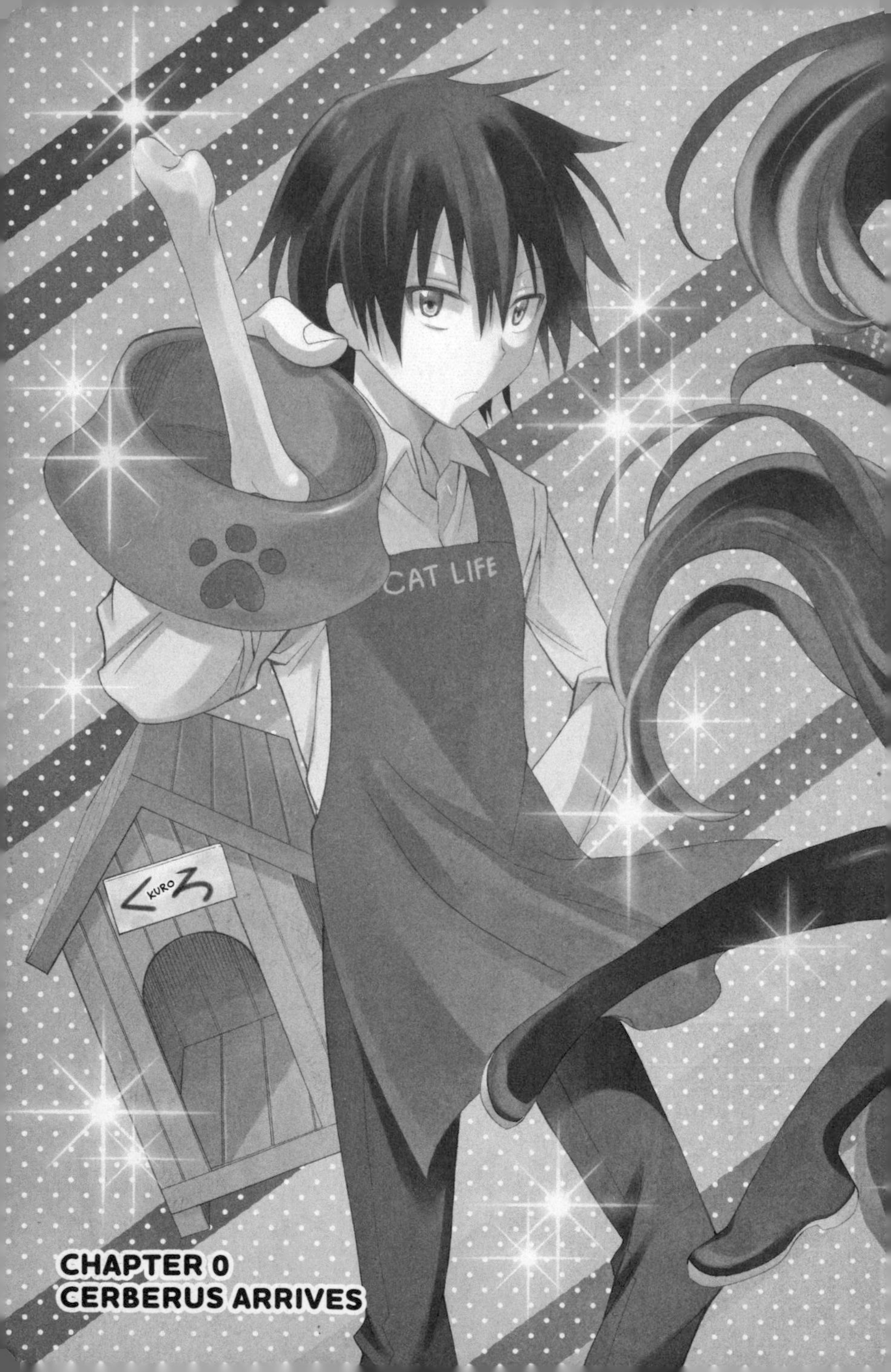
CAT LIFE
くKUROろ
CHAPTER 0
CERBERUS ARRIVES

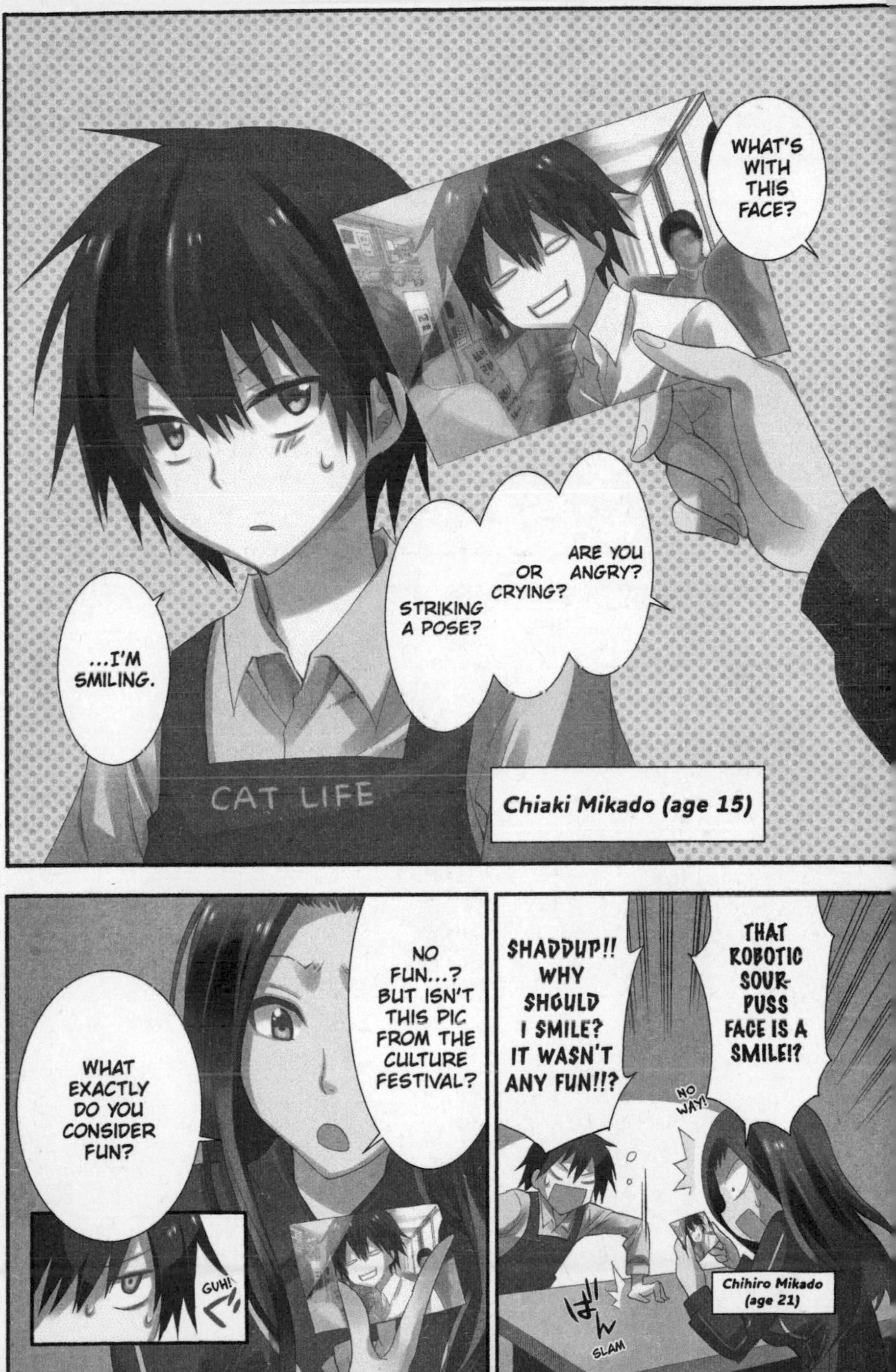
WHAT'S WITH THIS FACE?
ARE YOU ANGRY? OR CRYING? STRIKING A POSE?
...I'M SMILING.
Chiaki Mikado (age 15)
THAT ROBOTIC SOUR-PUSS FACE IS A SMILE!?
NO WAY!
SHADDUP!! WHY SHOULD I SMILE? IT WASN'T ANY FUN!!?
Chihiro Mikado (age 21)
SLAM
NO FUN...? BUT ISN'T THIS PIC FROM THE CULTURE FESTIVAL?
WHAT EXACTLY DO YOU CONSIDER FUN?
GUH!

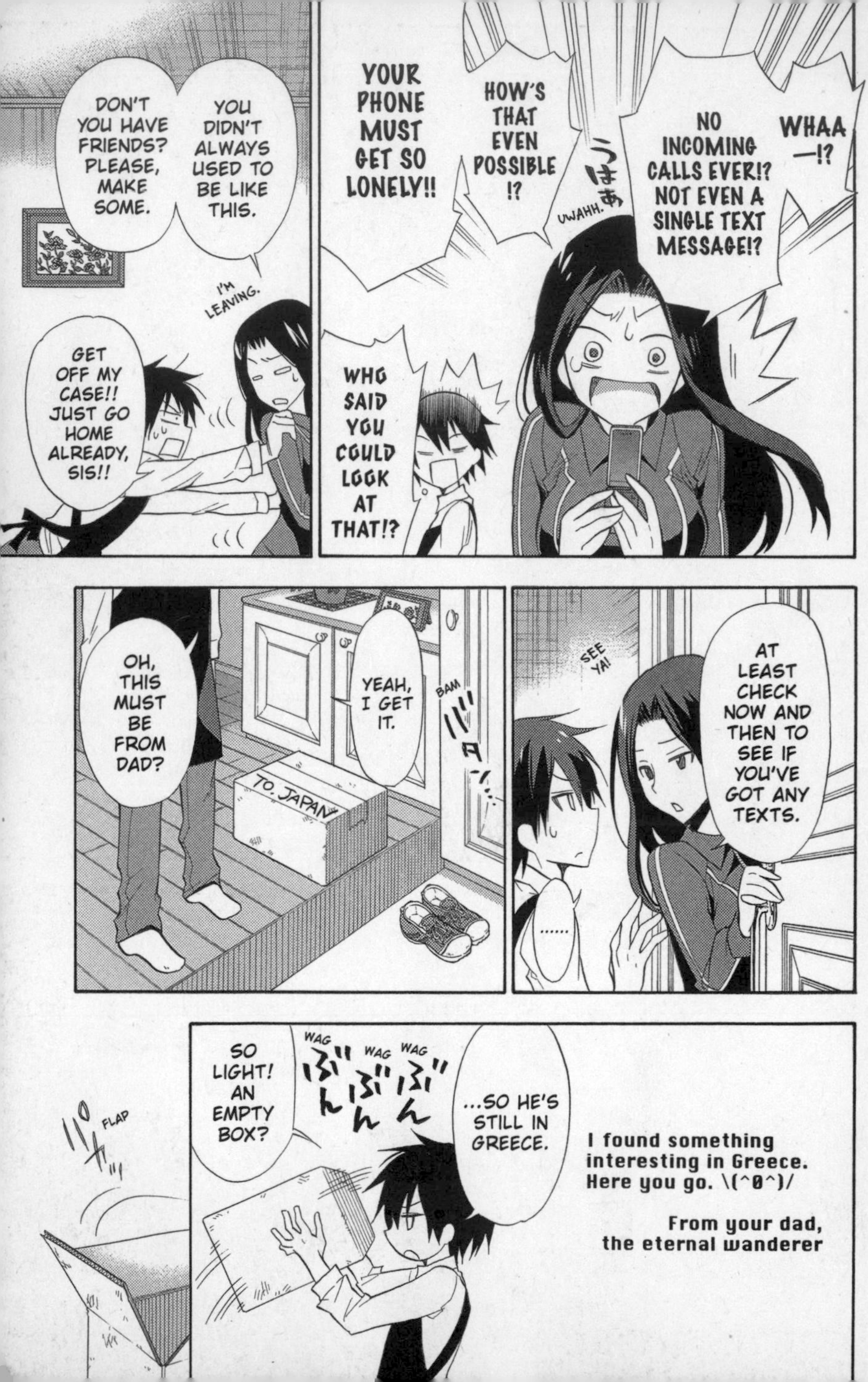
WHAA—!?
NO INCOMING CALLS EVER!? NOT EVEN A SINGLE TEXT MESSAGE!?
うはぁ
UWAHH.
HOW'S THAT EVEN POSSIBLE!?
YOUR PHONE MUST GET SO LONELY!!
WHO SAID YOU COULD LOOK AT THAT!?
YOU DIDN'T ALWAYS USED TO BE LIKE THIS.
DON'T YOU HAVE FRIENDS? PLEASE, MAKE SOME.
I'M LEAVING.
GET OFF MY CASE!! JUST GO HOME ALREADY, SIS!!
AT LEAST CHECK NOW AND THEN TO SEE IF YOU'VE GOT ANY TEXTS.
SEE YA!
......
BAM
バタン
YEAH, I GET IT.
OH, THIS MUST BE FROM DAD?
TO: JAPAN
I found something interesting in Greece. Here you go. \(^0^)/
From your dad, the eternal wanderer
...SO HE'S STILL IN GREECE.
ぶんぶんぶん
WAG WAG WAG
SO LIGHT! AN EMPTY BOX?
パカ
FLAP

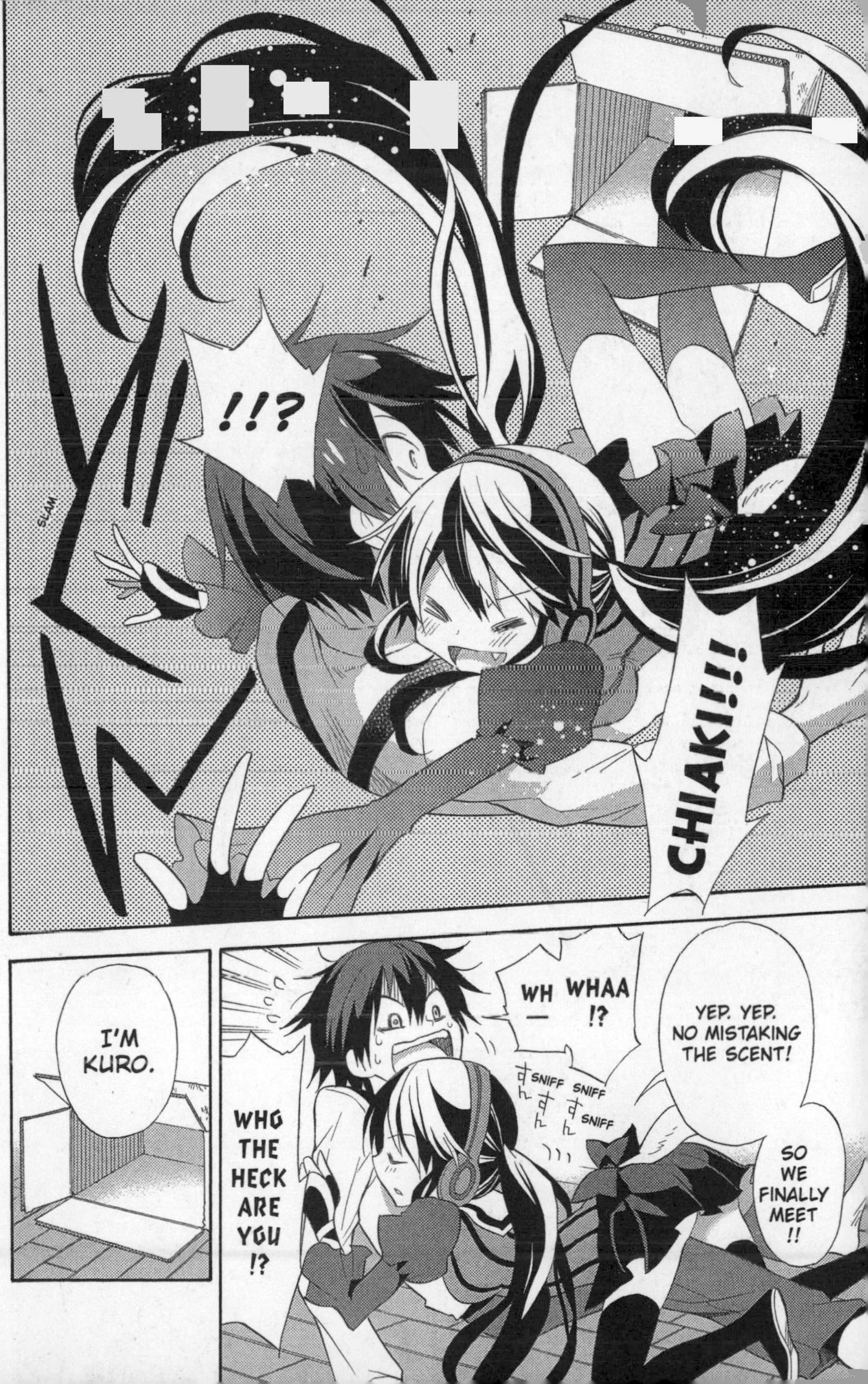
CHIAKI!!!!
SLAM
!!?
YEP. YEP. NO MISTAKING THE SCENT!
WH— WHAA!?
すんすん SNIFF SNIFF
すん SNIFF
SO WE FINALLY MEET!!
WHO THE HECK ARE YOU!?
I'M KURO.

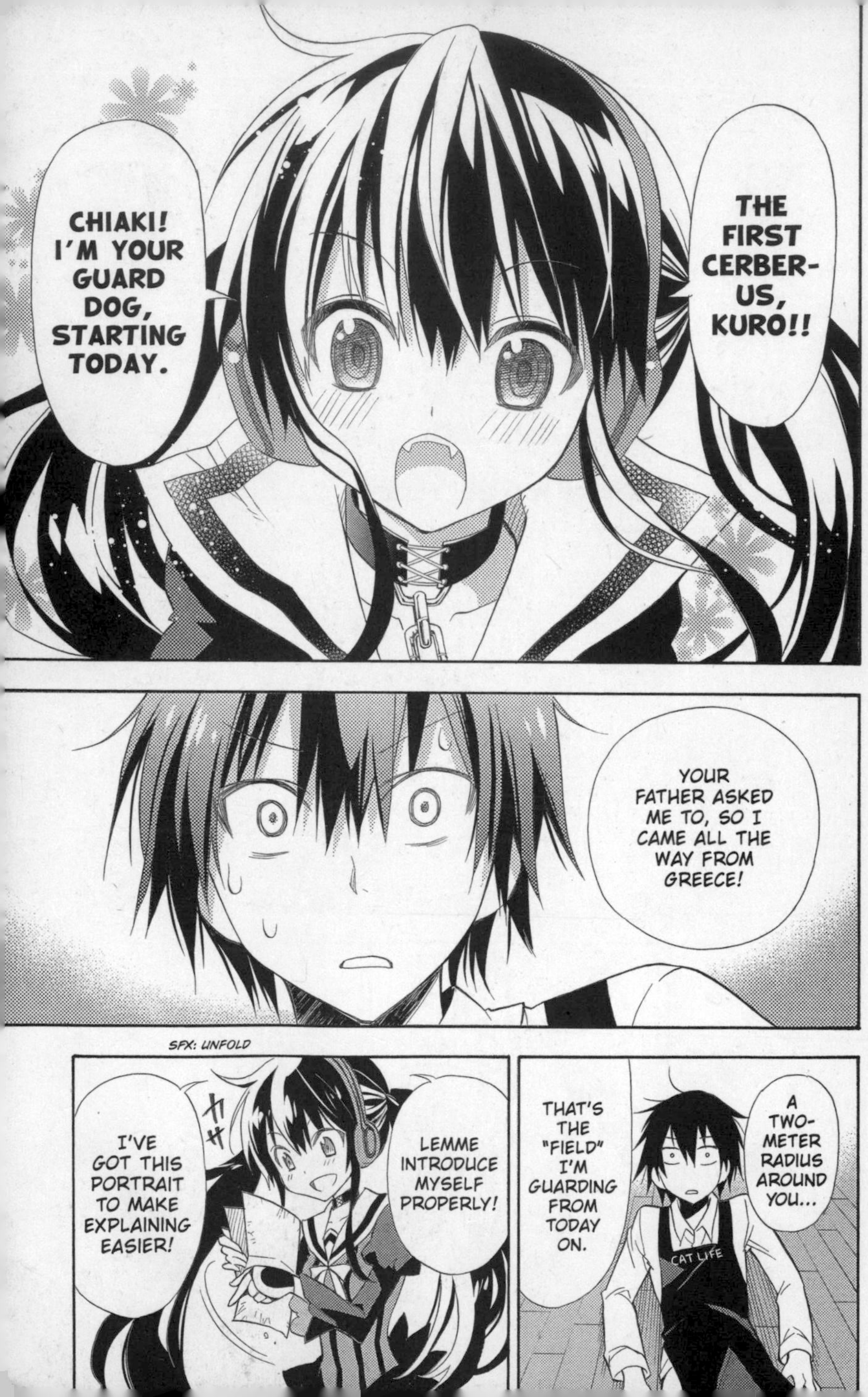
THE FIRST CERBER-US, KURO!!
CHIAKI! I'M YOUR GUARD DOG, STARTING TODAY.
YOUR FATHER ASKED ME TO, SO I CAME ALL THE WAY FROM GREECE!
A TWO-METER RADIUS AROUND YOU...
THAT'S THE "FIELD" I'M GUARDING FROM TODAY ON.
CAT LIFE
SFX: UNFOLD
LEMME INTRODUCE MYSELF PROPERLY!
I'VE GOT THIS PORTRAIT TO MAKE EXPLAINING EASIER!

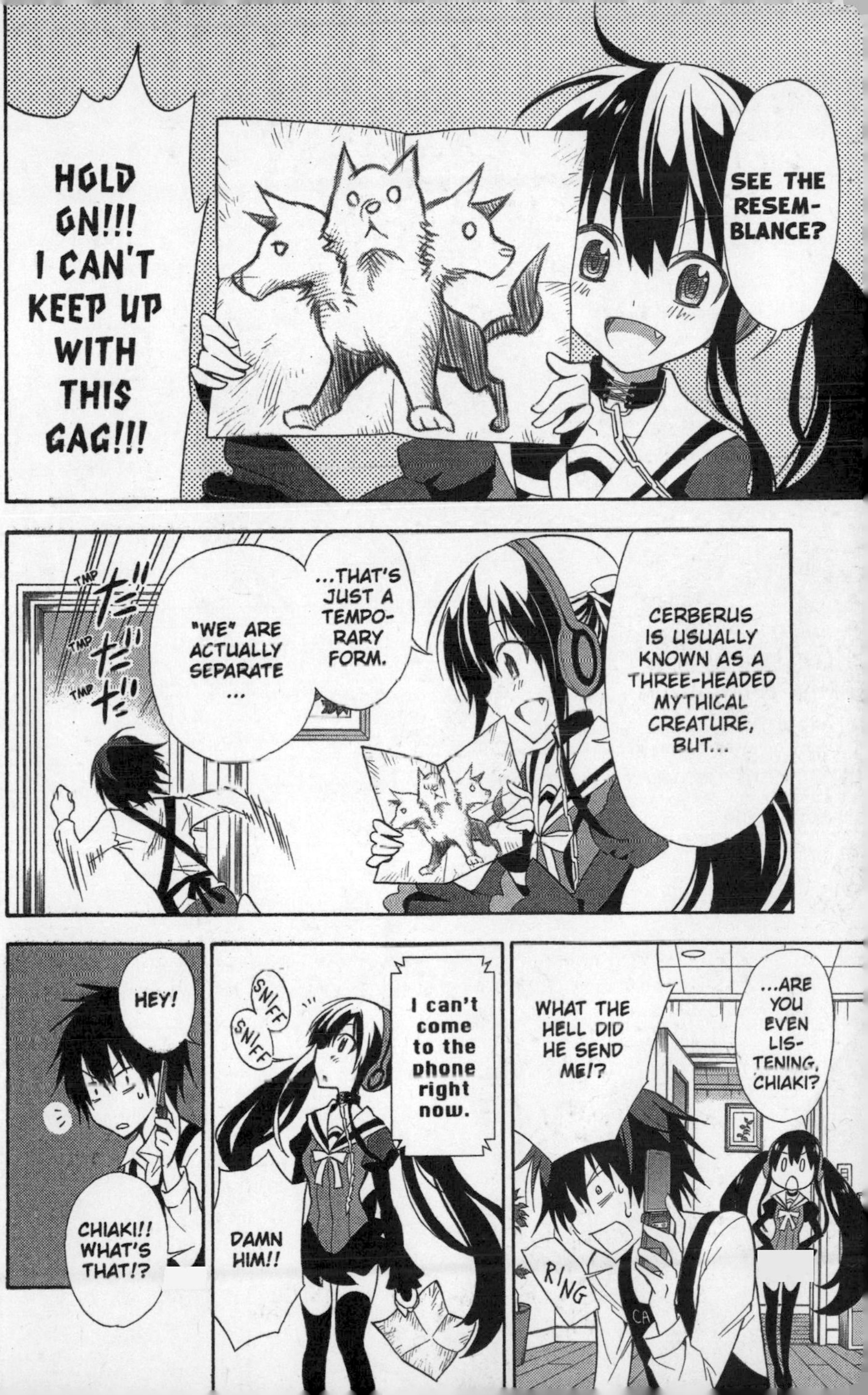
SEE THE RESEM-BLANCE?
HOLD ON!!! I CAN'T KEEP UP WITH THIS GAG!!!
CERBERUS IS USUALLY KNOWN AS A THREE-HEADED MYTHICAL CREATURE, BUT...
...THAT'S JUST A TEMPORARY FORM.
"WE" ARE ACTUALLY SEPARATE ...
TMP
TMP
TMP
...ARE YOU EVEN LIS-TENING, CHIAKI?
WHAT THE HELL DID HE SEND ME!?
RING
I can't come to the phone right now.
SNIFF
SNIFF
DAMN HIM!!
HEY!
CHIAKI!! WHAT'S THAT!?

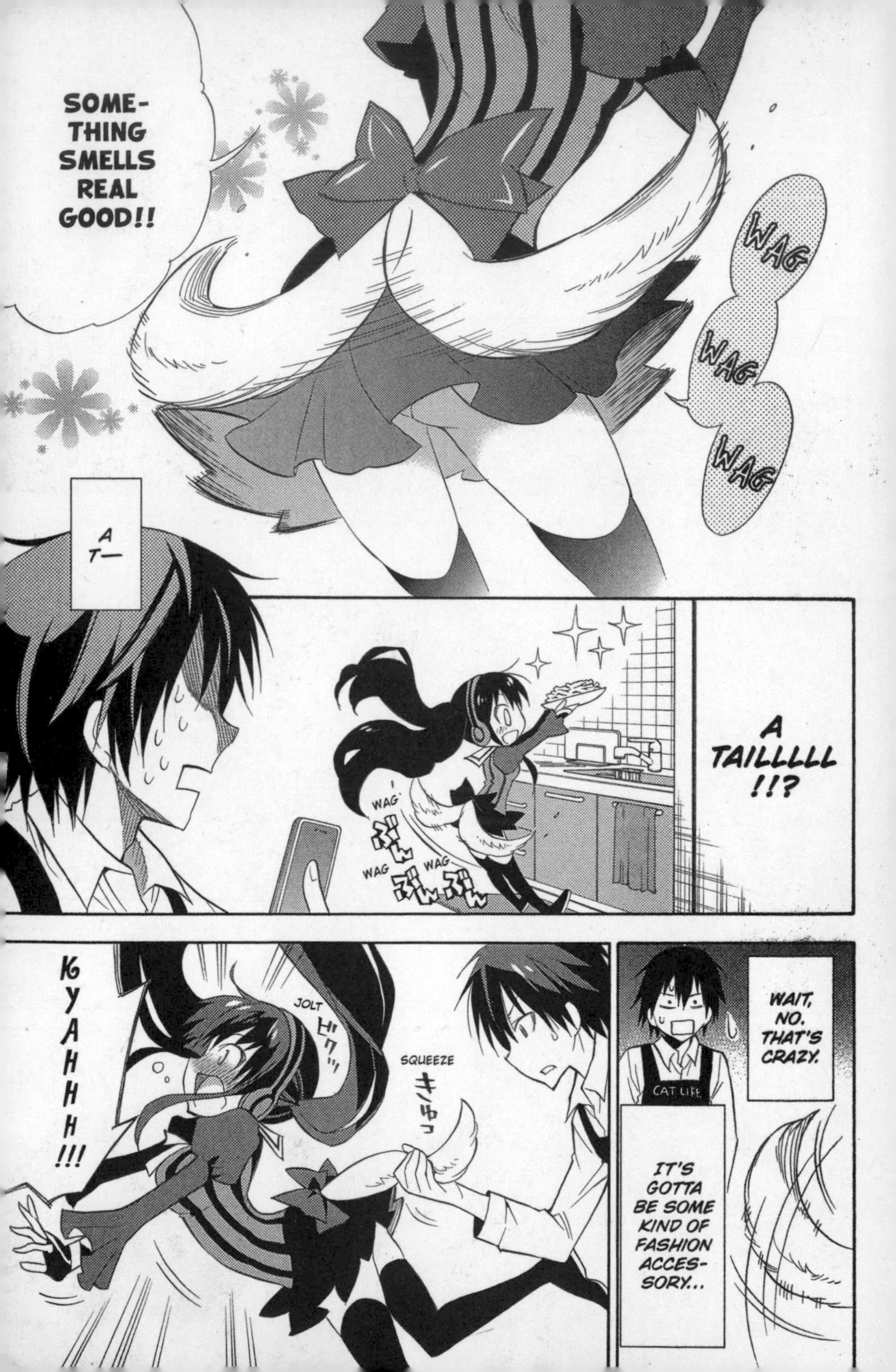
SOME-THING SMELLS REAL GOOD!!
WAG
WAG
WAG
A T—
A TAILLLLLL!!?
WAG
ぶん
WAG
ぶん
WAG
ぶん
WAIT, NO. THAT'S CRAZY.
CAT LIFE
IT'S GOTTA BE SOME KIND OF FASHION ACCES-SORY...
SQUEEZE
キュッ
JOLT
ビクッ
KYAHHHH!!!

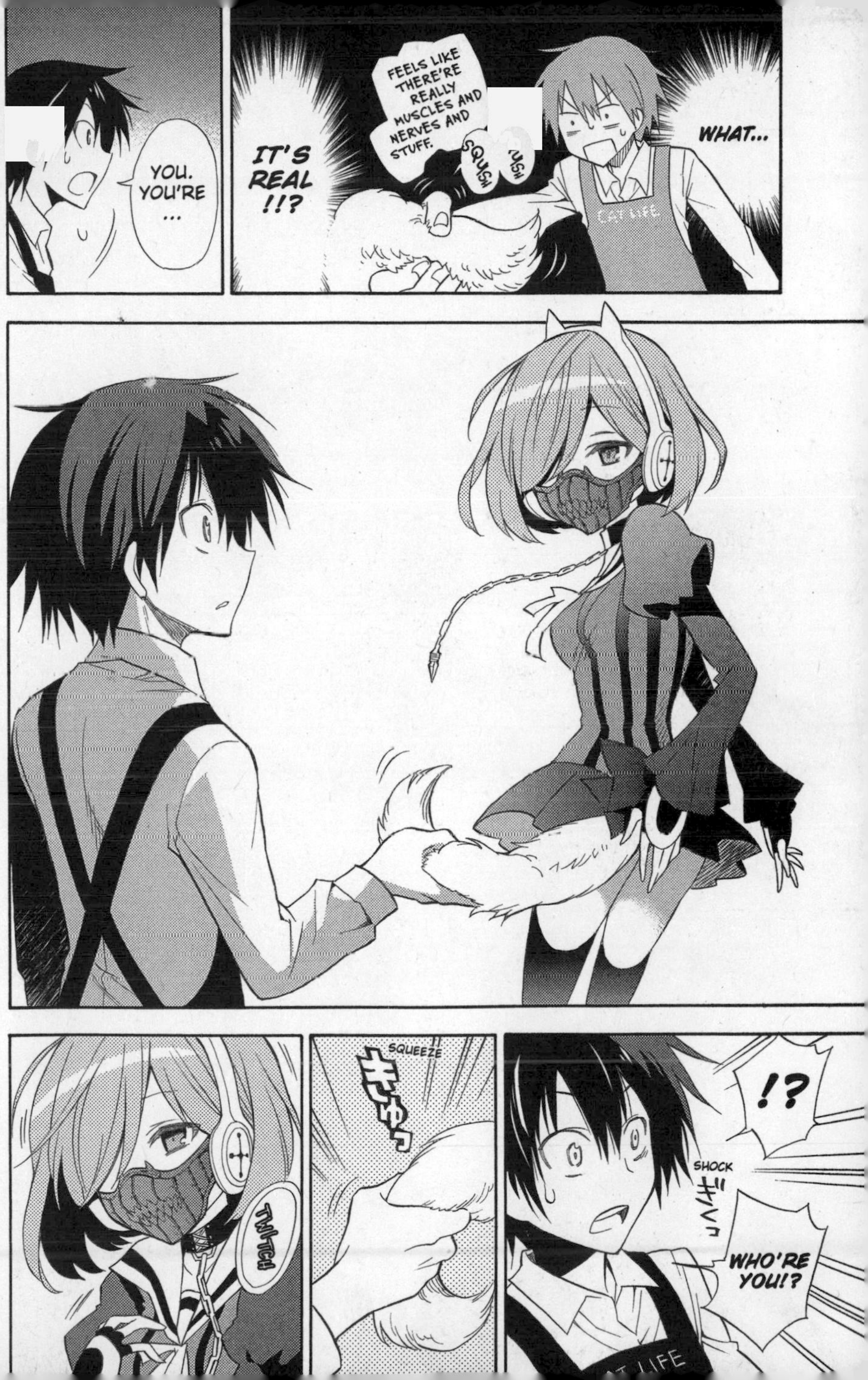
WHAT...
FEELS LIKE THERE'RE REALLY MUSCLES AND NERVES AND STUFF.
SQUISH
IT'S REAL !!?
YOU. YOU'RE ...
!?
SHOCK
WHO'RE YOU!?
SQUEEZE
TWITCH

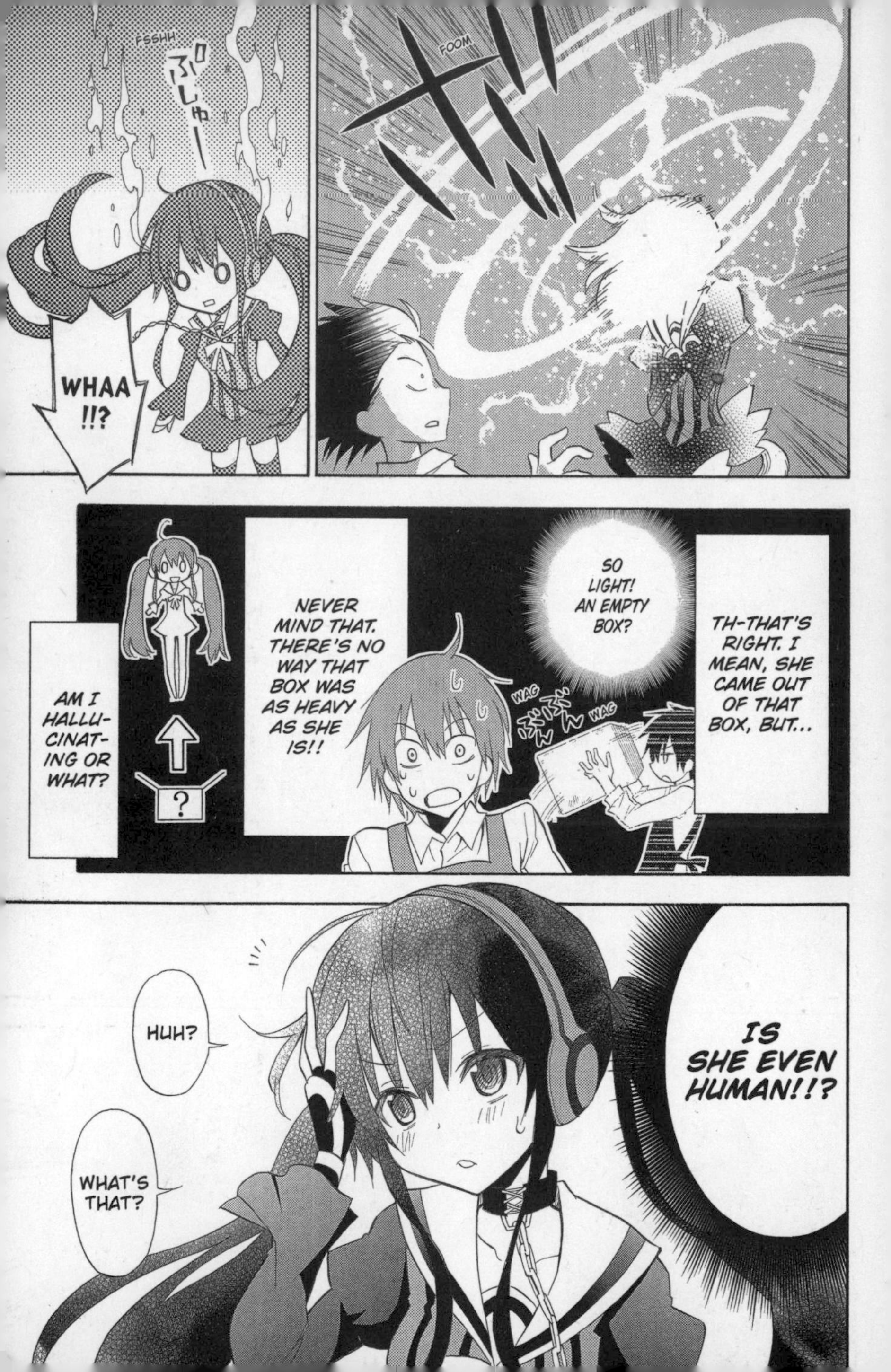
FOOM
FSSHH
ぷしゅー
WHAA!!?
TH-THAT'S RIGHT. I MEAN, SHE CAME OUT OF THAT BOX, BUT...
SO LIGHT! AN EMPTY BOX?
WAG
ぶんぶん
WAG
NEVER MIND THAT. THERE'S NO WAY THAT BOX WAS AS HEAVY AS SHE IS!!
?
AM I HALLUCINATING OR WHAT?
IS SHE EVEN HUMAN!!?
HUH?
WHAT'S THAT?

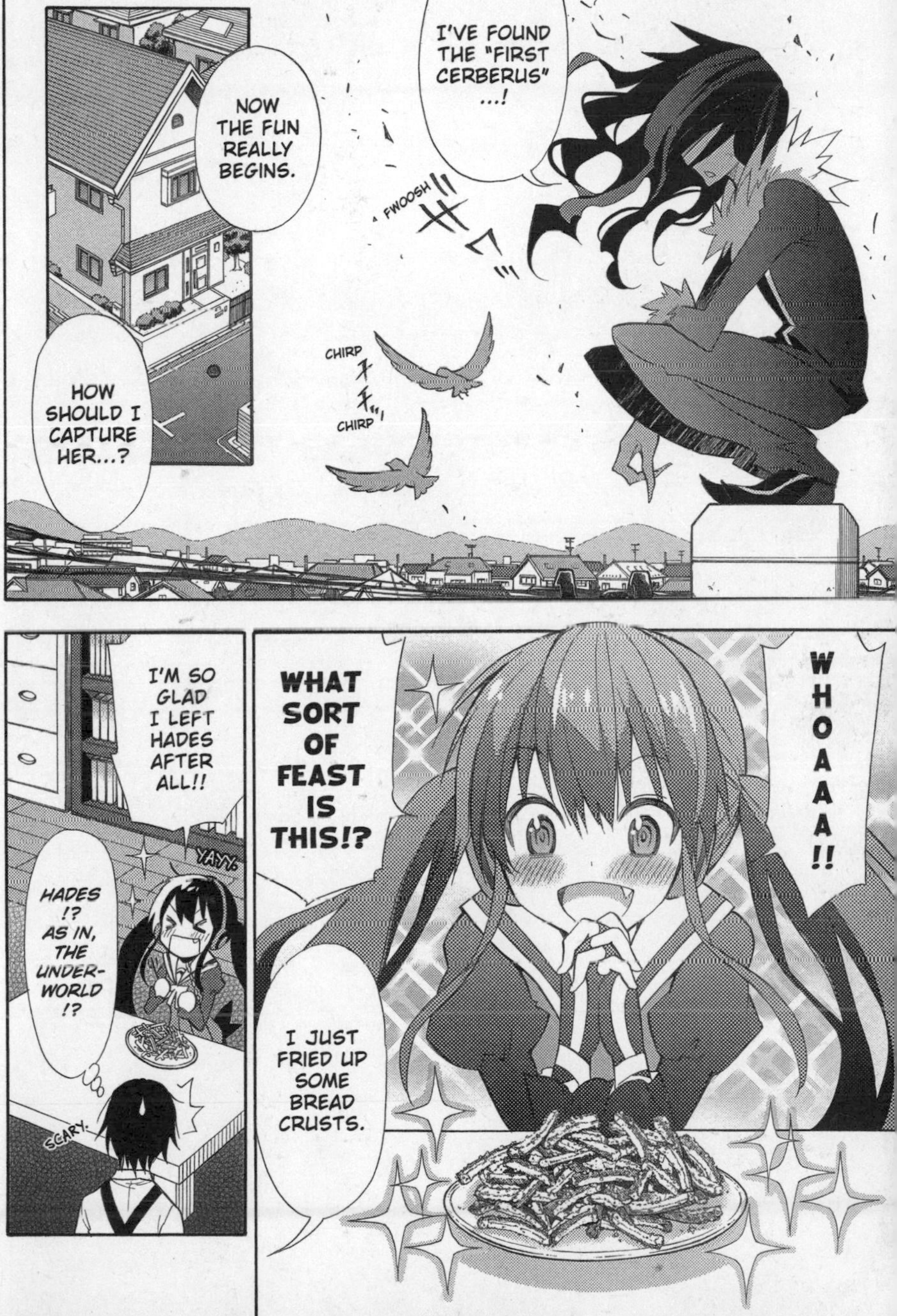

I'VE FOUND THE "FIRST CERBERUS" ...!
FWOOSH
CHIRP
CHIRP
NOW THE FUN REALLY BEGINS.
HOW SHOULD I CAPTURE HER...?
WHOAAA!!
WHAT SORT OF FEAST IS THIS!?
I JUST FRIED UP SOME BREAD CRUSTS.
I'M SO GLAD I LEFT HADES AFTER ALL!!
YAYY.
HADES!? AS IN, THE UNDER-WORLD!?
SCARY.

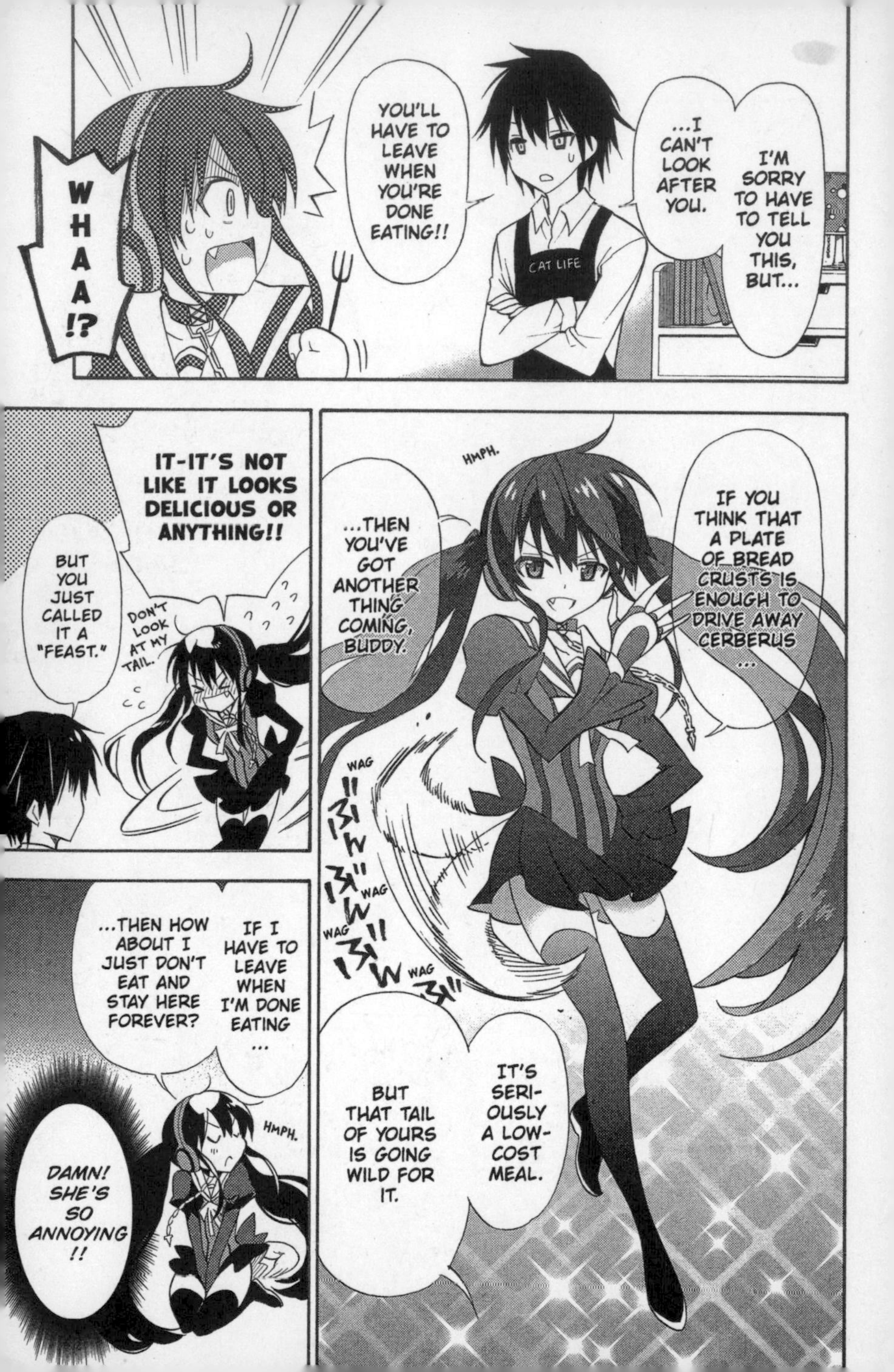

I'M SORRY TO HAVE TO TELL YOU THIS, BUT...
...I CAN'T LOOK AFTER YOU.
CAT LIFE
YOU'LL HAVE TO LEAVE WHEN YOU'RE DONE EATING!!
WHAA!?
HMPH.
IF YOU THINK THAT A PLATE OF BREAD CRUSTS IS ENOUGH TO DRIVE AWAY CERBERUS...
...THEN YOU'VE GOT ANOTHER THING COMING, BUDDY.
WAG
WAG
WAG
WAG
IT'S SERIOUSLY A LOW-COST MEAL.
BUT THAT TAIL OF YOURS IS GOING WILD FOR IT.
IT-IT'S NOT LIKE IT LOOKS DELICIOUS OR ANYTHING!!
DON'T LOOK AT MY TAIL.
BUT YOU JUST CALLED IT A "FEAST."
IF I HAVE TO LEAVE WHEN I'M DONE EATING...
...THEN HOW ABOUT I JUST DON'T EAT AND STAY HERE FOREVER?
HMPH.
DAMN! SHE'S SO ANNOYING!!

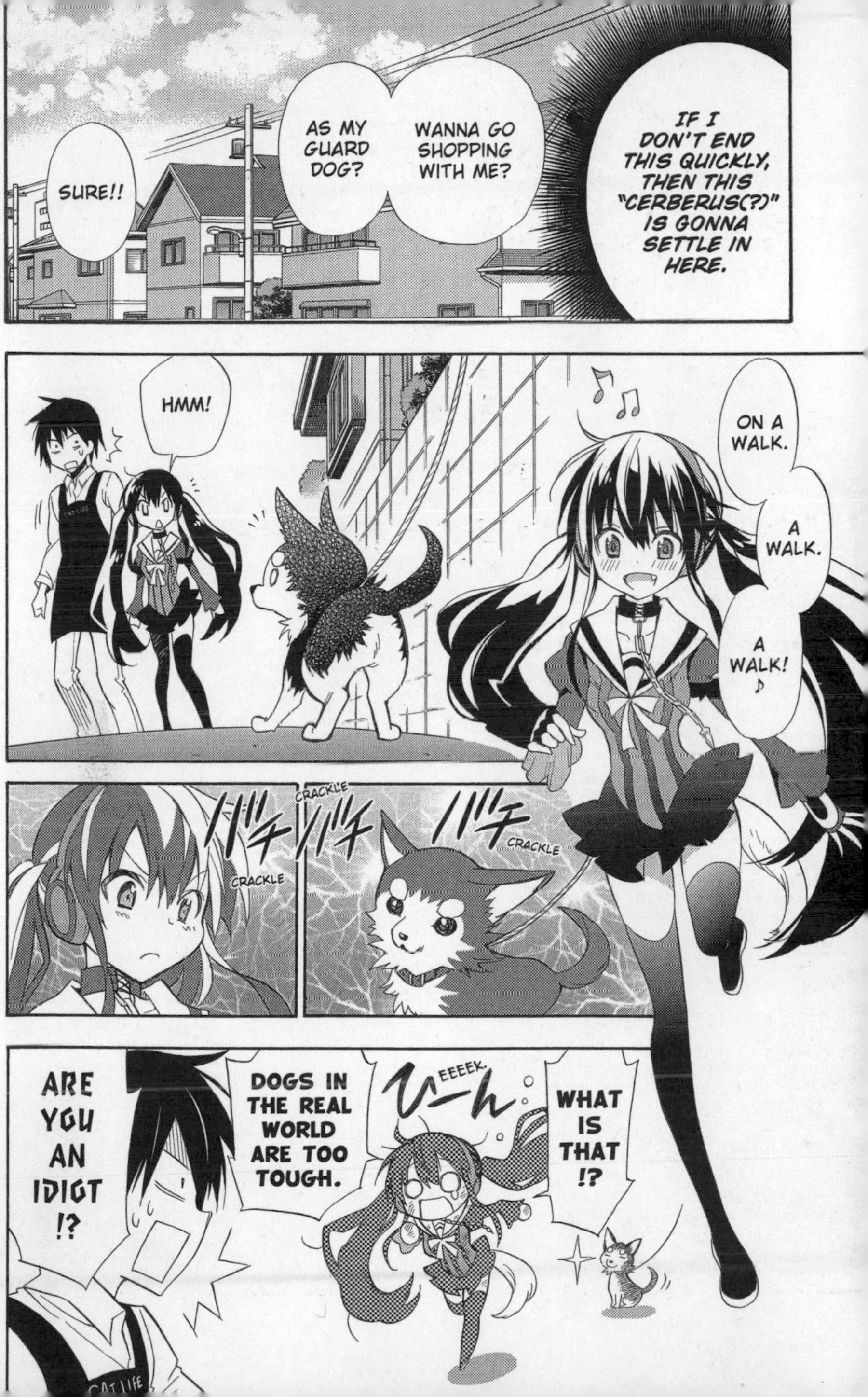
IF I DON'T END THIS QUICKLY, THEN THIS "CERBERUS(?)" IS GONNA SETTLE IN HERE.
WANNA GO SHOPPING WITH ME?
AS MY GUARD DOG?
SURE!!
♪ ♫
ON A WALK.
A WALK.
A WALK! ♪
HMM!
バチ
CRACKLE
バチ
CRACKLE
バチ
CRACKLE
WHAT IS THAT!?
ひーん
EEEEK.
DOGS IN THE REAL WORLD ARE TOO TOUGH.
ARE YOU AN IDIOT!?
CAT LIFE

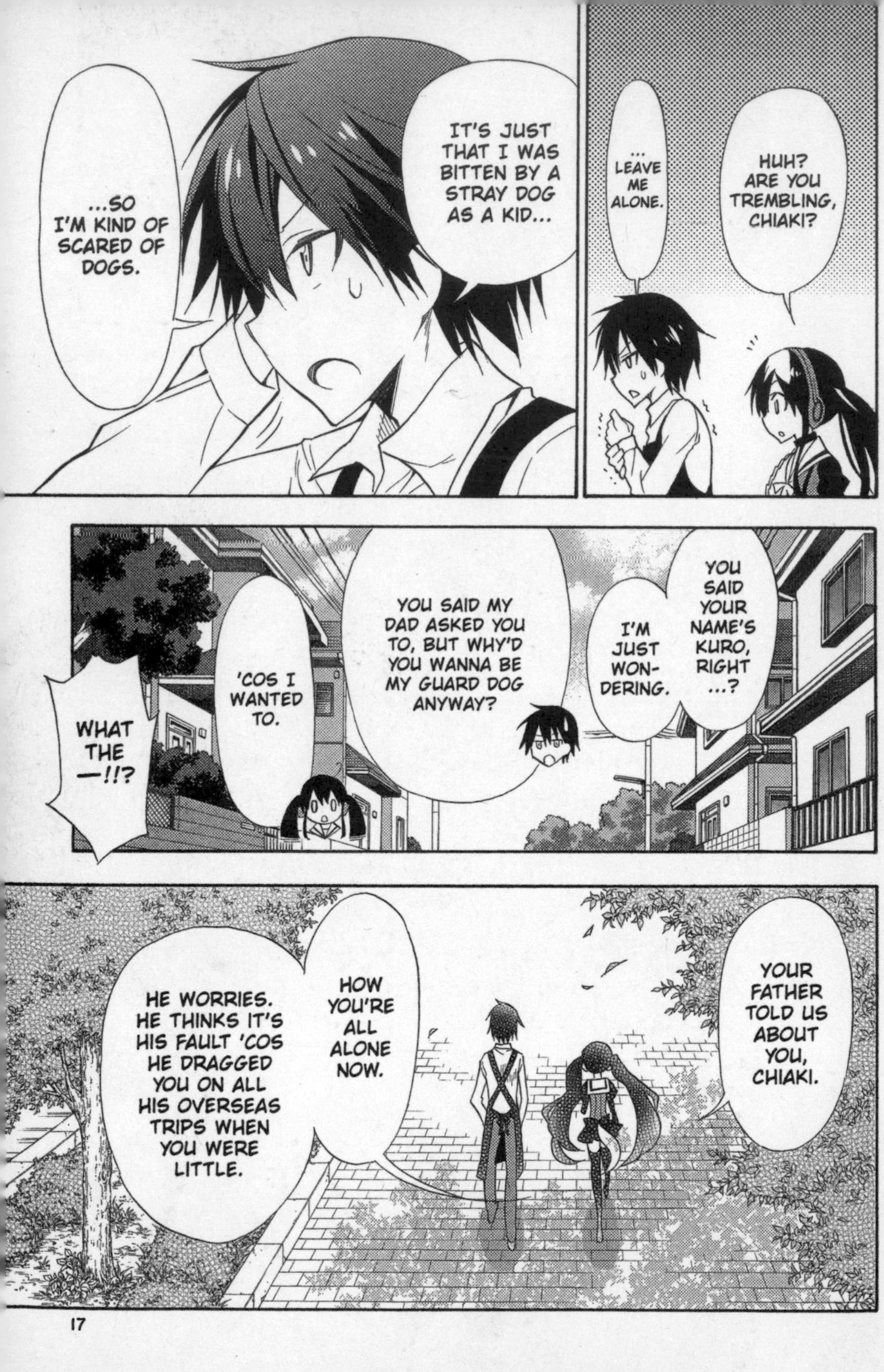
HUH? ARE YOU TREMBLING, CHIAKI?
... LEAVE ME ALONE.
IT'S JUST THAT I WAS BITTEN BY A STRAY DOG AS A KID...
...SO I'M KIND OF SCARED OF DOGS.
YOU SAID YOUR NAME'S KURO, RIGHT ...?
I'M JUST WON-DERING.
YOU SAID MY DAD ASKED YOU TO, BUT WHY'D YOU WANNA BE MY GUARD DOG ANYWAY?
'COS I WANTED TO.
WHAT THE—!!?
YOUR FATHER TOLD US ABOUT YOU, CHIAKI.
HOW YOU'RE ALL ALONE NOW.
HE WORRIES. HE THINKS IT'S HIS FAULT 'COS HE DRAGGED YOU ON ALL HIS OVERSEAS TRIPS WHEN YOU WERE LITTLE.

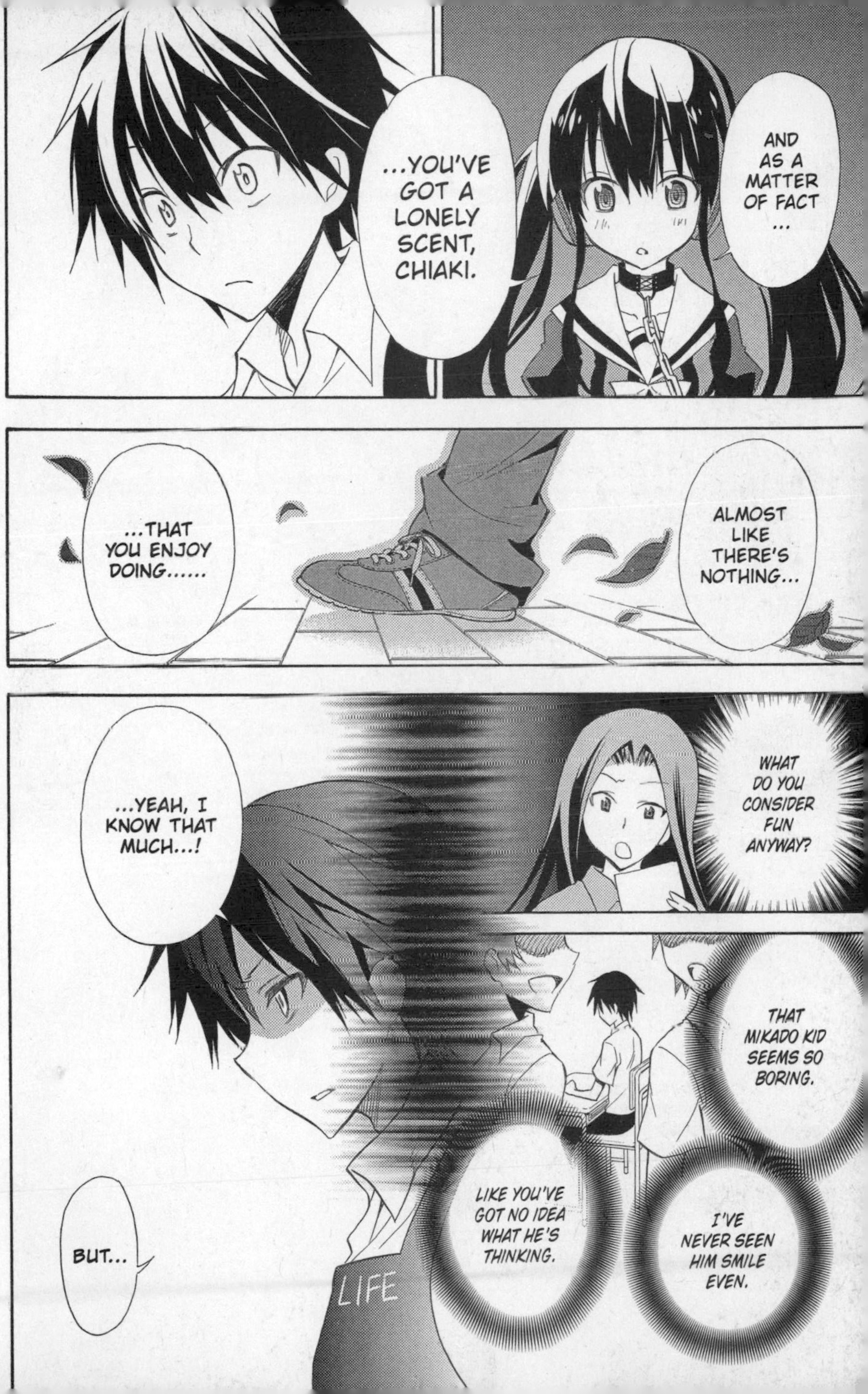
AND AS A MATTER OF FACT...
...YOU'VE GOT A LONELY SCENT, CHIAKI.
ALMOST LIKE THERE'S NOTHING...
...THAT YOU ENJOY DOING......
WHAT DO YOU CONSIDER FUN ANYWAY?
THAT MIKADO KID SEEMS SO BORING.
I'VE NEVER SEEN HIM SMILE EVEN.
LIKE YOU'VE GOT NO IDEA WHAT HE'S THINKING.
...YEAH, I KNOW THAT MUCH...!
BUT...
LIFE

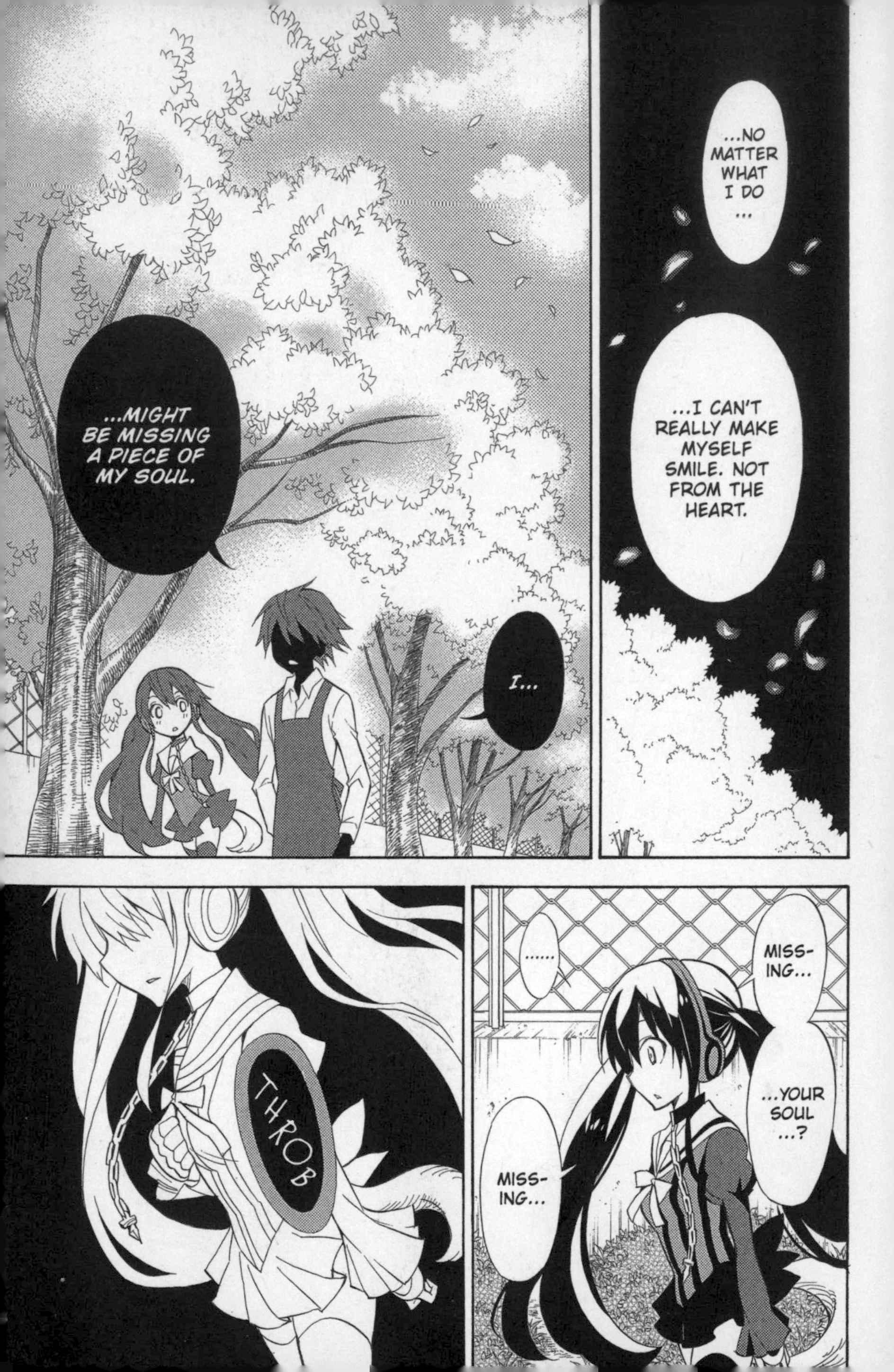
...NO MATTER WHAT I DO ...
...I CAN'T REALLY MAKE MYSELF SMILE. NOT FROM THE HEART.
I...
...MIGHT BE MISSING A PIECE OF MY SOUL.
MISS-ING...
...YOUR SOUL ...?
......
MISS-ING...
THROB

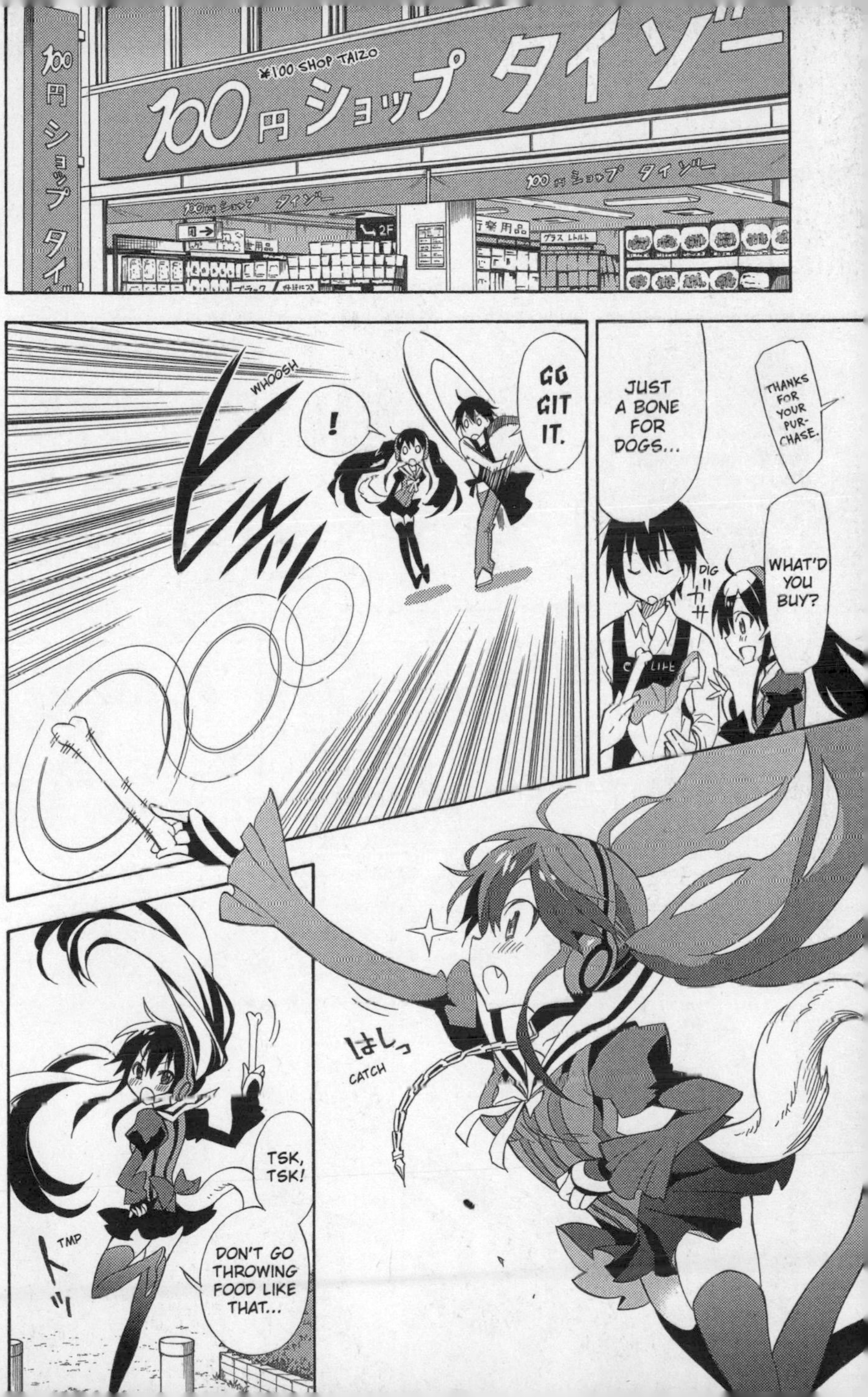

¥100 SHOP TAIZO
100円ショップ タイゾー
THANKS FOR YOUR PUR-CHASE.
WHAT'D YOU BUY?
DIG
JUST A BONE FOR DOGS...
GO GIT IT.
!
WHOOSH
はしっ
CATCH
TSK, TSK!
DON'T GO THROWING FOOD LIKE THAT...
TMP

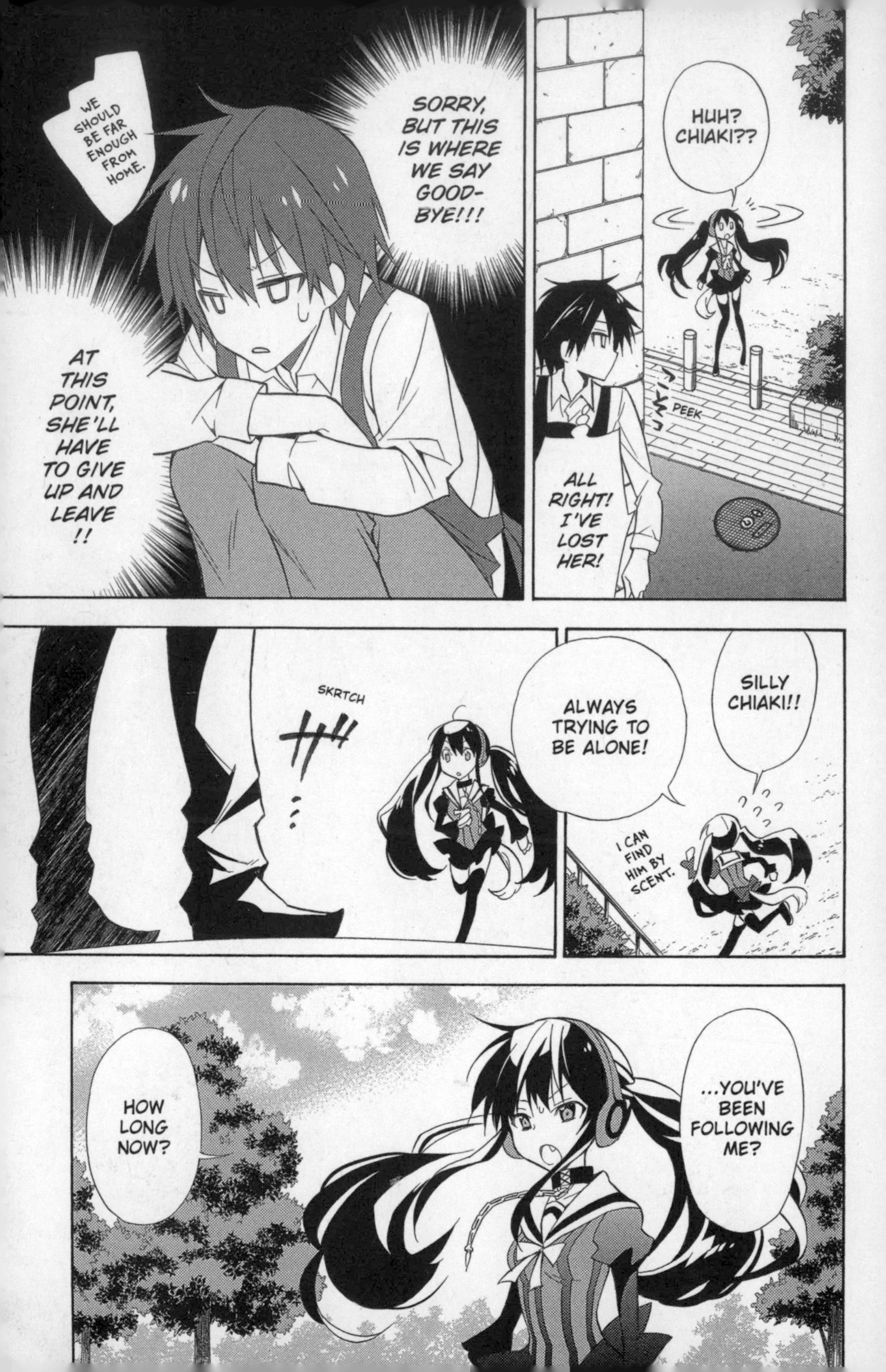
HUH? CHIAKI??
PEEK
ALL RIGHT! I'VE LOST HER!
WE SHOULD BE FAR ENOUGH FROM HOME.
SORRY, BUT THIS IS WHERE WE SAY GOOD-BYE!!!
AT THIS POINT, SHE'LL HAVE TO GIVE UP AND LEAVE!!
SILLY CHIAKI!!
I CAN FIND HIM BY SCENT.
ALWAYS TRYING TO BE ALONE!
SKRTCH
...YOU'VE BEEN FOLLOWING ME?
HOW LONG NOW?

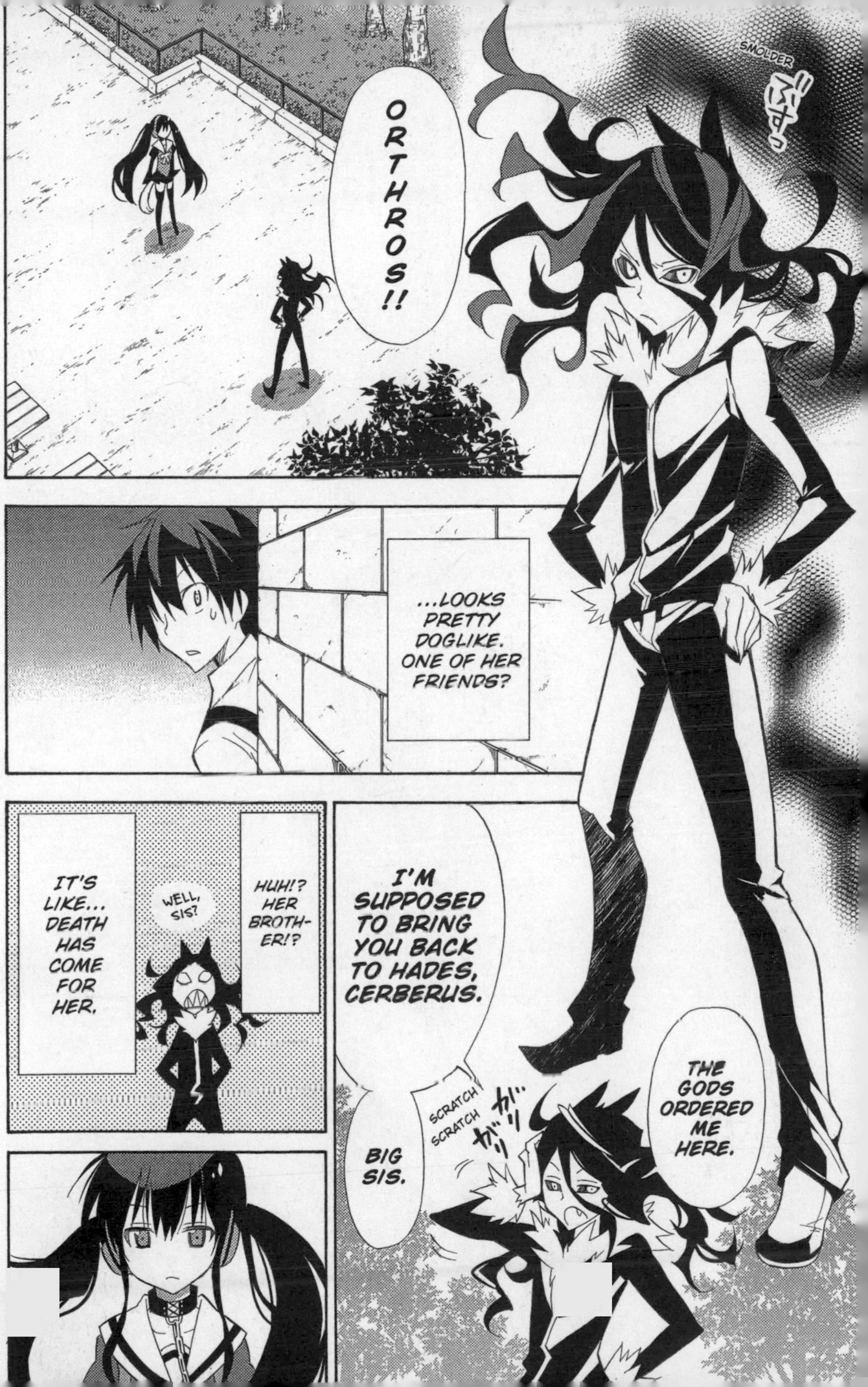

SMOLDER
ぶすっ
ORTHROS!!
...LOOKS PRETTY DOGLIKE. ONE OF HER FRIENDS?
THE GODS ORDERED ME HERE.
I'M SUPPOSED TO BRING YOU BACK TO HADES, CERBERUS.
SCRATCH SCRATCH
BIG SIS.
HUH!? HER BROTHER!?
WELL, SIS?
IT'S LIKE... DEATH HAS COME FOR HER.

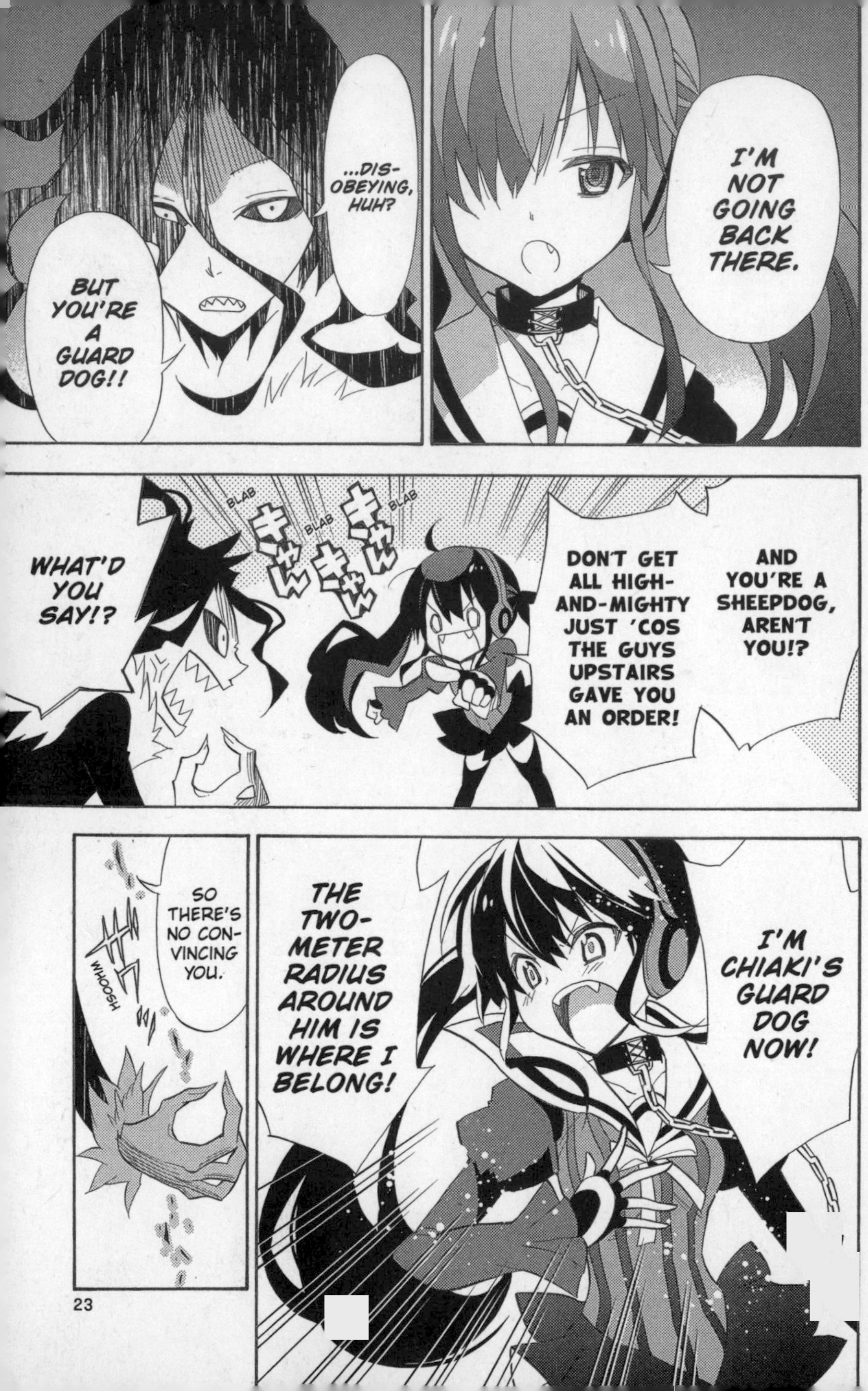
I'M NOT GOING BACK THERE.
...DIS-OBEYING, HUH?
BUT YOU'RE A GUARD DOG!!
AND YOU'RE A SHEEPDOG, AREN'T YOU!?
DON'T GET ALL HIGH-AND-MIGHTY JUST 'COS THE GUYS UPSTAIRS GAVE YOU AN ORDER!
BLAB
BLAB
BLAB
WHAT'D YOU SAY!?
I'M CHIAKI'S GUARD DOG NOW!
THE TWO-METER RADIUS AROUND HIM IS WHERE I BELONG!
SO THERE'S NO CON-VINCING YOU.
WHOOSH

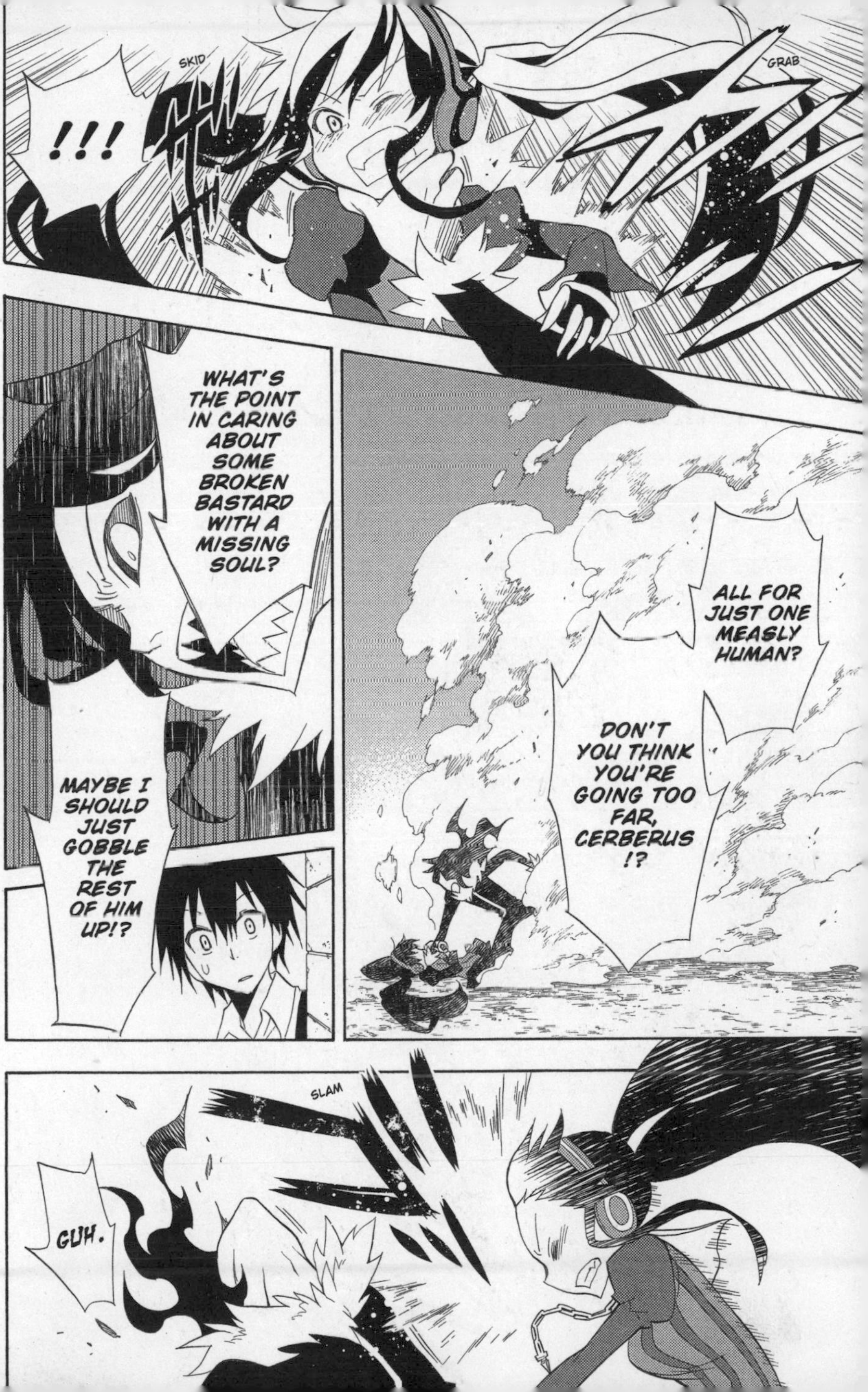
GRAB
SKID
!!!
ALL FOR JUST ONE MEASLY HUMAN?
DON'T YOU THINK YOU'RE GOING TOO FAR, CERBERUS!?
WHAT'S THE POINT IN CARING ABOUT SOME BROKEN BASTARD WITH A MISSING SOUL?
MAYBE I SHOULD JUST GOBBLE THE REST OF HIM UP!?
SLAM
GUH.

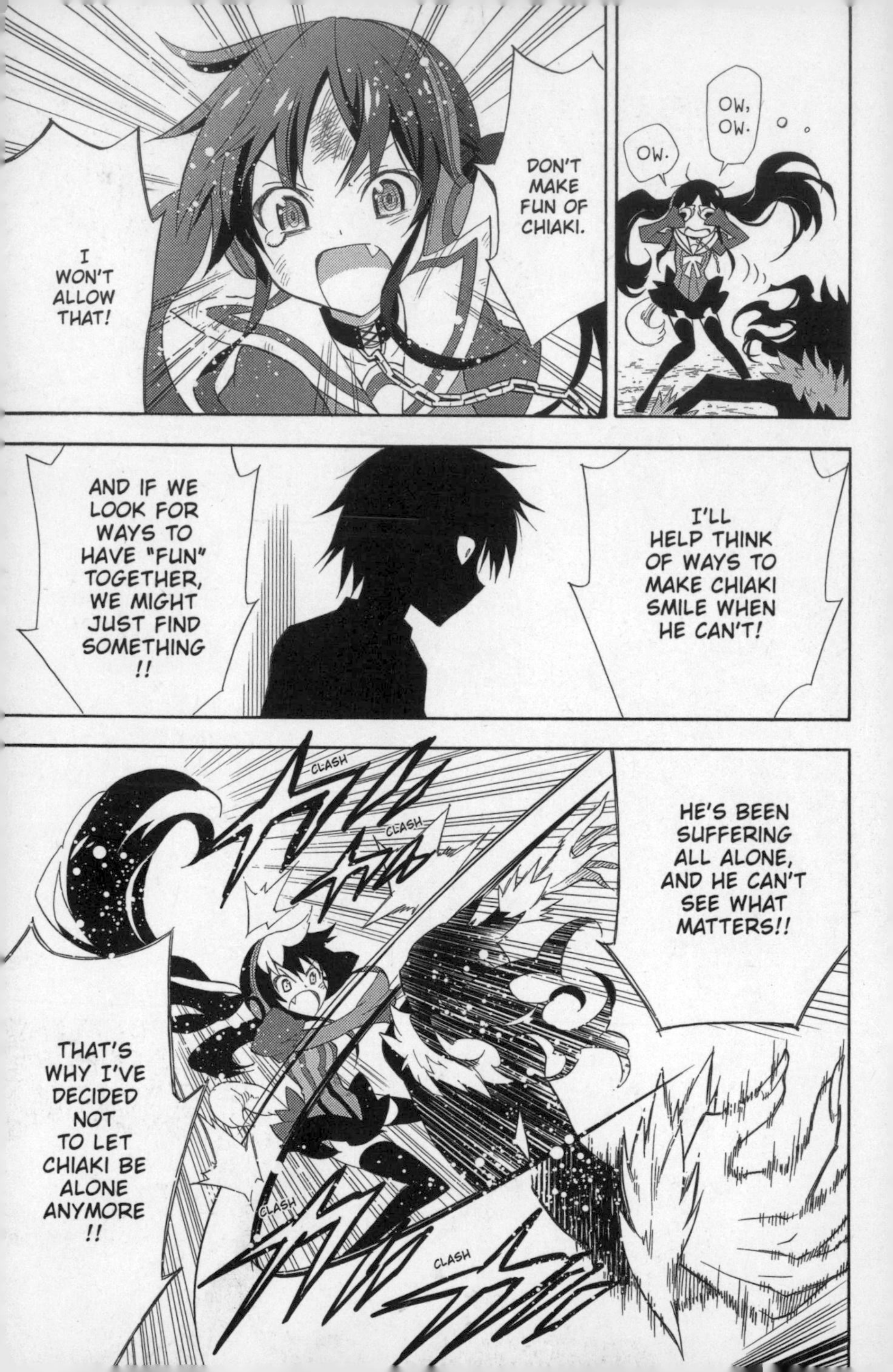
OW, OW.
OW.
DON'T MAKE FUN OF CHIAKI.
I WON'T ALLOW THAT!
I'LL HELP THINK OF WAYS TO MAKE CHIAKI SMILE WHEN HE CAN'T!
AND IF WE LOOK FOR WAYS TO HAVE "FUN" TOGETHER, WE MIGHT JUST FIND SOMETHING!!
HE'S BEEN SUFFERING ALL ALONE, AND HE CAN'T SEE WHAT MATTERS!!
CLASH
CLASH
THAT'S WHY I'VE DECIDED NOT TO LET CHIAKI BE ALONE ANYMORE!!
CLASH
CLASH

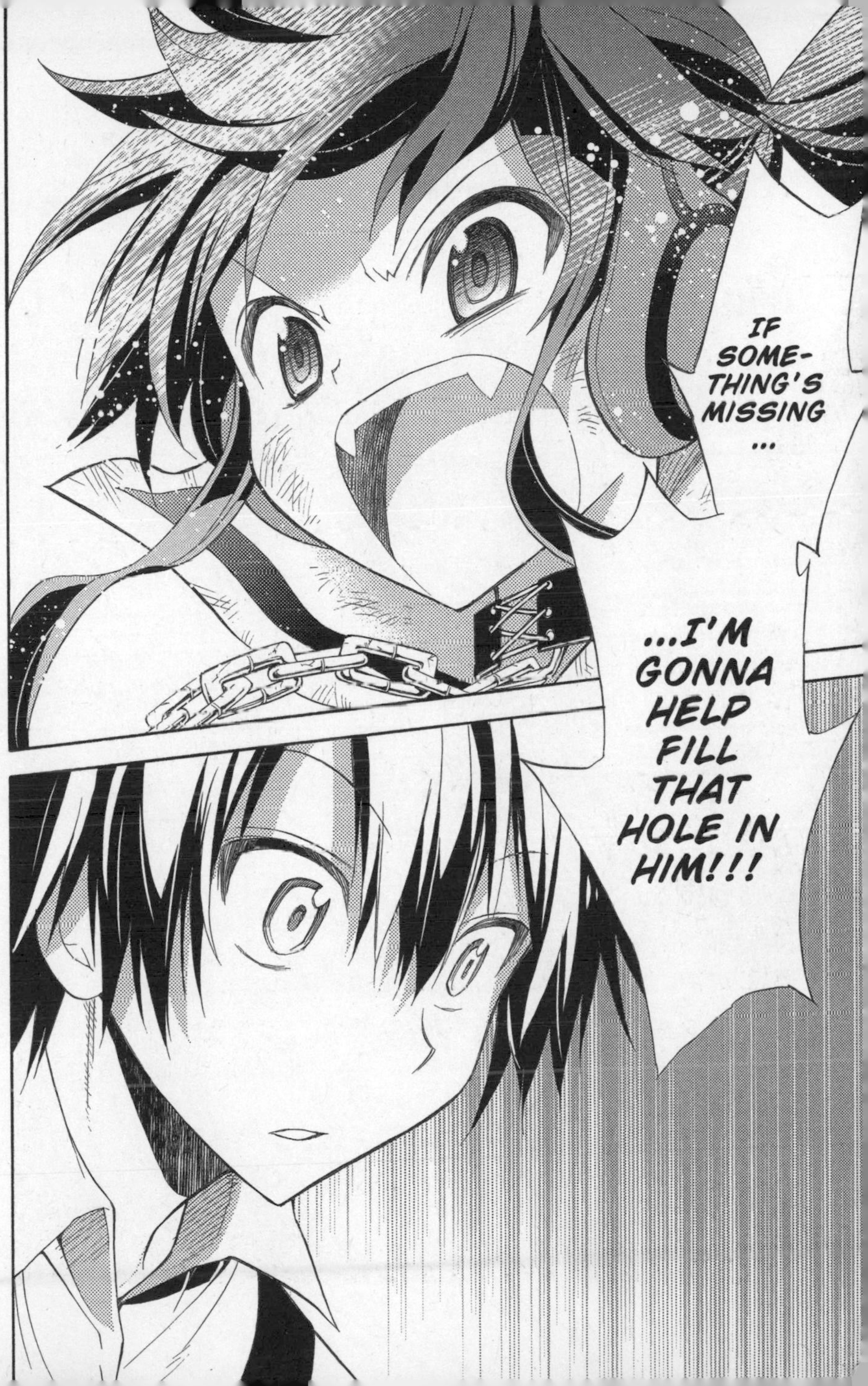
IF SOME-THING'S MISSING ...
...I'M GONNA HELP FILL THAT HOLE IN HIM!!!

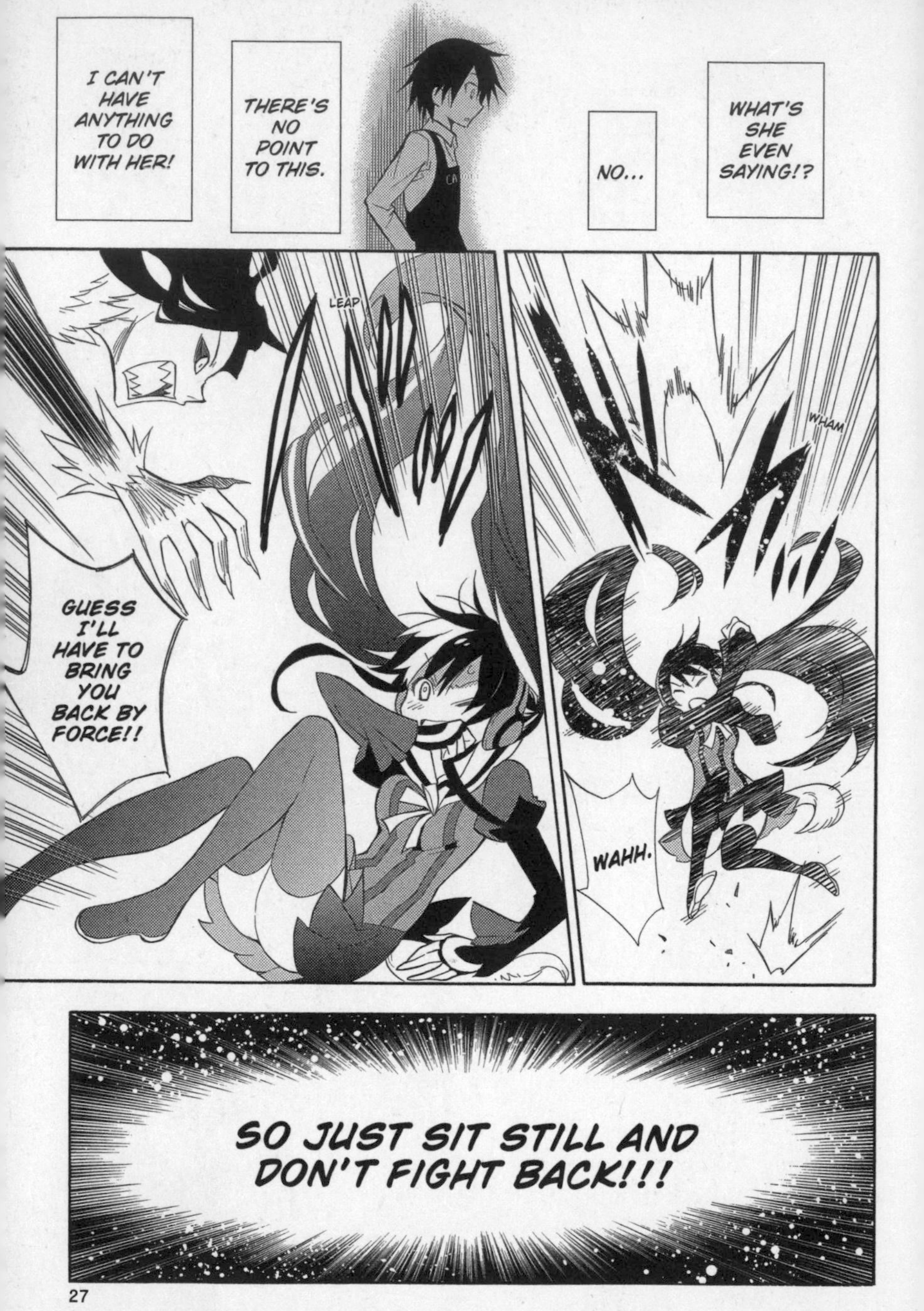
WHAT'S SHE EVEN SAYING!?
NO...
THERE'S NO POINT TO THIS.
I CAN'T HAVE ANYTHING TO DO WITH HER!
WHAM
WAHH.
LEAP
GUESS I'LL HAVE TO BRING YOU BACK BY FORCE!!
SO JUST SIT STILL AND DON'T FIGHT BACK!!!

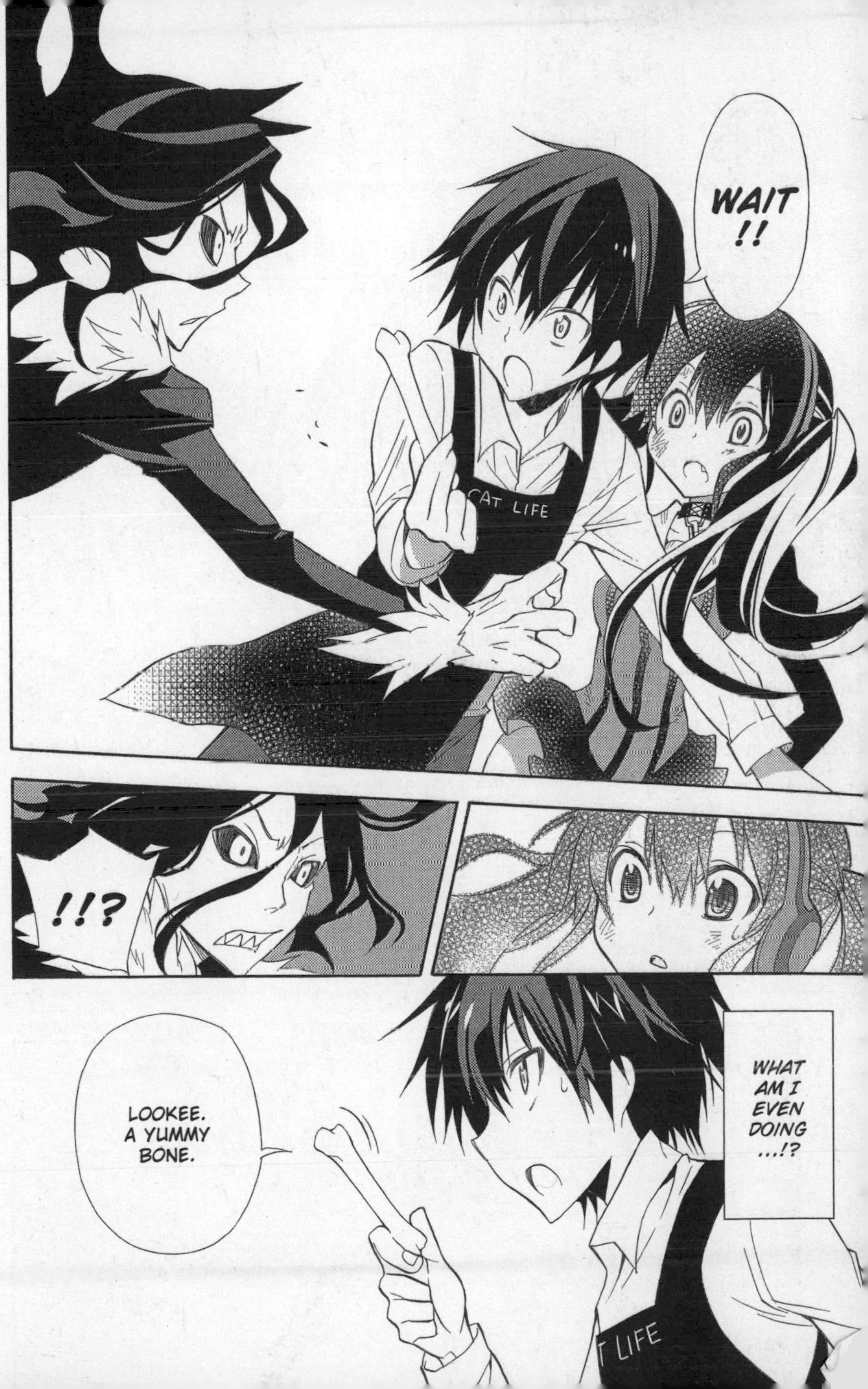
WAIT !!
CAT LIFE
!!?
WHAT AM I EVEN DOING ...!?
LOOKEE. A YUMMY BONE.

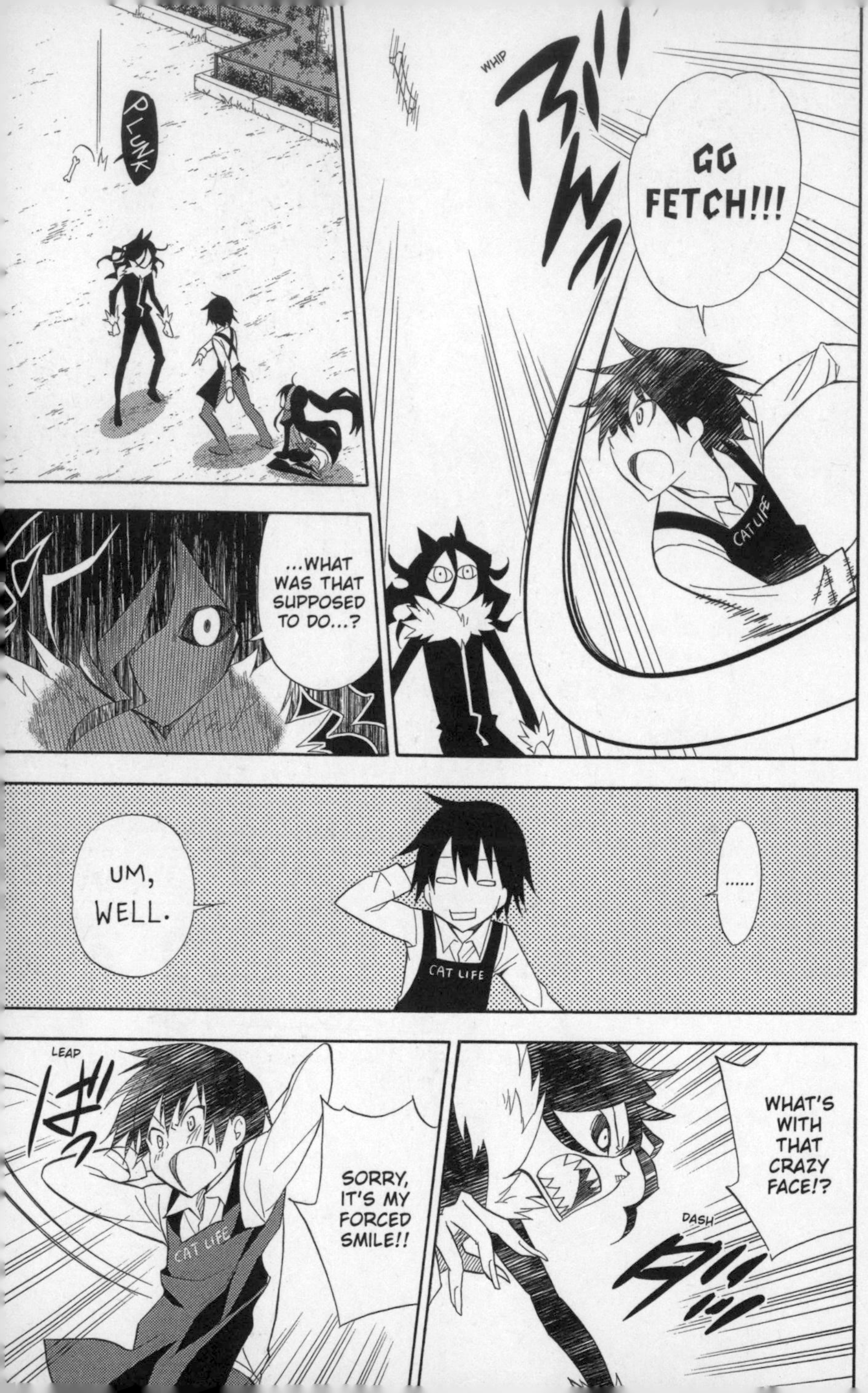
WHIP
GO FETCH!!!
PLUNK
...WHAT WAS THAT SUPPOSED TO DO...?
......
UM, WELL.
CAT LIFE
WHAT'S WITH THAT CRAZY FACE!?
DASH
LEAP
SORRY, IT'S MY FORCED SMILE!!
CAT LIFE

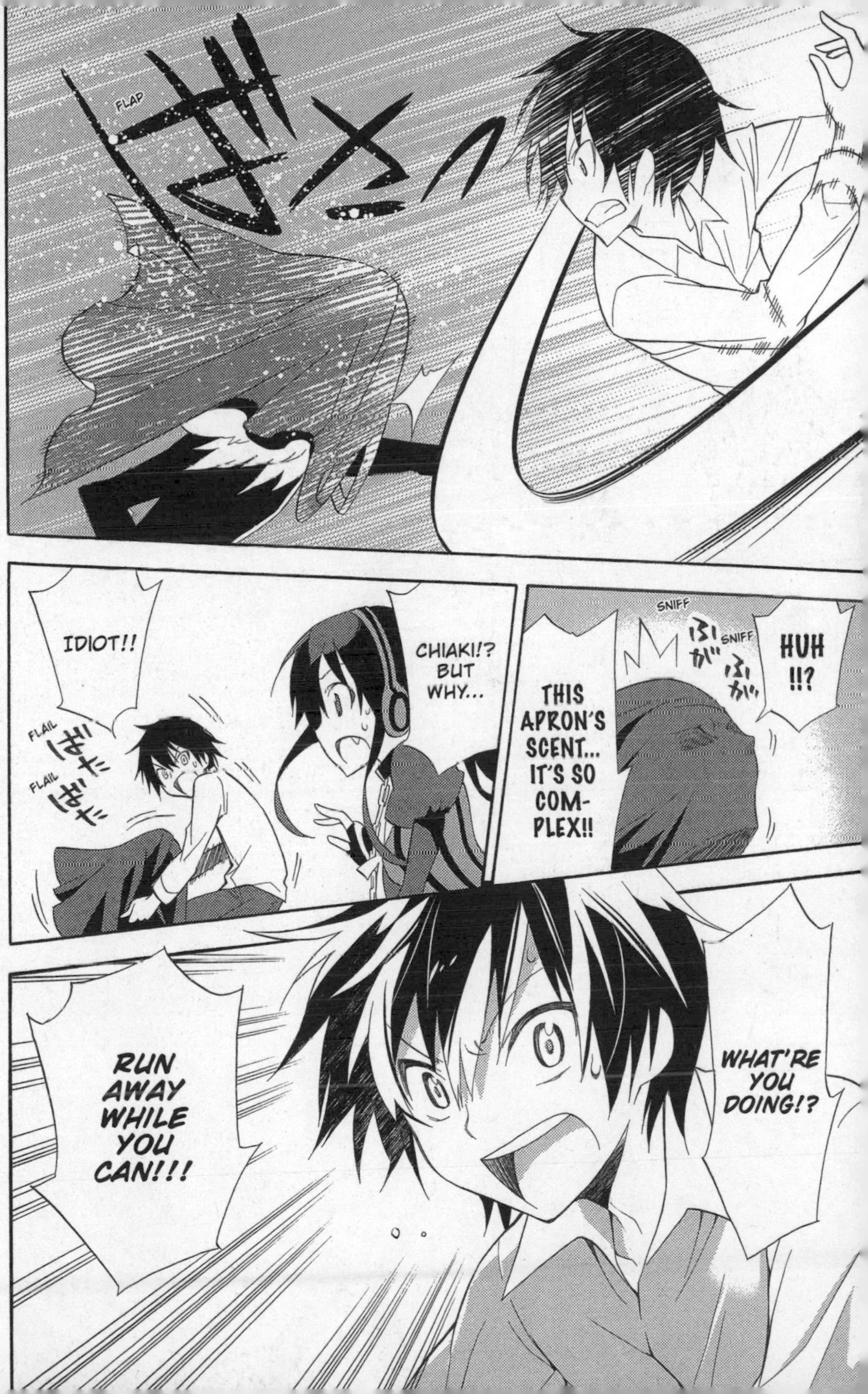
FLAP
HUH!!?
SNIFF
ふが
SNIFF
ふが
THIS APRON'S SCENT... IT'S SO COMPLEX!!
CHIAKI!? BUT WHY...
IDIOT!!
FLAIL
ばた
FLAIL
ばた
WHAT'RE YOU DOING!?
RUN AWAY WHILE YOU CAN!!!

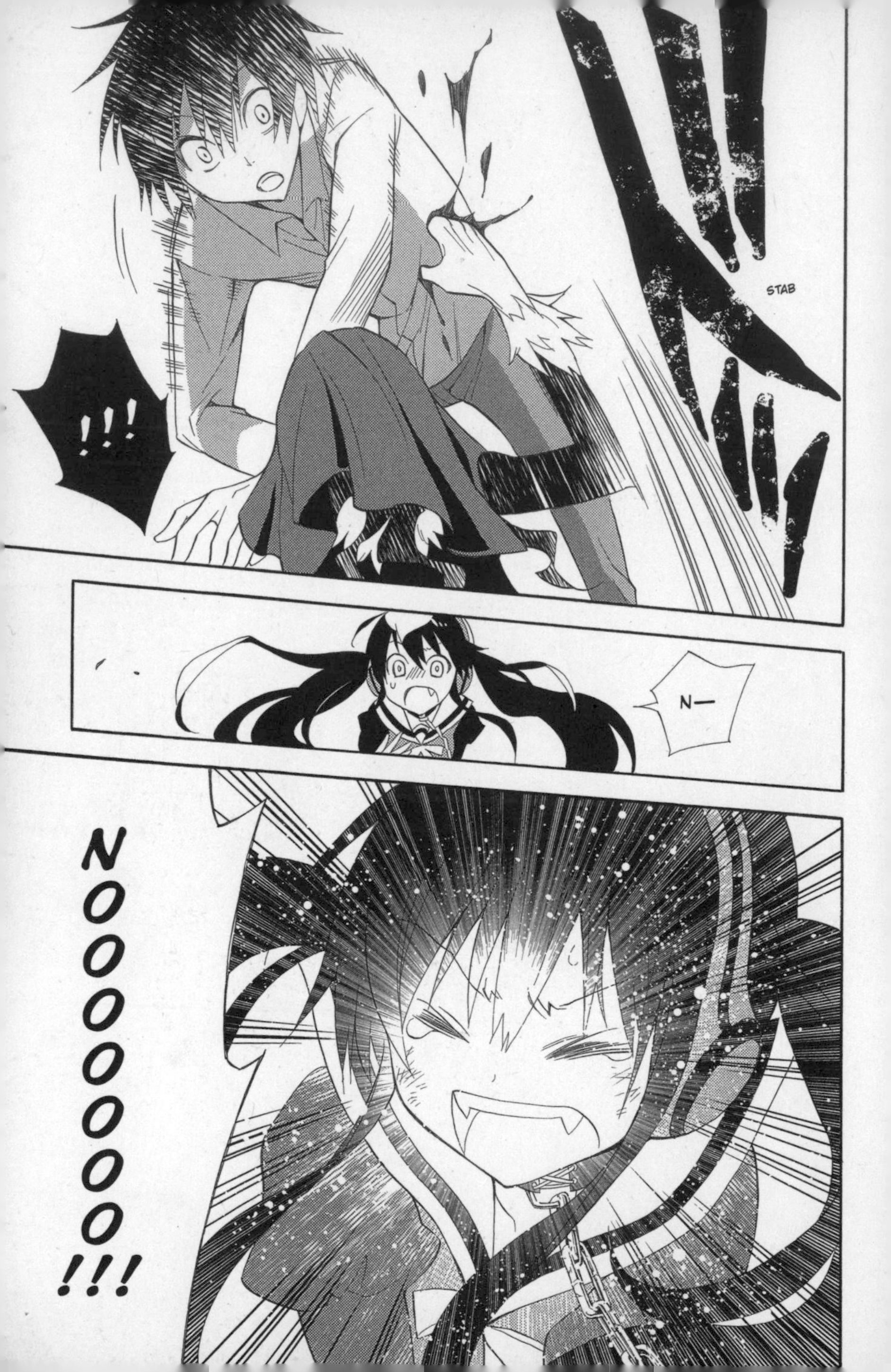
STAB
!!!
N—
NOOOOOOO!!!

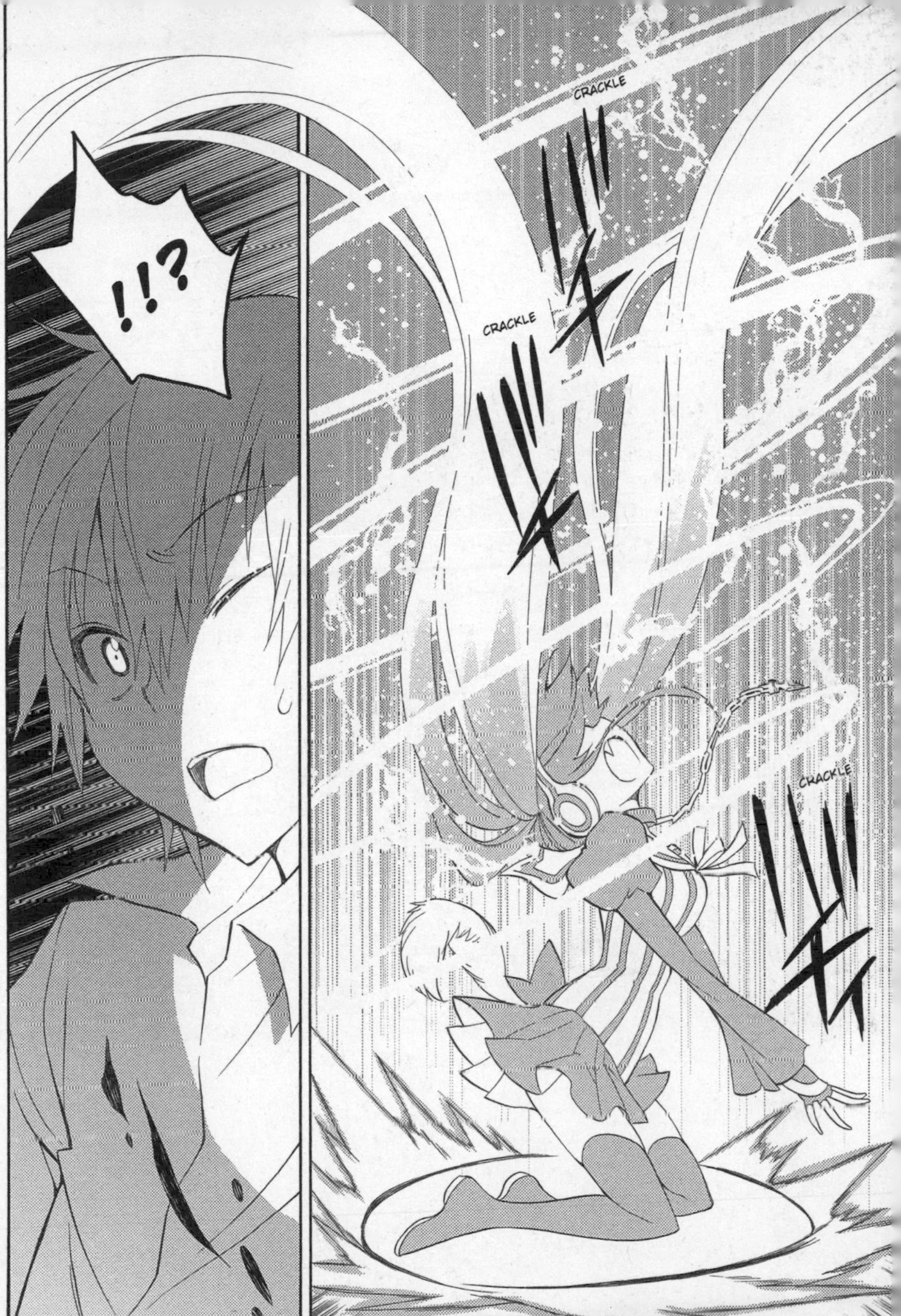
CRACKLE
CRACKLE
CRACKLE
!!?

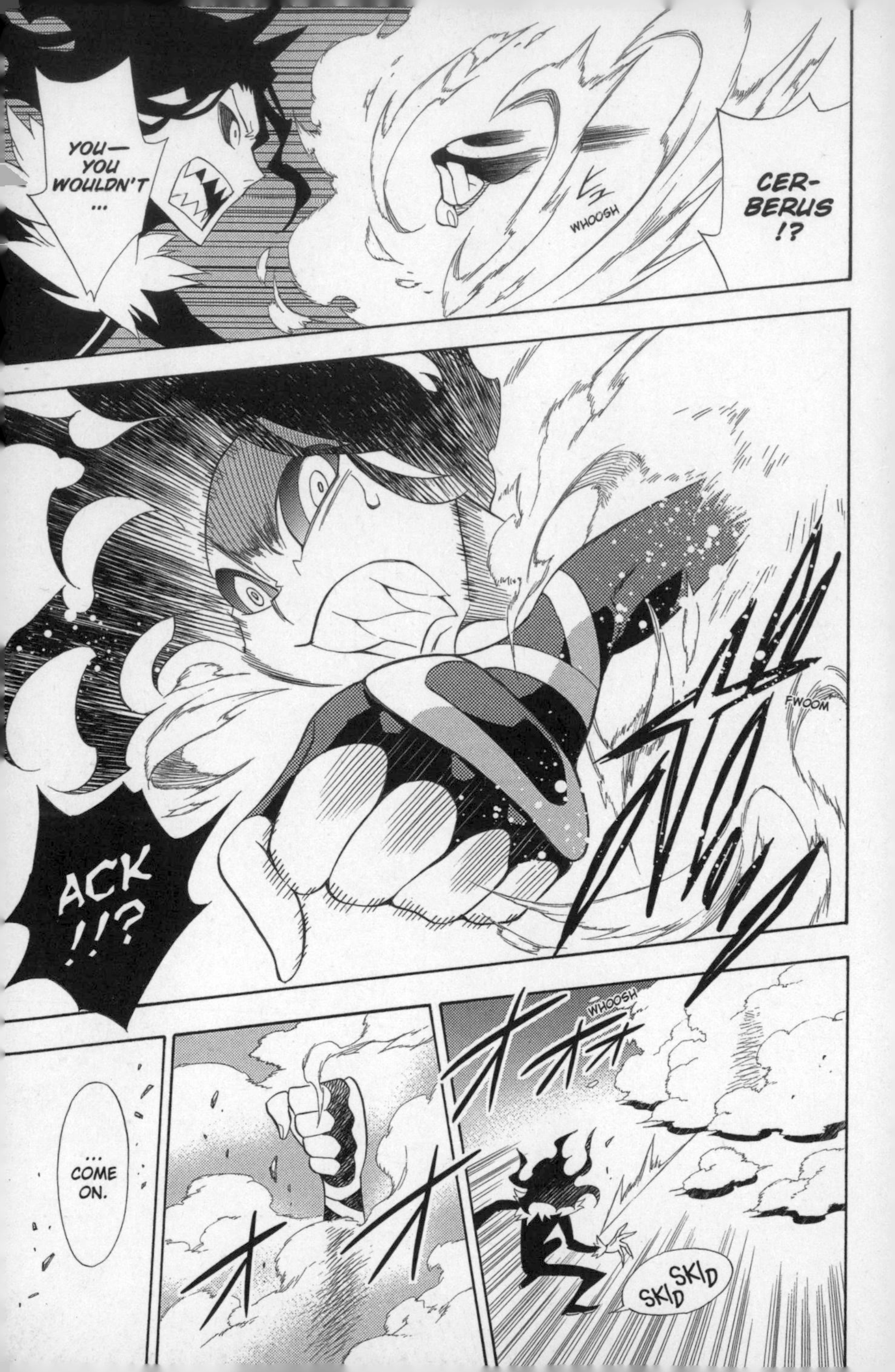
CER-BERUS !?
WHOOSH
YOU— YOU WOULDN'T ...
FWOOM
ACK !!?
WHOOSH
SKID SKID
... COME ON.

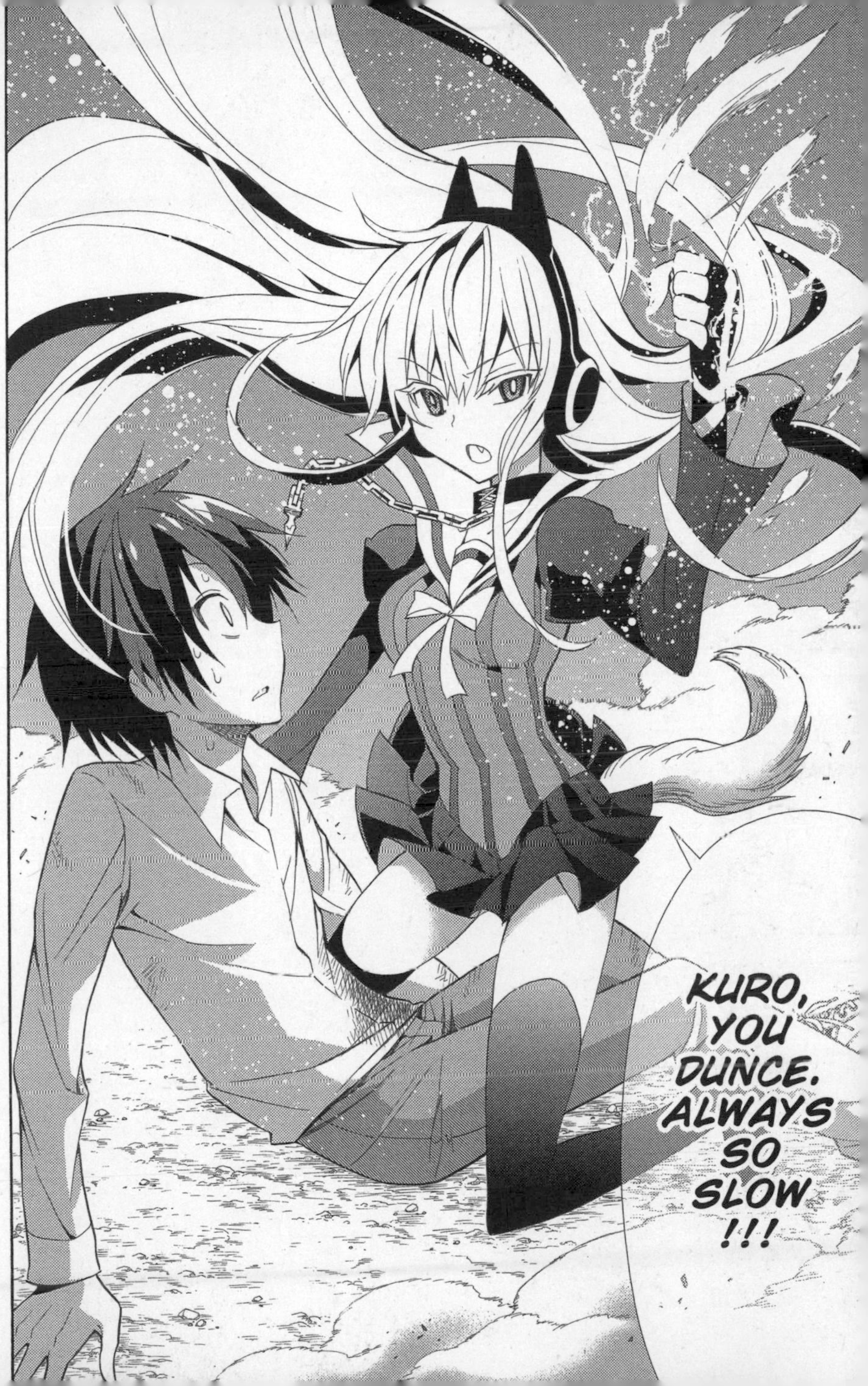
KURO, YOU DUNCE. ALWAYS SO SLOW!!!

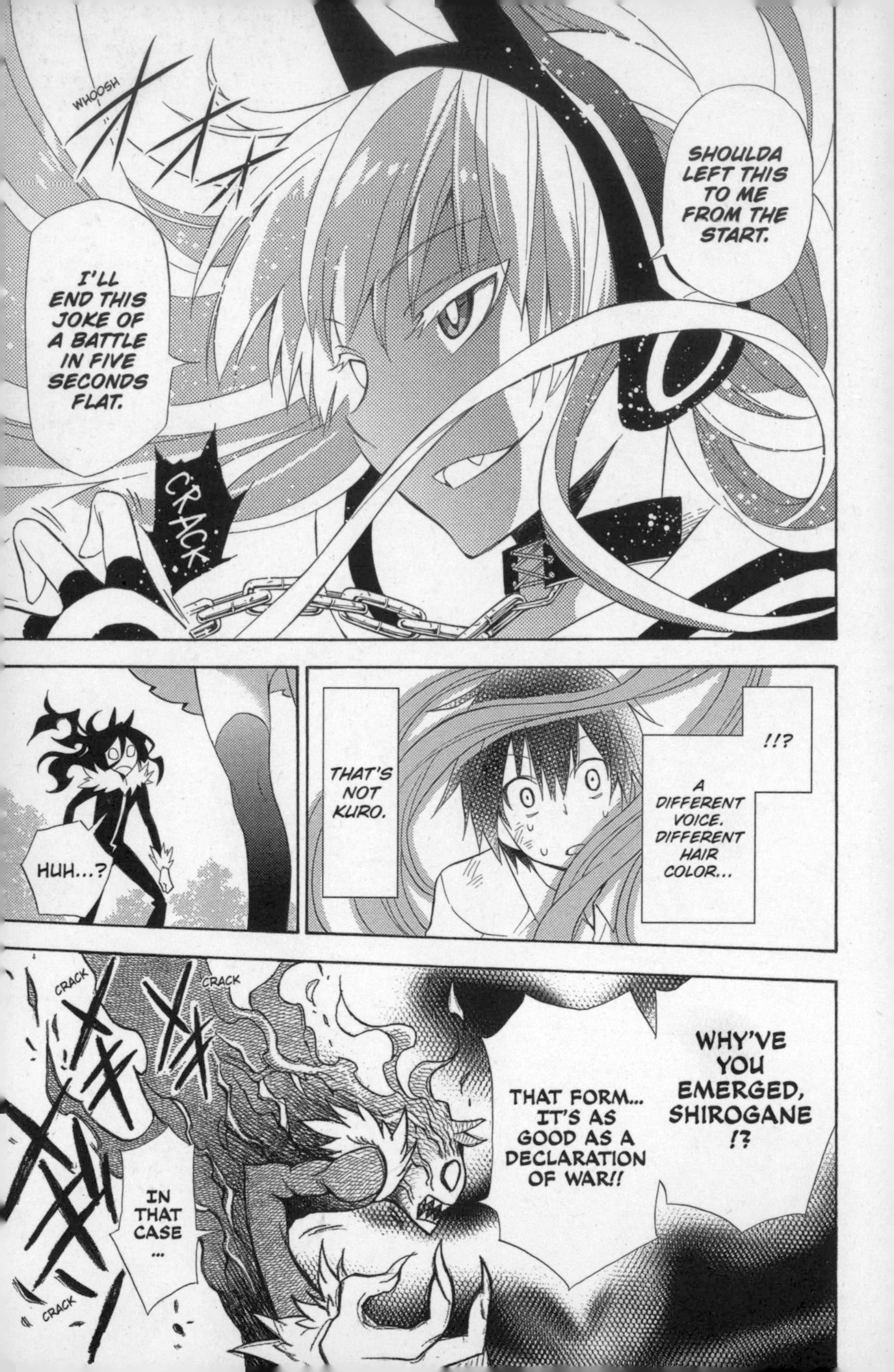
SHOULDA LEFT THIS TO ME FROM THE START.
WHOOSH
I'LL END THIS JOKE OF A BATTLE IN FIVE SECONDS FLAT.
CRACK
!!?
A DIFFERENT VOICE. DIFFERENT HAIR COLOR...
THAT'S NOT KURO.
HUH...?
WHY'VE YOU EMERGED, SHIROGANE!?
THAT FORM... IT'S AS GOOD AS A DECLARATION OF WAR!!
CRACK
CRACK
IN THAT CASE ...
CRACK

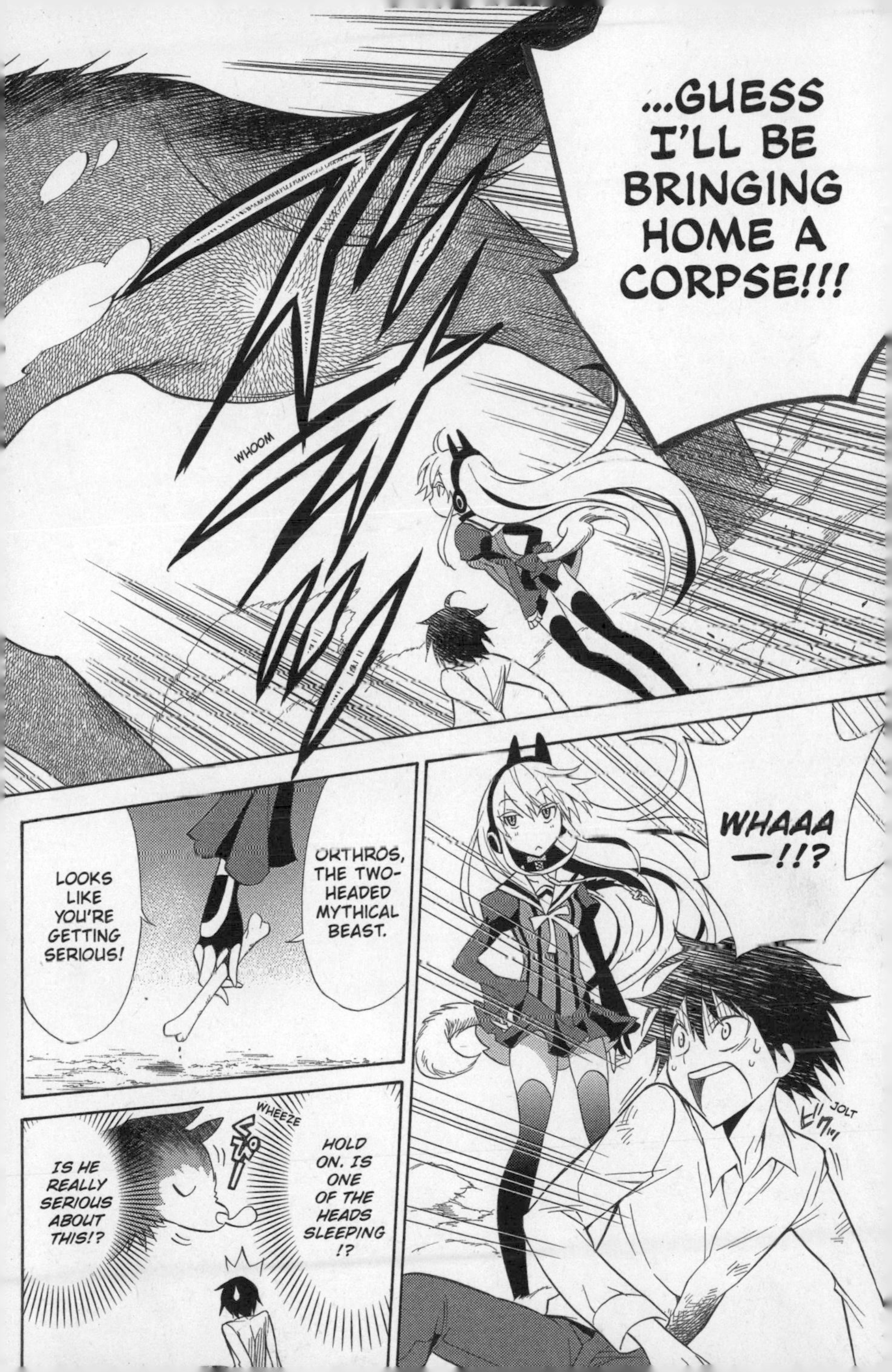
...GUESS I'LL BE BRINGING HOME A CORPSE!!!
WHOOM
WHAAA—!!?
JOLT
ORTHROS, THE TWO-HEADED MYTHICAL BEAST.
LOOKS LIKE YOU'RE GETTING SERIOUS!
HOLD ON. IS ONE OF THE HEADS SLEEPING!?
WHEEZE
IS HE REALLY SERIOUS ABOUT THIS!?

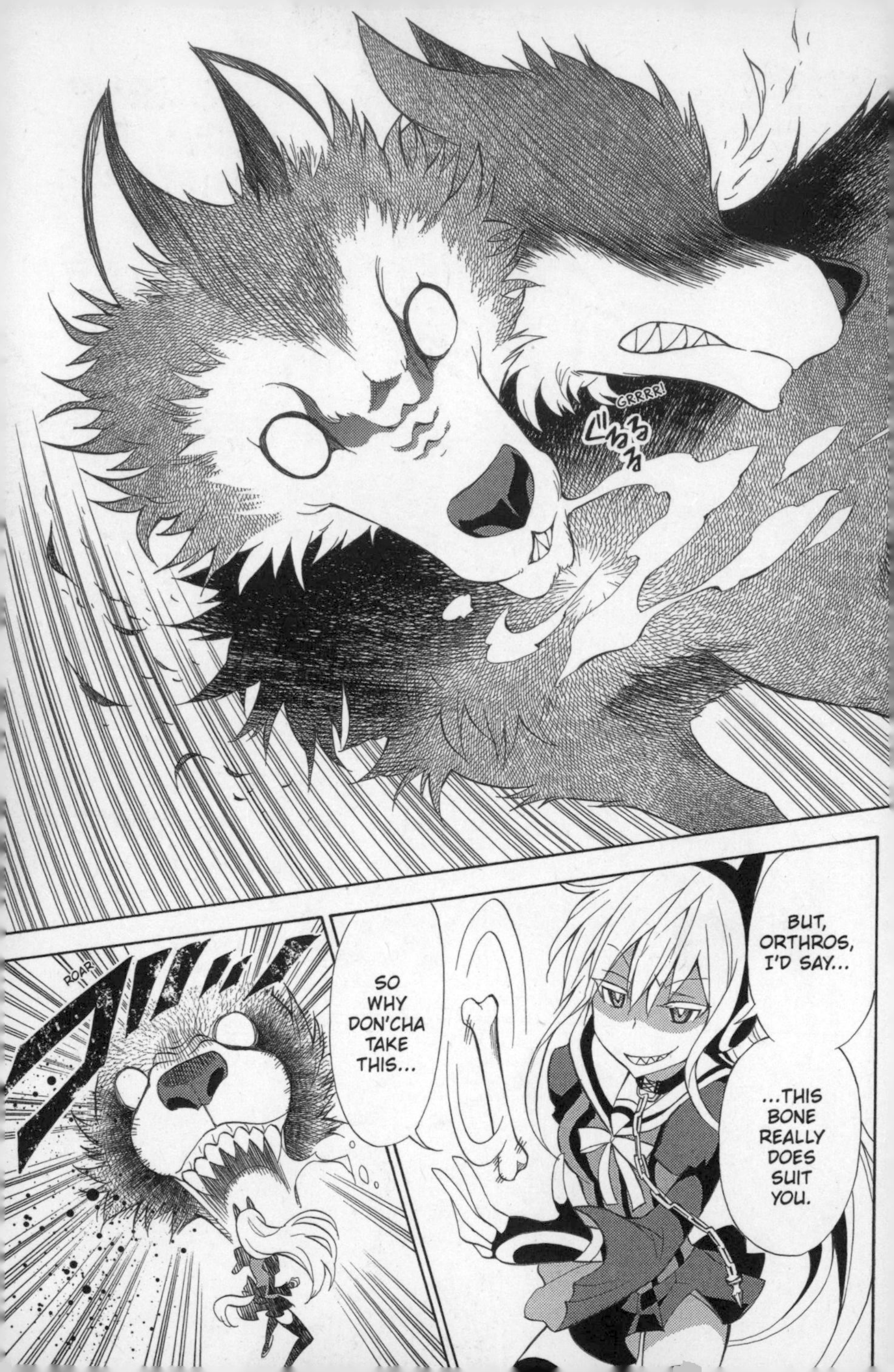
GRRRR!
ぐるるる
BUT, ORTHROS, I'D SAY...
...THIS BONE REALLY DOES SUIT YOU.
SO WHY DON'CHA TAKE THIS...
ROAR

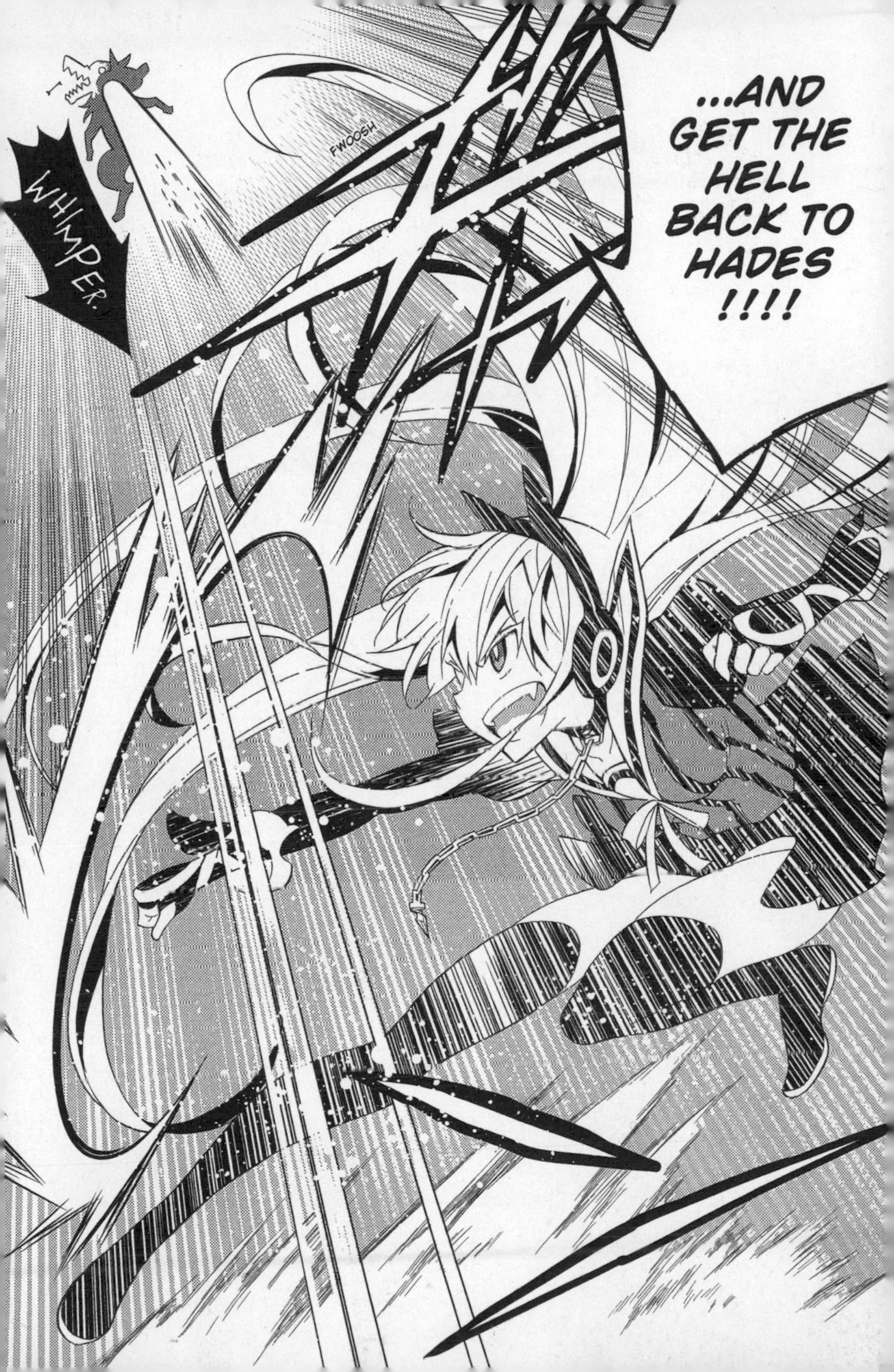
...AND GET THE HELL BACK TO HADES !!!!
FWOOSH
WHIMPER.

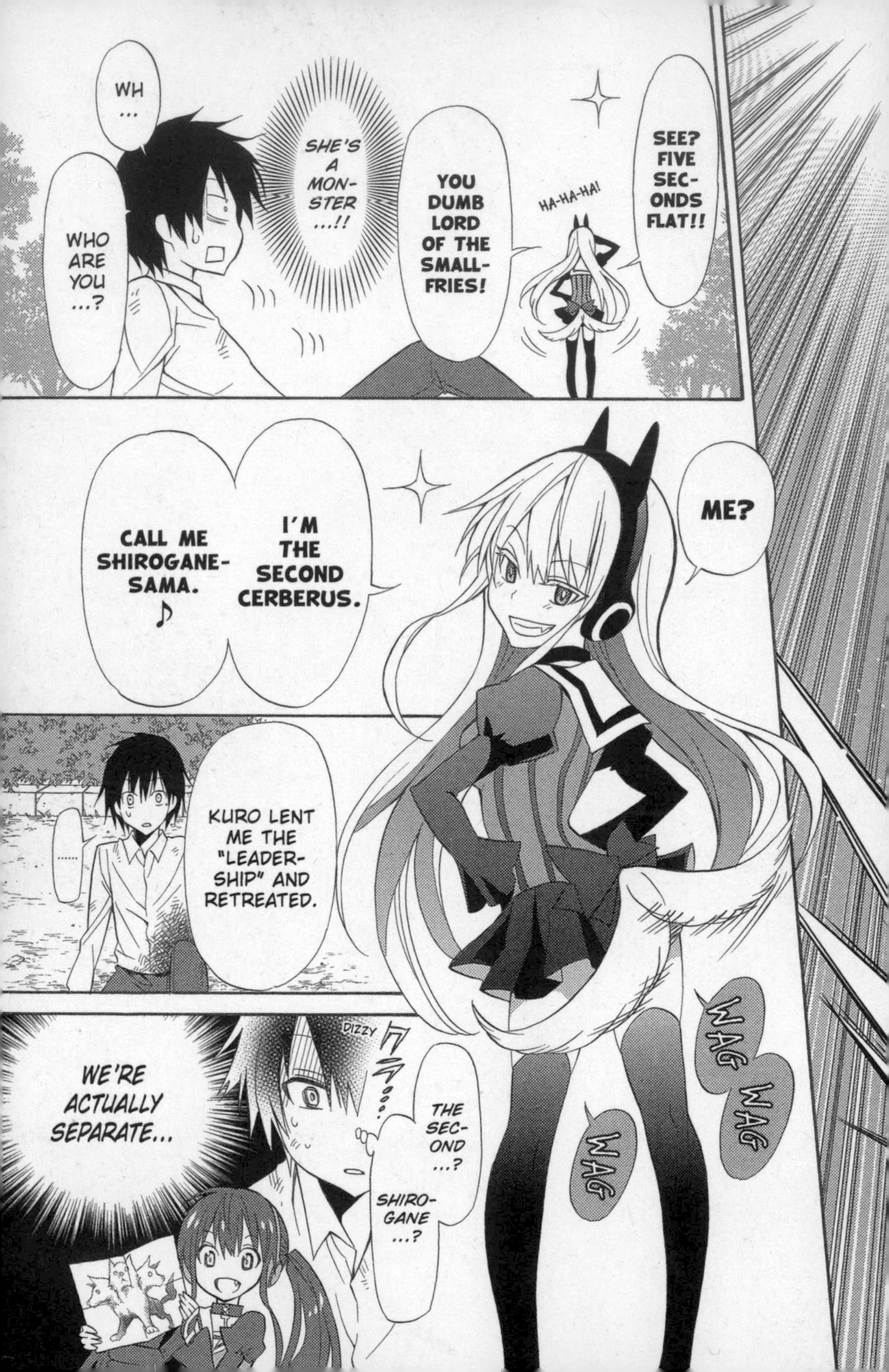
SEE? FIVE SEC-ONDS FLAT!!
HA-HA-HA!
YOU DUMB LORD OF THE SMALL-FRIES!
SHE'S A MON-STER ...!!
WH ...
WHO ARE YOU ...?
ME?
I'M THE SECOND CERBERUS.
CALL ME SHIROGANE-SAMA. ♪
KURO LENT ME THE "LEADER-SHIP" AND RETREATED.
......
WAG WAG
WAG
THE SEC-OND ...?
SHIRO-GANE ...?
DIZZY
WE'RE ACTUALLY SEPARATE...

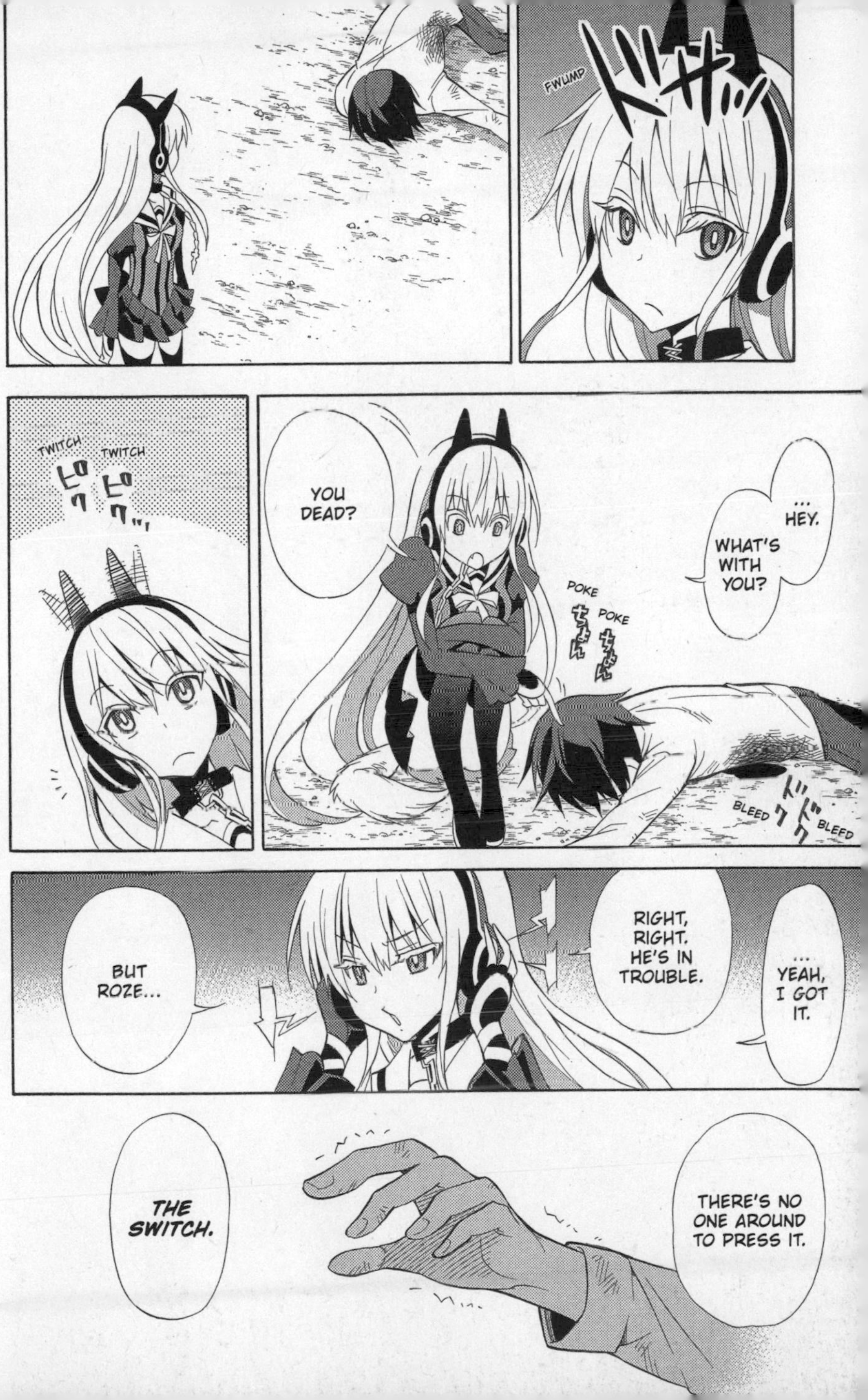
FWUMP
... HEY.
WHAT'S WITH YOU?
YOU DEAD?
POKE
POKE
BLEED
BLEED
TWITCH
TWITCH
... YEAH, I GOT IT.
RIGHT, RIGHT. HE'S IN TROUBLE.
BUT ROZE...
THERE'S NO ONE AROUND TO PRESS IT.
THE SWITCH.

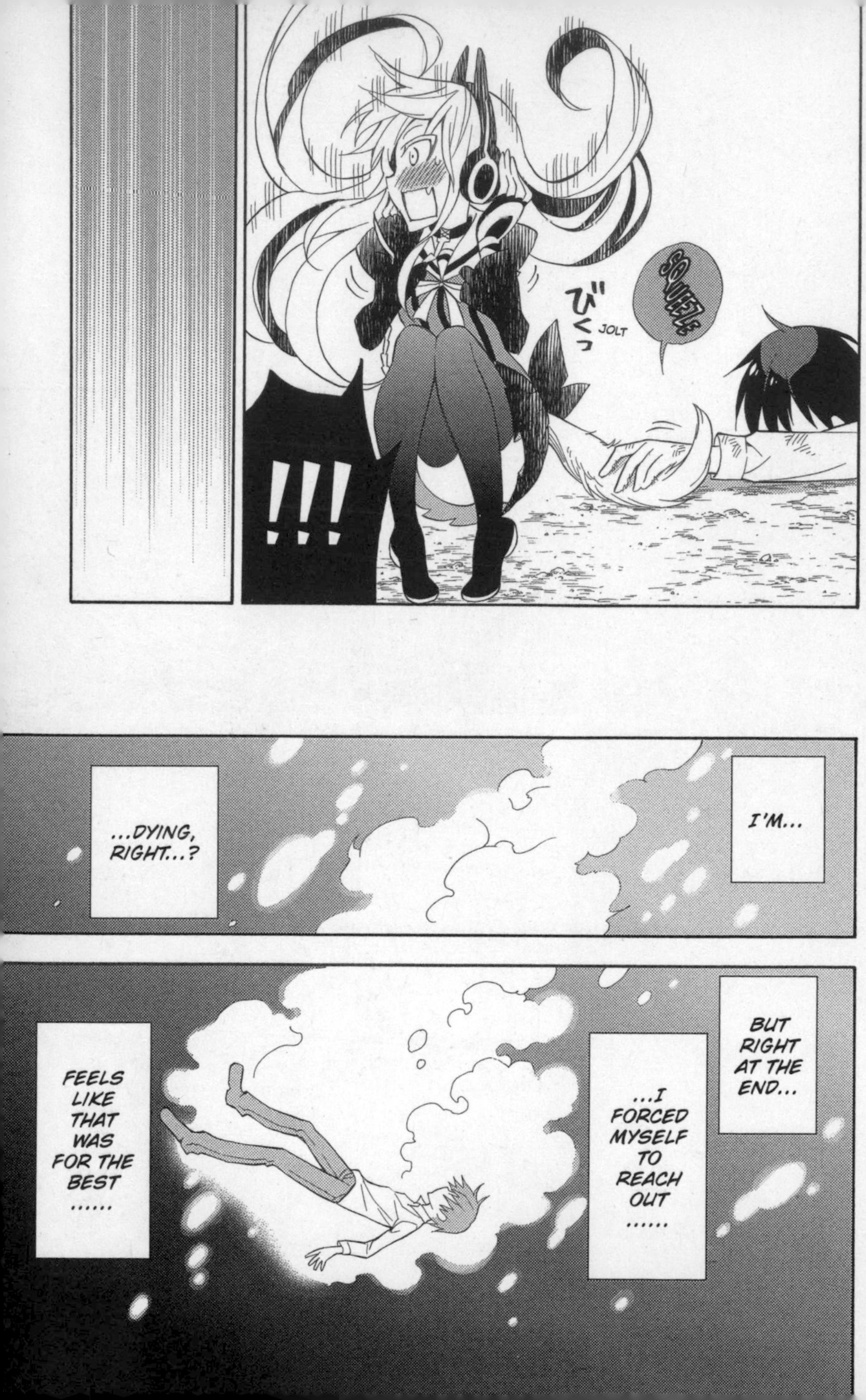
SQUEEZE
びくっ
JOLT
!!!
I'M...
...DYING, RIGHT...?
BUT RIGHT AT THE END...
...I FORCED MYSELF TO REACH OUT......
FEELS LIKE THAT WAS FOR THE BEST......

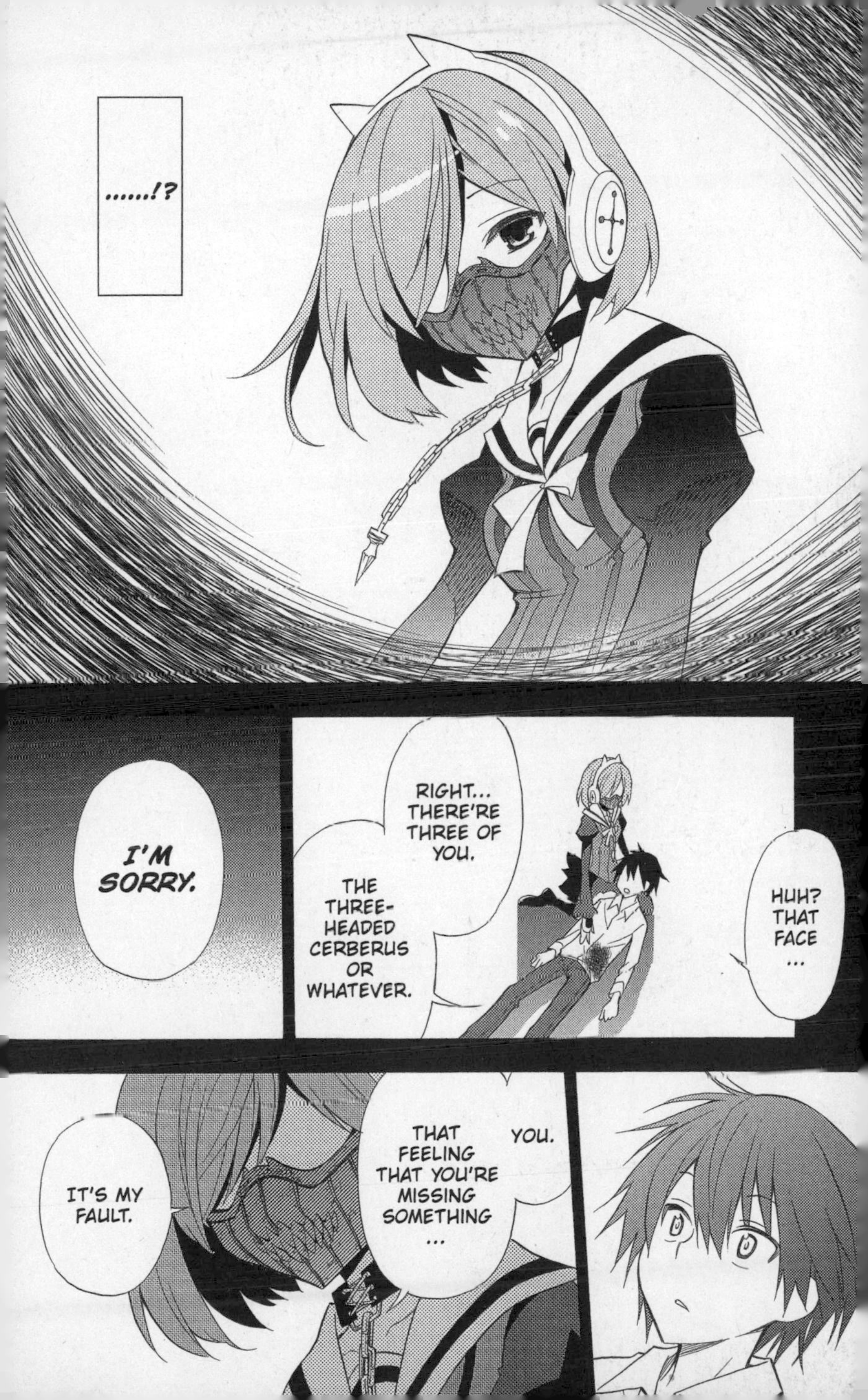
......!?
HUH? THAT FACE ...
RIGHT... THERE'RE THREE OF YOU.
THE THREE-HEADED CERBERUS OR WHATEVER.
I'M SORRY.
YOU.
THAT FEELING THAT YOU'RE MISSING SOMETHING ...
IT'S MY FAULT.

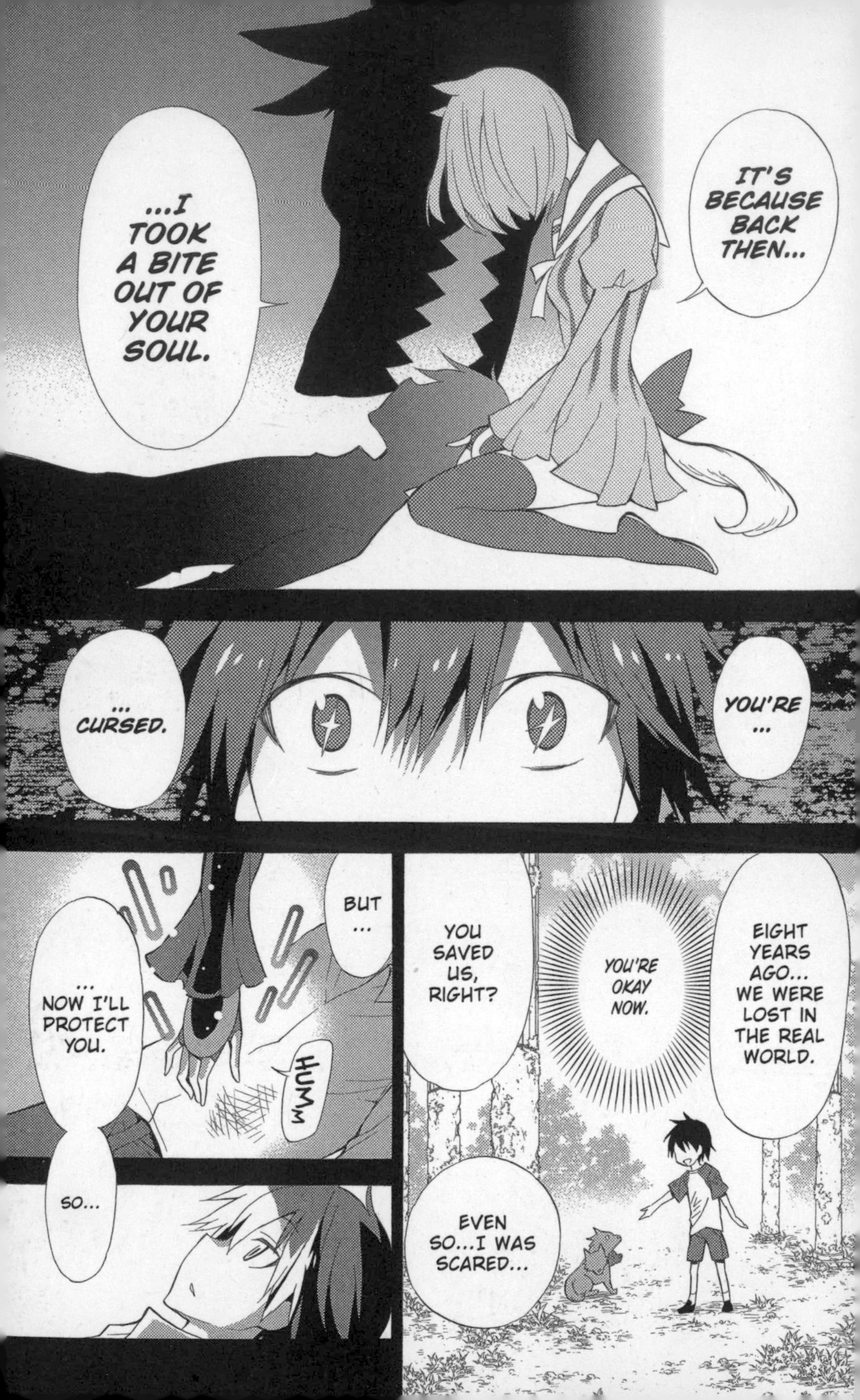
IT'S BECAUSE BACK THEN...
...I TOOK A BITE OUT OF YOUR SOUL.
YOU'RE ...
... CURSED.
EIGHT YEARS AGO... WE WERE LOST IN THE REAL WORLD.
YOU'RE OKAY NOW.
YOU SAVED US, RIGHT?
EVEN SO...I WAS SCARED...
BUT ...
HUMM
... NOW I'LL PROTECT YOU.
SO...

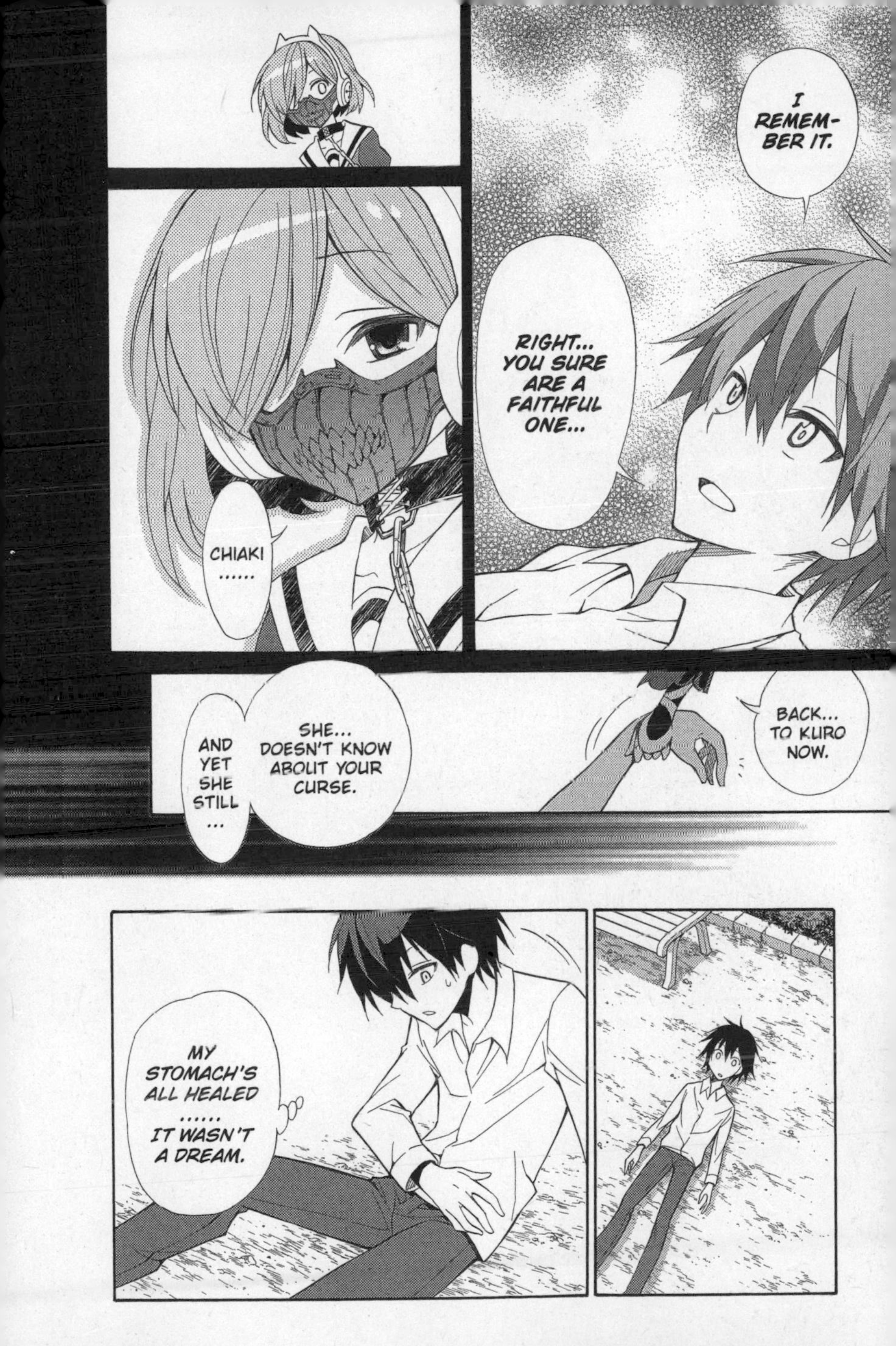
I REMEMBER IT.
RIGHT... YOU SURE ARE A FAITHFUL ONE...
CHIAKI ......
BACK... TO KURO NOW.
SHE... DOESN'T KNOW ABOUT YOUR CURSE.
AND YET SHE STILL ...
MY STOMACH'S ALL HEALED ...... IT WASN'T A DREAM.

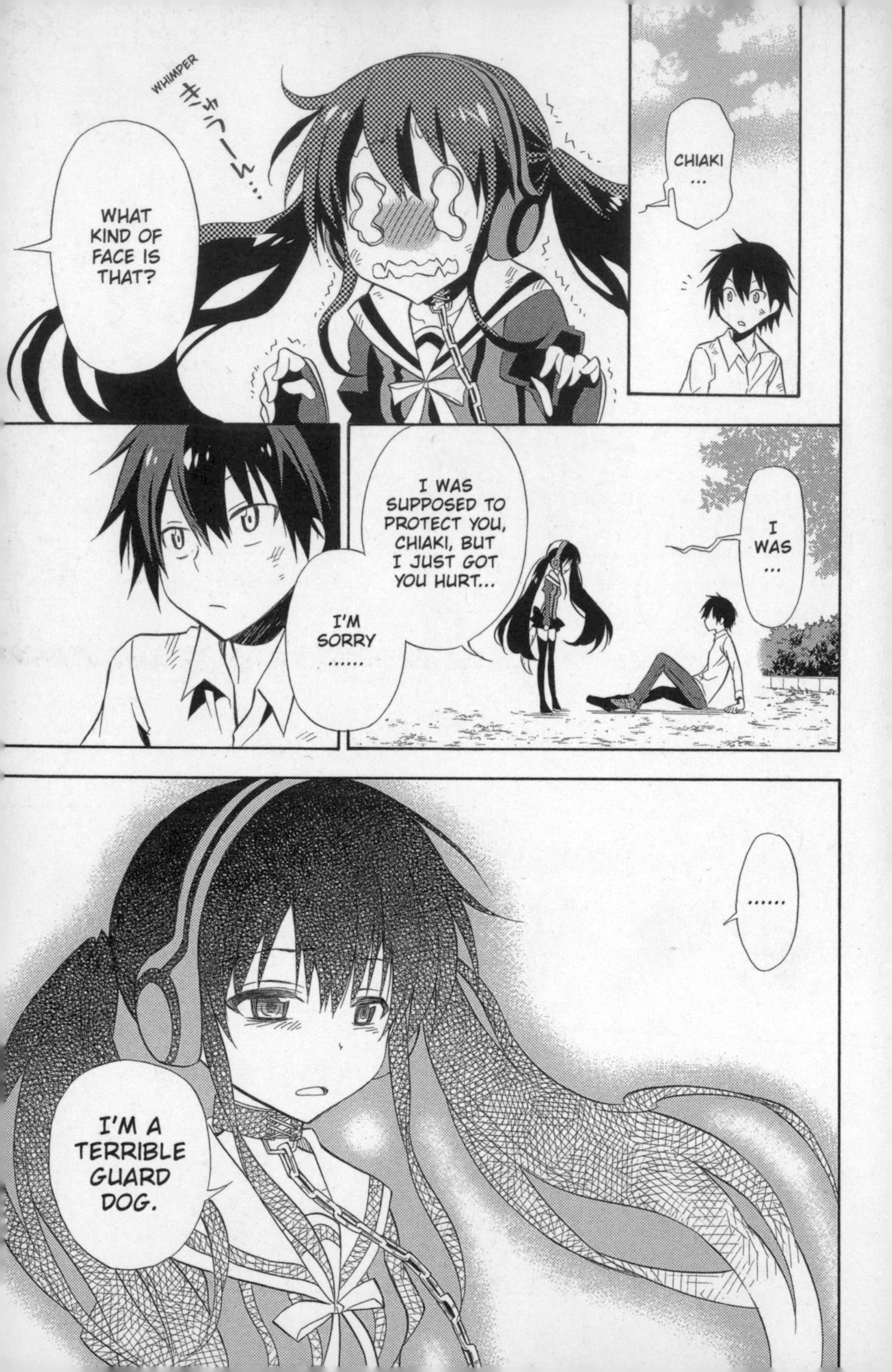
CHIAKI ...
WHIMPER
きゅうーん…
WHAT KIND OF FACE IS THAT?
I WAS ...
I WAS SUPPOSED TO PROTECT YOU, CHIAKI, BUT I JUST GOT YOU HURT...
I'M SORRY ......
......
I'M A TERRIBLE GUARD DOG.

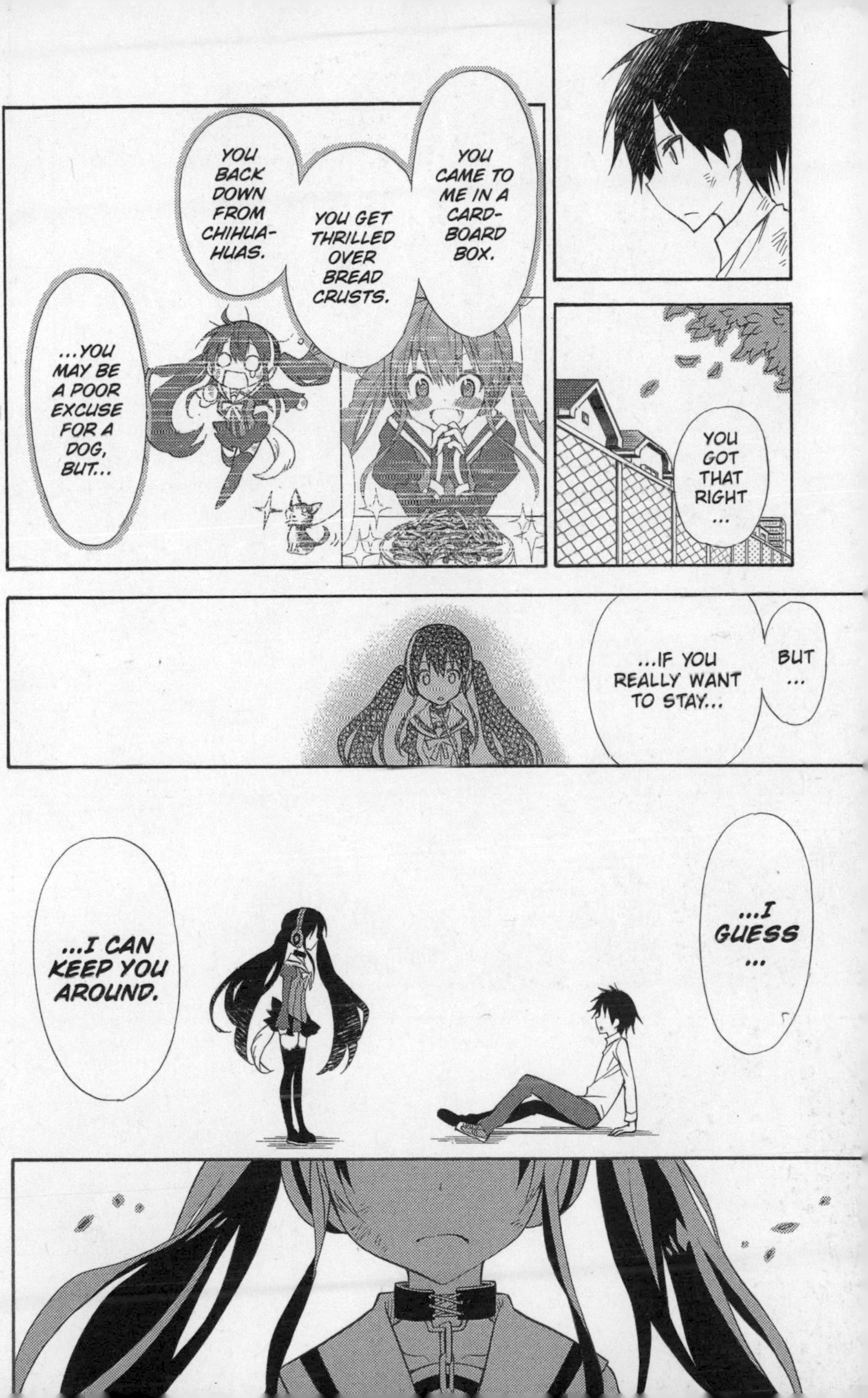
YOU GOT THAT RIGHT ...
YOU CAME TO ME IN A CARD-BOARD BOX.
YOU GET THRILLED OVER BREAD CRUSTS.
YOU BACK DOWN FROM CHIHUA-HUAS.
...YOU MAY BE A POOR EXCUSE FOR A DOG, BUT...
BUT ...
...IF YOU REALLY WANT TO STAY...
...I GUESS ...
...I CAN KEEP YOU AROUND.

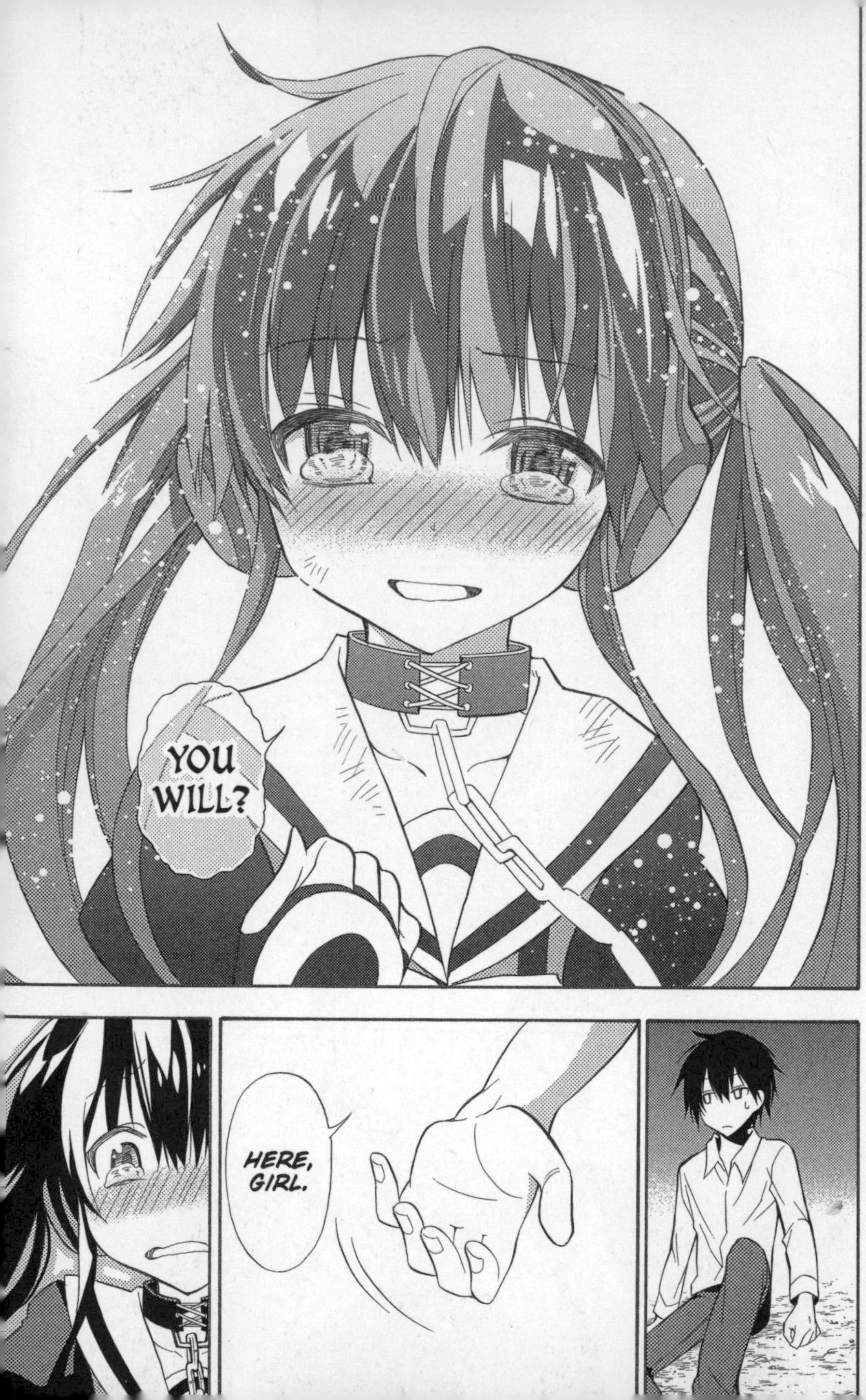
YOU WILL?
HERE, GIRL.

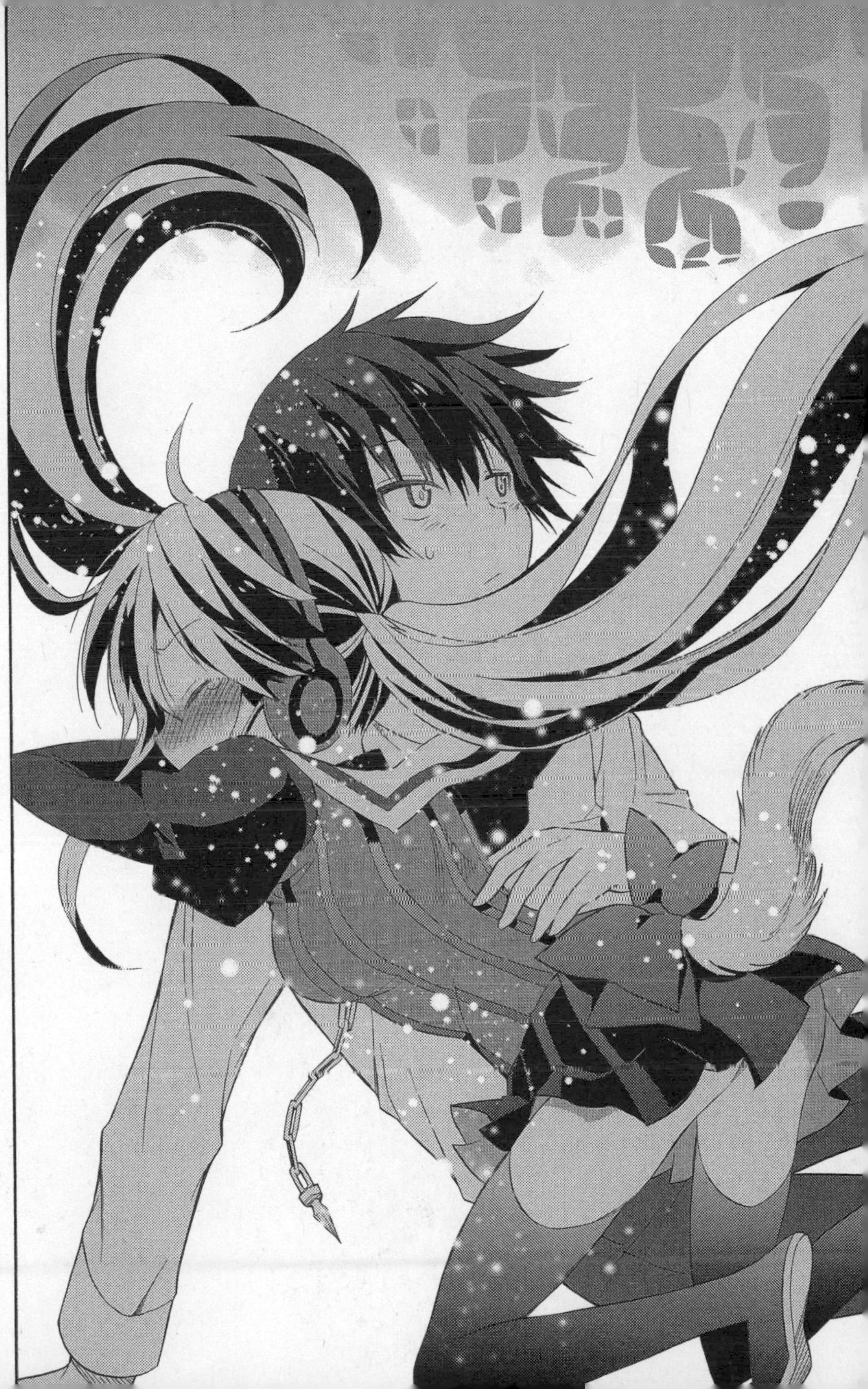

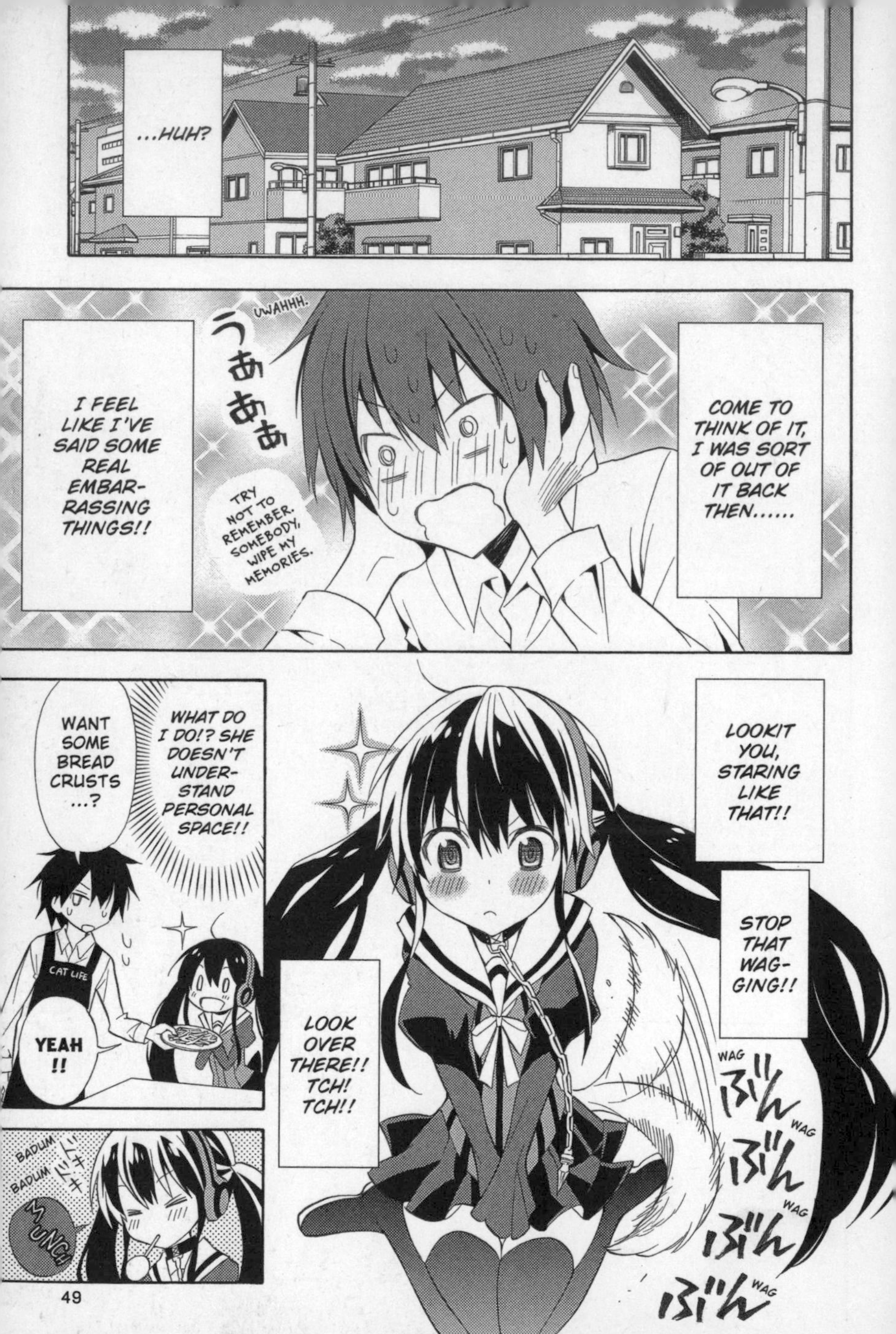
...HUH?
COME TO THINK OF IT, I WAS SORT OF OUT OF IT BACK THEN......
うあぁ
UWAHHH.
TRY NOT TO REMEMBER. SOMEBODY, WIPE MY MEMORIES.
I FEEL LIKE I'VE SAID SOME REAL EMBAR-RASSING THINGS!!
LOOKIT YOU, STARING LIKE THAT!!
STOP THAT WAG-GING!!
LOOK OVER THERE!! TCH! TCH!!
ぶん WAG
ぶん WAG
ぶん WAG
ぶん WAG
WHAT DO I DO!? SHE DOESN'T UNDER-STAND PERSONAL SPACE!!
WANT SOME BREAD CRUSTS ...?
CAT LIFE
YEAH !!
ドキドキ
BADUM BADUM
MUNCH

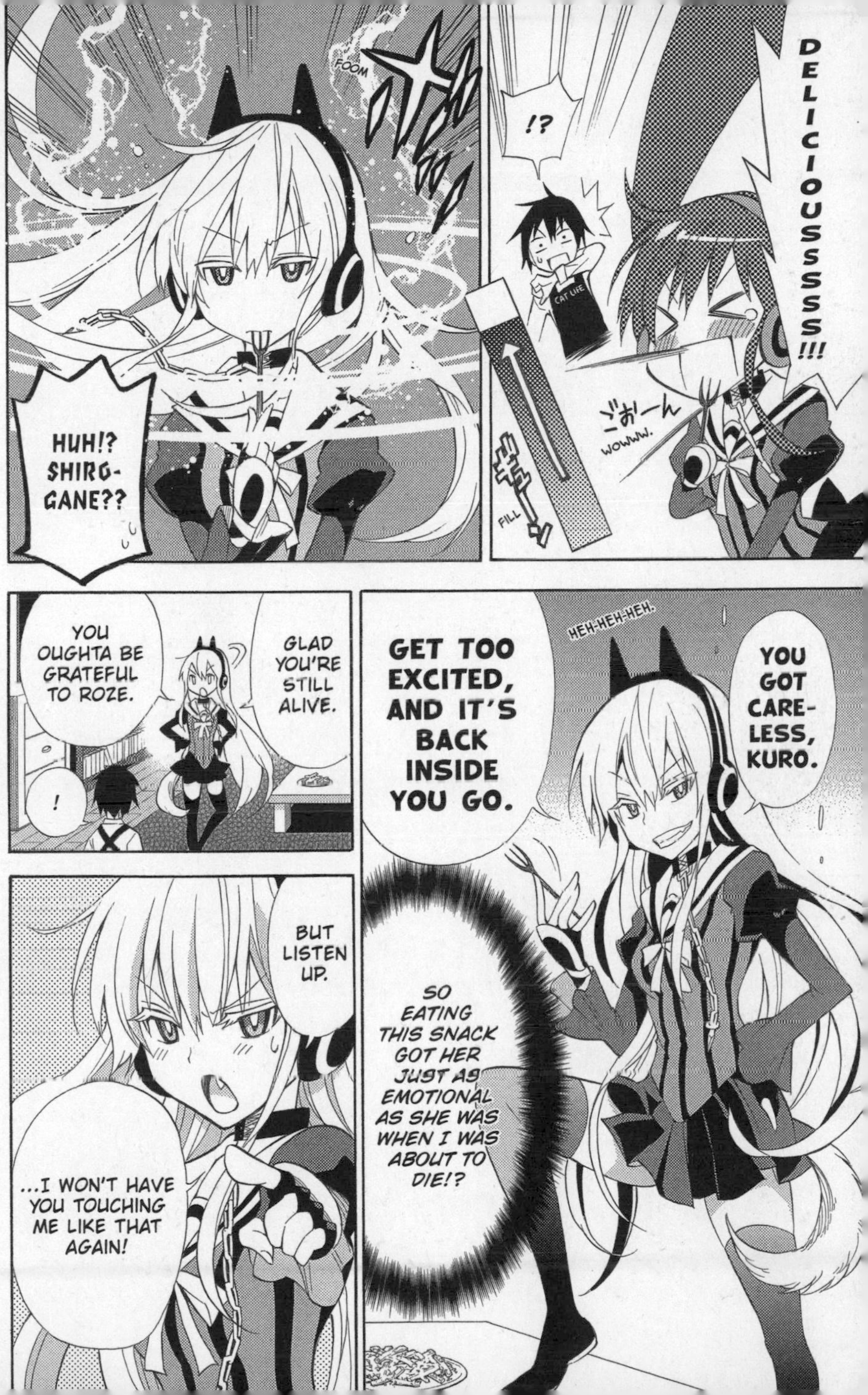

!?
DELICIOUSSSSSS!!!
ごおーん
WOWWW.
FILL
FOOM
HUH!? SHIRO-GANE??
HEH-HEH-HEH.
YOU GOT CARE-LESS, KURO.
GET TOO EXCITED, AND IT'S BACK INSIDE YOU GO.
SO EATING THIS SNACK GOT HER JUST AS EMOTIONAL AS SHE WAS WHEN I WAS ABOUT TO DIE!?
GLAD YOU'RE STILL ALIVE.
YOU OUGHTA BE GRATEFUL TO ROZE.
!
BUT LISTEN UP.
...I WON'T HAVE YOU TOUCHING ME LIKE THAT AGAIN!

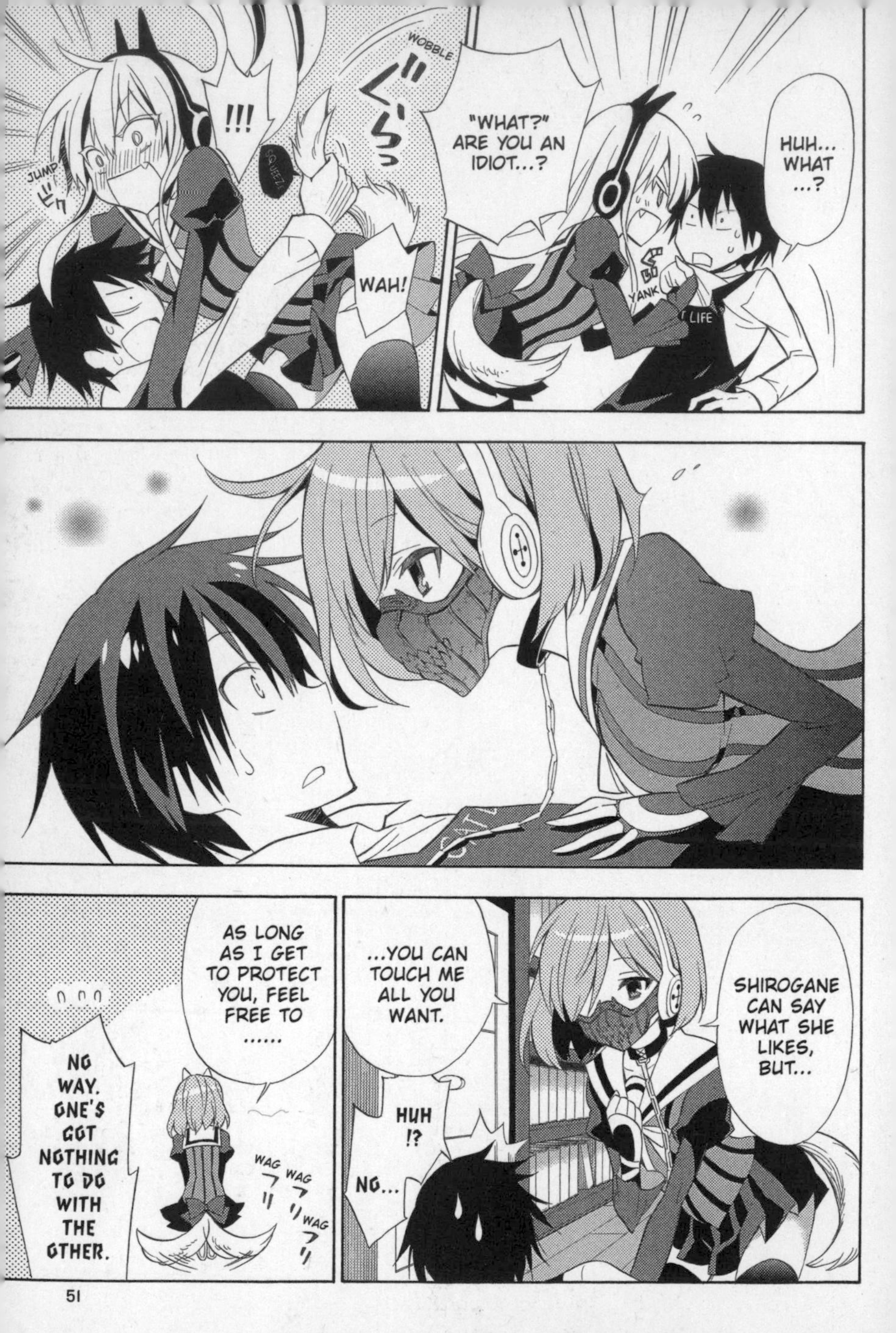
HUH... WHAT ...?
"WHAT?" ARE YOU AN IDIOT...?
YANK
WOBBLE
!!!
SQUEEZE
JUMP
WAH!
SHIROGANE CAN SAY WHAT SHE LIKES, BUT...
...YOU CAN TOUCH ME ALL YOU WANT.
HUH !?
NO...
AS LONG AS I GET TO PROTECT YOU, FEEL FREE TO ......
NO WAY. ONE'S GOT NOTHING TO DO WITH THE OTHER.
WAG
WAG
WAG

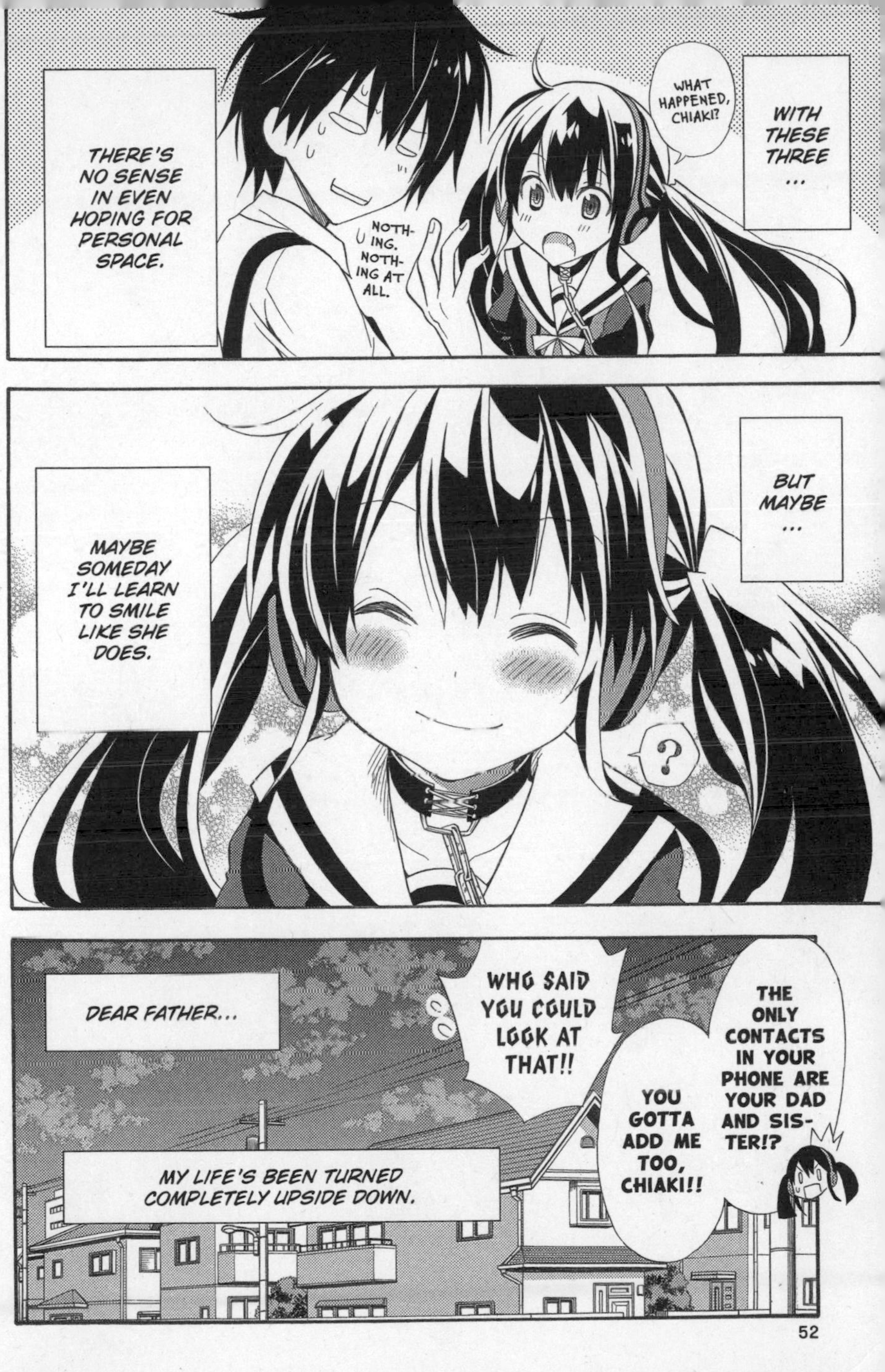
WITH THESE THREE ...
WHAT HAPPENED, CHIAKI?
NOTH-ING. NOTH-ING AT ALL.
THERE'S NO SENSE IN EVEN HOPING FOR PERSONAL SPACE.
BUT MAYBE ...
?
MAYBE SOMEDAY I'LL LEARN TO SMILE LIKE SHE DOES.
THE ONLY CONTACTS IN YOUR PHONE ARE YOUR DAD AND SIS-TER!?
YOU GOTTA ADD ME TOO, CHIAKI!!
WHO SAID YOU COULD LOOK AT THAT!!
DEAR FATHER...
MY LIFE'S BEEN TURNED COMPLETELY UPSIDE DOWN.

TODAY'S CERBERUS

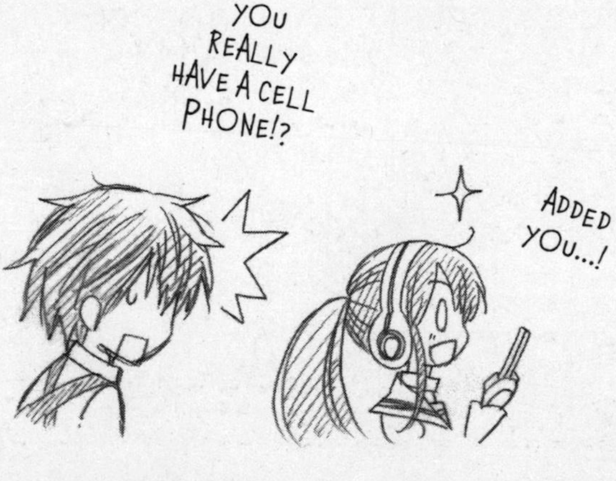
YOU REALLY HAVE A CELL PHONE!?
ADDED YOU...!

TODAY'S CERBERUS

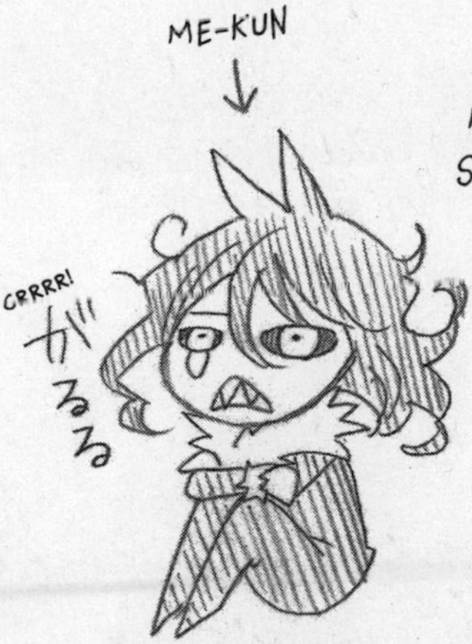
ME-KUN
CRRRR!
がるる

ME-KUN IS SUFFERING.

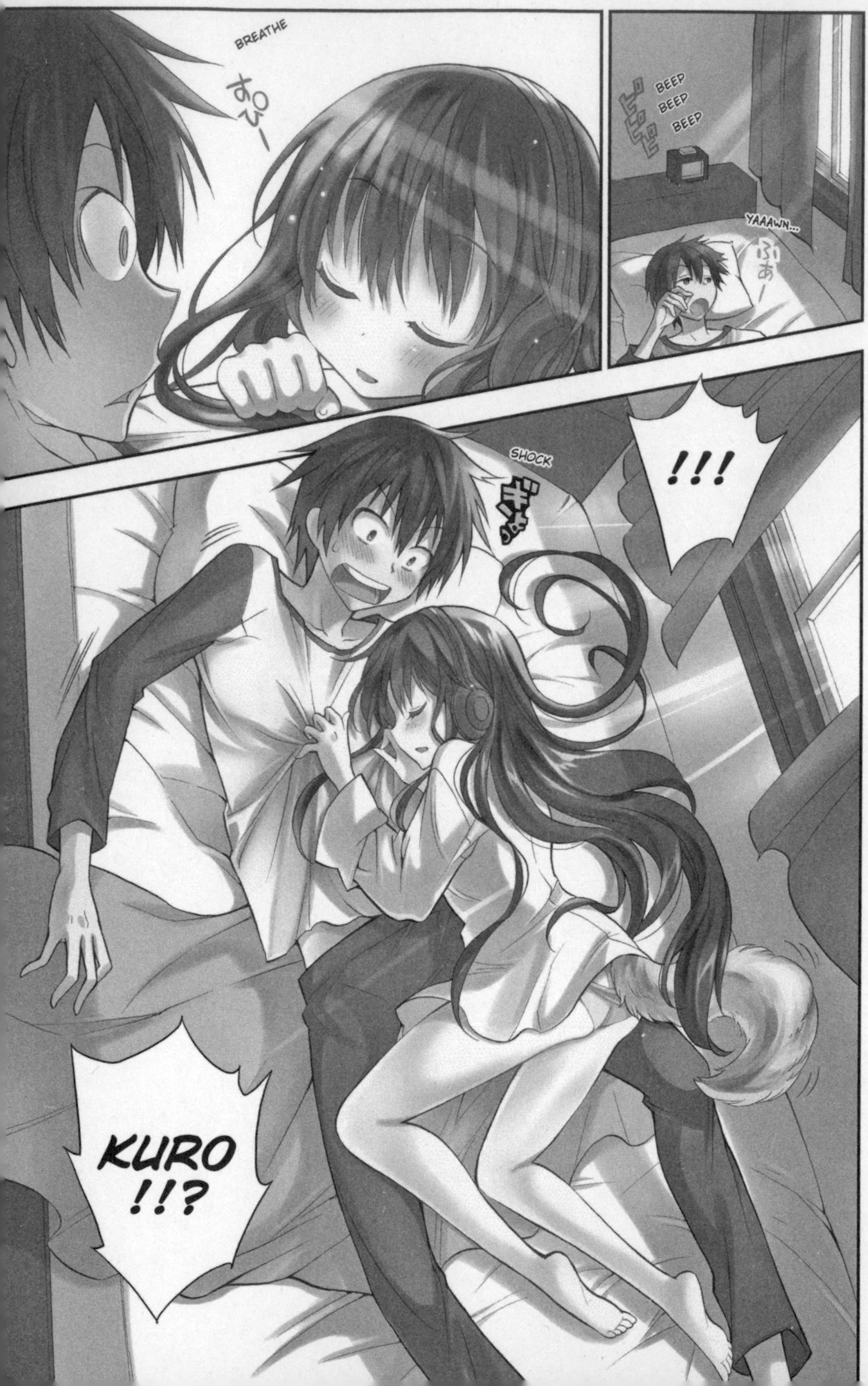

BEEP
BEEP
BEEP
ピピピ
YAAAWN...
ふあー
BREATHE
すぴー
!!!
SHOCK
KURO !!?

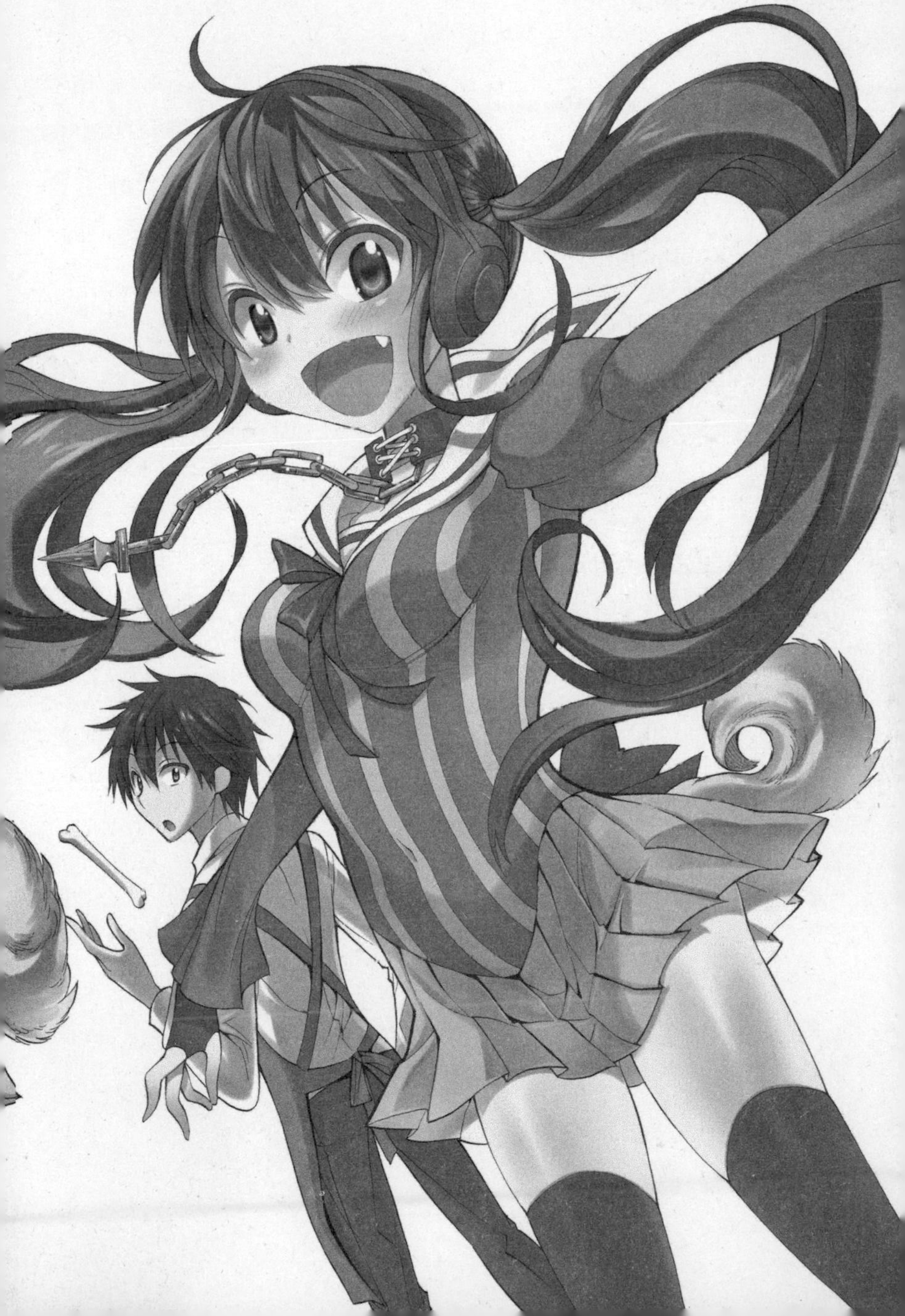

CHAPTER 1
FIRST ERRAND

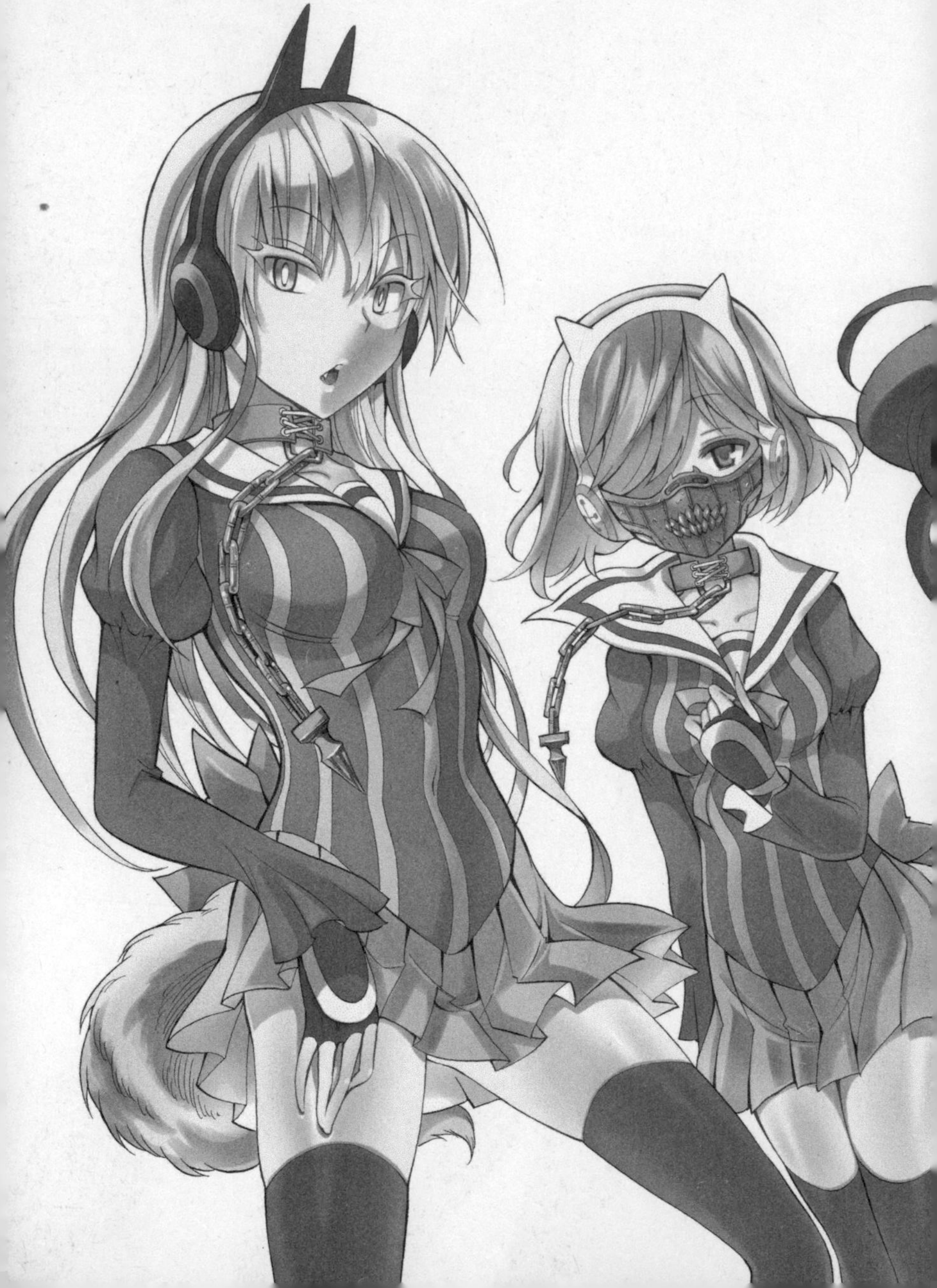

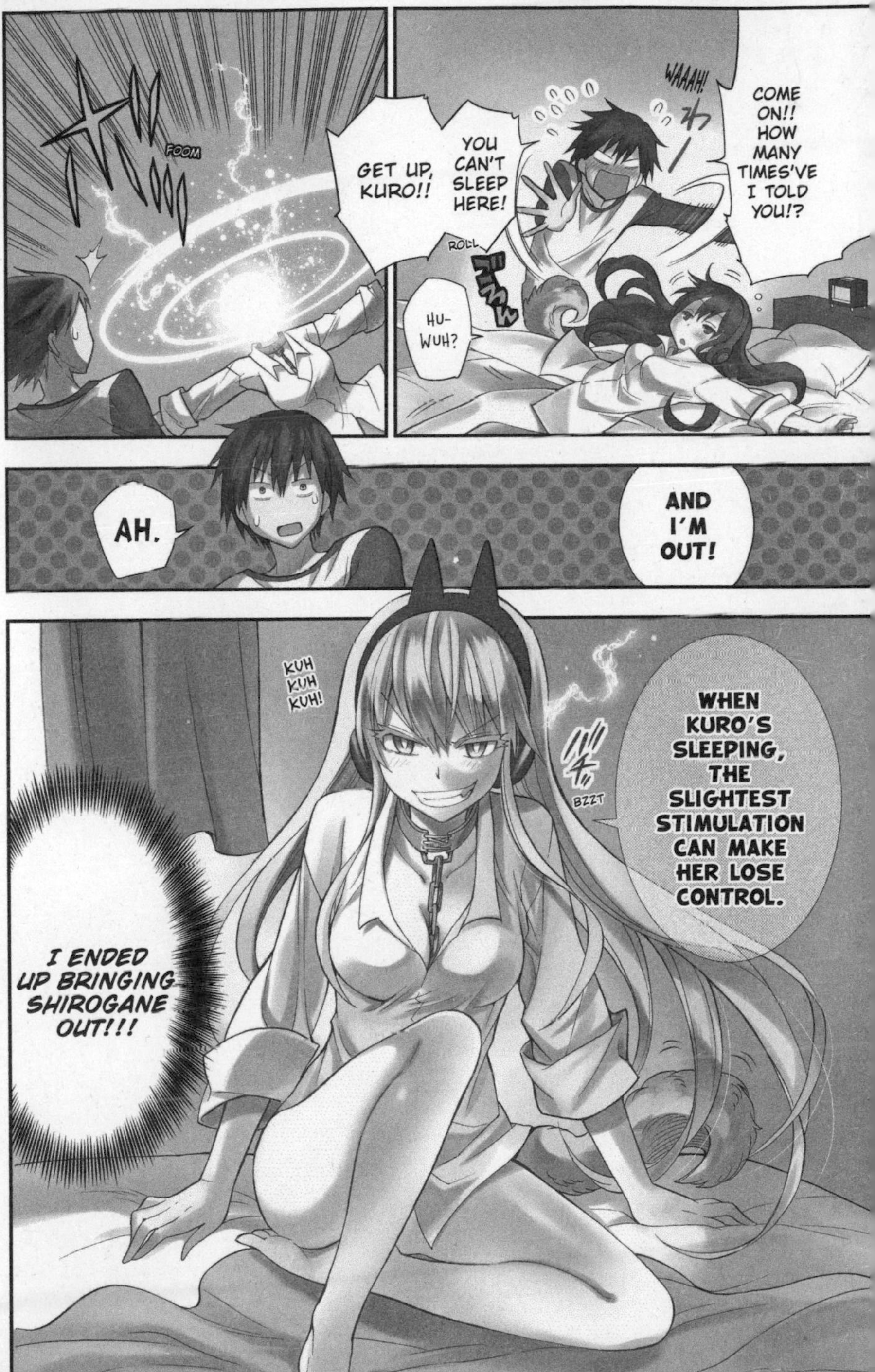

WAAAH!
COME ON!! HOW MANY TIMES'VE I TOLD YOU!?
YOU CAN'T SLEEP HERE!
GET UP, KURO!!
ROLL
HU-WUH?
FOOM
AND I'M OUT!
AH.
WHEN KURO'S SLEEPING, THE SLIGHTEST STIMULATION CAN MAKE HER LOSE CONTROL.
BZZT
KUH KUH KUH!
I ENDED UP BRINGING SHIROGANE OUT!!!

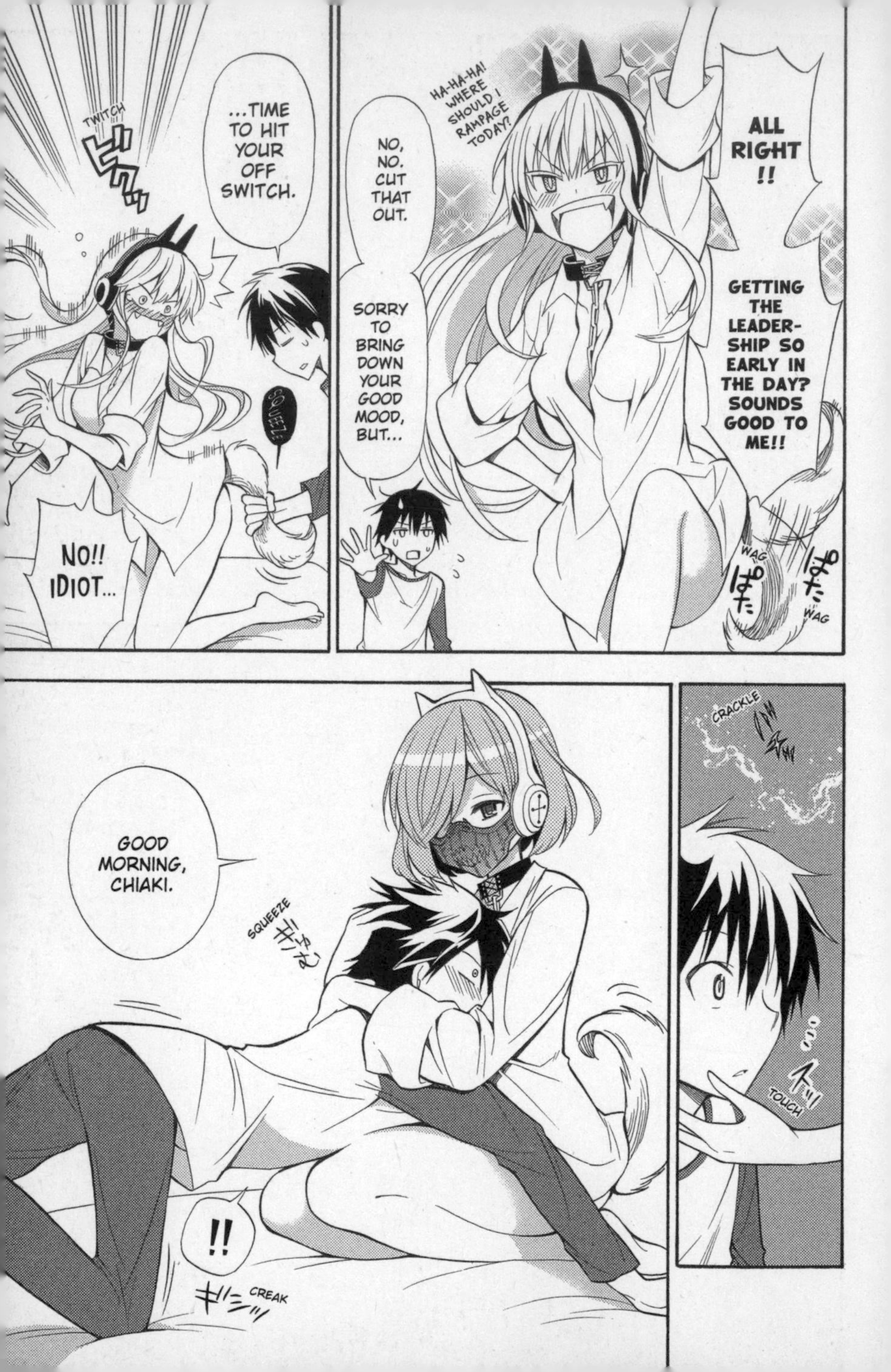
ALL RIGHT!!
GETTING THE LEADERSHIP SO EARLY IN THE DAY? SOUNDS GOOD TO ME!!
HA-HA-HA! WHERE SHOULD I RAMPAGE TODAY?
NO, NO. CUT THAT OUT.
SORRY TO BRING DOWN YOUR GOOD MOOD, BUT...
WAG
WAG
...TIME TO HIT YOUR OFF SWITCH.
TWITCH
SQUEEZE
NO!! IDIOT...
CRACKLE
TOUCH
...
GOOD MORNING, CHIAKI.
SQUEEZE
!!
CREAK

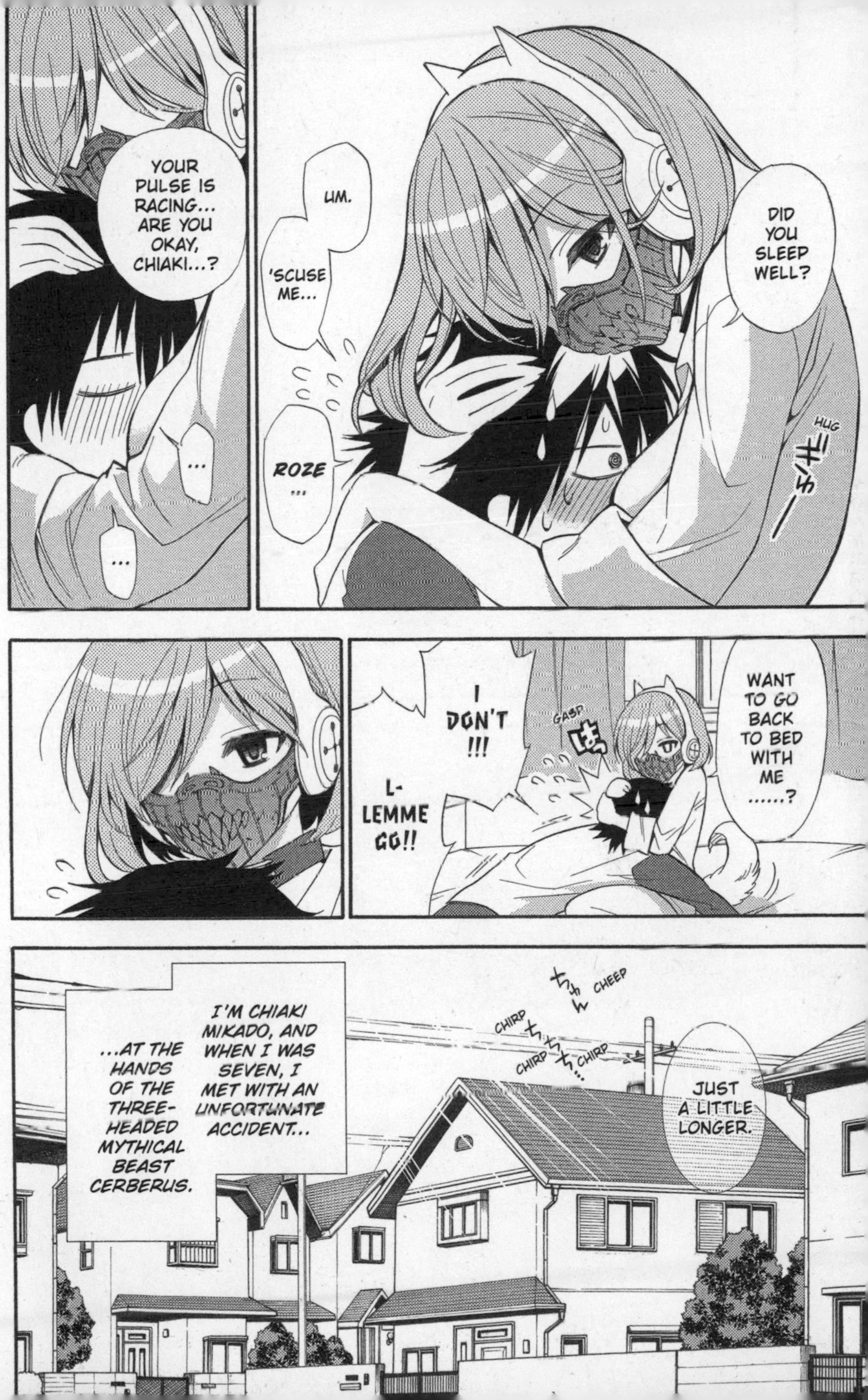

DID YOU SLEEP WELL?
HUG
UM.
'SCUSE ME...
ROZE...
YOUR PULSE IS RACING... ARE YOU OKAY, CHIAKI...?
...
...
WANT TO GO BACK TO BED WITH ME ......?
GASP
I DON'T!!!
L-LEMME GO!!
CHEEP
CHIRP
CHIRP
CHIRP
JUST A LITTLE LONGER.
I'M CHIAKI MIKADO, AND WHEN I WAS SEVEN, I MET WITH AN UNFORTUNATE ACCIDENT...
...AT THE HANDS OF THE THREE-HEADED MYTHICAL BEAST CERBERUS.

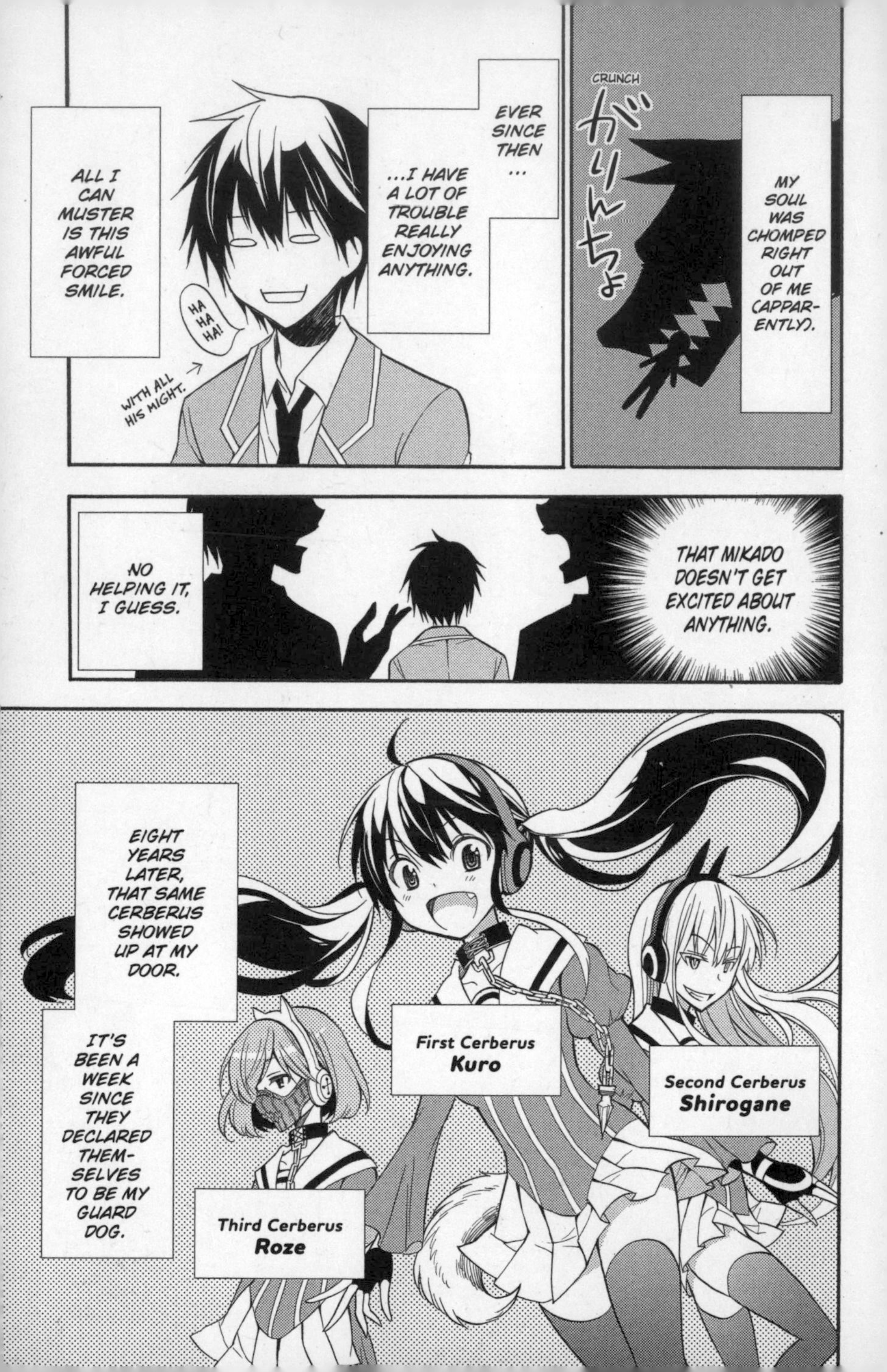
CRUNCH
がりんちょ
MY SOUL WAS CHOMPED RIGHT OUT OF ME (APPARENTLY).
EVER SINCE THEN...
...I HAVE A LOT OF TROUBLE REALLY ENJOYING ANYTHING.
ALL I CAN MUSTER IS THIS AWFUL FORCED SMILE.
HA HA HA!
WITH ALL HIS MIGHT.
THAT MIKADO DOESN'T GET EXCITED ABOUT ANYTHING.
NO HELPING IT, I GUESS.
EIGHT YEARS LATER, THAT SAME CERBERUS SHOWED UP AT MY DOOR.
IT'S BEEN A WEEK SINCE THEY DECLARED THEM-SELVES TO BE MY GUARD DOG.
First Cerberus Kuro
Second Cerberus Shirogane
Third Cerberus Roze

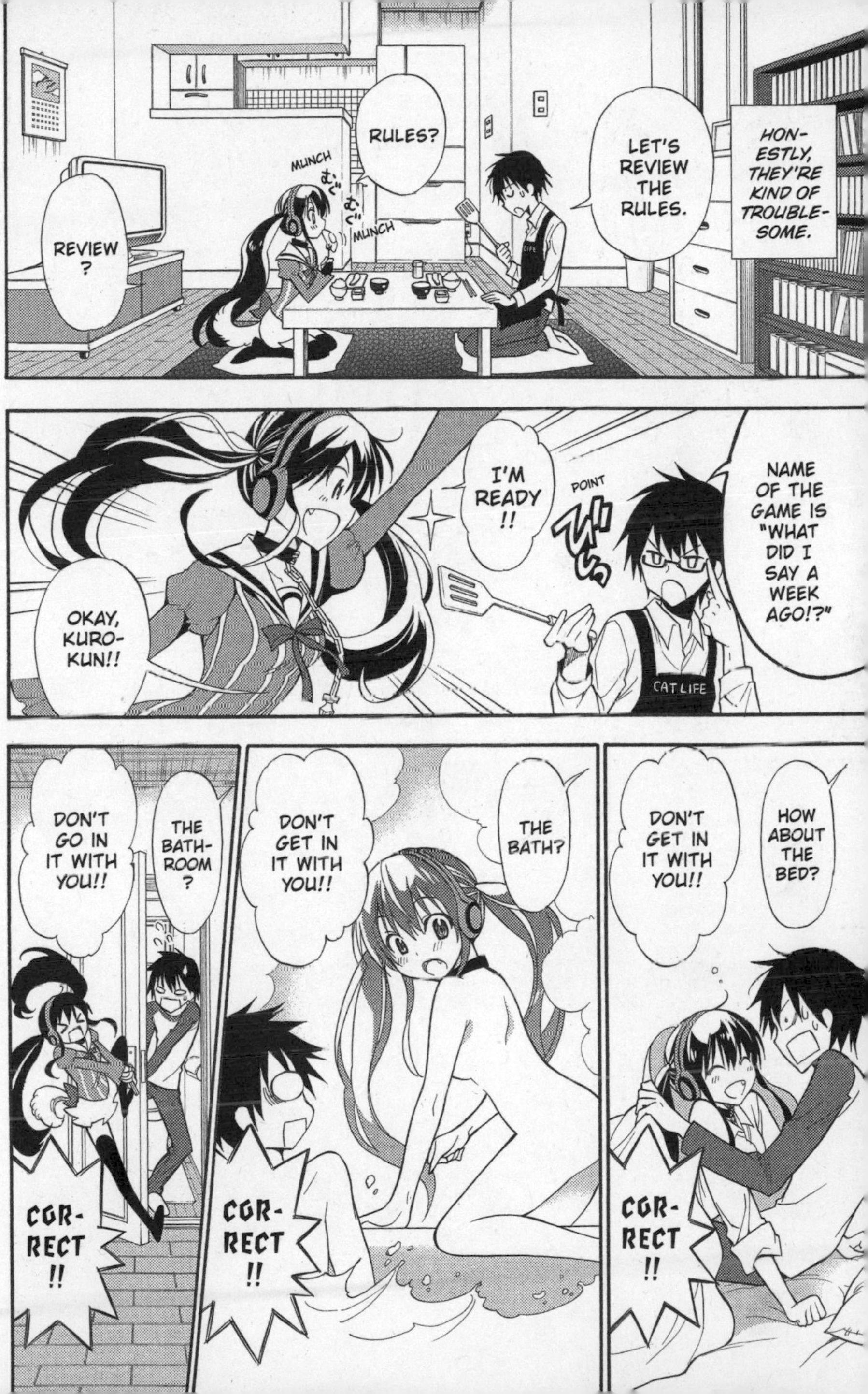
HON-ESTLY, THEY'RE KIND OF TROUBLE-SOME.
LET'S REVIEW THE RULES.
RULES?
MUNCH
むぐ
むぐ
MUNCH
REVIEW?
NAME OF THE GAME IS "WHAT DID I SAY A WEEK AGO!?"
POINT
I'M READY!!
OKAY, KURO-KUN!!
HOW ABOUT THE BED?
DON'T GET IN IT WITH YOU!!
COR-RECT!!
THE BATH?
DON'T GET IN IT WITH YOU!!
COR-RECT!!
THE BATH-ROOM?
DON'T GO IN IT WITH YOU!!
COR-RECT!!

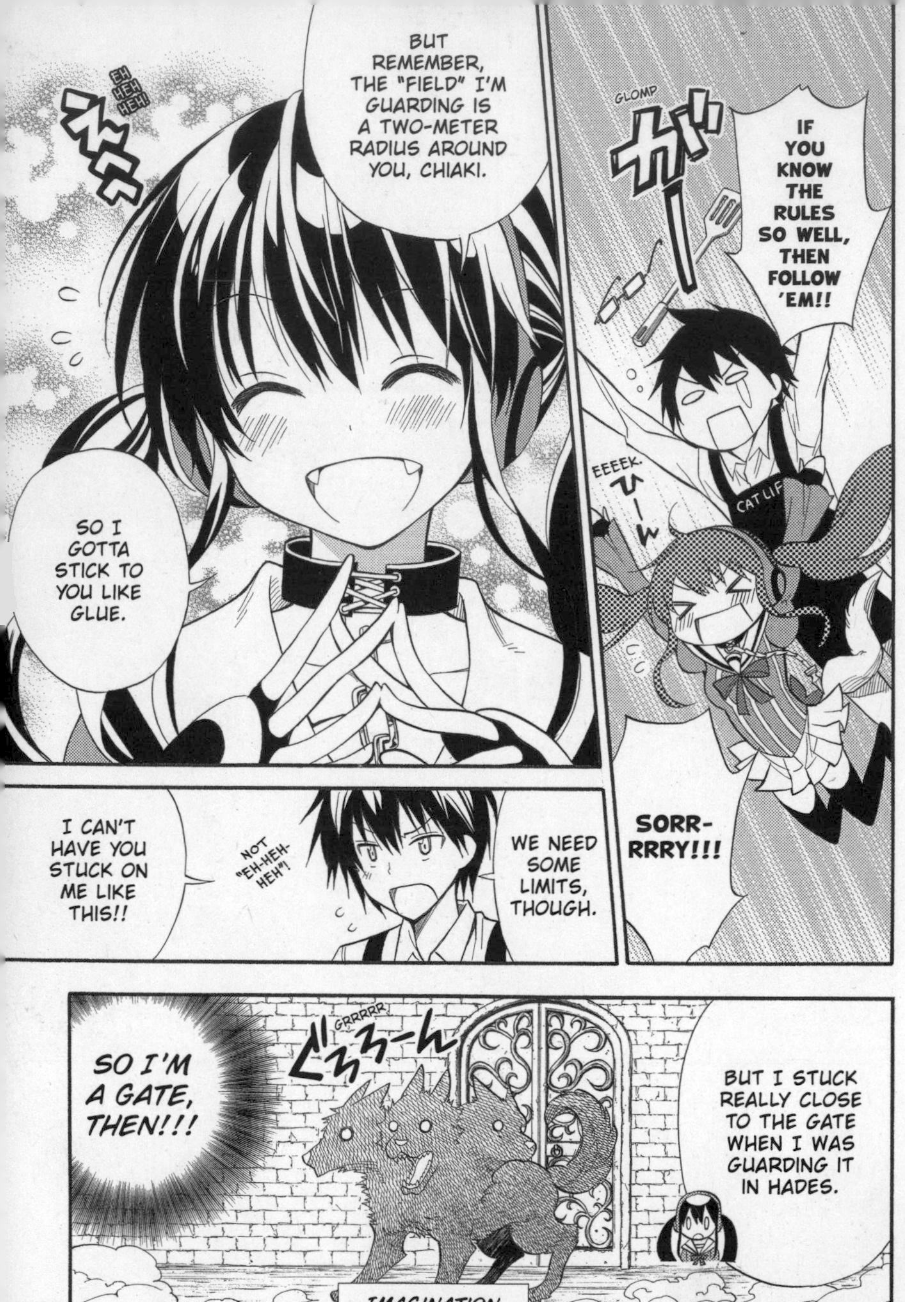
GLOMP
IF YOU KNOW THE RULES SO WELL, THEN FOLLOW 'EM!!
EEEEK.
CAT LIF
SORR-RRRY!!!
BUT REMEMBER, THE "FIELD" I'M GUARDING IS A TWO-METER RADIUS AROUND YOU, CHIAKI.
EH HEH HEH!
SO I GOTTA STICK TO YOU LIKE GLUE.
WE NEED SOME LIMITS, THOUGH.
NOT "EH-HEH-HEH"!
I CAN'T HAVE YOU STUCK ON ME LIKE THIS!!
BUT I STUCK REALLY CLOSE TO THE GATE WHEN I WAS GUARDING IT IN HADES.
GRRRRRR
SO I'M A GATE, THEN!!!
IMAGINATION

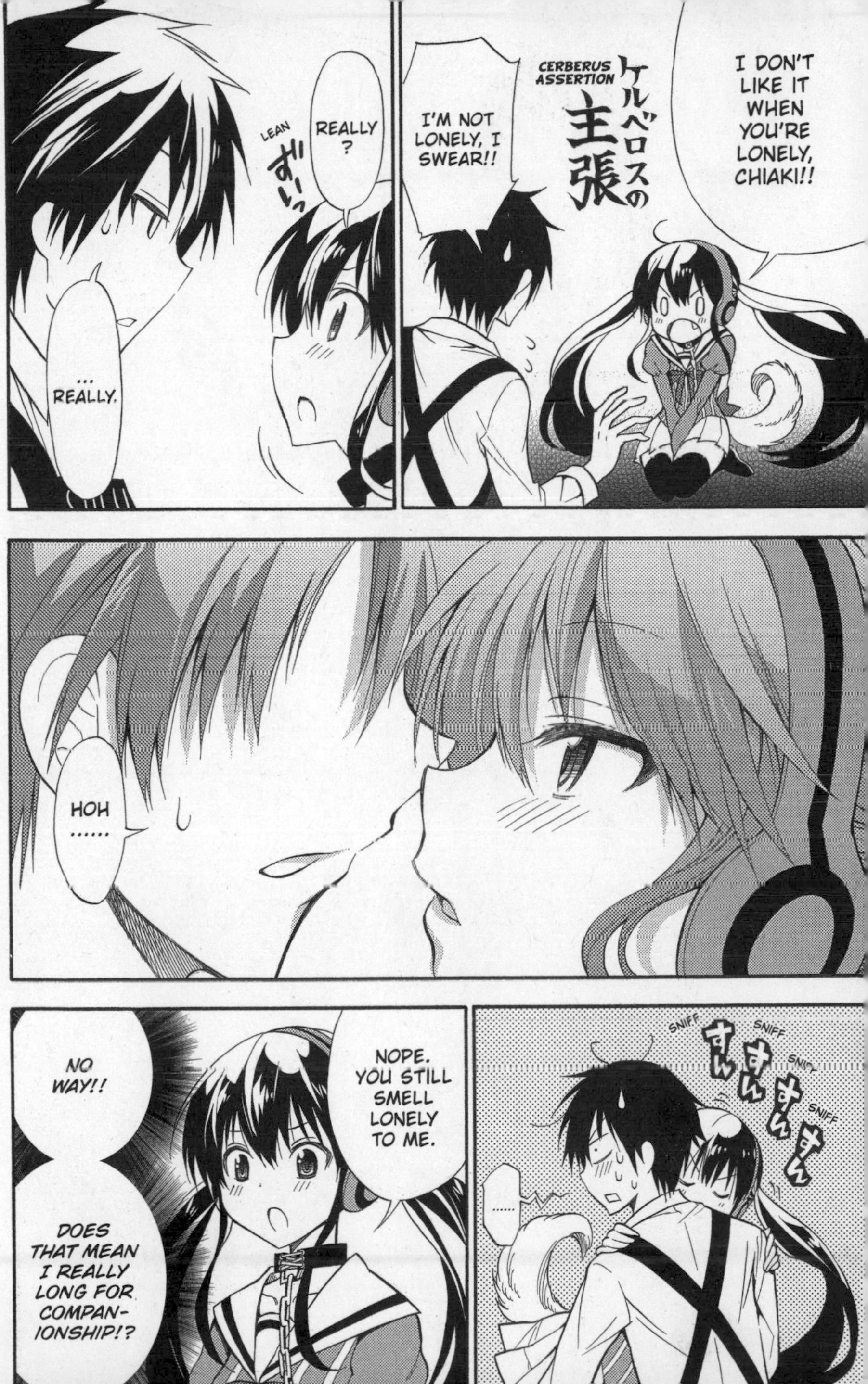
I DON'T LIKE IT WHEN YOU'RE LONELY, CHIAKI!!
CERBERUS ASSERTION
ケルベロスの主張
I'M NOT LONELY, I SWEAR!!
REALLY ?
LEAN
ずいっ
... REALLY.
HOH ......
SNIFF
SNIFF
SNIFF
SNIFF
すんすんすんすん
......
NOPE. YOU STILL SMELL LONELY TO ME.
NO WAY!!
DOES THAT MEAN I REALLY LONG FOR COMPAN-IONSHIP!?

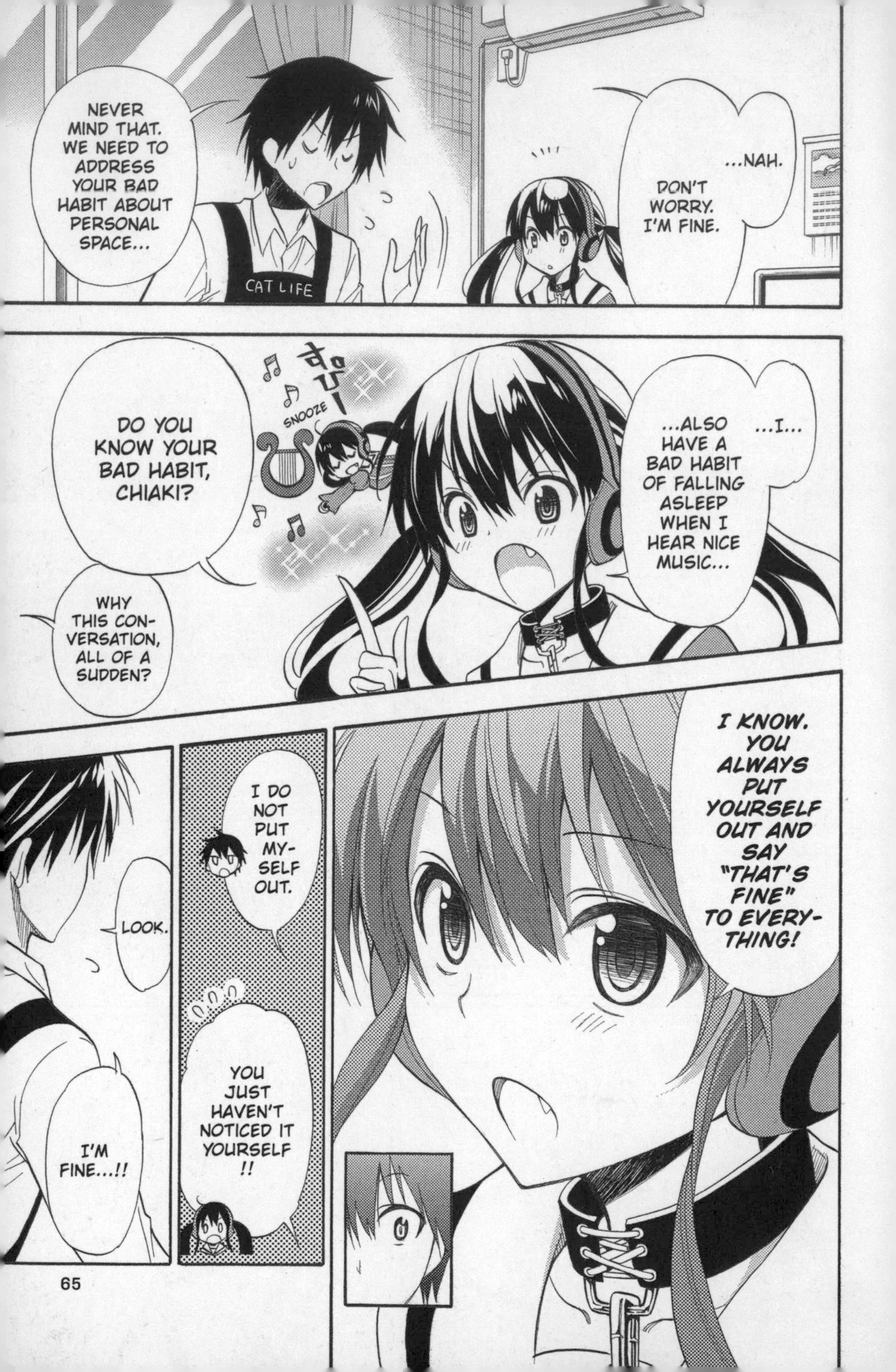
...NAH.
DON'T WORRY. I'M FINE.
NEVER MIND THAT. WE NEED TO ADDRESS YOUR BAD HABIT ABOUT PERSONAL SPACE...
CAT LIFE
...I...
...ALSO HAVE A BAD HABIT OF FALLING ASLEEP WHEN I HEAR NICE MUSIC...
SNOOZE
DO YOU KNOW YOUR BAD HABIT, CHIAKI?
WHY THIS CON-VERSATION, ALL OF A SUDDEN?
I KNOW. YOU ALWAYS PUT YOURSELF OUT AND SAY "THAT'S FINE" TO EVERY-THING!
I DO NOT PUT MY-SELF OUT.
YOU JUST HAVEN'T NOTICED IT YOURSELF !!
LOOK.
I'M FINE...!!

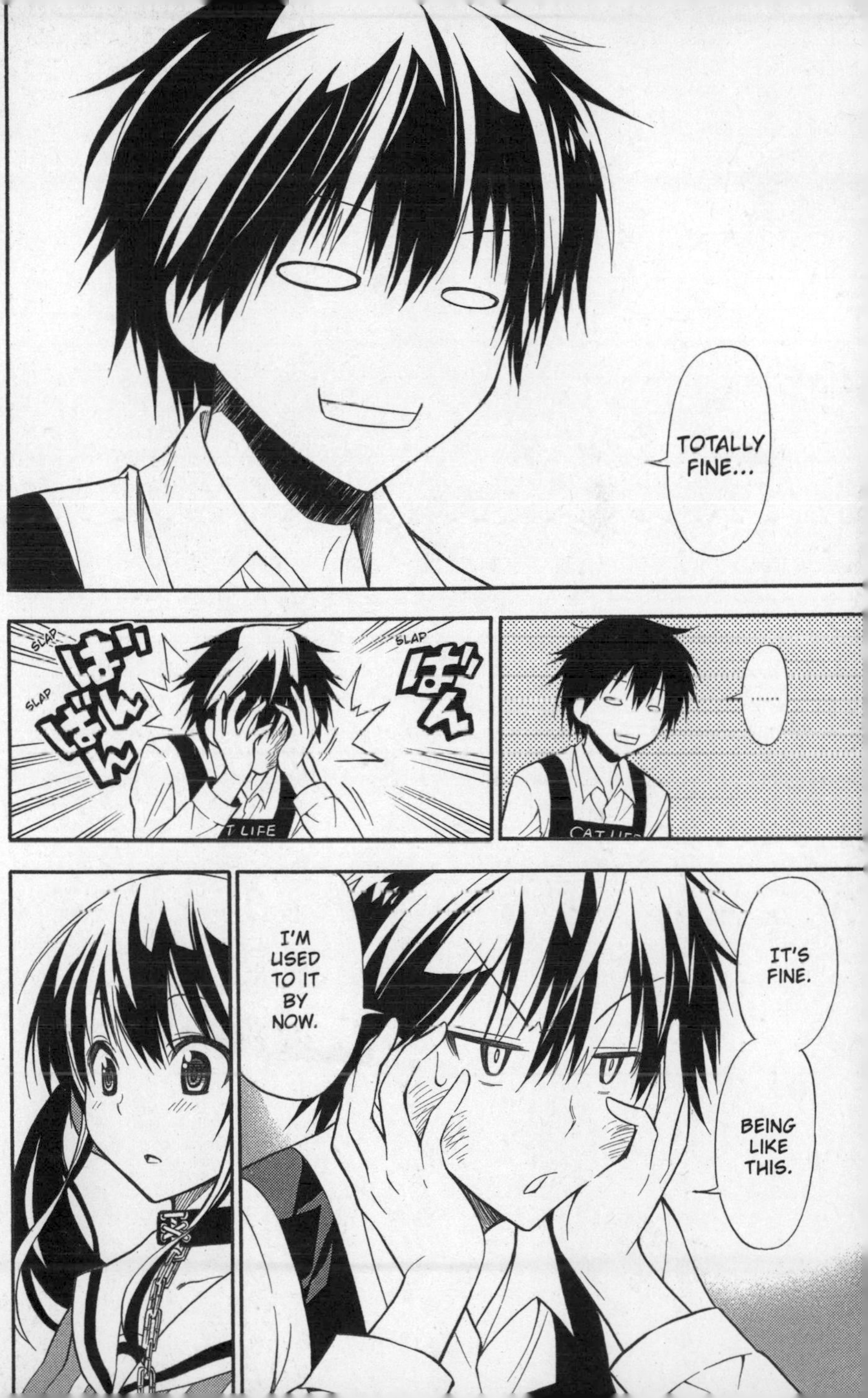
TOTALLY FINE...
......
SLAP
SLAP
SLAP
IT'S FINE.
BEING LIKE THIS.
I'M USED TO IT BY NOW.

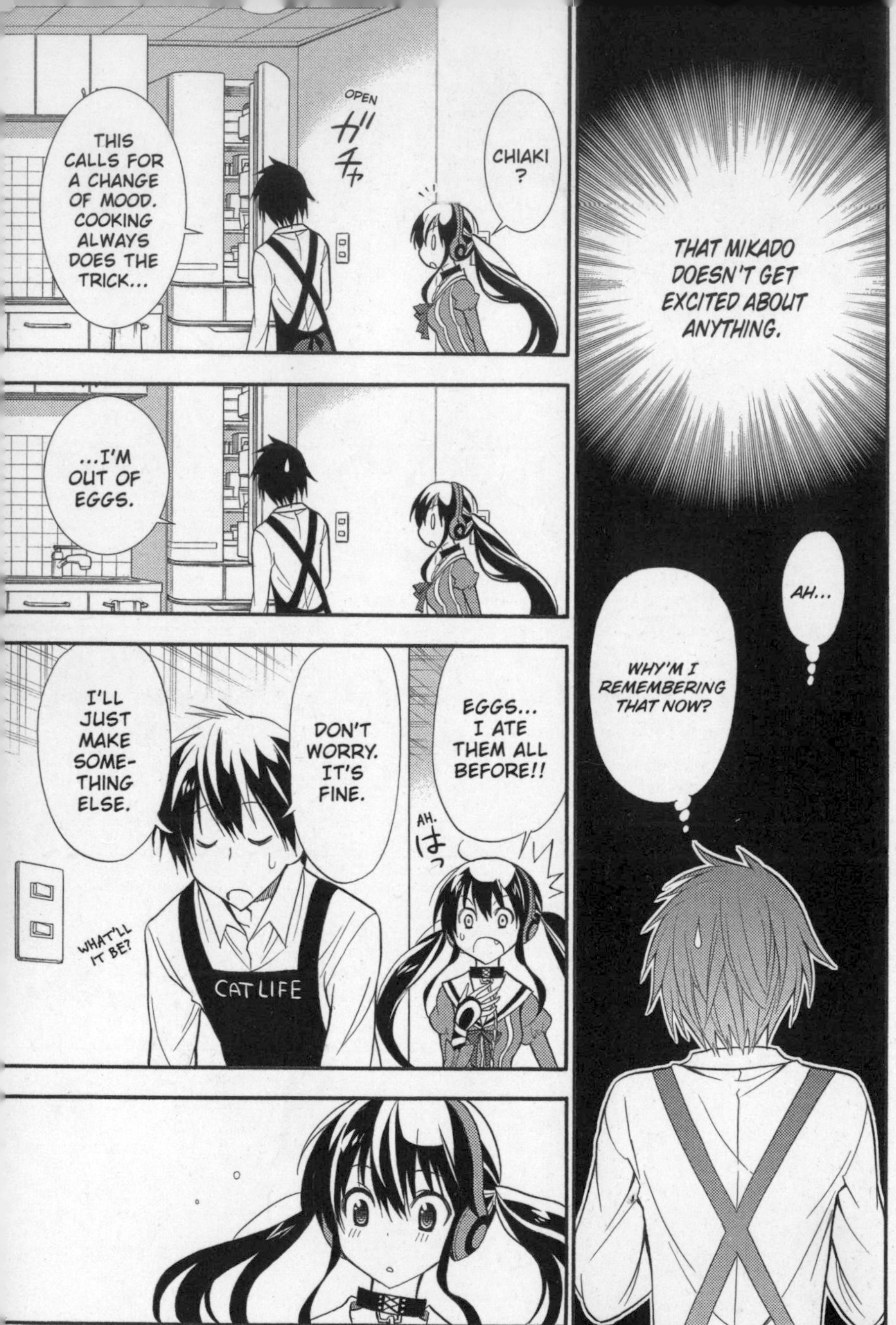
THAT MIKADO DOESN'T GET EXCITED ABOUT ANYTHING.
AH...
WHY'M I REMEMBERING THAT NOW?
CHIAKI?
OPEN
ガチャ
THIS CALLS FOR A CHANGE OF MOOD. COOKING ALWAYS DOES THE TRICK...
...I'M OUT OF EGGS.
EGGS... I ATE THEM ALL BEFORE!!
AH.
はっ
DON'T WORRY. IT'S FINE.
I'LL JUST MAKE SOME-THING ELSE.
WHAT'LL IT BE?
CAT LIFE

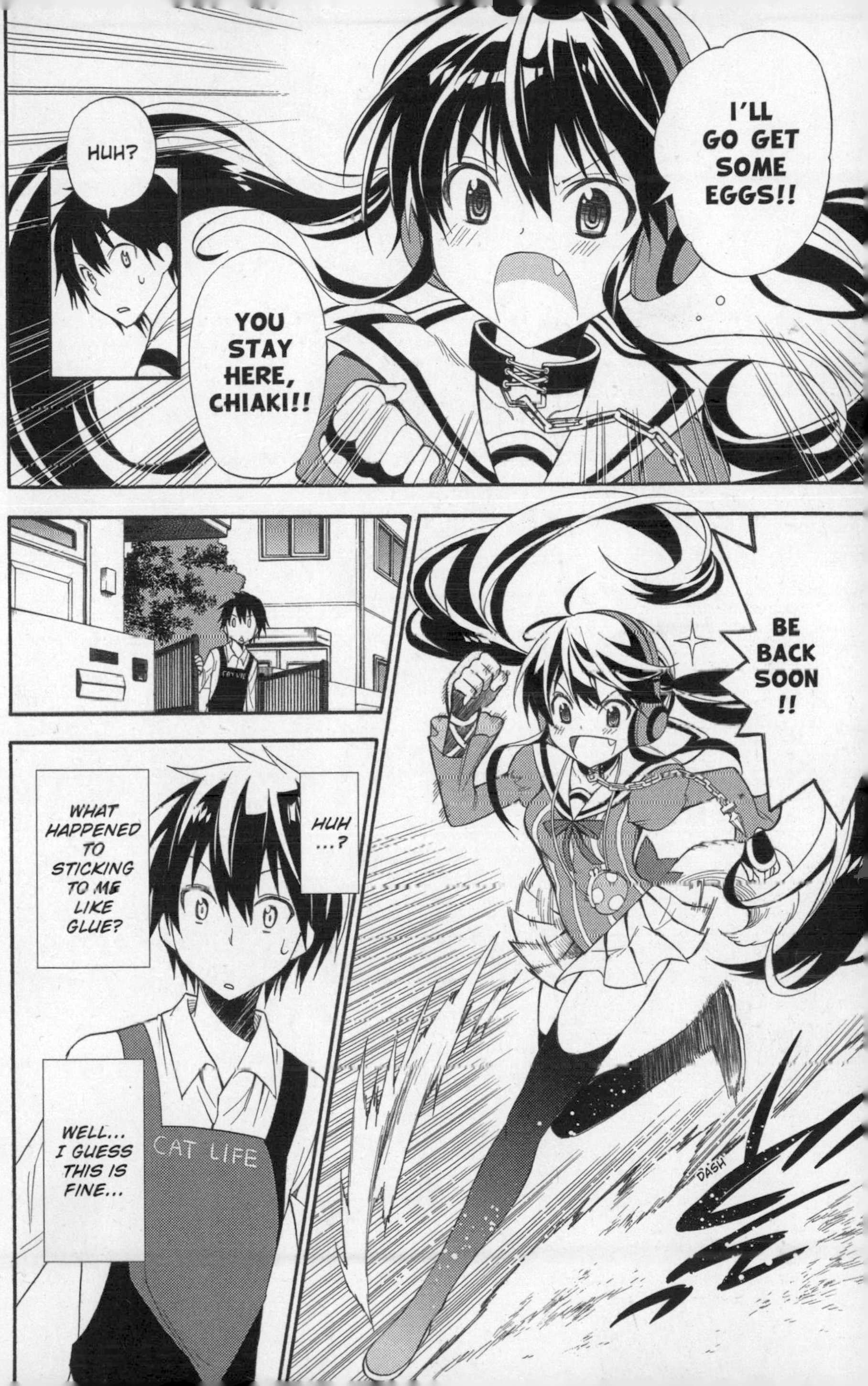
I'LL GO GET SOME EGGS!!
YOU STAY HERE, CHIAKI!!
HUH?
BE BACK SOON!!
DASH
HUH ...?
WHAT HAPPENED TO STICKING TO ME LIKE GLUE?
CAT LIFE
WELL... I GUESS THIS IS FINE...

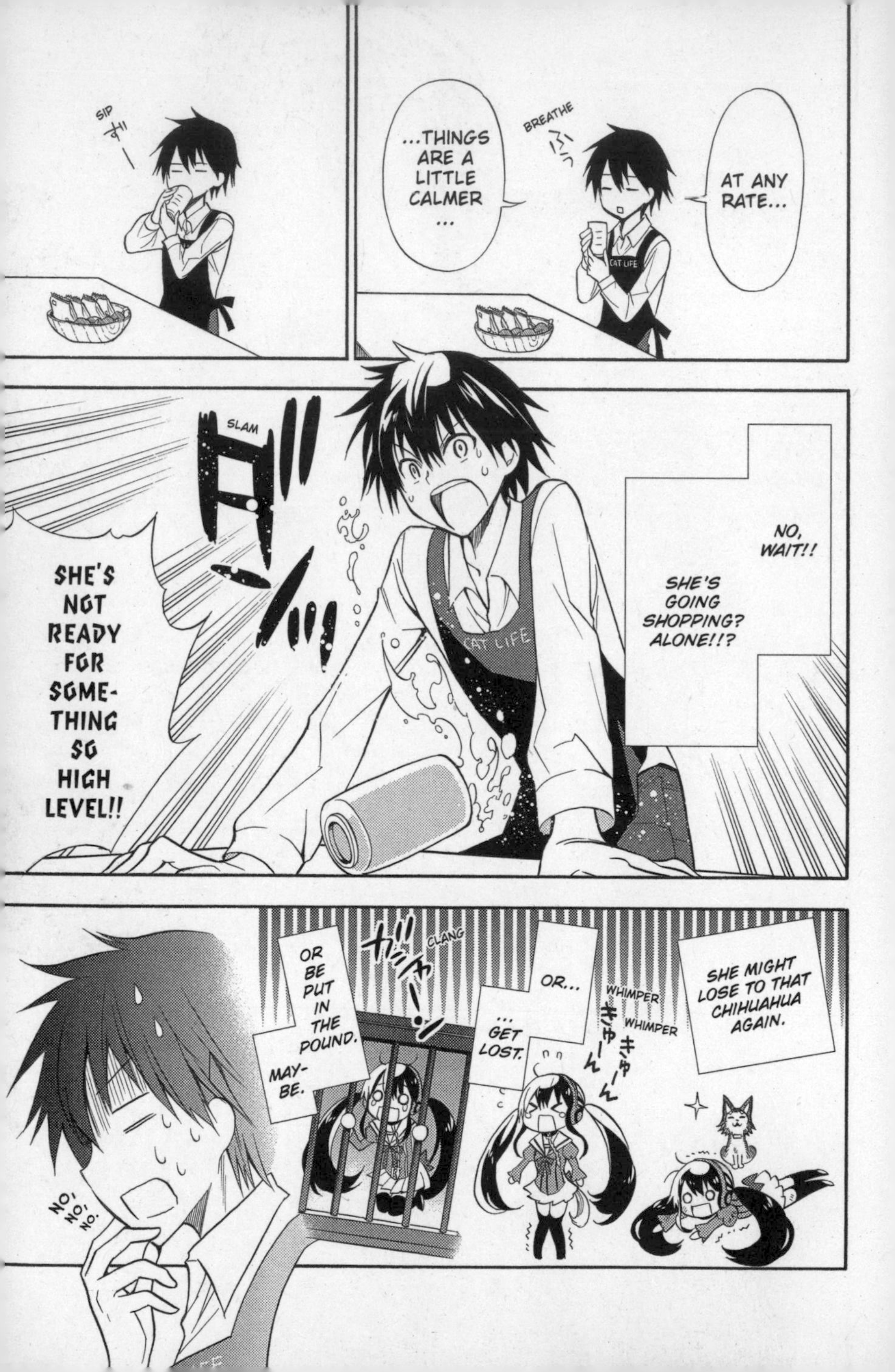
BREATHE
ふぅ
AT ANY RATE...
...THINGS ARE A LITTLE CALMER...
SIP
ずー
NO, WAIT!!
SHE'S GOING SHOPPING? ALONE!!?
SLAM
SHE'S NOT READY FOR SOME-THING SO HIGH LEVEL!!
SHE MIGHT LOSE TO THAT CHIHUAHUA AGAIN.
WHIMPER WHIMPER
OR...
...GET LOST.
CLANG
OR BE PUT IN THE POUND.
MAY-BE.
NO, NO, NO.

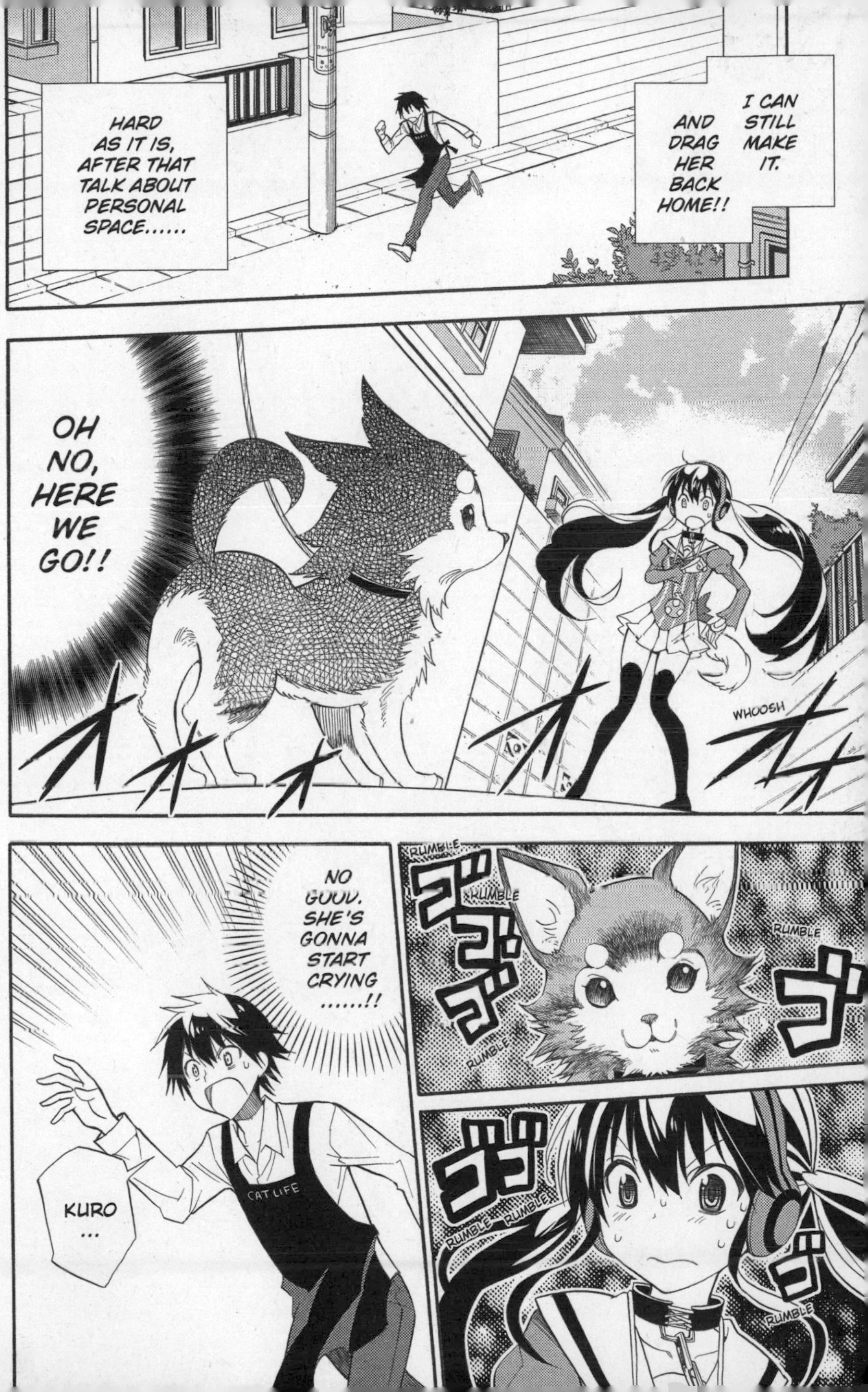

I CAN STILL MAKE IT. AND DRAG HER BACK HOME!!
HARD AS IT IS, AFTER THAT TALK ABOUT PERSONAL SPACE......
WHOOSH
OH NO, HERE WE GO!!
RUMBLE
RUMBLE
RUMBLE
RUMBLE
RUMBLE RUMBLE
RUMBLE
RUMBLE
NO GOOD. SHE'S GONNA START CRYING ......!!
KURO ...
CAT LIFE

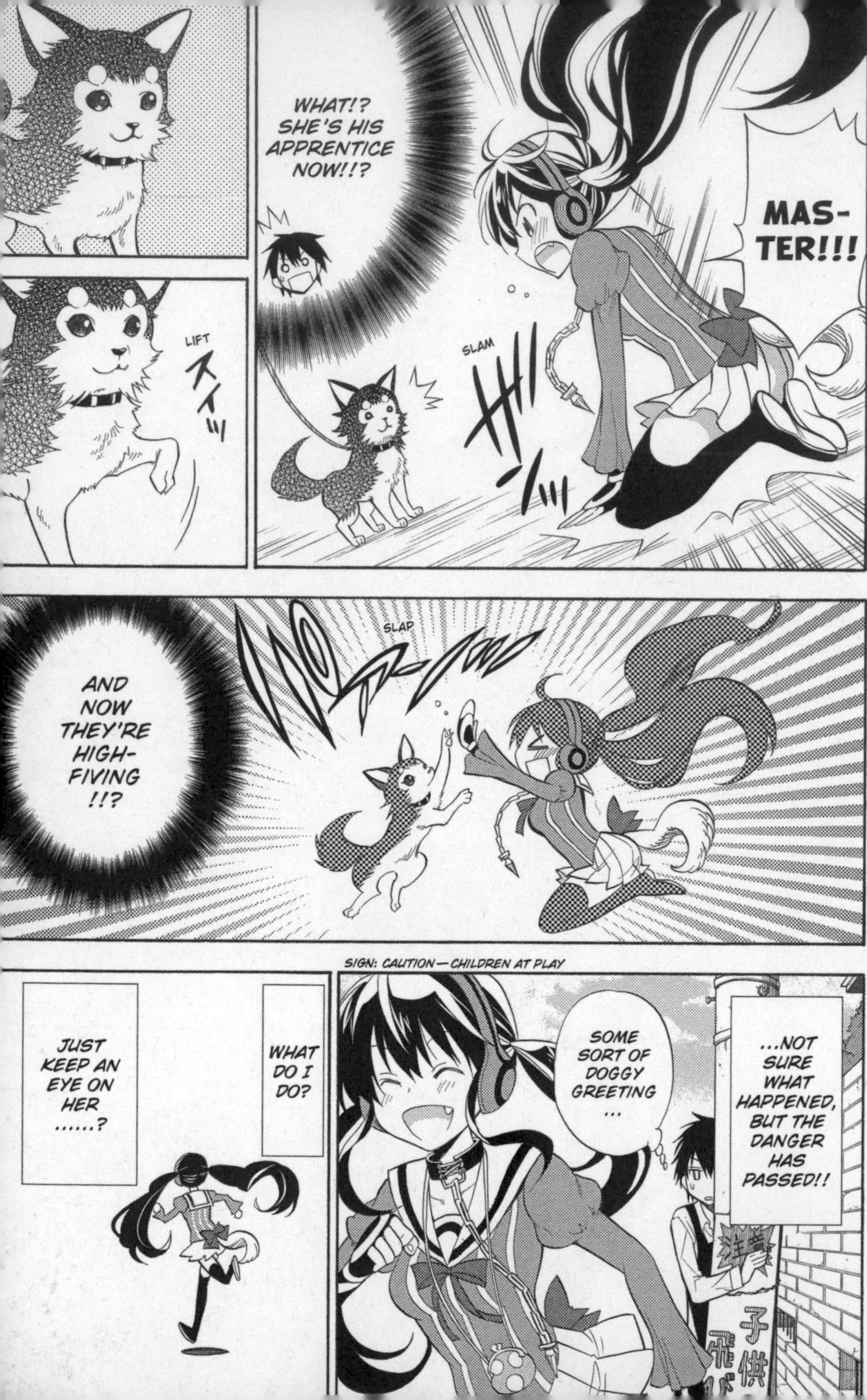
MAS-TER!!!
WHAT!? SHE'S HIS APPRENTICE NOW!!?
SLAM
LIFT
スイッ
SLAP
AND NOW THEY'RE HIGH-FIVING!!?
SIGN: CAUTION—CHILDREN AT PLAY
...NOT SURE WHAT HAPPENED, BUT THE DANGER HAS PASSED!!
SOME SORT OF DOGGY GREETING ...
WHAT DO I DO?
JUST KEEP AN EYE ON HER ......?

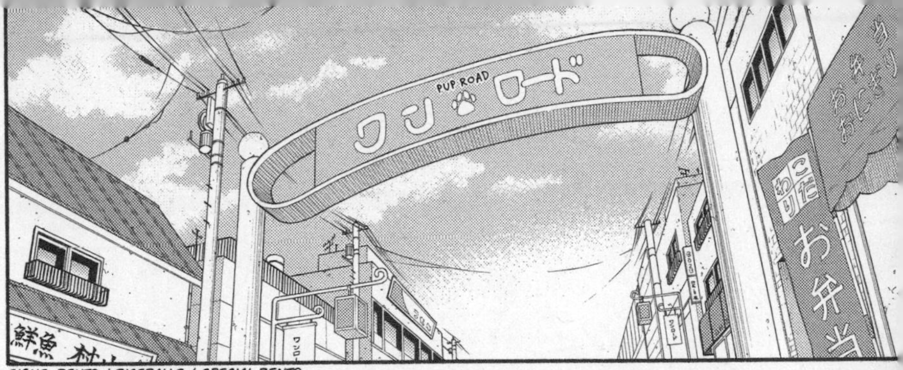
PUP ROAD
ワン ロード
お弁当
こだわり
SIGNS: BENTO / RICEBALLS / SPECIAL BENTO

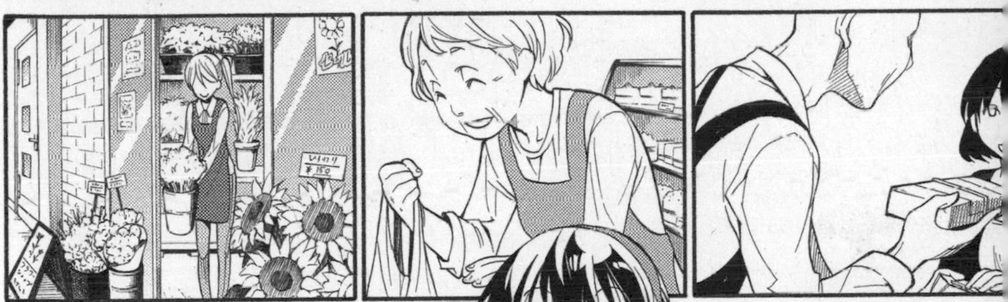
SIGNS: SPECIAL SALE TODAY / SHIMIZU PHARMACY

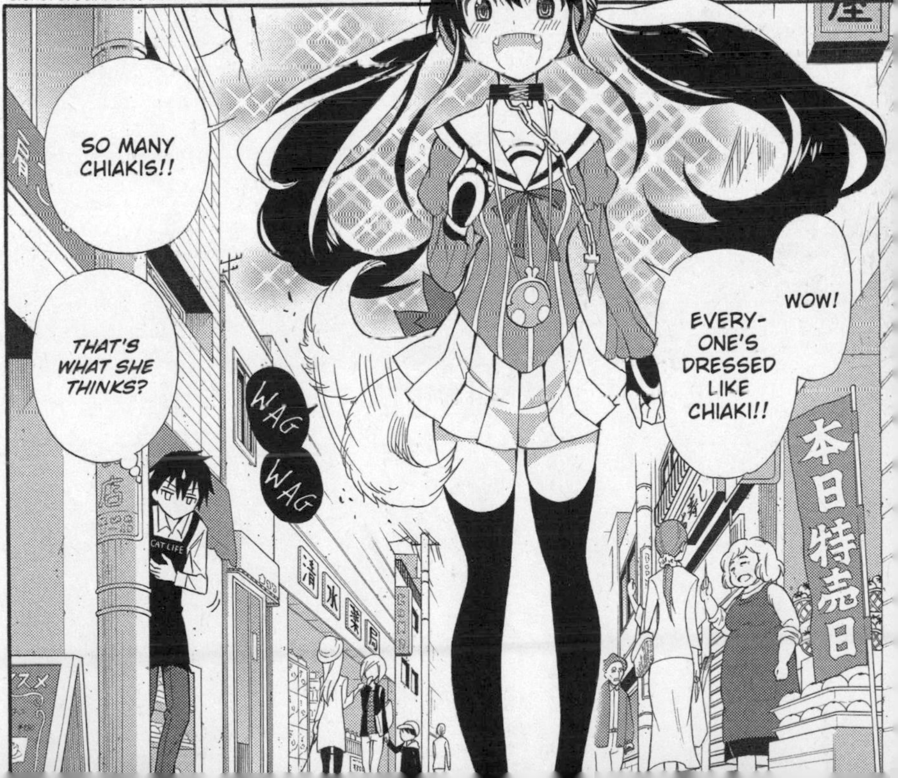
WOW!
EVERY-ONE'S DRESSED LIKE CHIAKI!!
SO MANY CHIAKIS!!
WAG WAG
THAT'S WHAT SHE THINKS?
本日特売日
清水薬局
CAT LIFE

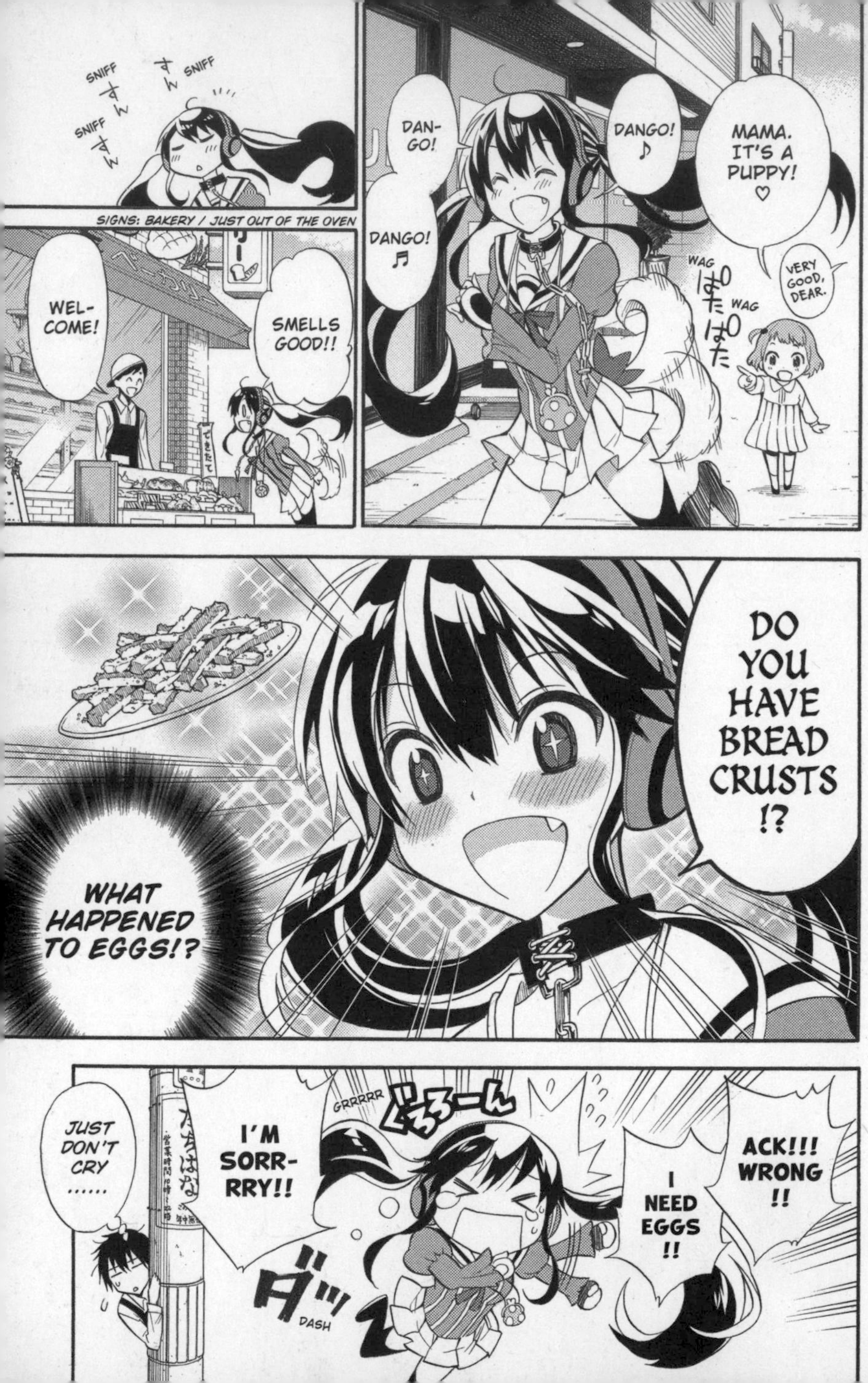

MAMA. IT'S A PUPPY! ♡
VERY GOOD, DEAR.
WAG ぱた WAG ぱた
DANGO! ♪
DAN-GO!
DANGO! ♬
SNIFF すん SNIFF すん SNIFF すん
SIGNS: BAKERY / JUST OUT OF THE OVEN
SMELLS GOOD!!
WEL-COME!
DO YOU HAVE BREAD CRUSTS !?
WHAT HAPPENED TO EGGS!?
ACK!!! WRONG !!
I NEED EGGS !!
GRRRRR ぐるるーん
I'M SORR-RRY!!
ダッ DASH
JUST DON'T CRY ......

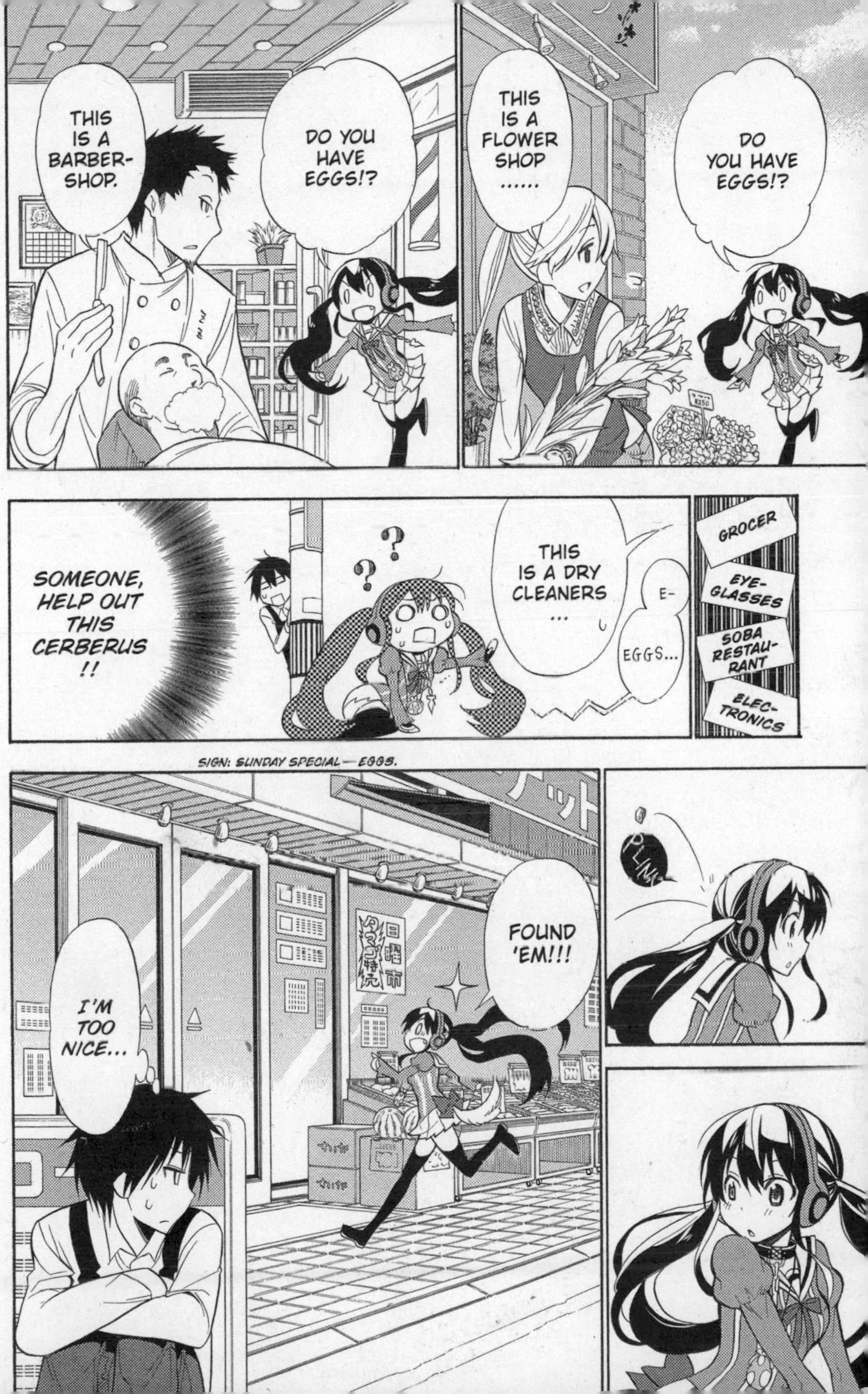
DO YOU HAVE EGGS!?
THIS IS A FLOWER SHOP ......
DO YOU HAVE EGGS!?
THIS IS A BARBER-SHOP.
GROCER
EYE-GLASSES
SOBA RESTAU-RANT
ELEC-TRONICS
E- EGGS...
THIS IS A DRY CLEANERS ...
SOMEONE, HELP OUT THIS CERBERUS !!
PLINK
SIGN: SUNDAY SPECIAL— EGGS.
FOUND 'EM!!!
I'M TOO NICE...

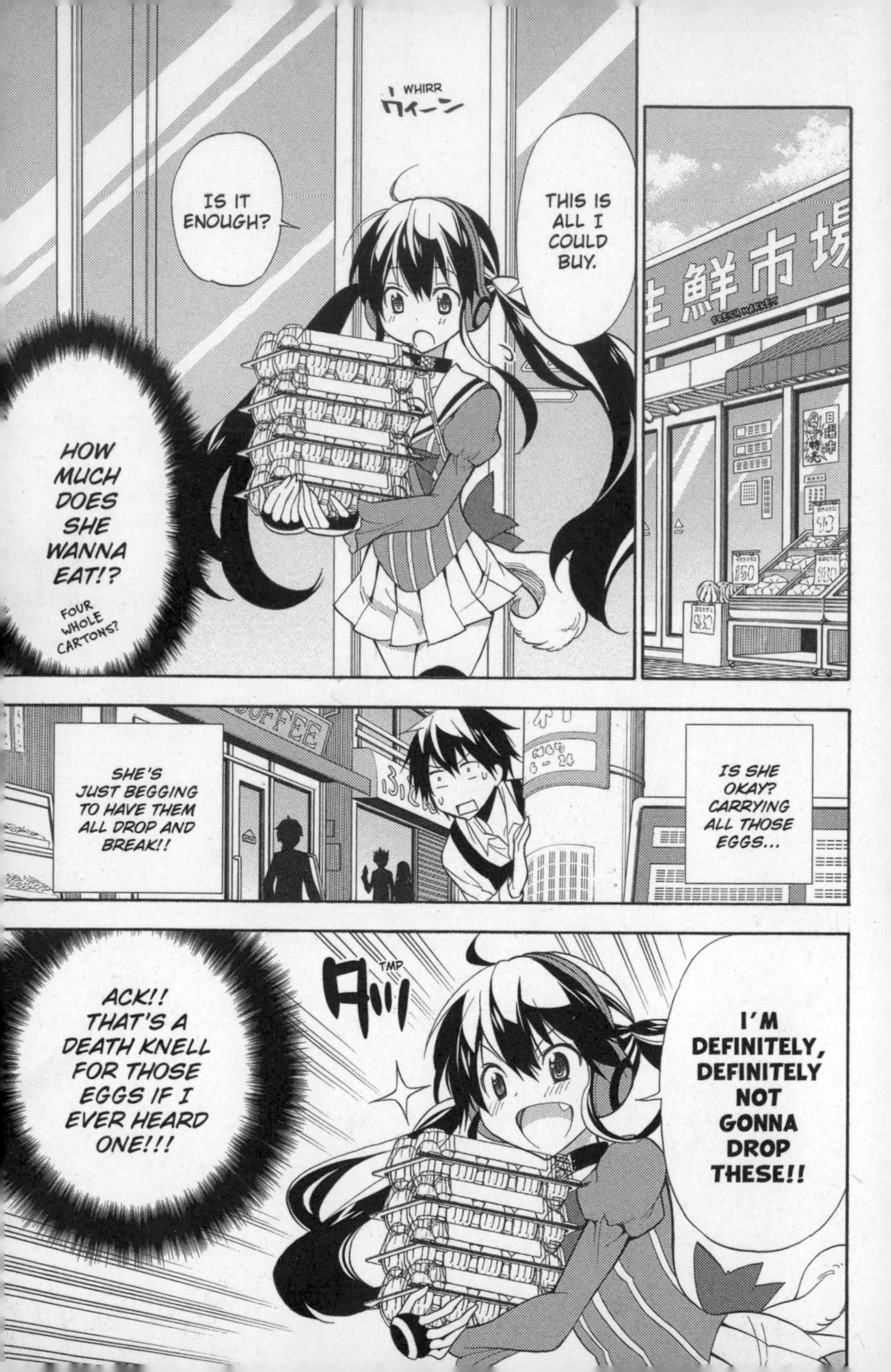

生鮮市場
FRESH MARKET
150
WHIRR
ウィーン
THIS IS ALL I COULD BUY.
IS IT ENOUGH?
HOW MUCH DOES SHE WANNA EAT!?
FOUR WHOLE CARTONS?
IS SHE OKAY? CARRYING ALL THOSE EGGS...
SHE'S JUST BEGGING TO HAVE THEM ALL DROP AND BREAK!!
I'M DEFINITELY, DEFINITELY NOT GONNA DROP THESE!!
TMP
ダッ
ACK!! THAT'S A DEATH KNELL FOR THOSE EGGS IF I EVER HEARD ONE!!!

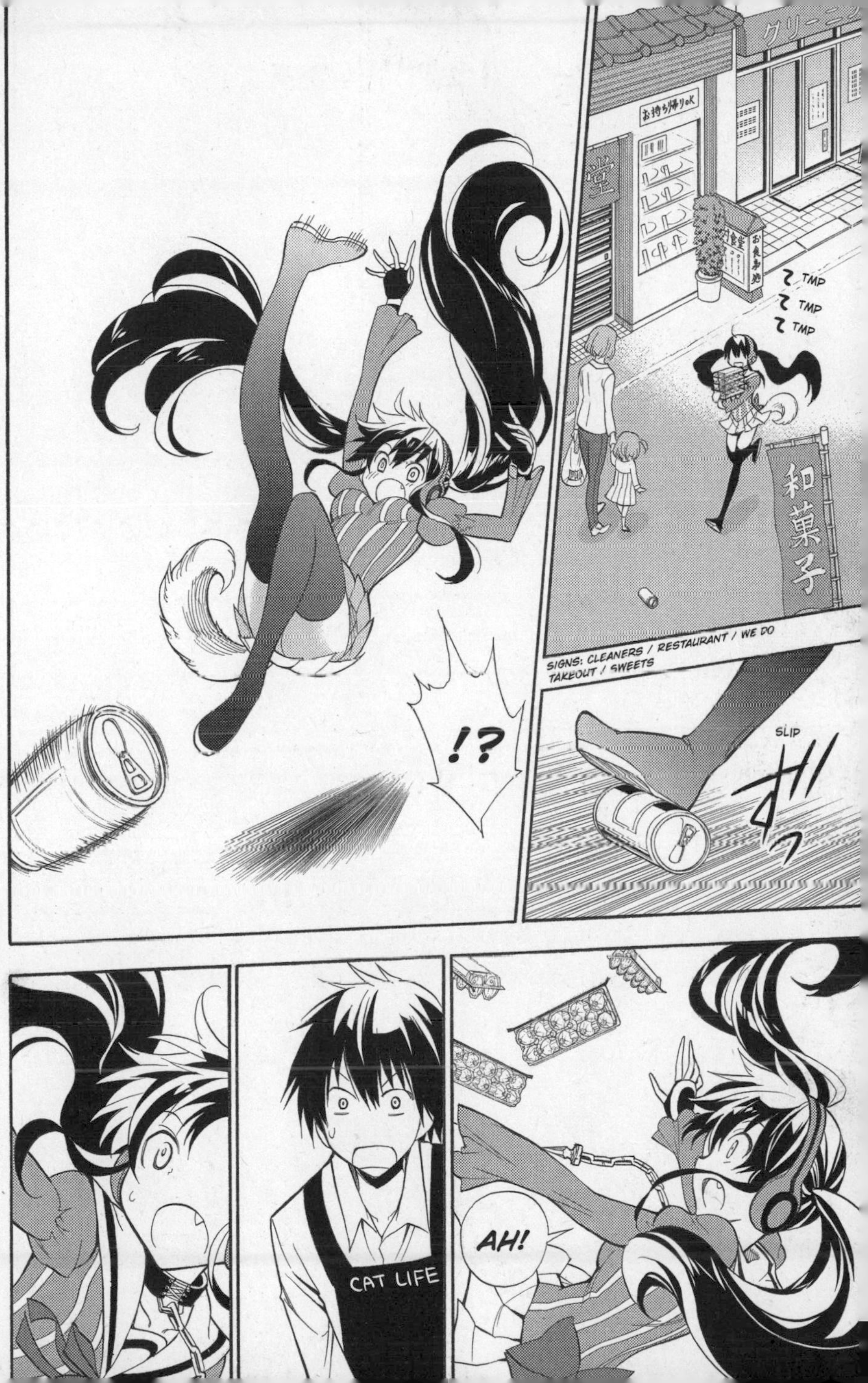

お持ち帰りOK
和菓子
TMP
TMP
TMP
SIGNS: CLEANERS / RESTAURANT / WE DO TAKEOUT / SWEETS
SLIP
!?
AH!
CAT LIFE

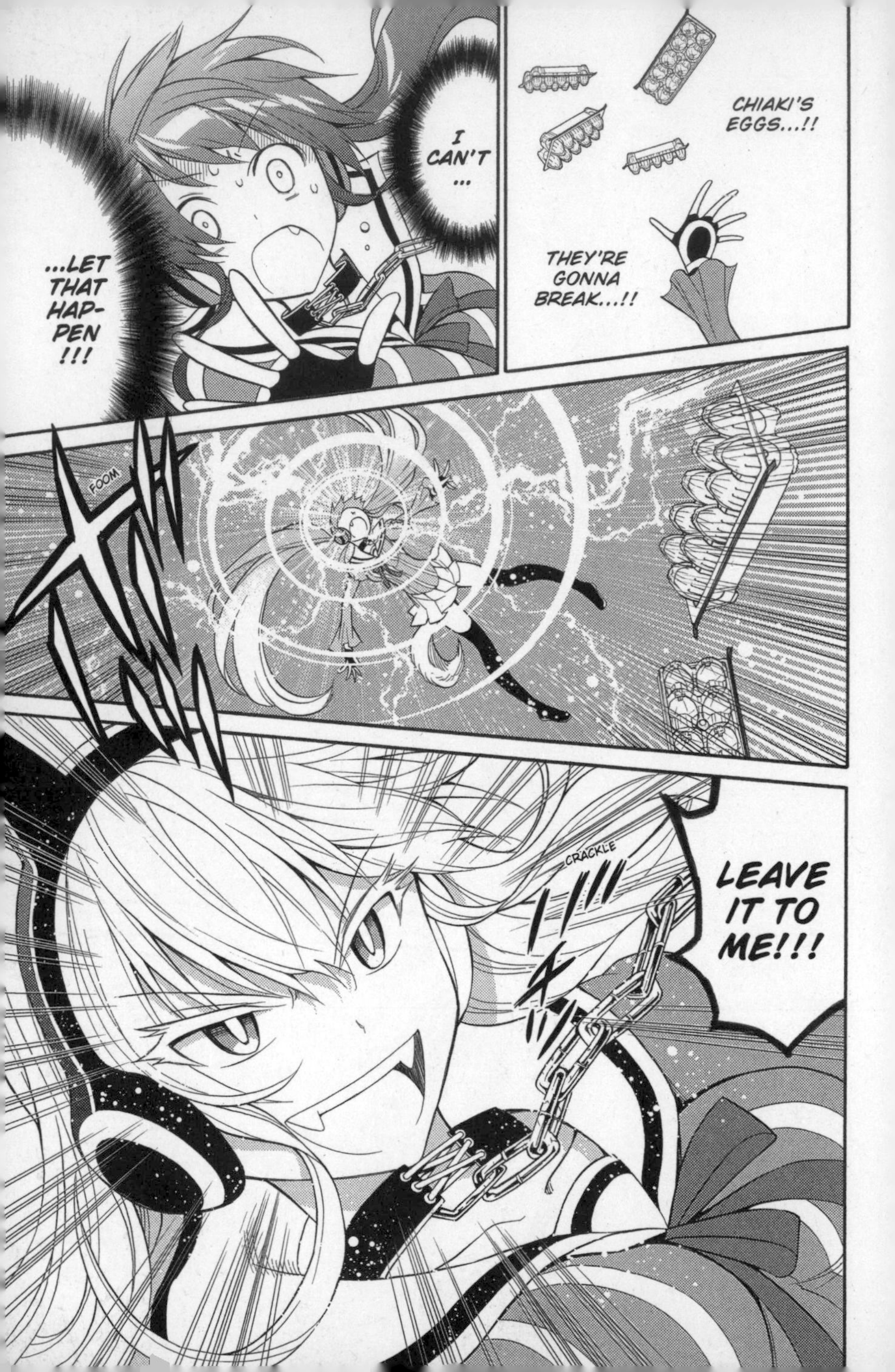
CHIAKI'S EGGS...!!
THEY'RE GONNA BREAK...!!
I CAN'T ...
...LET THAT HAP-PEN!!!
FOOM
CRACKLE
LEAVE IT TO ME!!!

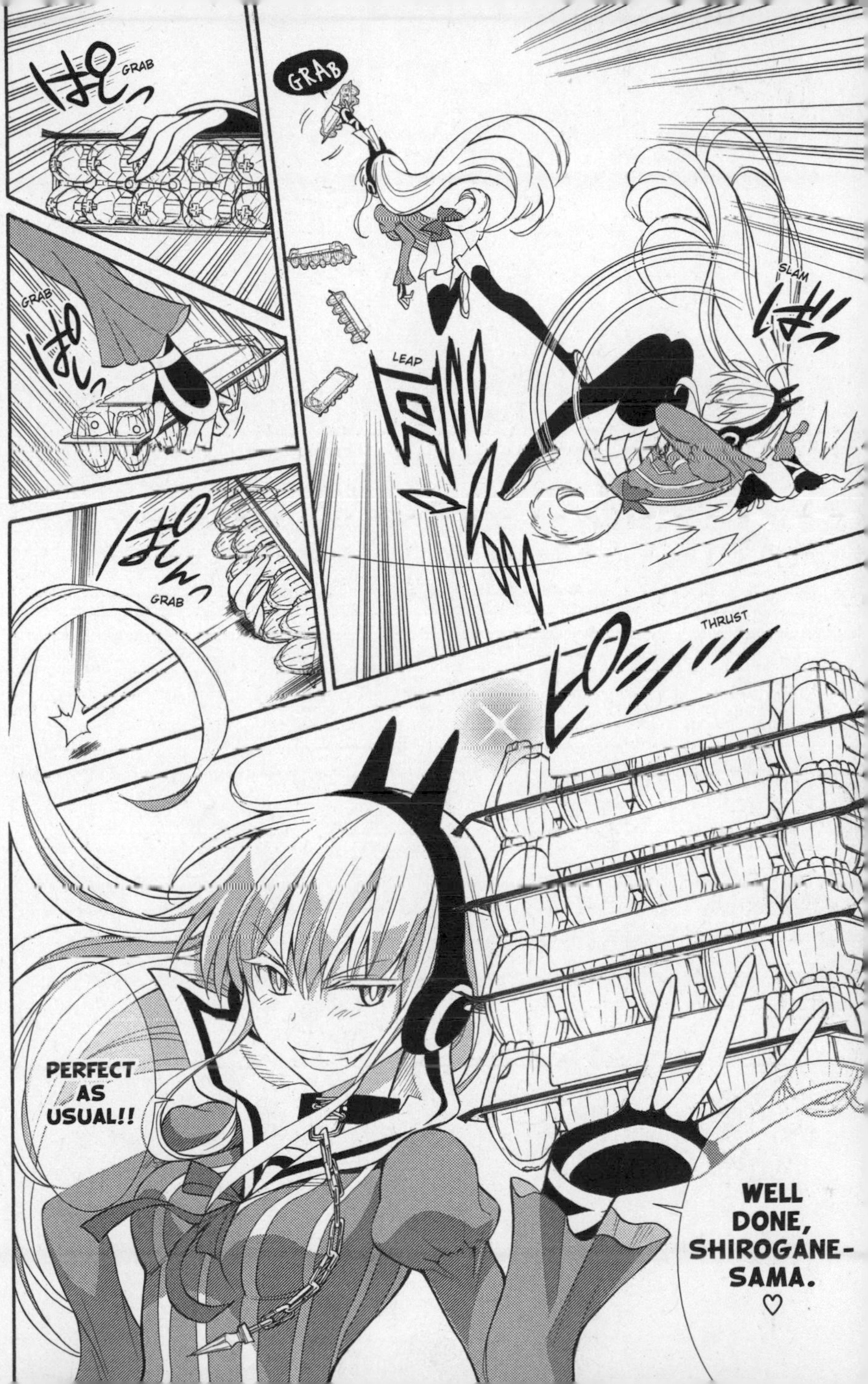
GRAB
LEAP
SLAM
GRAB
GRAB
GRAB
THRUST
WELL DONE, SHIROGANE-SAMA. ♡
PERFECT AS USUAL!!

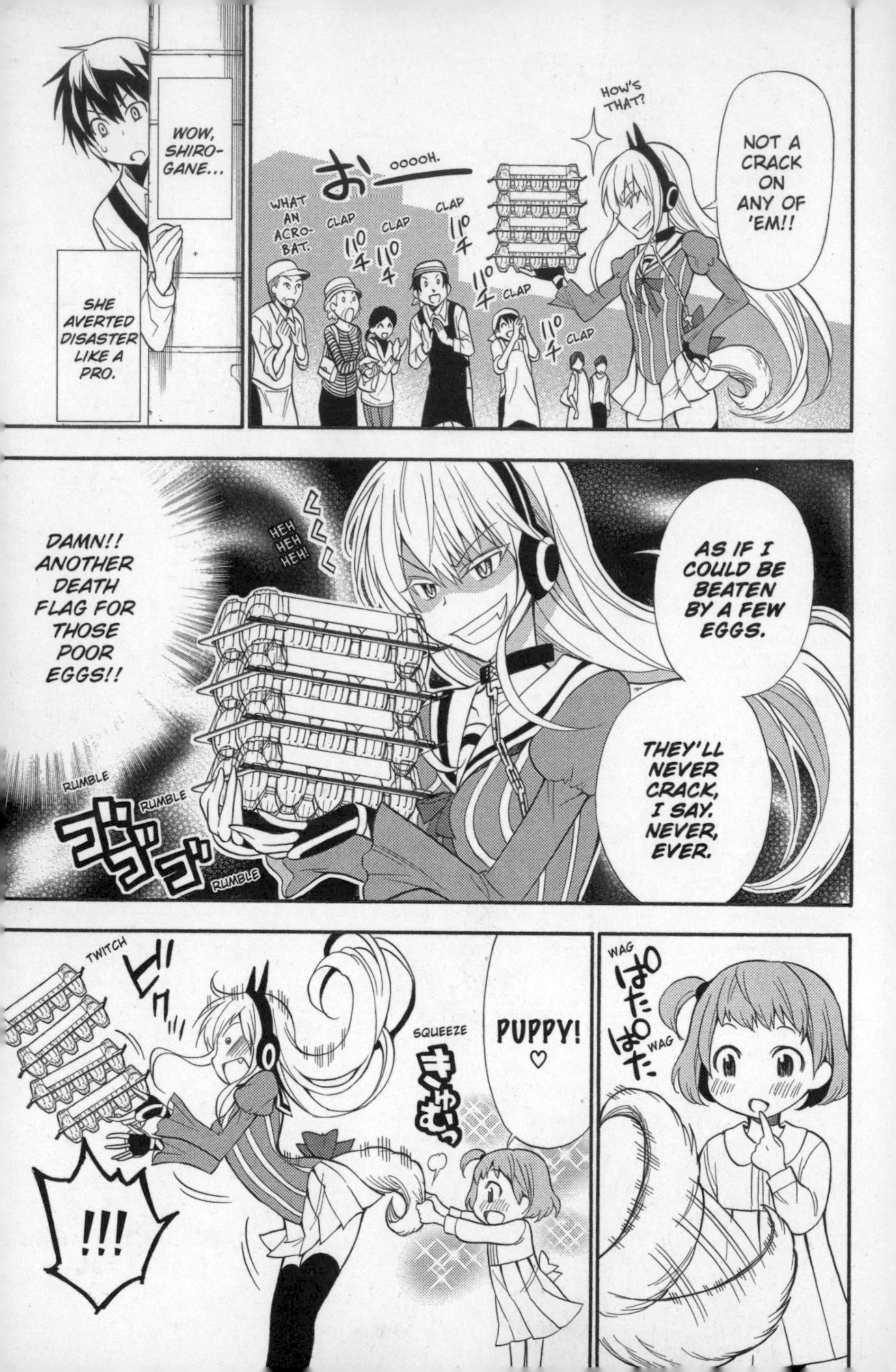
NOT A CRACK ON ANY OF 'EM!!
HOW'S THAT?
OOOOH.
CLAP
CLAP
CLAP
CLAP
CLAP
WHAT AN ACRO-BAT.
WOW, SHIRO-GANE...
SHE AVERTED DISASTER LIKE A PRO.
AS IF I COULD BE BEATEN BY A FEW EGGS.
THEY'LL NEVER CRACK, I SAY. NEVER, EVER.
HEH HEH HEH!
DAMN!! ANOTHER DEATH FLAG FOR THOSE POOR EGGS!!
RUMBLE
RUMBLE
RUMBLE
WAG
WAG
PUPPY! ♡
SQUEEZE
TWITCH
!!!

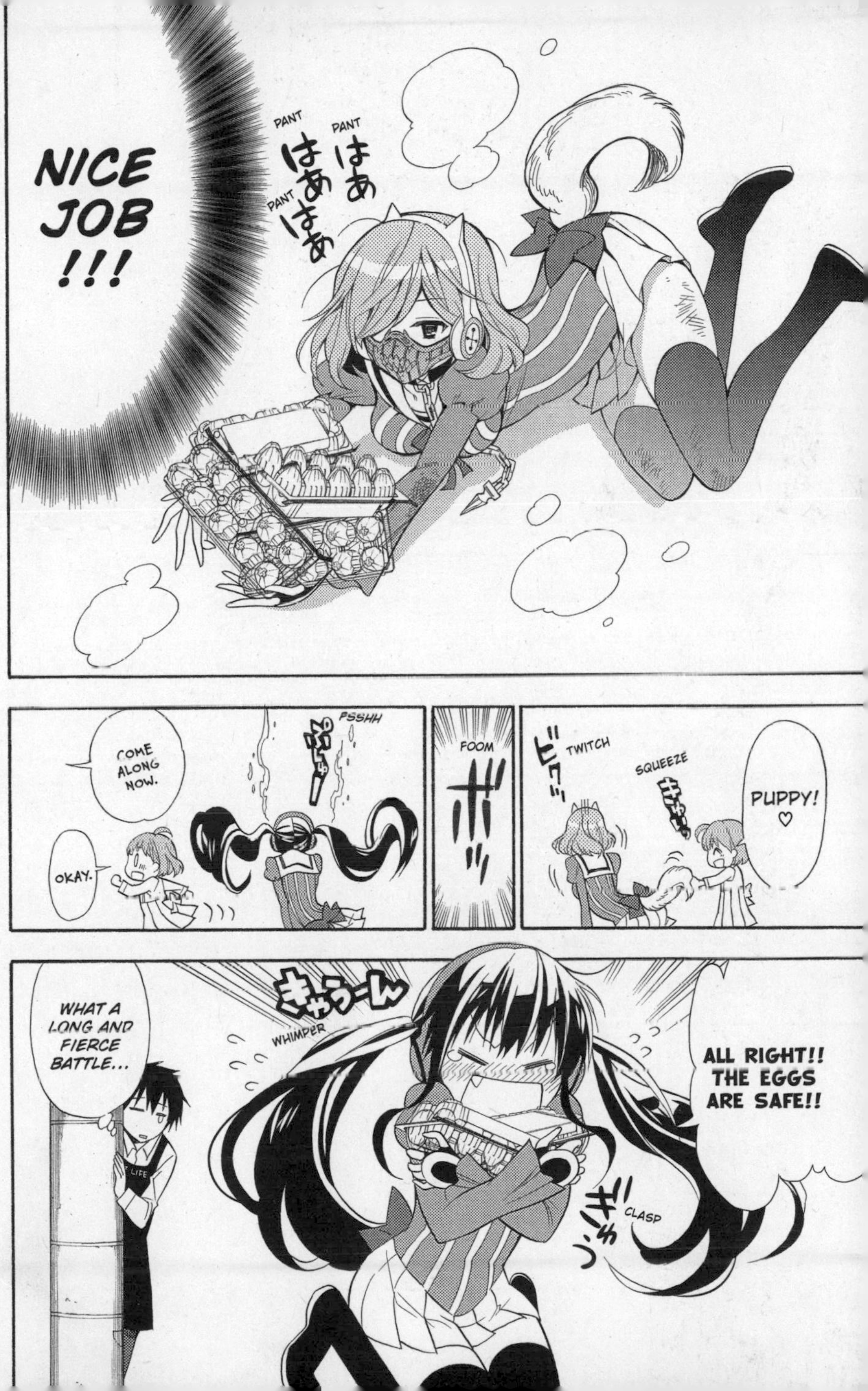
PANT
はぁ
PANT
PANT
はぁはぁ
NICE JOB!!!
PUPPY! ♡
SQUEEZE
TWITCH
FOOM
FSSHH
COME ALONG NOW.
OKAY.
ALL RIGHT!! THE EGGS ARE SAFE!!
CLASP
きゅうーん
WHIMPER
WHAT A LONG AND FIERCE BATTLE...

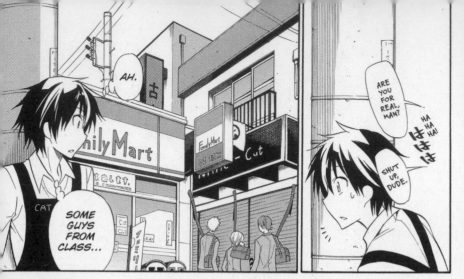

AH.

ARE YOU FOR REAL, MAN?

HA HA HA!

SHUT UP, DUDE.

SOME GUYS FROM CLASS...

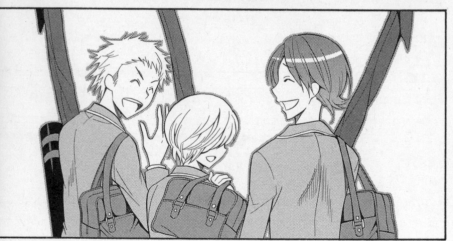

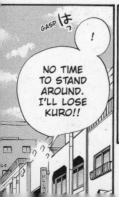

GASP

!

NO TIME TO STAND AROUND. I'LL LOSE KURO!!

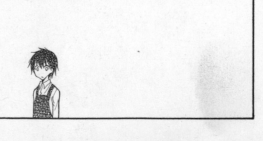

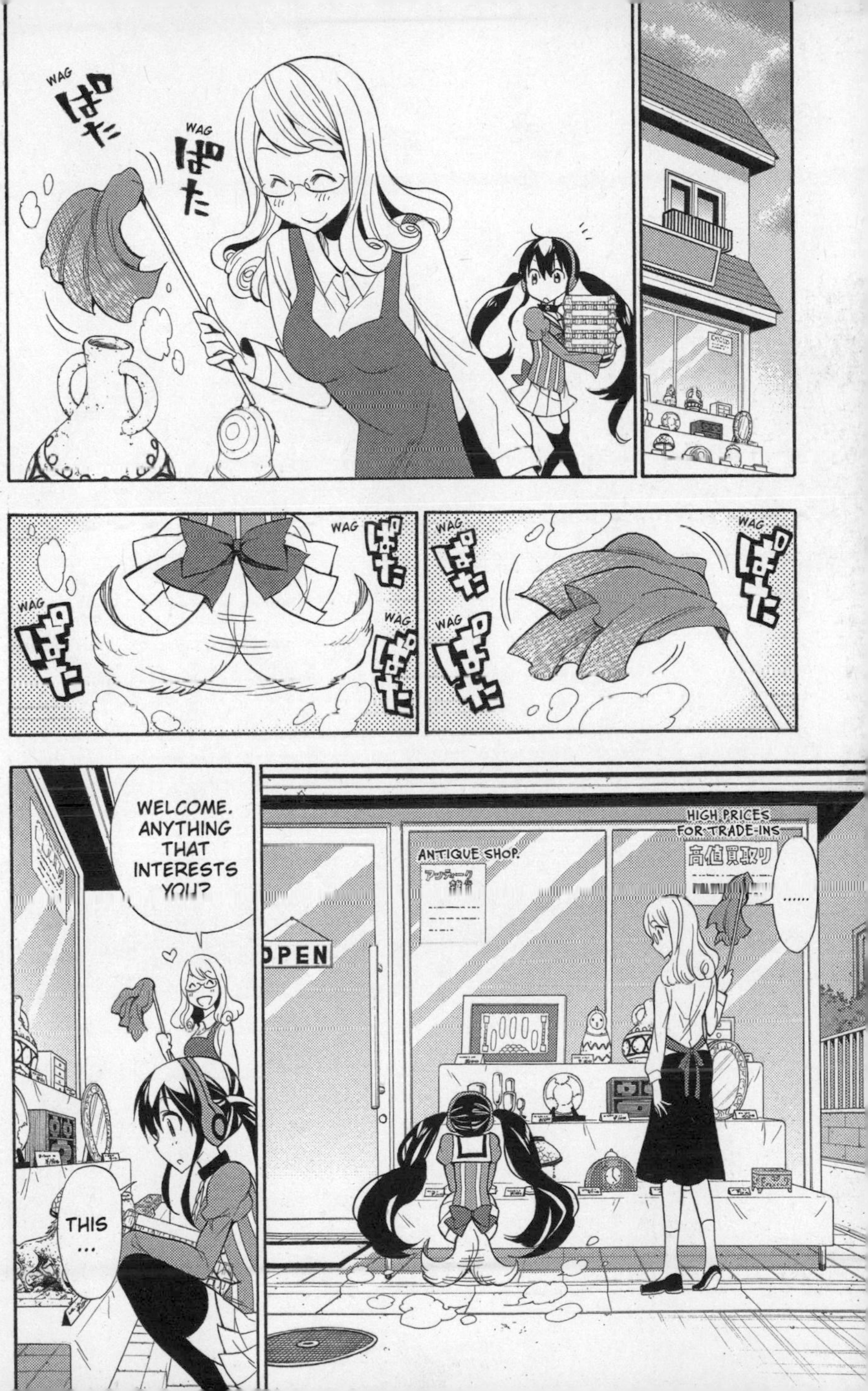
WAG
ぱた
WAG
ぱた
WAG
ぱた
WAG
ぱた
WAG
ぱた
WAG
ぱた
WAG
ぱた
HIGH PRICES FOR TRADE-INS
高値買取り
ANTIQUE SHOP.
OPEN
......
WELCOME. ANYTHING THAT INTERESTS YOU?
THIS ...

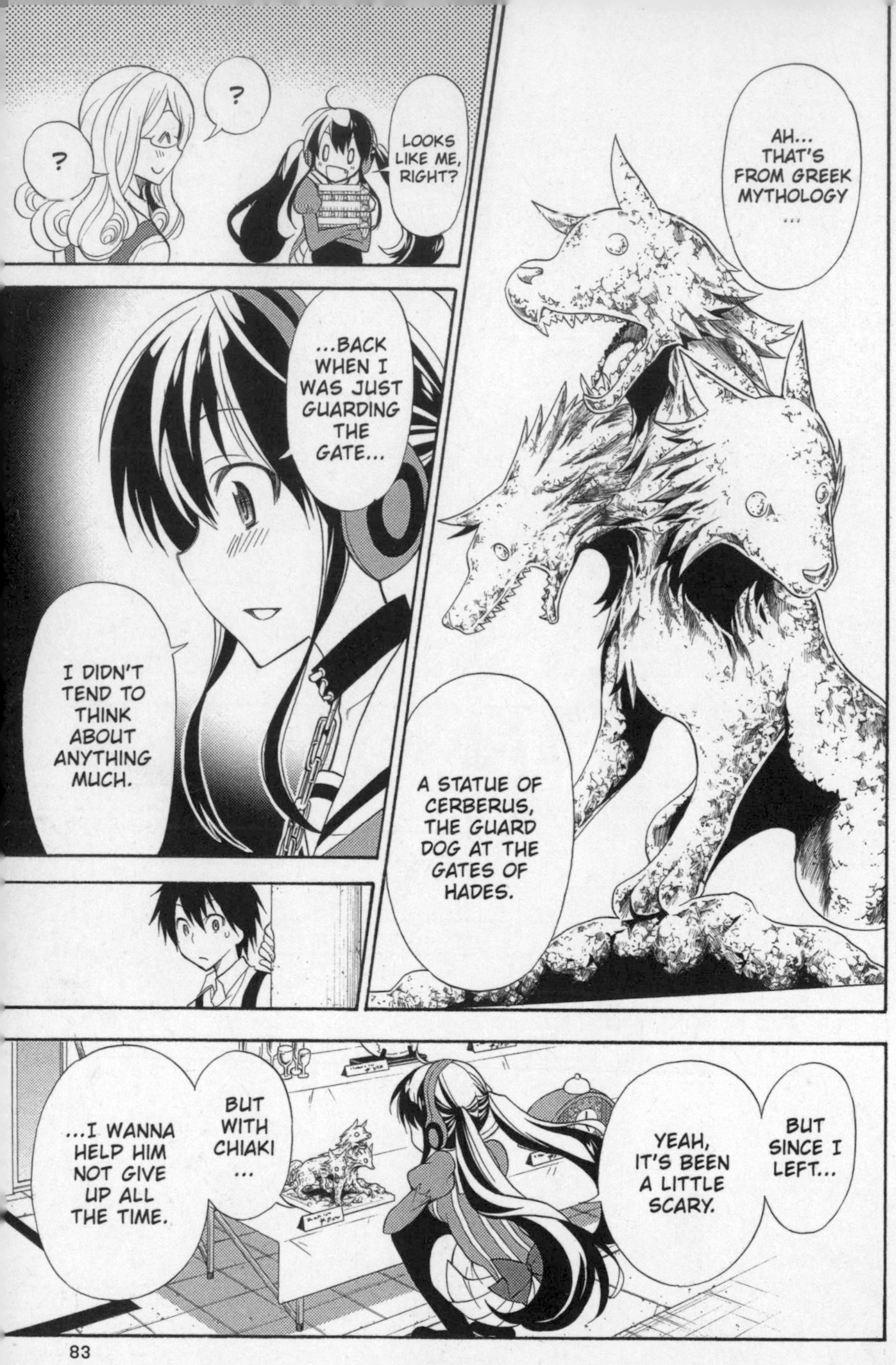
AH... THAT'S FROM GREEK MYTHOLOGY ...
A STATUE OF CERBERUS, THE GUARD DOG AT THE GATES OF HADES.
LOOKS LIKE ME, RIGHT?
?
?
...BACK WHEN I WAS JUST GUARDING THE GATE...
I DIDN'T TEND TO THINK ABOUT ANYTHING MUCH.
BUT SINCE I LEFT...
YEAH, IT'S BEEN A LITTLE SCARY.
BUT WITH CHIAKI ...
...I WANNA HELP HIM NOT GIVE UP ALL THE TIME.

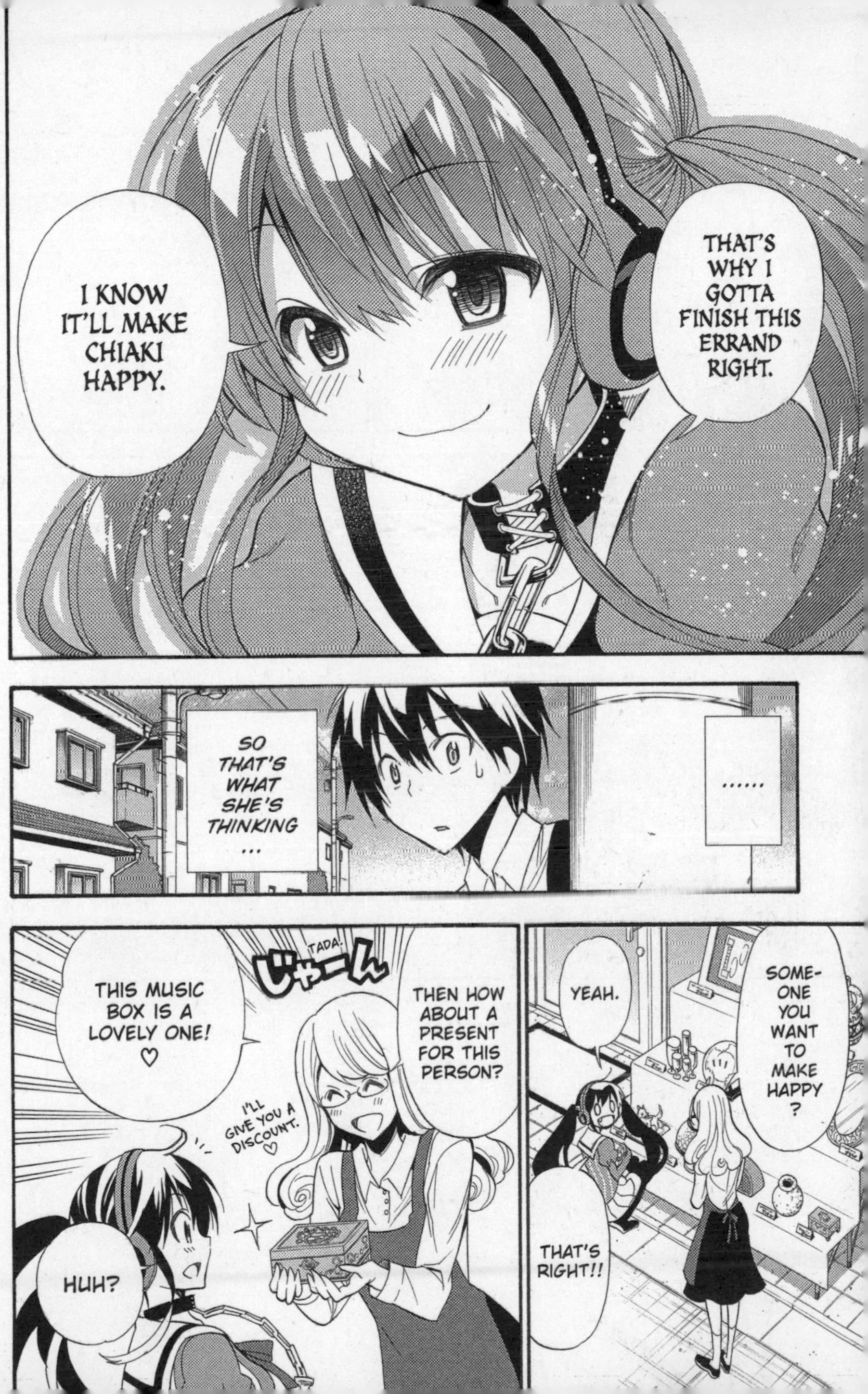
THAT'S WHY I GOTTA FINISH THIS ERRAND RIGHT.
I KNOW IT'LL MAKE CHIAKI HAPPY.
......
SO THAT'S WHAT SHE'S THINKING ...
SOME-ONE YOU WANT TO MAKE HAPPY?
YEAH.
THAT'S RIGHT!!
THEN HOW ABOUT A PRESENT FOR THIS PERSON?
じゃーん
TADA!
THIS MUSIC BOX IS A LOVELY ONE! ♡
I'LL GIVE YOU A DISCOUNT. ♡
HUH?

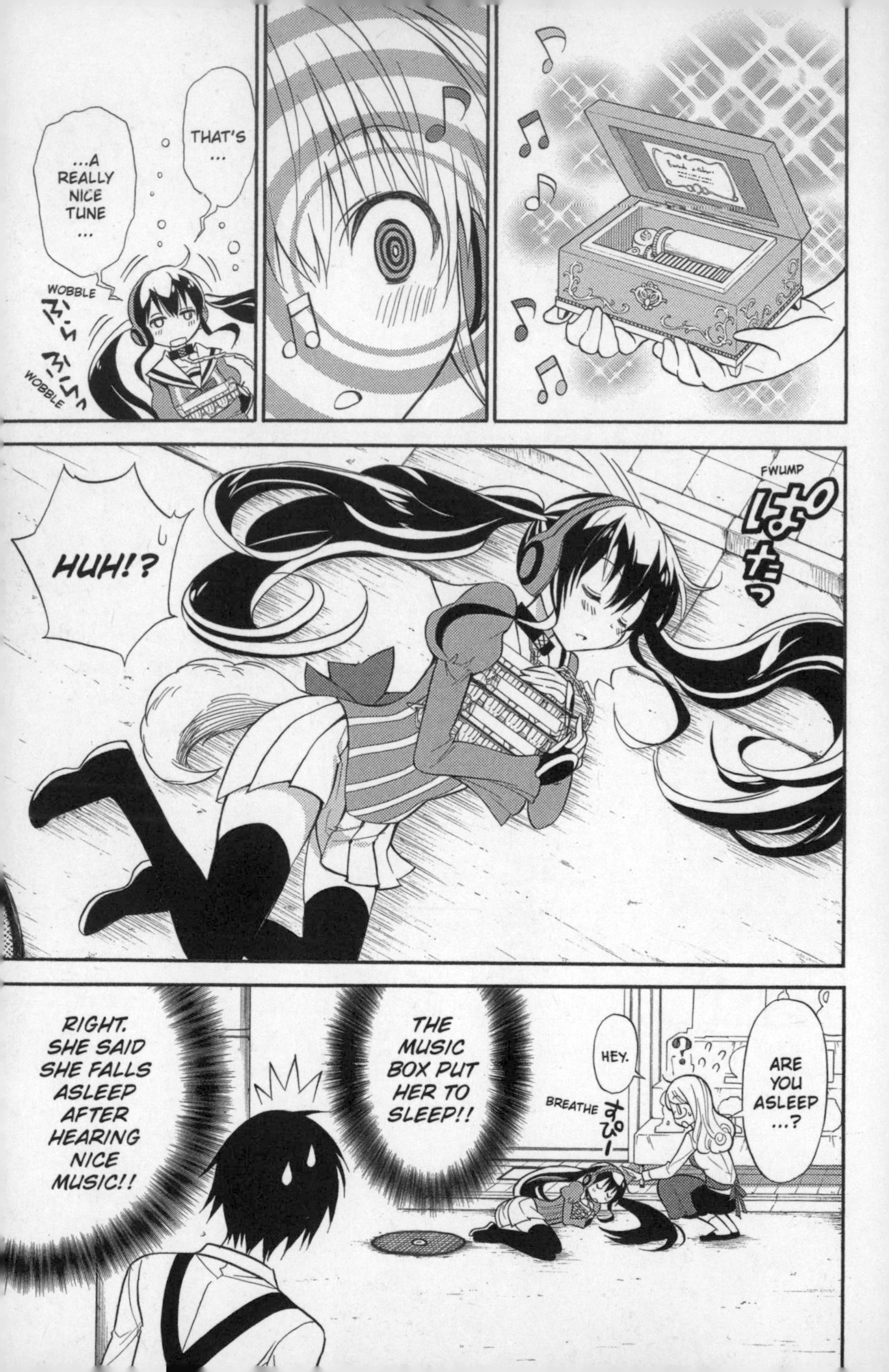
THAT'S ...
...A REALLY NICE TUNE ...
WOBBLE
ふら
WOBBLE
ふらっ
FWUMP
ぱたっ
HUH!?
ARE YOU ASLEEP ...?
HEY.
BREATHE
すぴー
THE MUSIC BOX PUT HER TO SLEEP!!
RIGHT. SHE SAID SHE FALLS ASLEEP AFTER HEARING NICE MUSIC!!

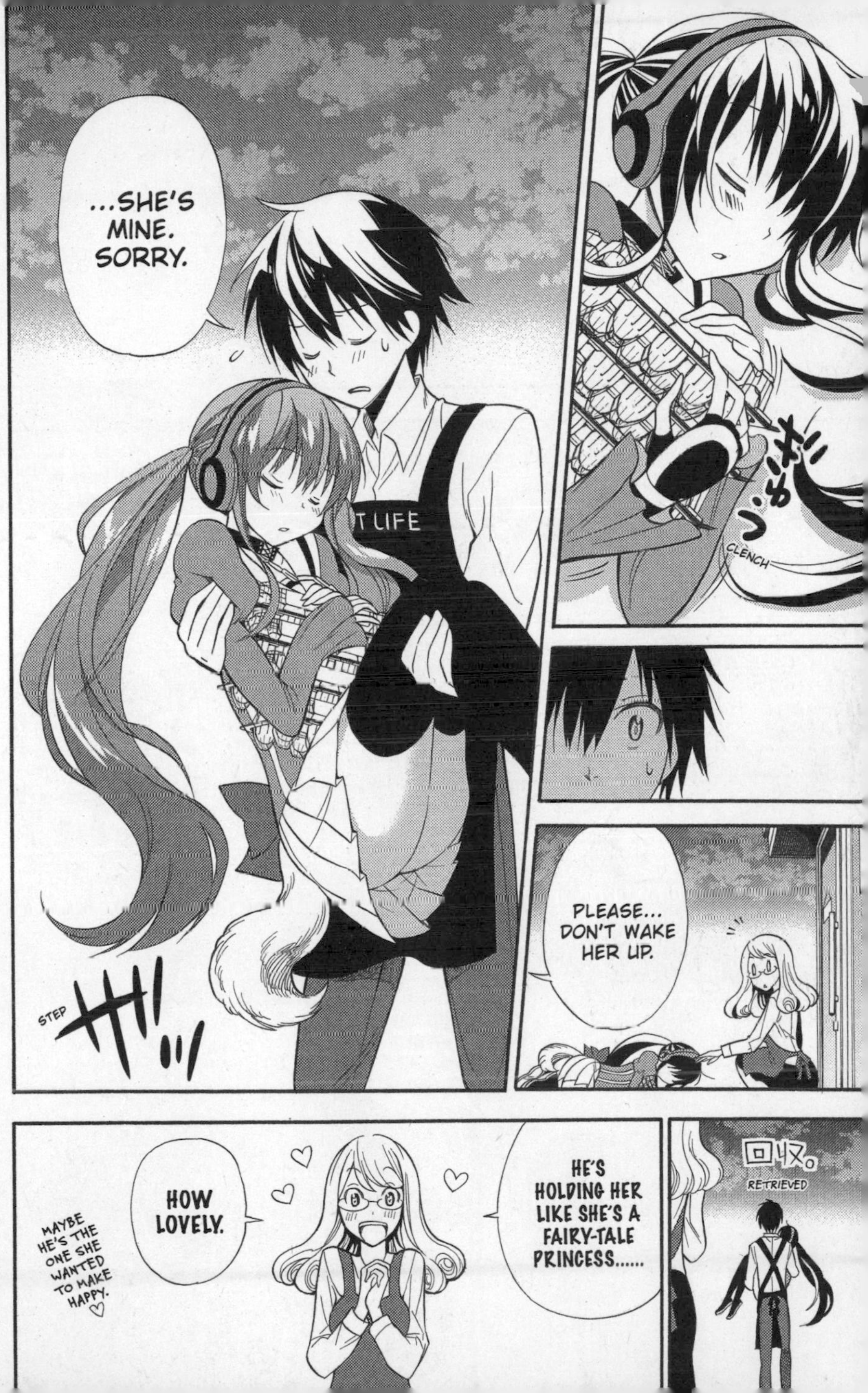
CLENCH
PLEASE... DON'T WAKE HER UP.
...SHE'S MINE. SORRY.
T LIFE
STEP
回収。
RETRIEVED
HE'S HOLDING HER LIKE SHE'S A FAIRY-TALE PRINCESS......
HOW LOVELY.
MAYBE HE'S THE ONE SHE WANTED TO MAKE HAPPY. ♡

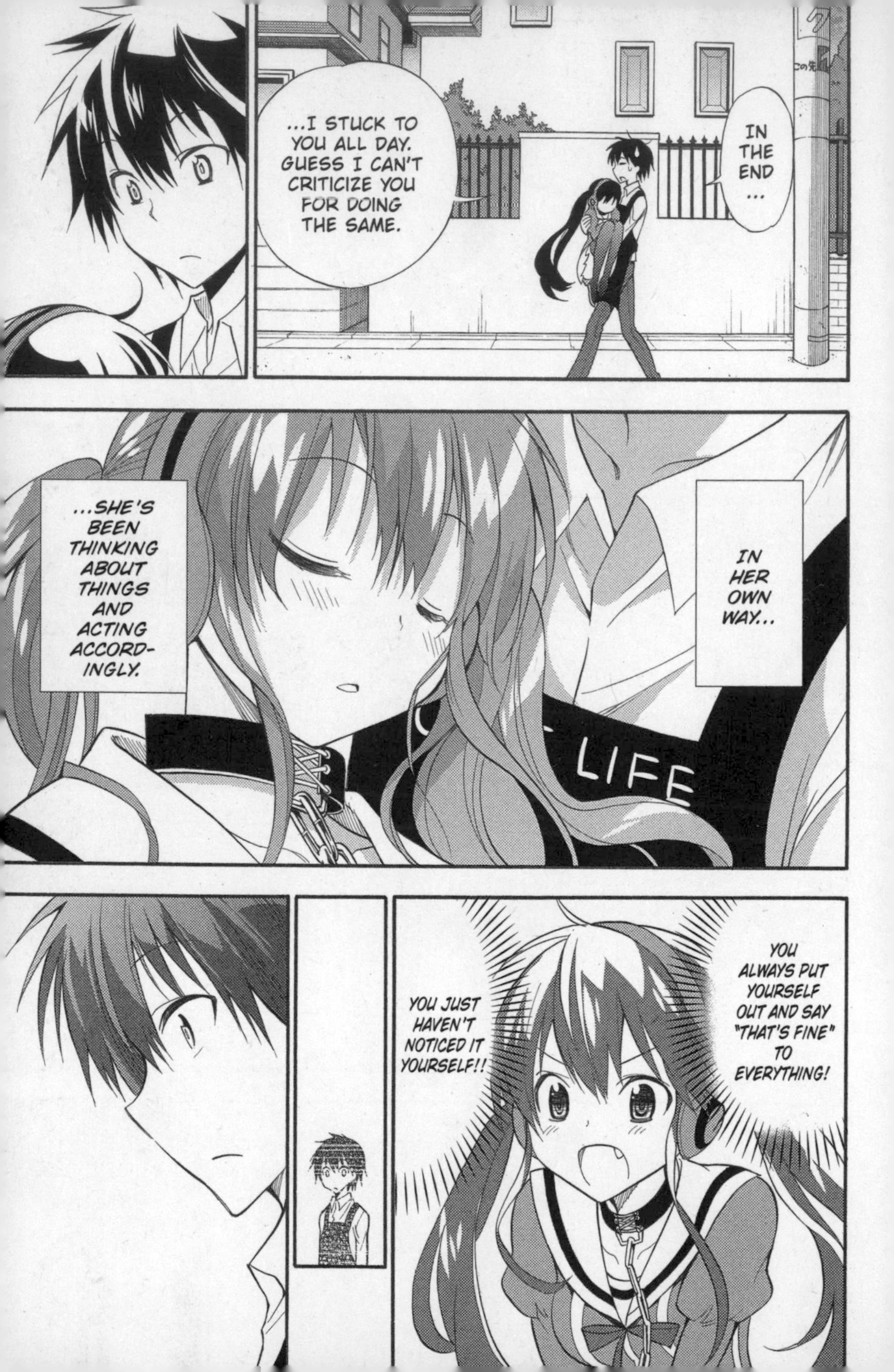
IN THE END...
...I STUCK TO YOU ALL DAY. GUESS I CAN'T CRITICIZE YOU FOR DOING THE SAME.
IN HER OWN WAY...
...SHE'S BEEN THINKING ABOUT THINGS AND ACTING ACCORD-INGLY.
LIFE
YOU ALWAYS PUT YOURSELF OUT AND SAY "THAT'S FINE" TO EVERYTHING!
YOU JUST HAVEN'T NOTICED IT YOURSELF!!

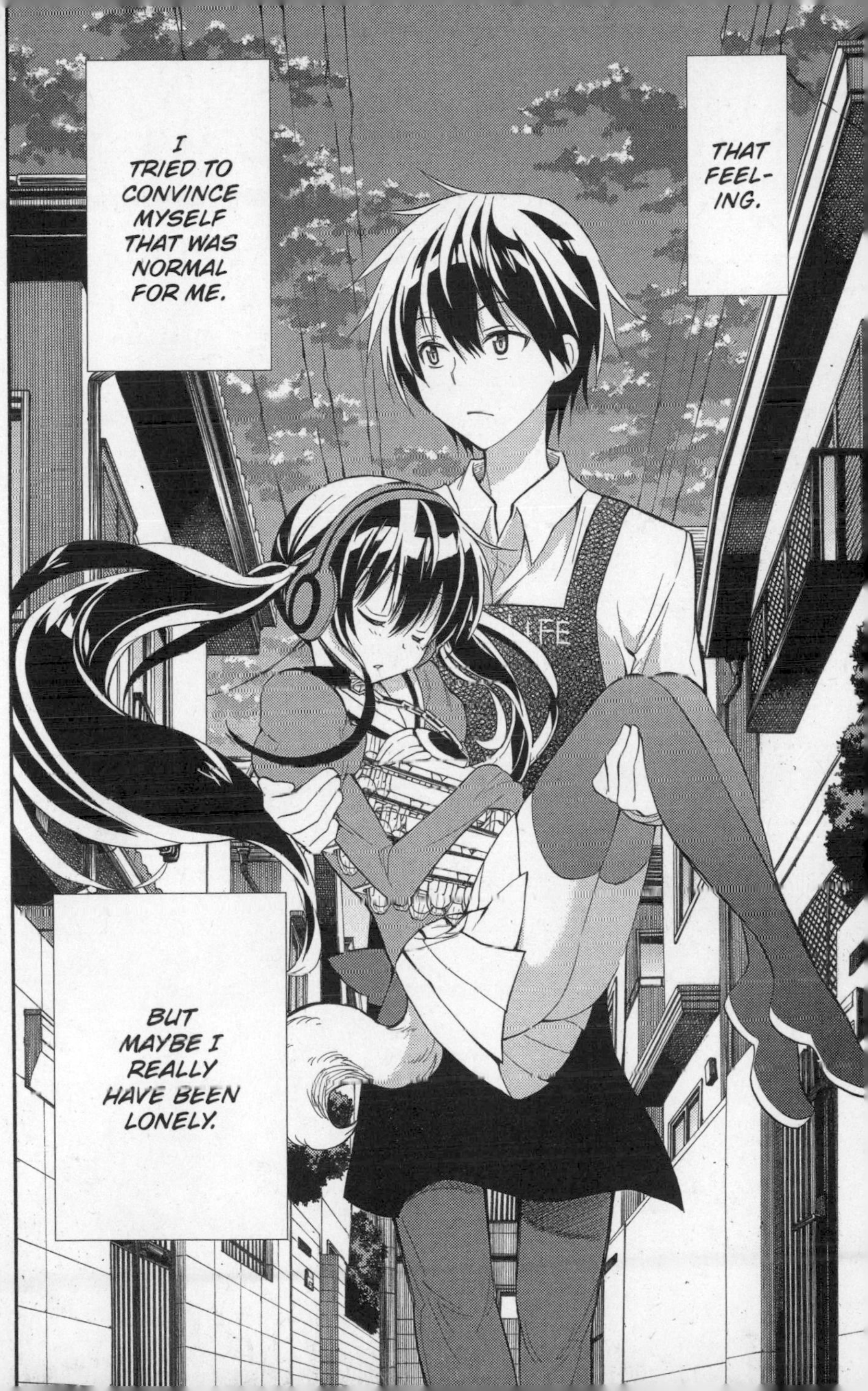
THAT FEELING.
I TRIED TO CONVINCE MYSELF THAT WAS NORMAL FOR ME.
BUT MAYBE I REALLY HAVE BEEN LONELY.

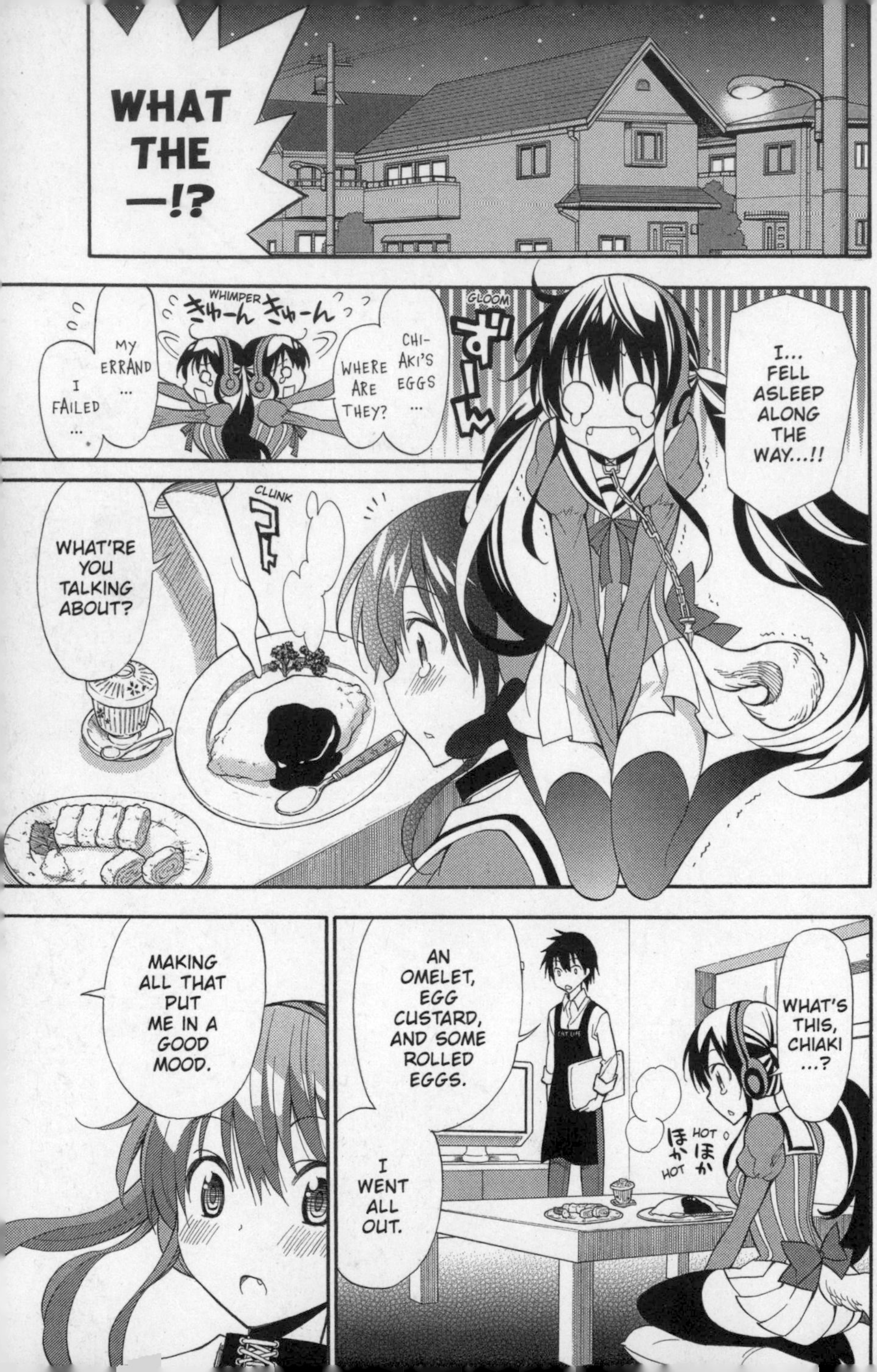
WHAT THE—!?
GLOOM
ずーん
I... FELL ASLEEP ALONG THE WAY...!!
WHIMPER
きゅーん きゅーん
CHI-AKI'S EGGS ...
WHERE ARE THEY?
MY ERRAND ...
I FAILED ...
CLUNK
コト
WHAT'RE YOU TALKING ABOUT?
WHAT'S THIS, CHIAKI ...?
HOT
ほか ほか
HOT
AN OMELET, EGG CUSTARD, AND SOME ROLLED EGGS.
I WENT ALL OUT.
MAKING ALL THAT PUT ME IN A GOOD MOOD.

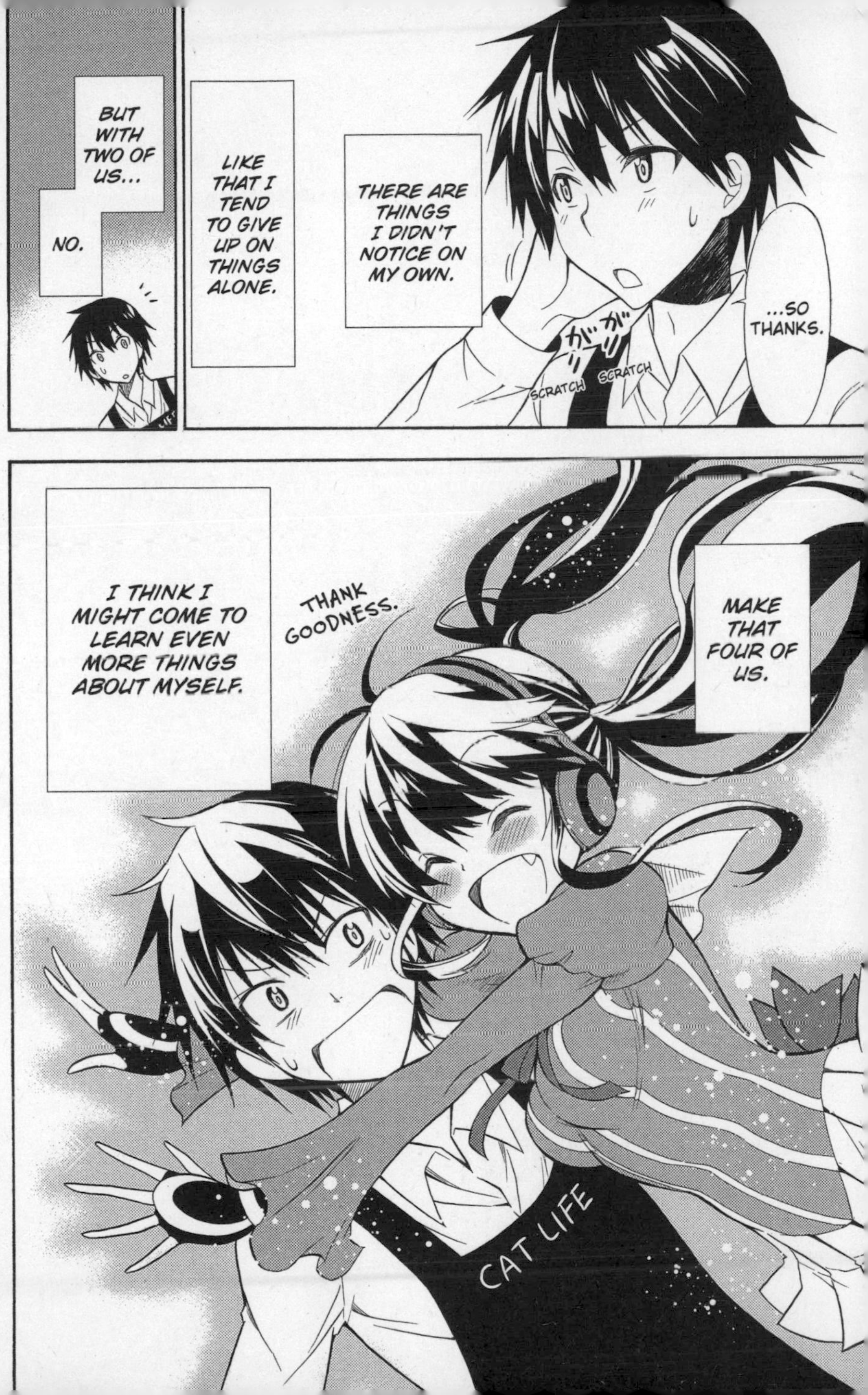
...SO THANKS.
THERE ARE THINGS I DIDN'T NOTICE ON MY OWN.
ガリガリ
SCRATCH SCRATCH
LIKE THAT I TEND TO GIVE UP ON THINGS ALONE.
BUT WITH TWO OF US...
NO.
MAKE THAT FOUR OF US.
THANK GOODNESS.
I THINK I MIGHT COME TO LEARN EVEN MORE THINGS ABOUT MYSELF.
CAT LIFE

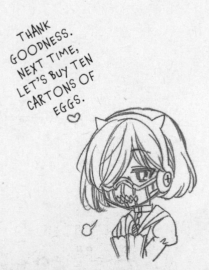

🐾 TODAY'S CERBERUS

THANK
GOODNESS.
NEXT TIME,
LET'S BUY TEN
CARTONS OF
EGGS.

TODAY'S CERBERUS

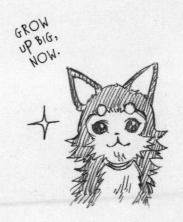

GROW
UP BIG,
NOW.

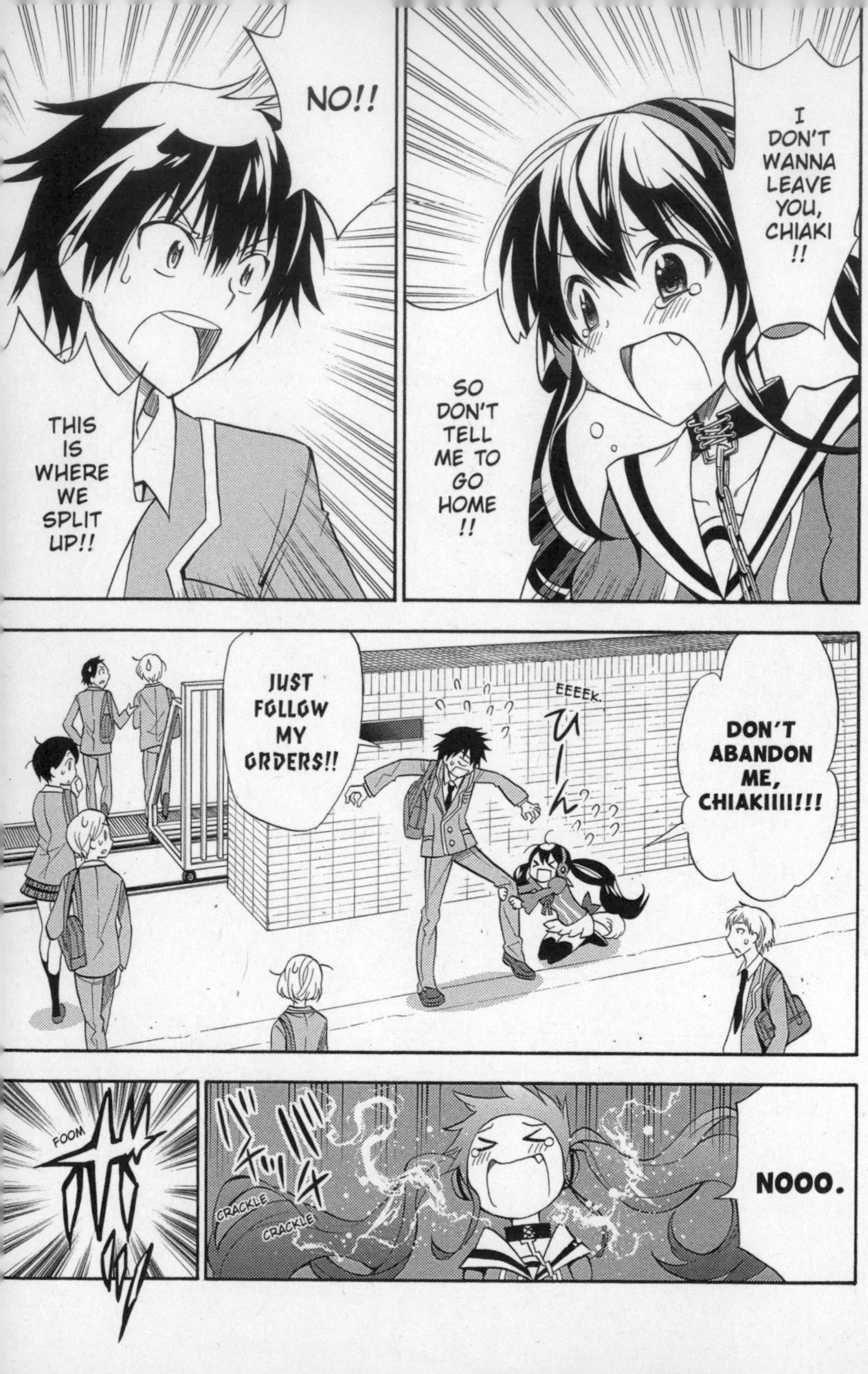
I DON'T WANNA LEAVE YOU, CHIAKI!!
SO DON'T TELL ME TO GO HOME!!
NO!!
THIS IS WHERE WE SPLIT UP!!
DON'T ABANDON ME, CHIAKIIIII!!!
EEEEK.
ひーん
JUST FOLLOW MY ORDERS!!
NOOO.
CRACKLE
CRACKLE
FOOM

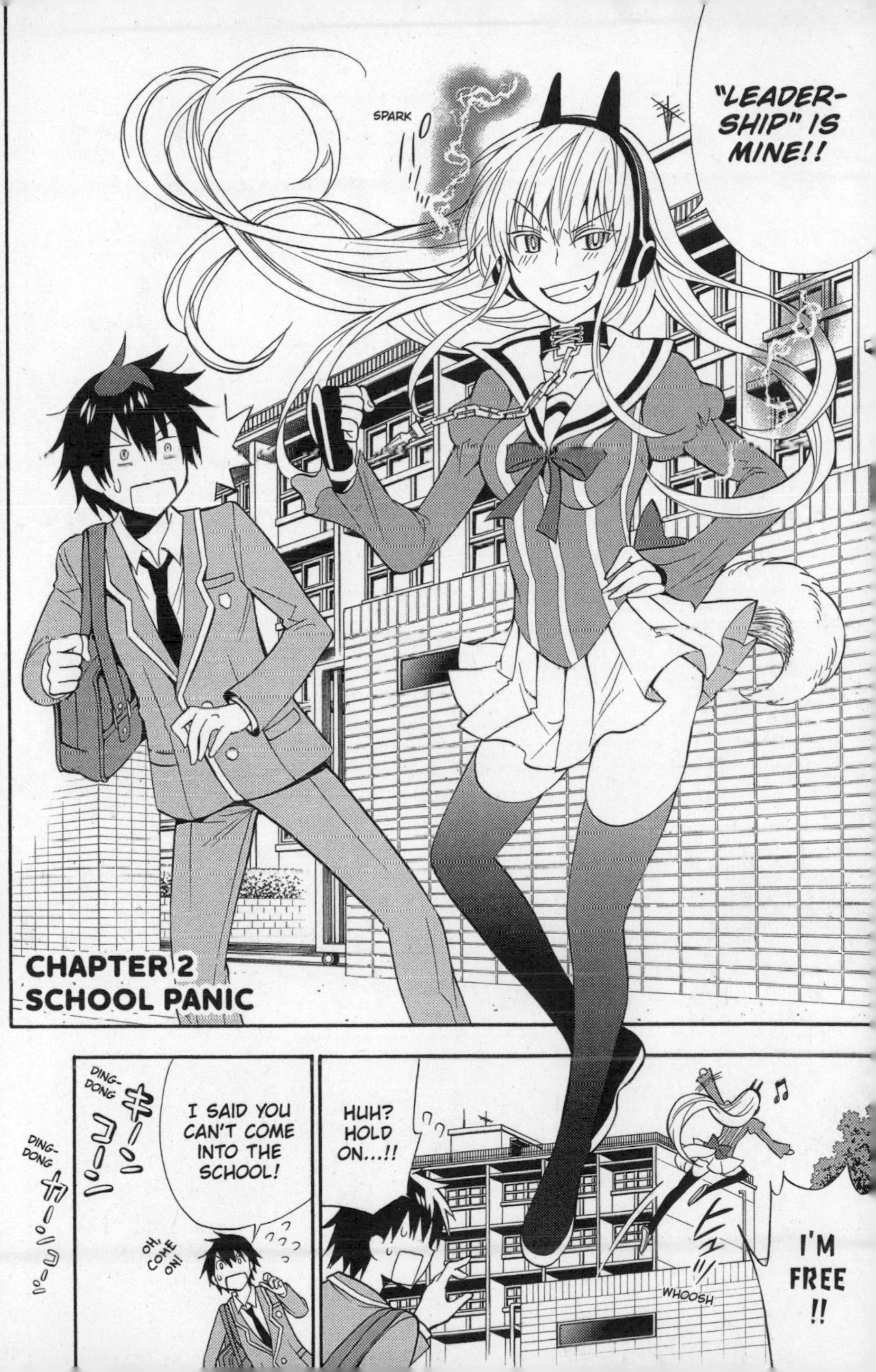
"LEADER-SHIP" IS MINE!!
SPARK
CHAPTER 2
SCHOOL PANIC
I'M FREE!!
HUH? HOLD ON...!!
WHOOSH
DING-DONG
DING-DONG
I SAID YOU CAN'T COME INTO THE SCHOOL!
OH, COME ON!

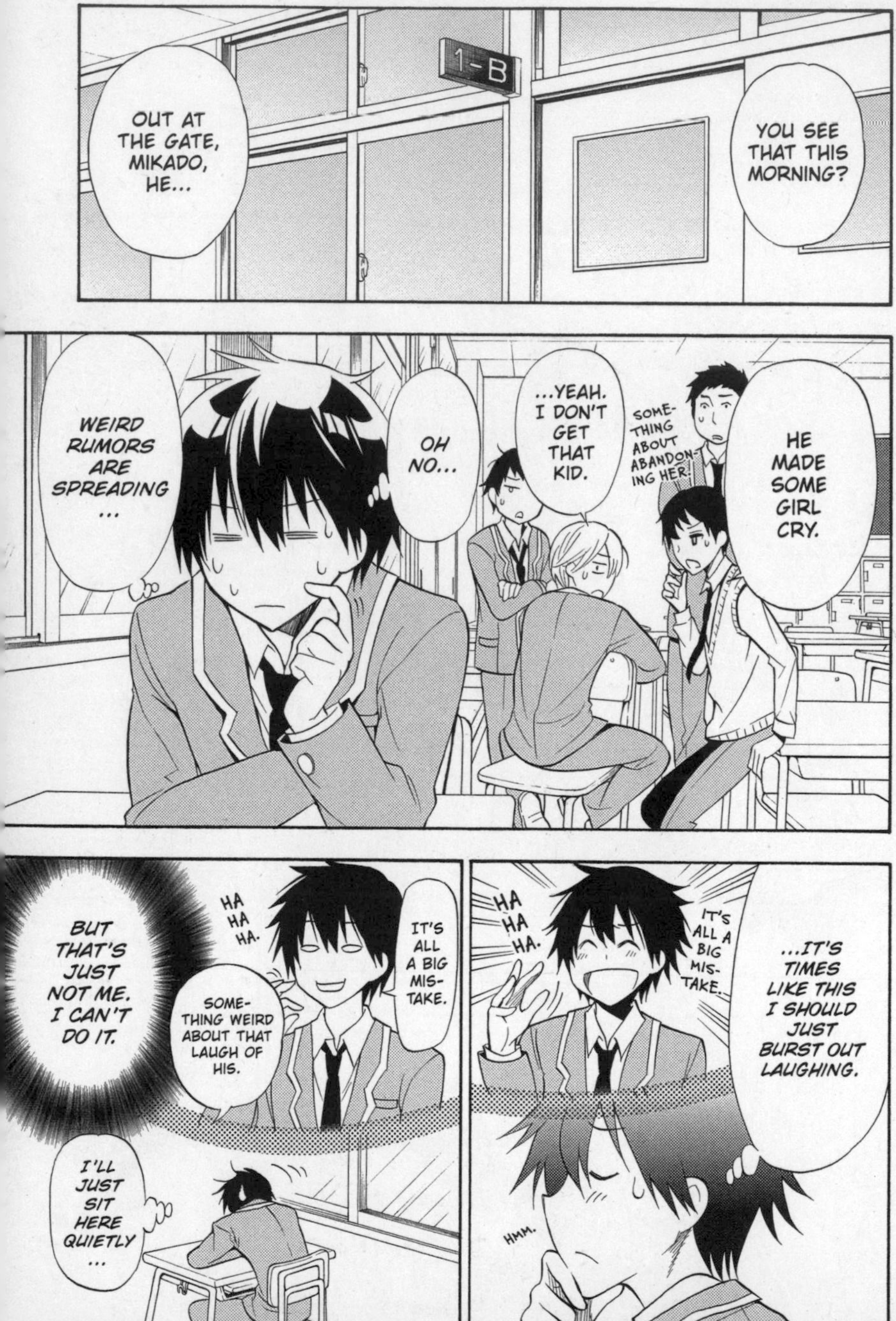

1-B
YOU SEE THAT THIS MORNING?
OUT AT THE GATE, MIKADO, HE...
HE MADE SOME GIRL CRY.
SOME-THING ABOUT ABANDON-ING HER.
...YEAH. I DON'T GET THAT KID.
OH NO...
WEIRD RUMORS ARE SPREADING ...
...IT'S TIMES LIKE THIS I SHOULD JUST BURST OUT LAUGHING.
HA HA HA.
IT'S ALL A BIG MIS-TAKE.
HMM.
HA HA HA.
IT'S ALL A BIG MIS-TAKE.
SOME-THING WEIRD ABOUT THAT LAUGH OF HIS.
BUT THAT'S JUST NOT ME. I CAN'T DO IT.
I'LL JUST SIT HERE QUIETLY ...

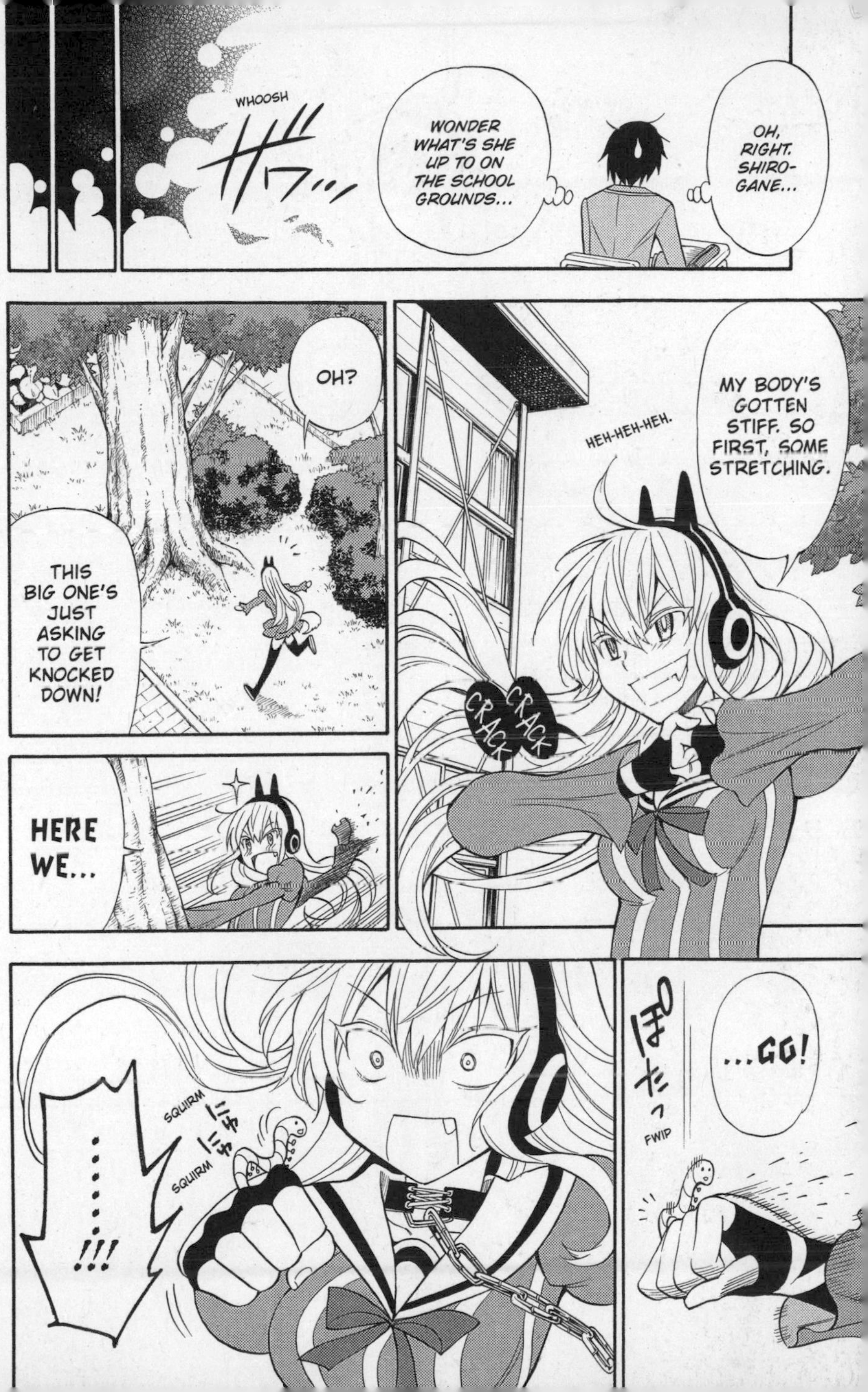
OH, RIGHT. SHIRO-GANE...
WONDER WHAT'S SHE UP TO ON THE SCHOOL GROUNDS...
WHOOSH
ザワッ
MY BODY'S GOTTEN STIFF. SO FIRST, SOME STRETCHING.
HEH-HEH-HEH.
CRACK
CRACK
OH?
THIS BIG ONE'S JUST ASKING TO GET KNOCKED DOWN!
HERE WE...
...GO!
ぽたっ
FWIP
SQUIRM
SQUIRM
......!!!

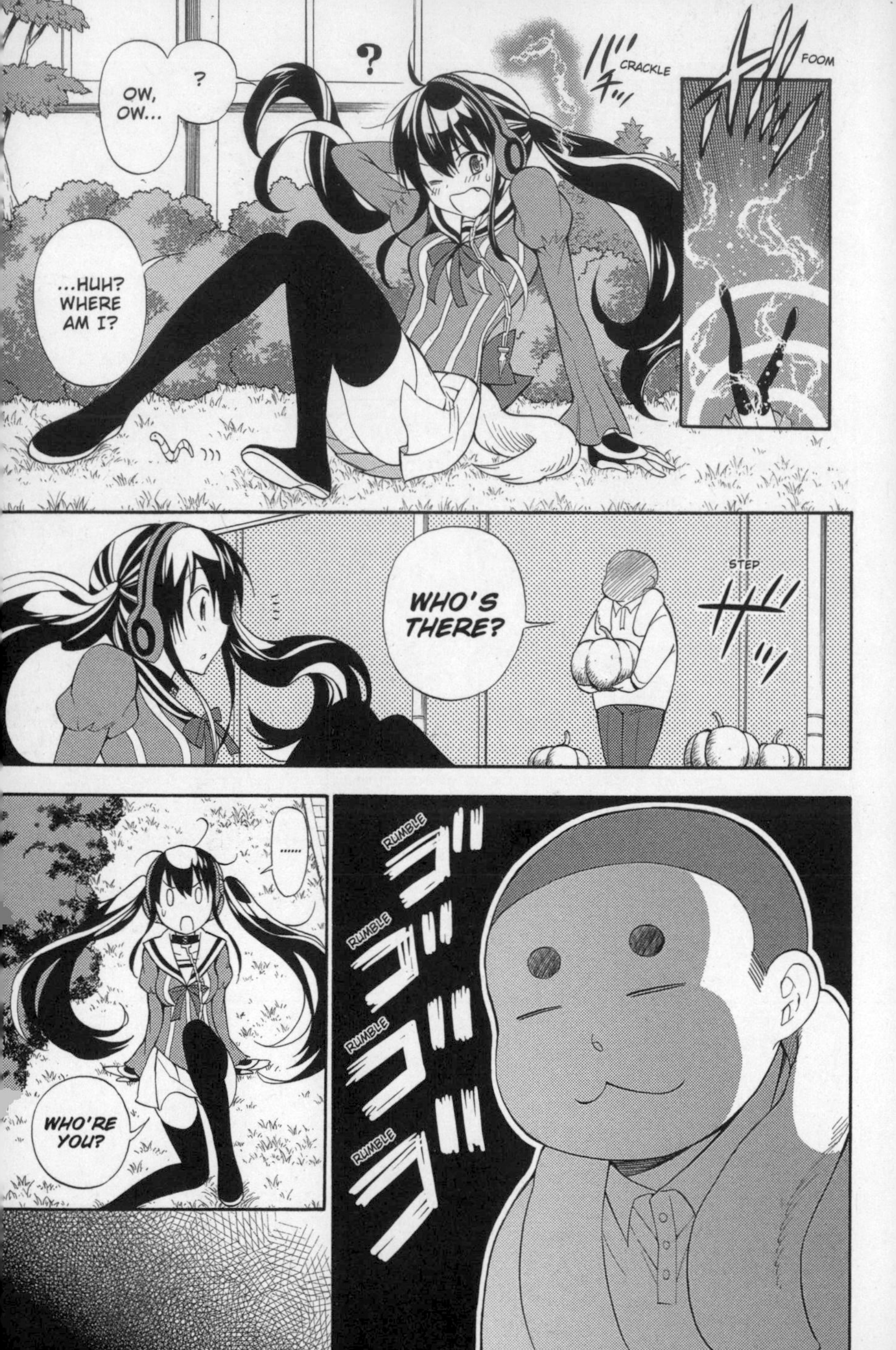
FOOM
CRACKLE
?
?
OW, OW...
...HUH? WHERE AM I?
STEP
WHO'S THERE?
RUMBLE
RUMBLE
RUMBLE
RUMBLE
......
WHO'RE YOU?

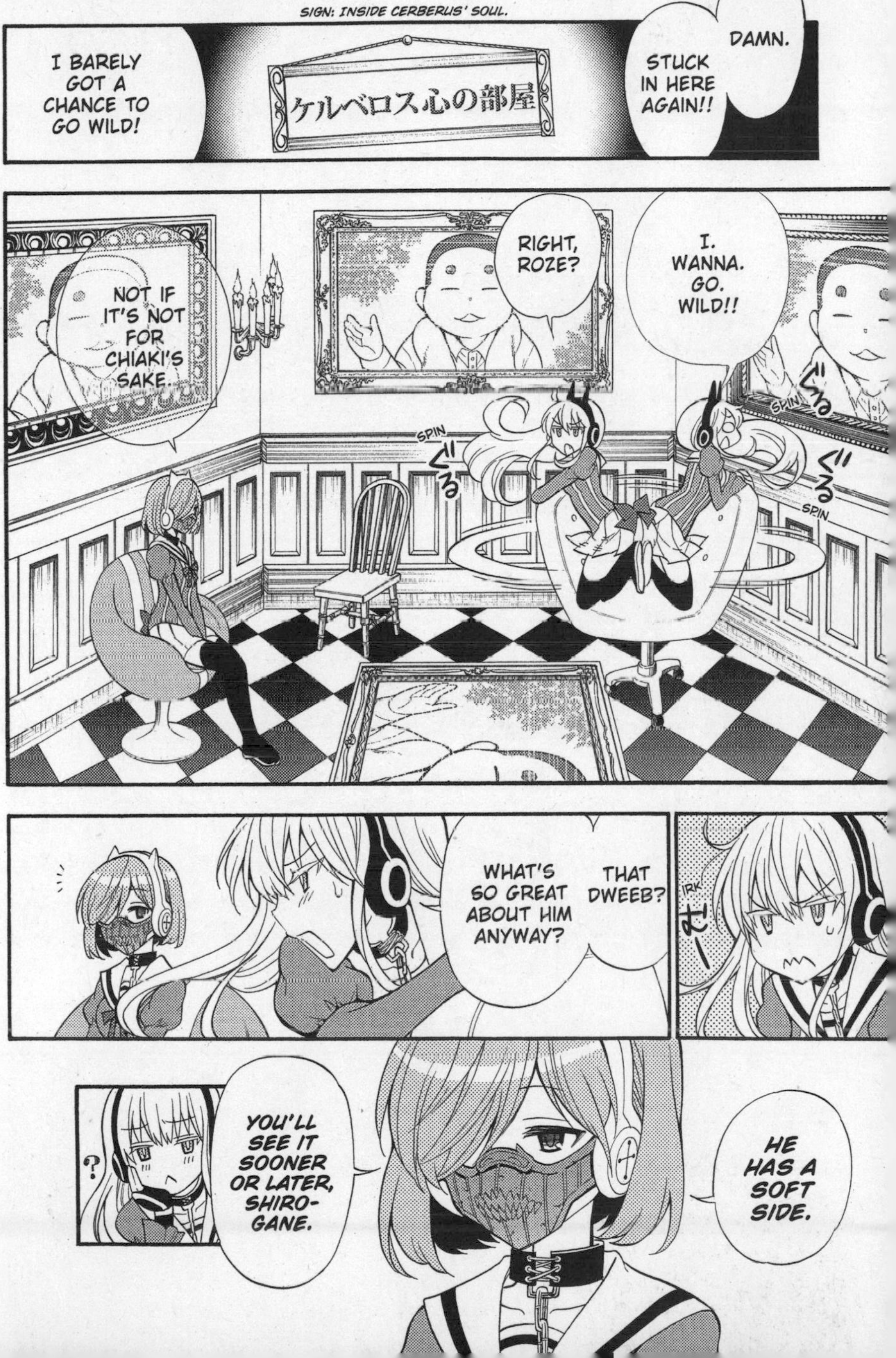
SIGN: INSIDE CERBERUS' SOUL.
DAMN.
STUCK IN HERE AGAIN!!
ケルベロス心の部屋
I BARELY GOT A CHANCE TO GO WILD!
I. WANNA. GO. WILD!!
ぐる SPIN
ぐる SPIN
RIGHT, ROZE?
ぐる SPIN
NOT IF IT'S NOT FOR CHIAKI'S SAKE.
IRK ムー
THAT DWEEB?
WHAT'S SO GREAT ABOUT HIM ANYWAY?
HE HAS A SOFT SIDE.
YOU'LL SEE IT SOONER OR LATER, SHIRO-GANE.
?

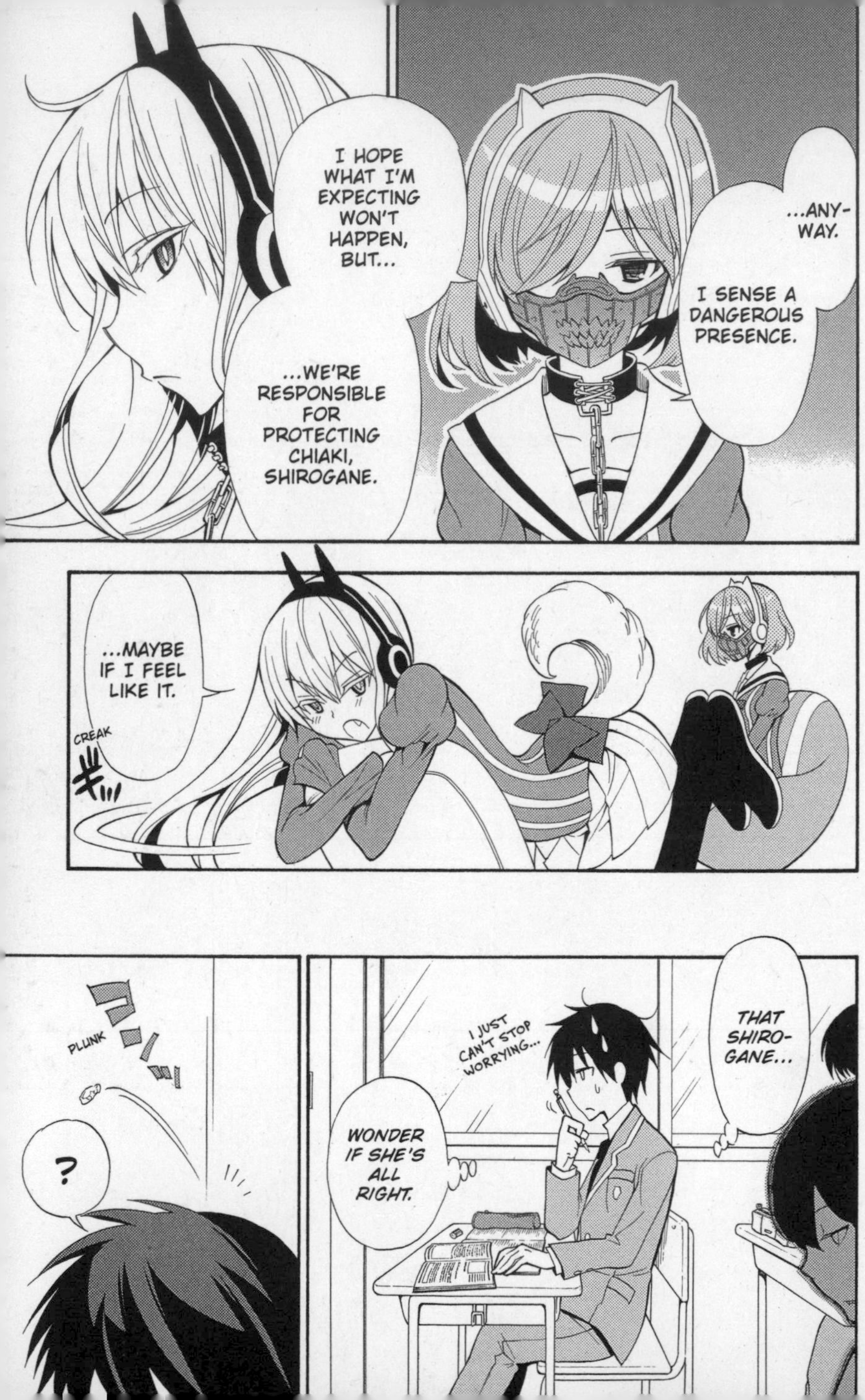
...ANY-WAY.
I SENSE A DANGEROUS PRESENCE.
I HOPE WHAT I'M EXPECTING WON'T HAPPEN, BUT...
...WE'RE RESPONSIBLE FOR PROTECTING CHIAKI, SHIROGANE.
...MAYBE IF I FEEL LIKE IT.
CREAK
THAT SHIRO-GANE...
I JUST CAN'T STOP WORRYING...
WONDER IF SHE'S ALL RIGHT.
PLUNK
?

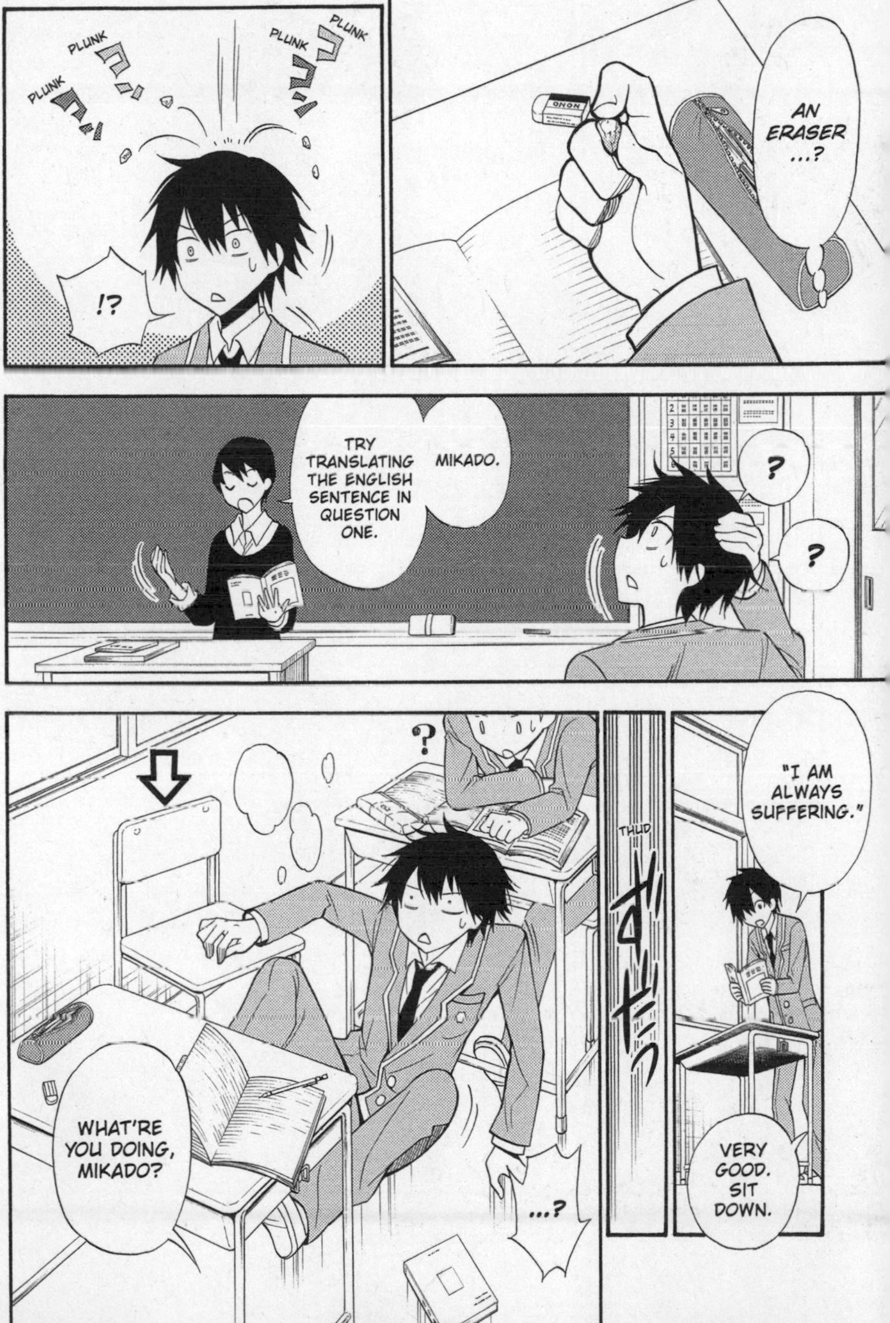
AN ERASER ...?
PLUNK
PLUNK
PLUNK
PLUNK
!?
MIKADO.
TRY TRANSLATING THE ENGLISH SENTENCE IN QUESTION ONE.
?
?
"I AM ALWAYS SUFFERING."
VERY GOOD. SIT DOWN.
THUD
?
WHAT'RE YOU DOING, MIKADO?
...?

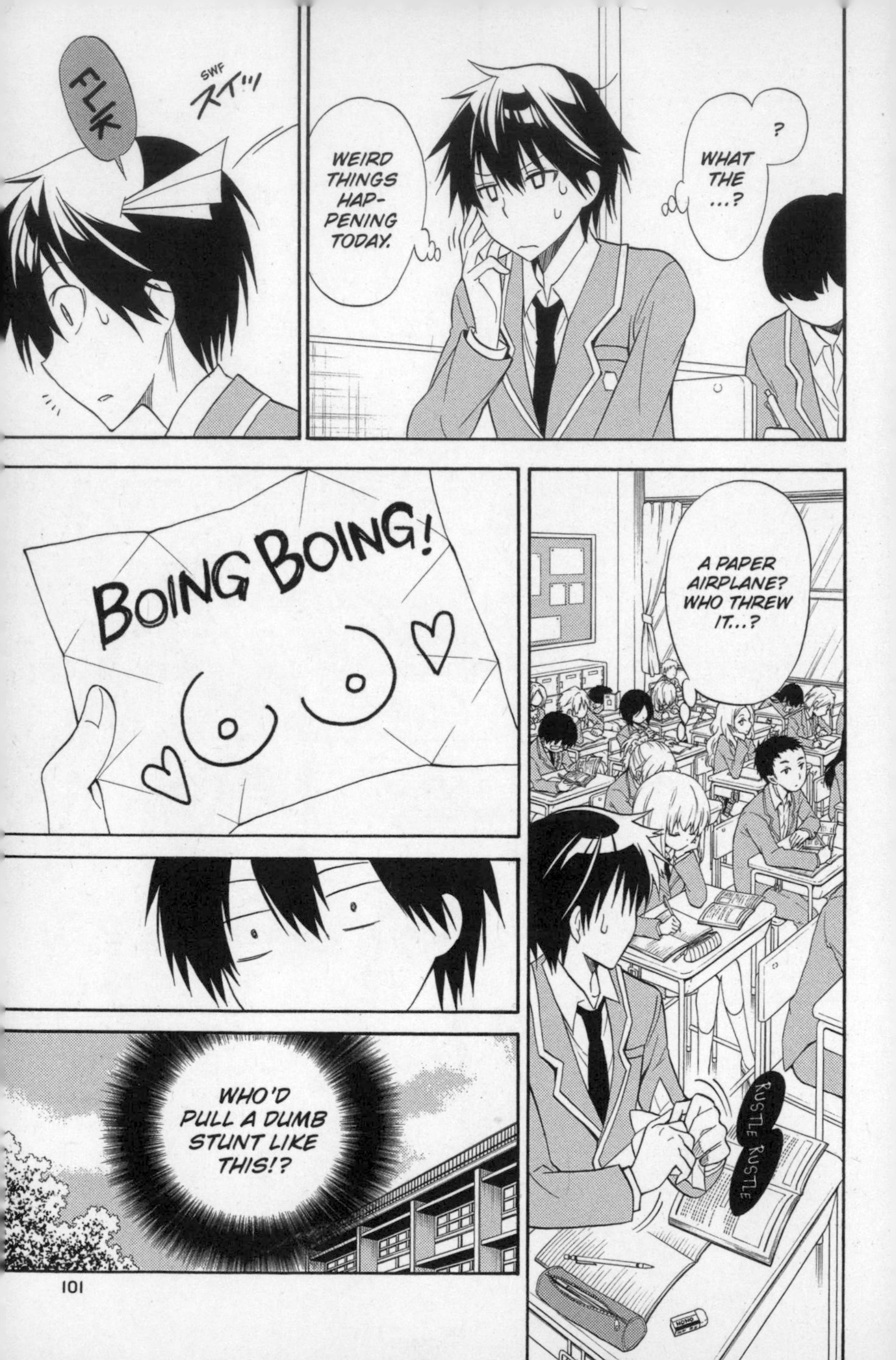
?
WHAT THE ...?
WEIRD THINGS HAP-PENING TODAY.
SWF
スイッ
FLIK
A PAPER AIRPLANE? WHO THREW IT...?
RUSTLE RUSTLE
BOING BOING!
WHO'D PULL A DUMB STUNT LIKE THIS!?

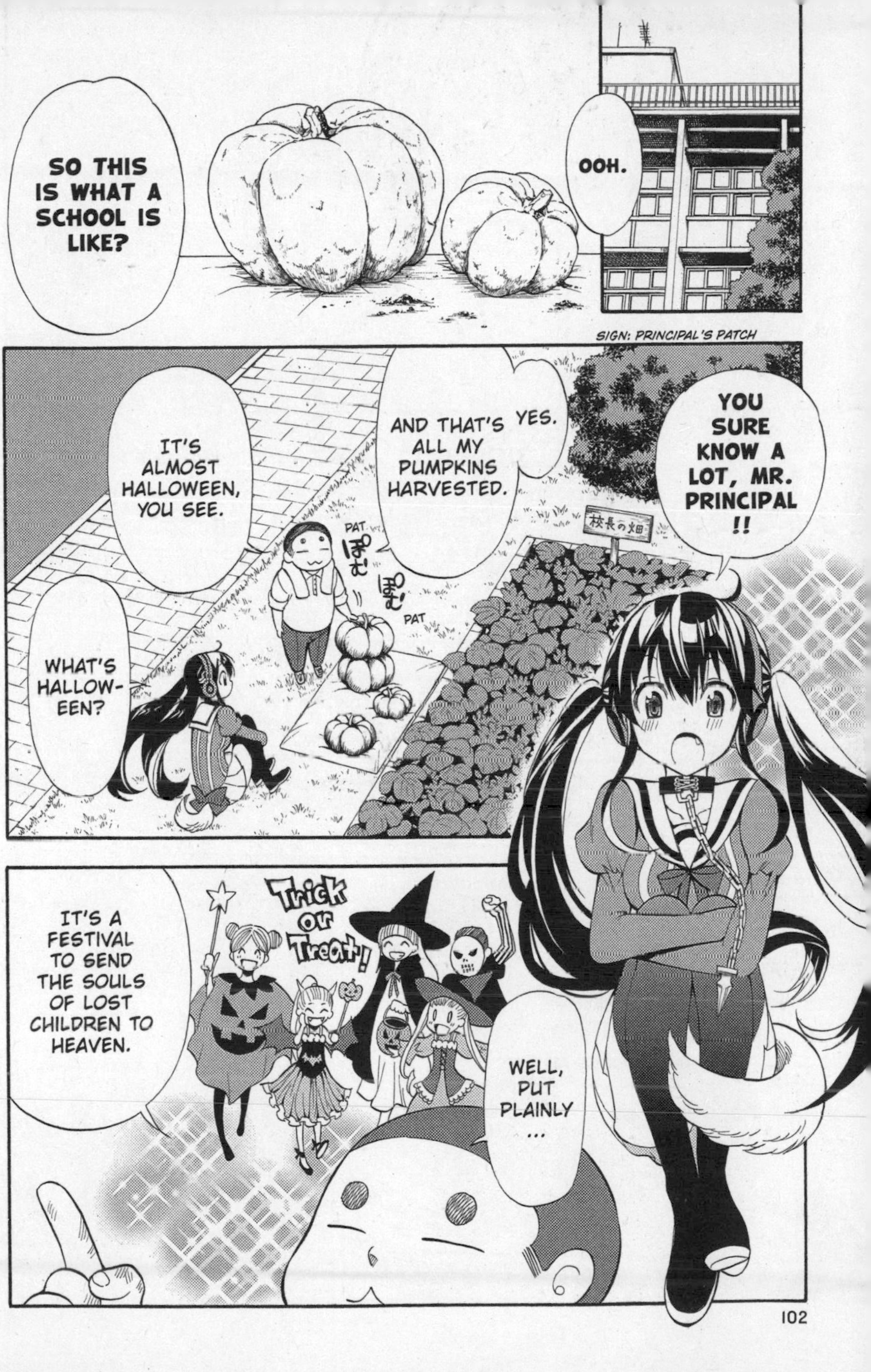
OOH.
SO THIS IS WHAT A SCHOOL IS LIKE?
SIGN: PRINCIPAL'S PATCH
YES.
AND THAT'S ALL MY PUMPKINS HARVESTED.
校長の畑
PAT ぽむ
ぽむ PAT
IT'S ALMOST HALLOWEEN, YOU SEE.
WHAT'S HALLOW-EEN?
WELL, PUT PLAINLY ...
Trick or Treat!
IT'S A FESTIVAL TO SEND THE SOULS OF LOST CHILDREN TO HEAVEN.
YOU SURE KNOW A LOT, MR. PRINCIPAL!!

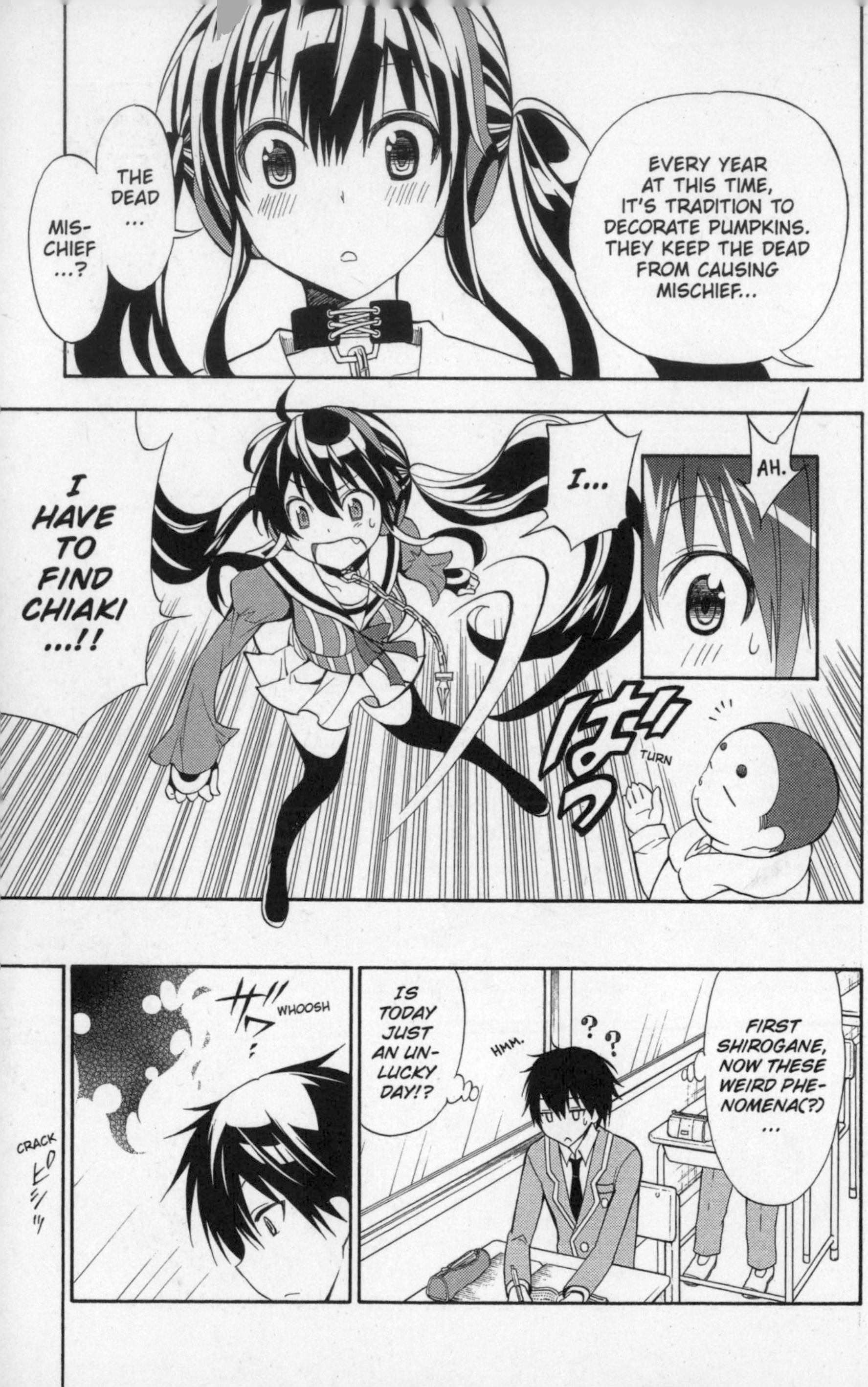
EVERY YEAR AT THIS TIME, IT'S TRADITION TO DECORATE PUMPKINS. THEY KEEP THE DEAD FROM CAUSING MISCHIEF...
THE DEAD ...
MIS-CHIEF ...?
AH.
I...
I HAVE TO FIND CHIAKI ...!!
TURN
FIRST SHIROGANE, NOW THESE WEIRD PHE-NOMENA(?) ...
HMM.
IS TODAY JUST AN UN-LUCKY DAY!?
WHOOSH
CRACK

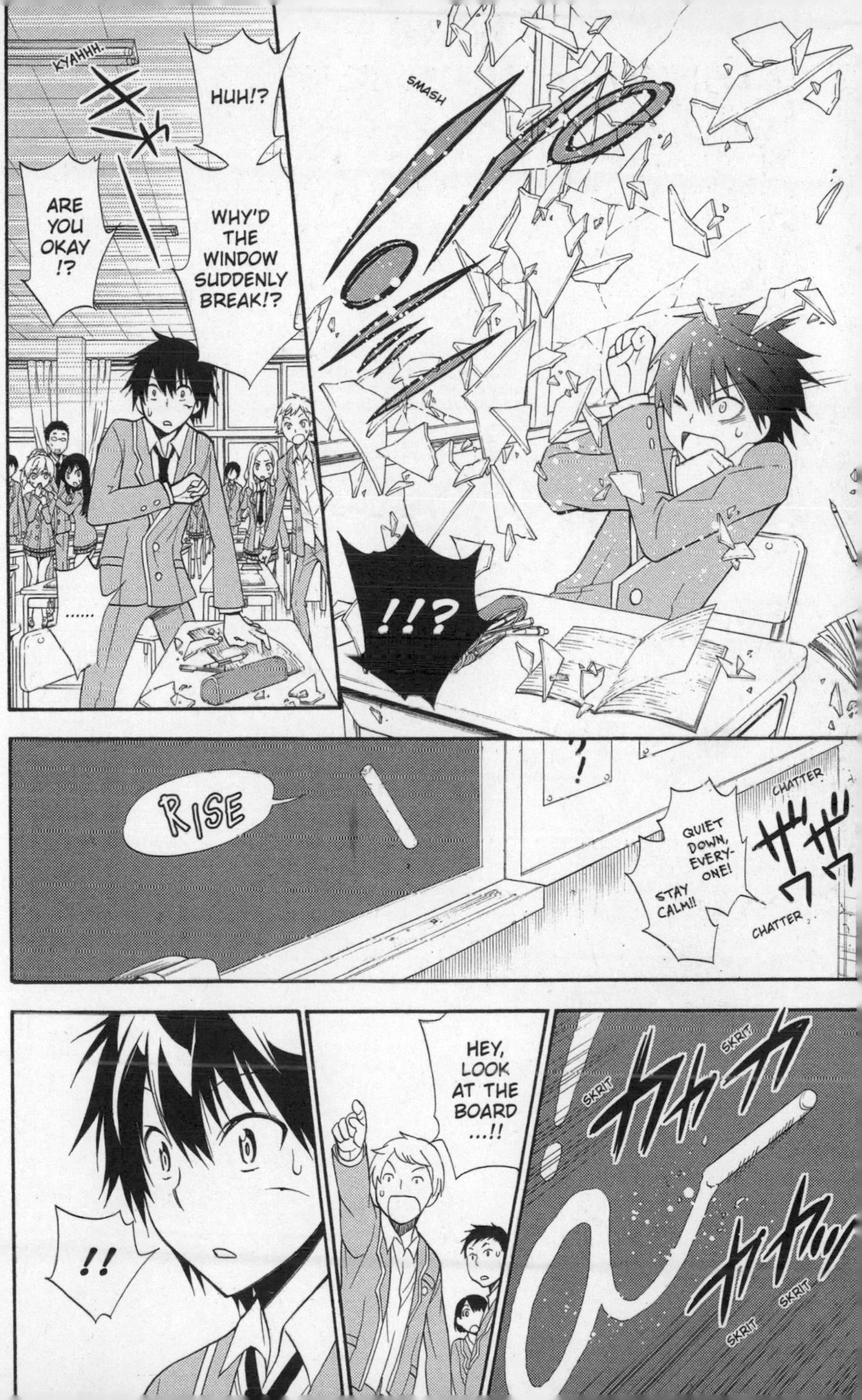
SMASH
!!?
KYAHHH.
HUH!?
WHY'D THE WINDOW SUDDENLY BREAK!?
ARE YOU OKAY !?
......
CHATTER
QUIET DOWN, EVERY-ONE!
STAY CALM!!
CHATTER
RISE
SKRIT
SKRIT
SKRIT
SKRIT
SKRIT
HEY, LOOK AT THE BOARD ...!!
!!

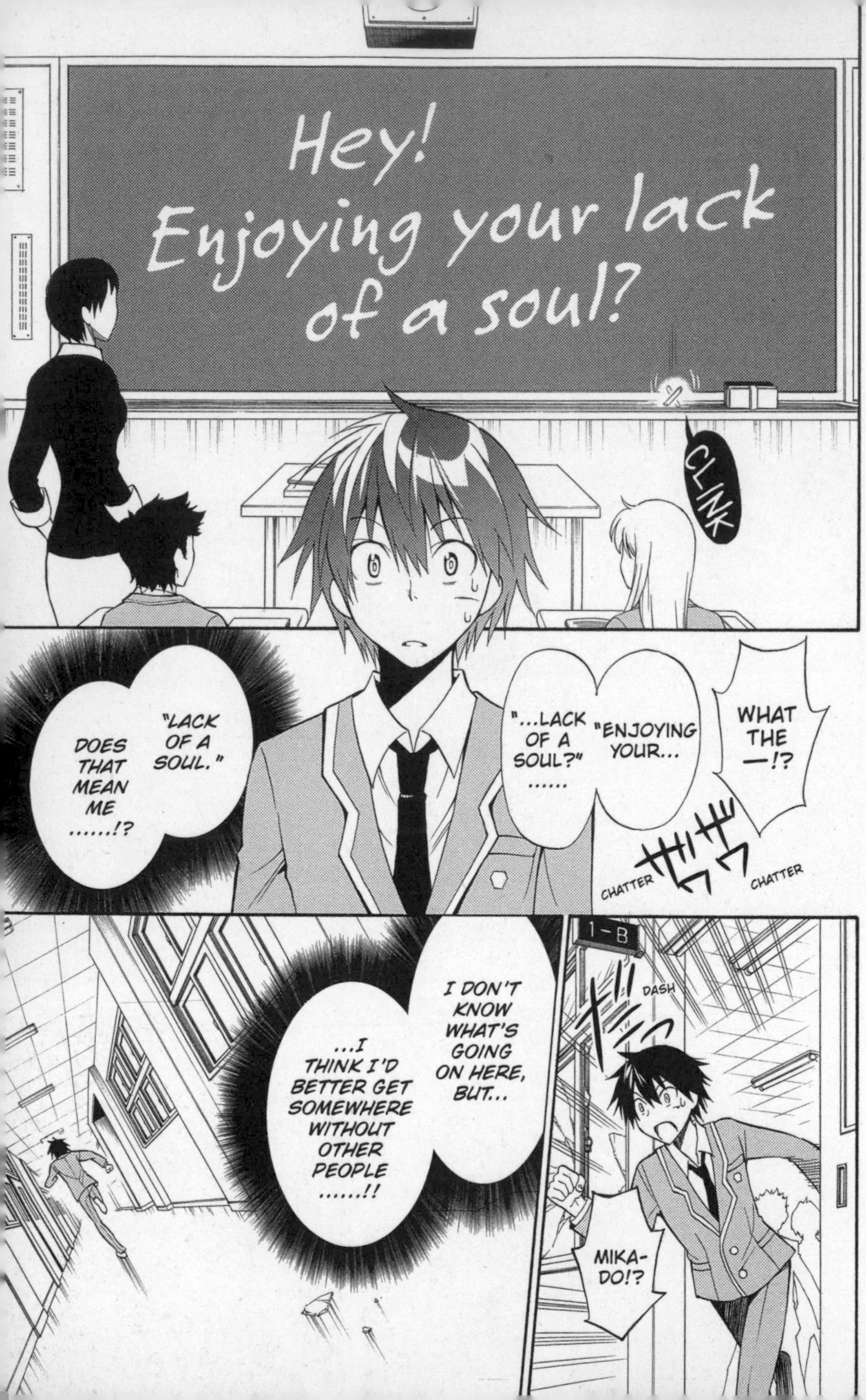
Hey! Enjoying your lack of a soul?
CLINK
WHAT THE —!?
"ENJOYING YOUR...
"...LACK OF A SOUL?" ......
"LACK OF A SOUL."
DOES THAT MEAN ME ......!?
CHATTER CHATTER
1-B
DASH
MIKA-DO!?
I DON'T KNOW WHAT'S GOING ON HERE, BUT...
...I THINK I'D BETTER GET SOMEWHERE WITHOUT OTHER PEOPLE ......!!

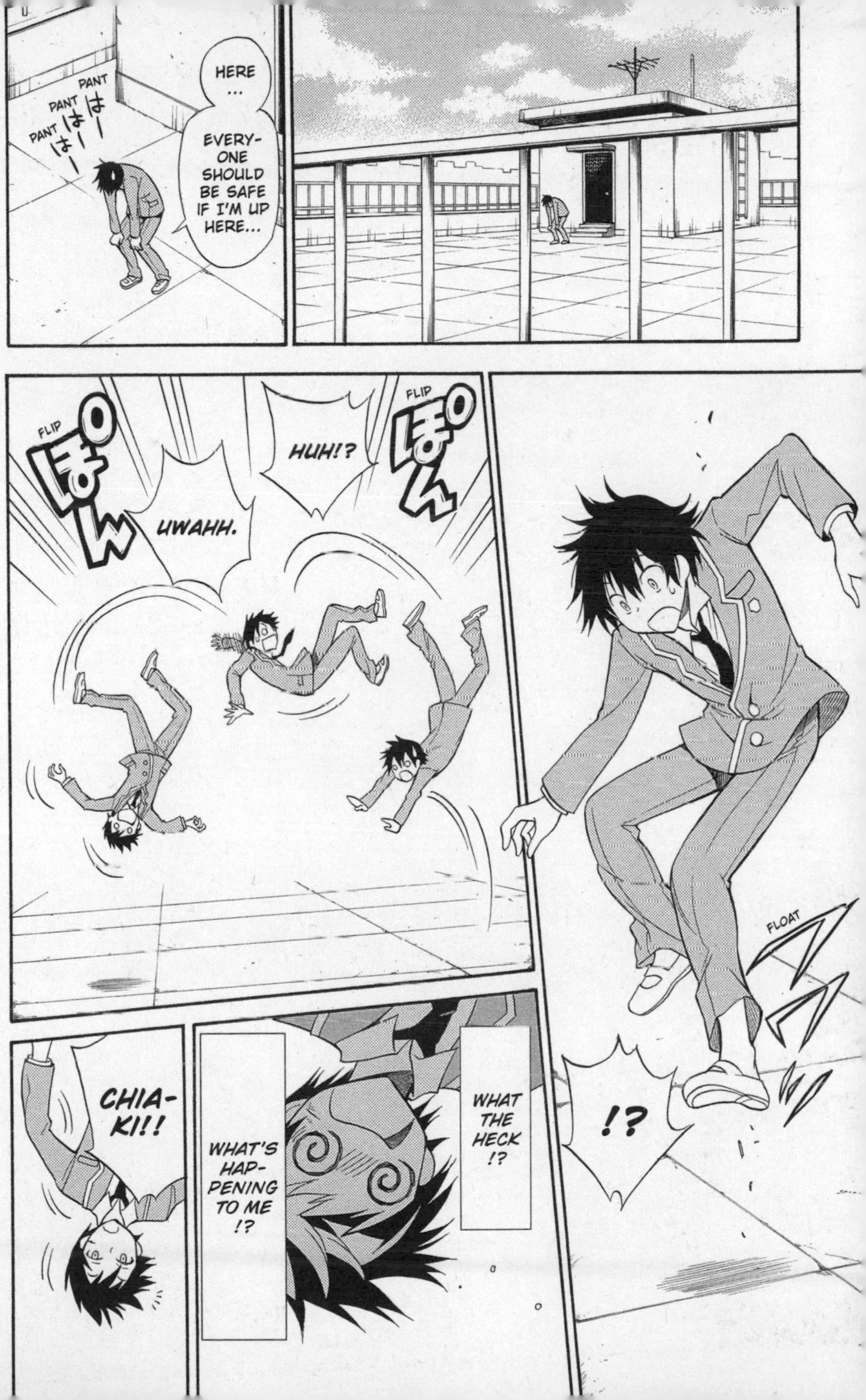
HERE ...
EVERY-ONE SHOULD BE SAFE IF I'M UP HERE...
PANT PANT PANT
はーはーはー
FLOAT
!?
FLIP
ぽん
HUH!?
FLIP
ぽん
UWAHH.
WHAT THE HECK !?
WHAT'S HAP-PENING TO ME !?
CHIA-KI!!

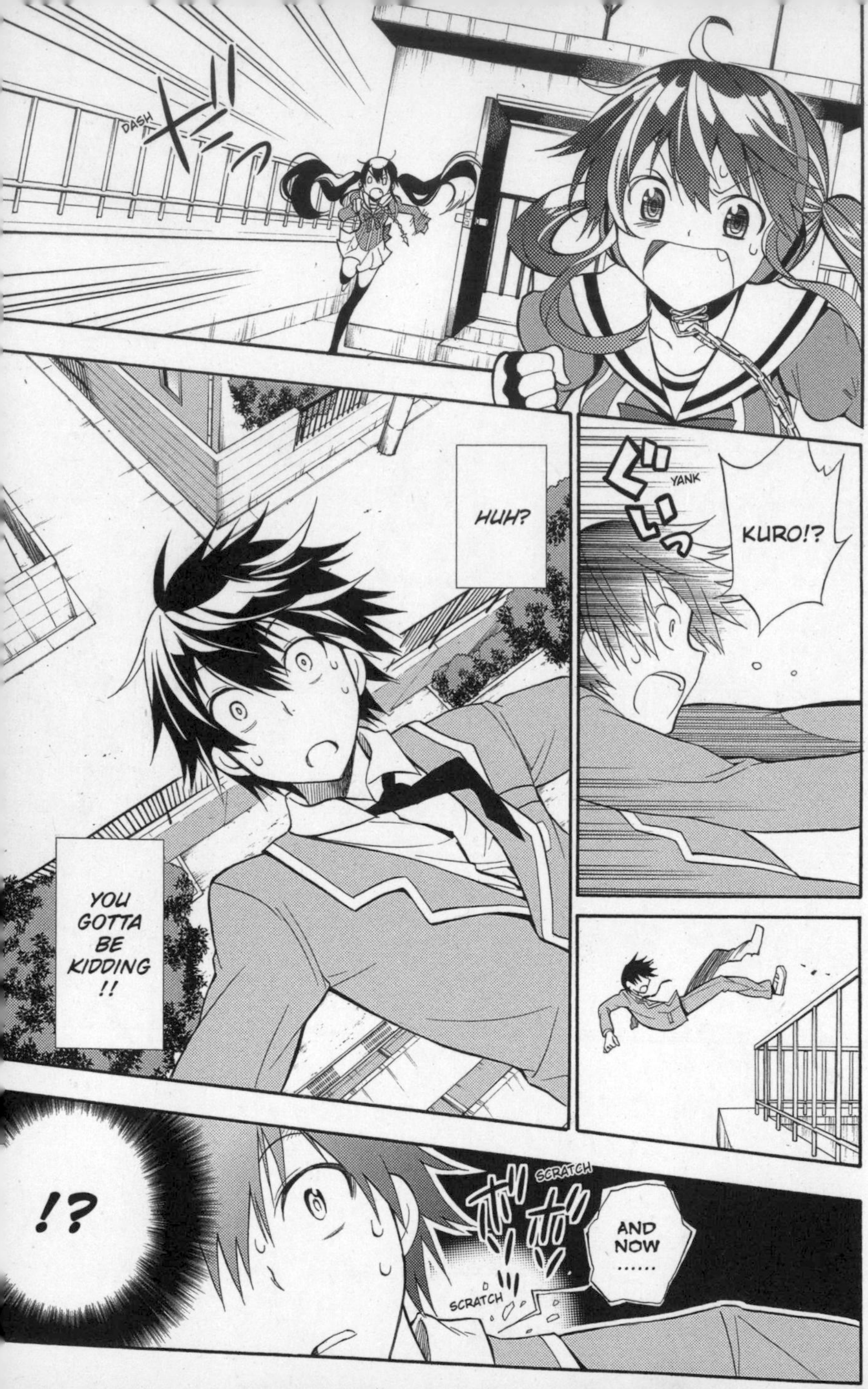
DASH
YANK
KURO!?
HUH?
YOU GOTTA BE KIDDING!!
AND NOW ......
SCRATCH
SCRATCH
!?

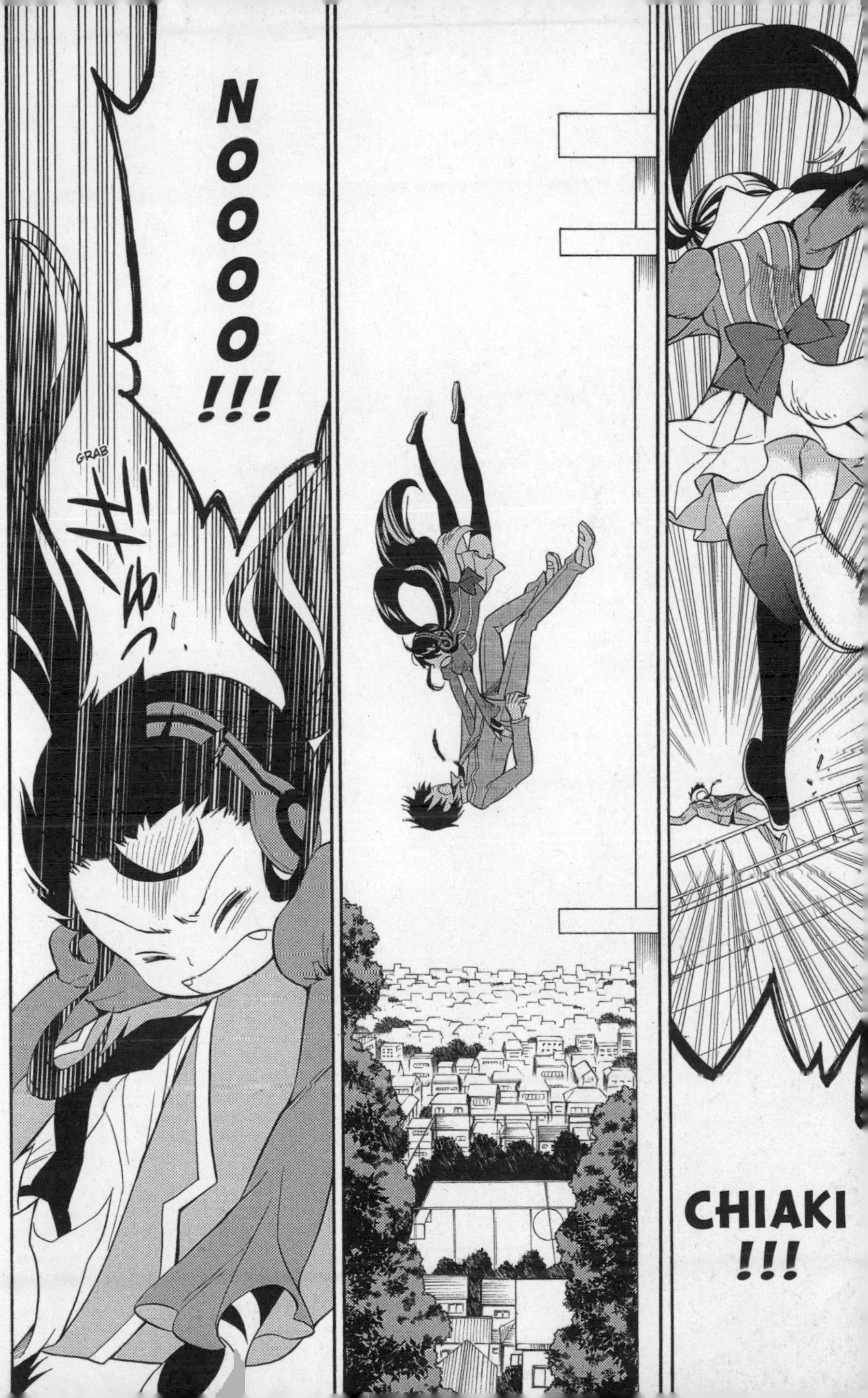
CHIAKI!!!
NOOOO!!!
GRAB

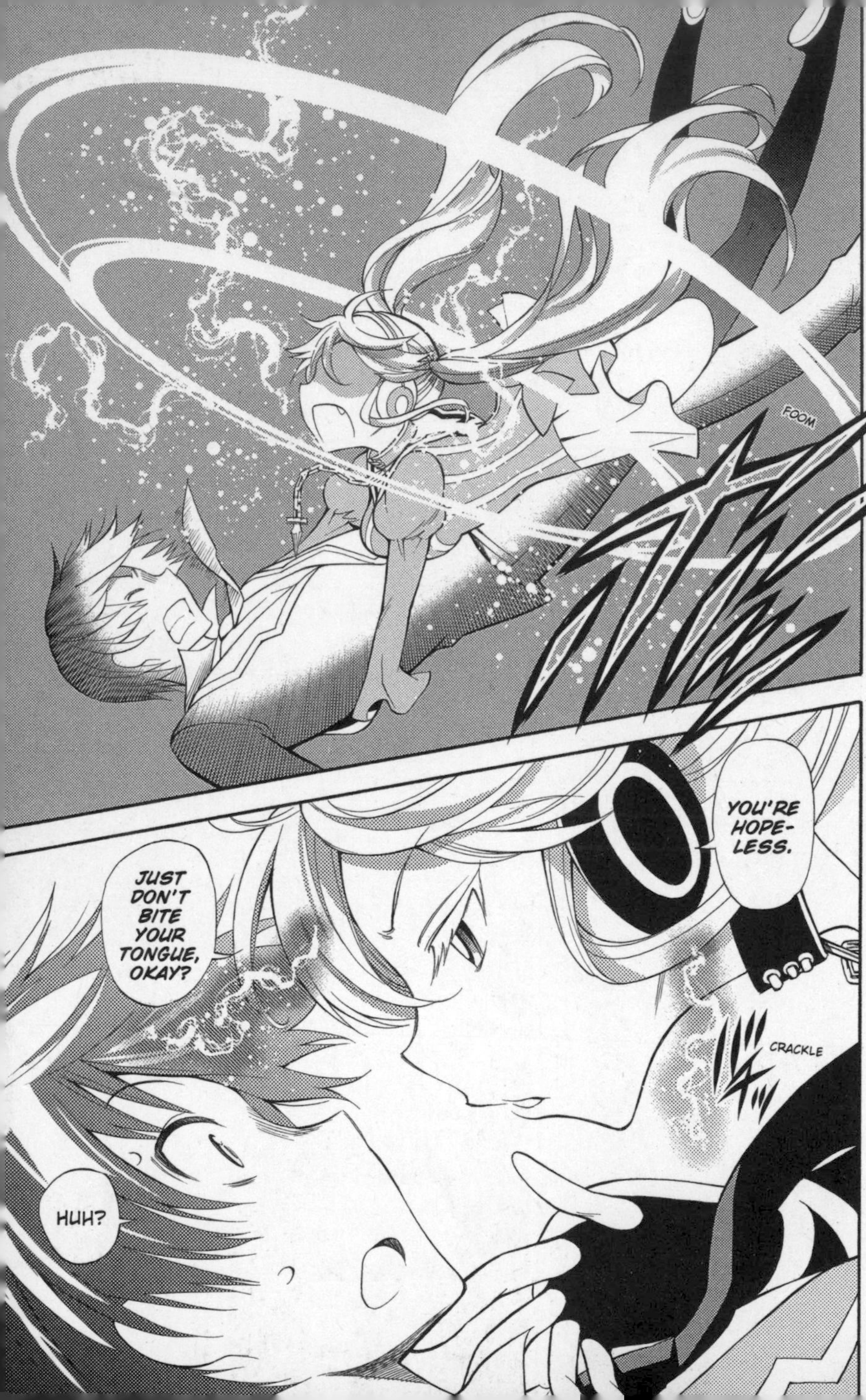
FOOM
YOU'RE HOPE-LESS.
JUST DON'T BITE YOUR TONGUE, OKAY?
CRACKLE
HUH?

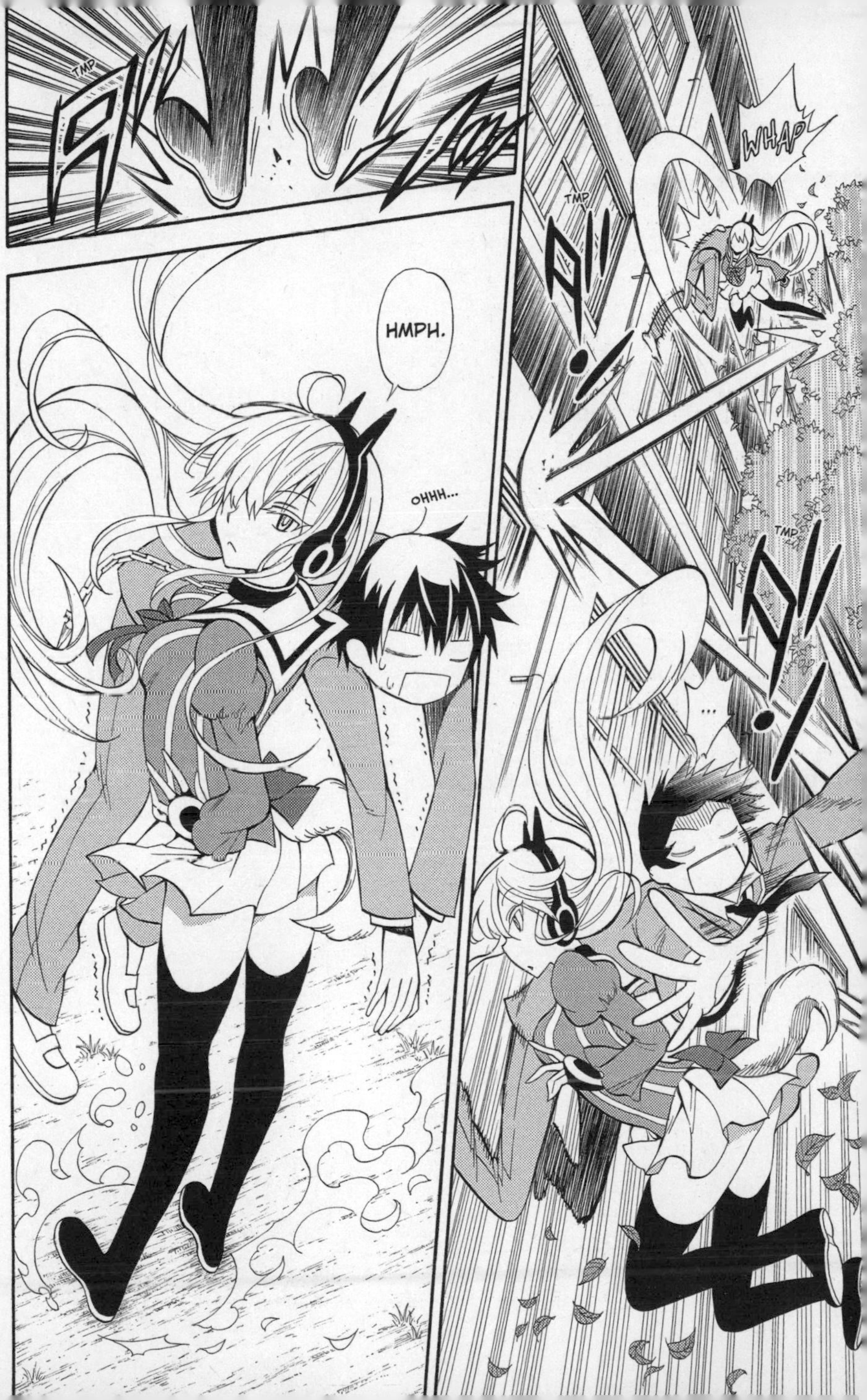
WHAP
TMP
TMP
...
TMP
HMPH.
OHHH...

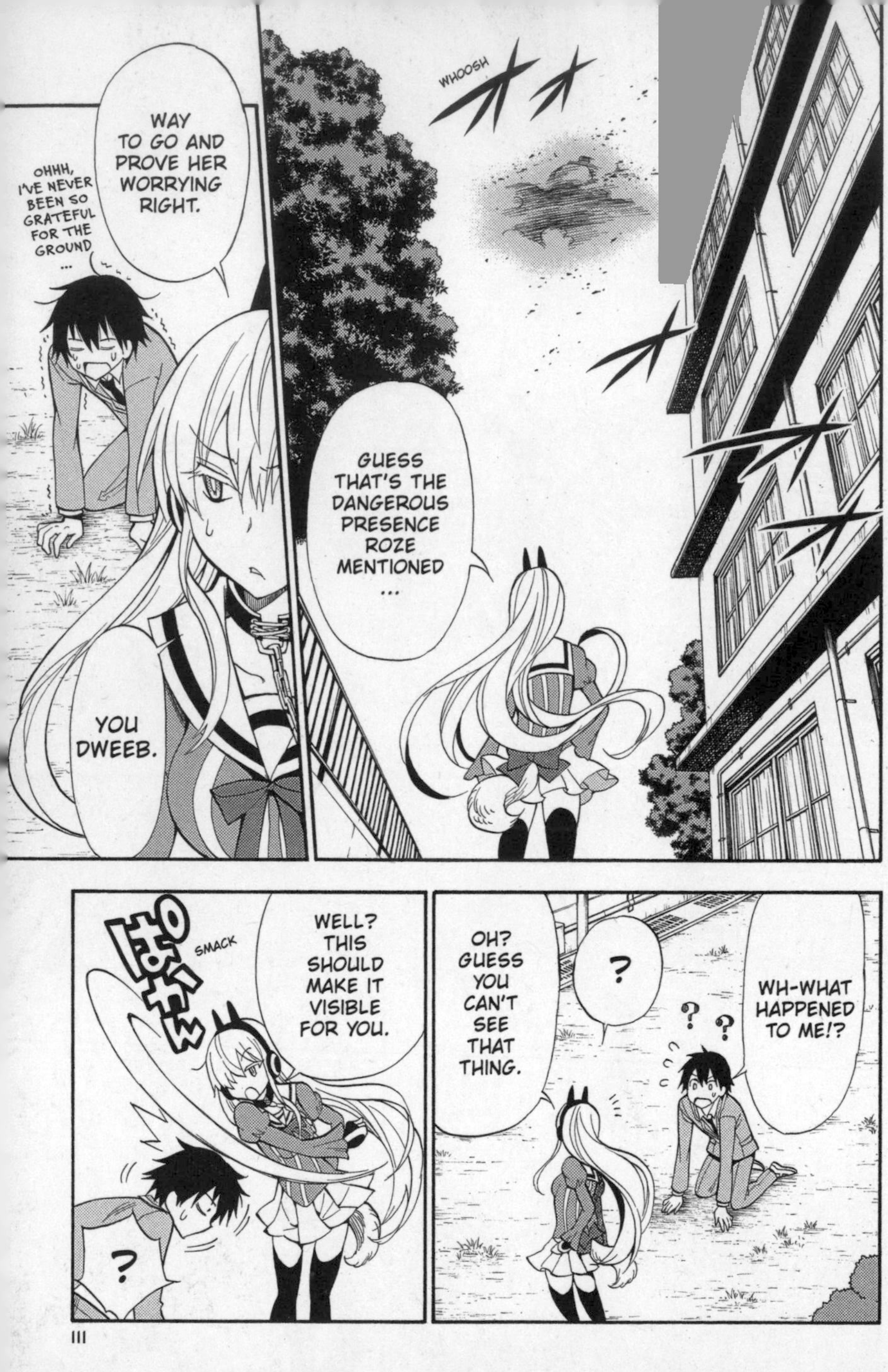
WHOOSH
GUESS THAT'S THE DANGEROUS PRESENCE ROZE MENTIONED ...
WAY TO GO AND PROVE HER WORRYING RIGHT.
OHHH, I'VE NEVER BEEN SO GRATEFUL FOR THE GROUND ...
YOU DWEEB.
WH-WHAT HAPPENED TO ME!?
?
OH? GUESS YOU CAN'T SEE THAT THING.
WELL? THIS SHOULD MAKE IT VISIBLE FOR YOU.
SMACK
?

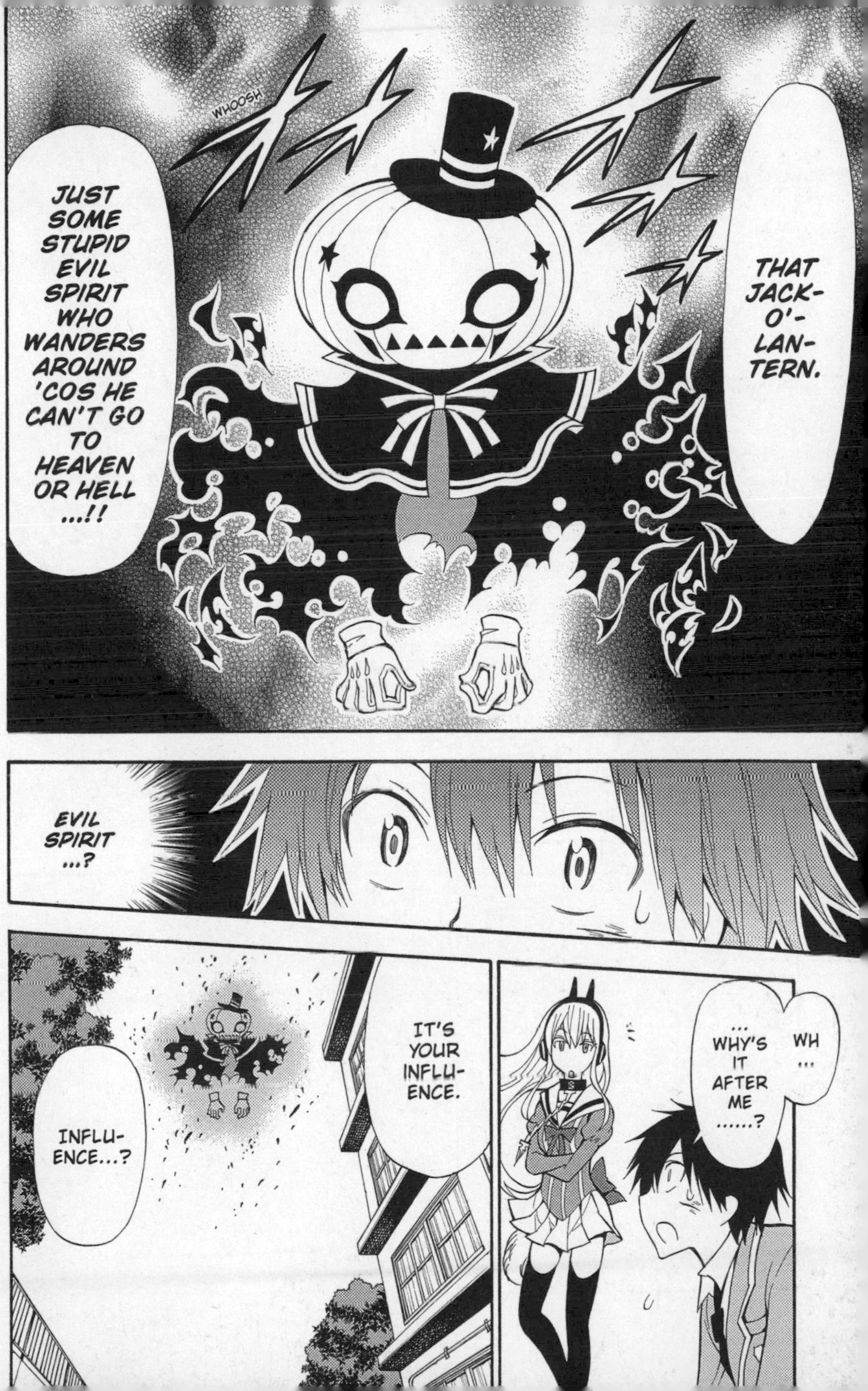
THAT JACK-O'-LANTERN.
WHOOSH
JUST SOME STUPID EVIL SPIRIT WHO WANDERS AROUND 'COS HE CAN'T GO TO HEAVEN OR HELL ...!!
EVIL SPIRIT ...?
WH ...
... WHY'S IT AFTER ME ......?
IT'S YOUR INFLU-ENCE.
INFLU-ENCE...?

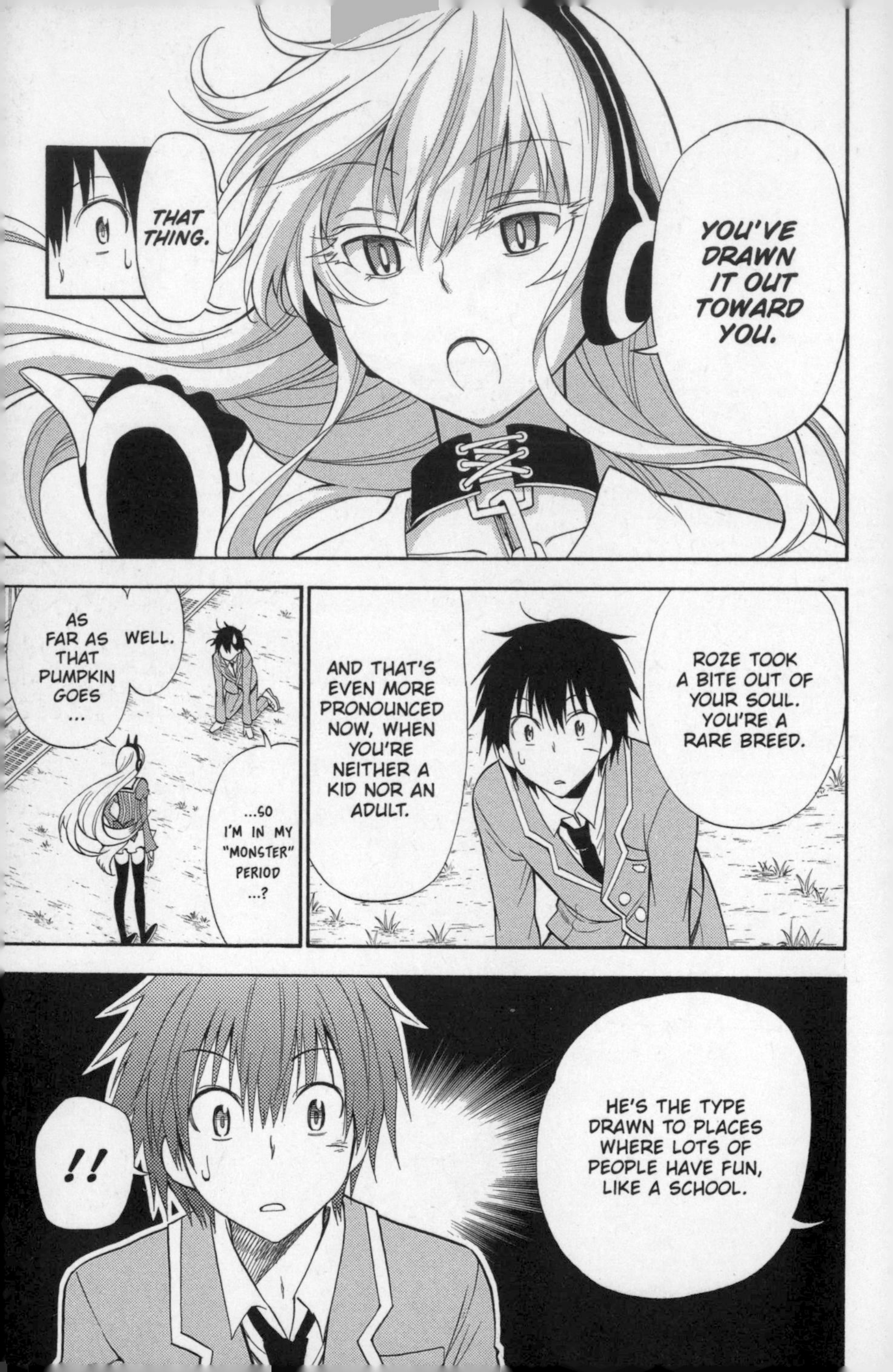
YOU'VE DRAWN IT OUT TOWARD YOU.
THAT THING.
ROZE TOOK A BITE OUT OF YOUR SOUL. YOU'RE A RARE BREED.
AND THAT'S EVEN MORE PRONOUNCED NOW, WHEN YOU'RE NEITHER A KID NOR AN ADULT.
...SO I'M IN MY "MONSTER" PERIOD ...?
WELL. AS FAR AS THAT PUMPKIN GOES ...
HE'S THE TYPE DRAWN TO PLACES WHERE LOTS OF PEOPLE HAVE FUN, LIKE A SCHOOL.
!!

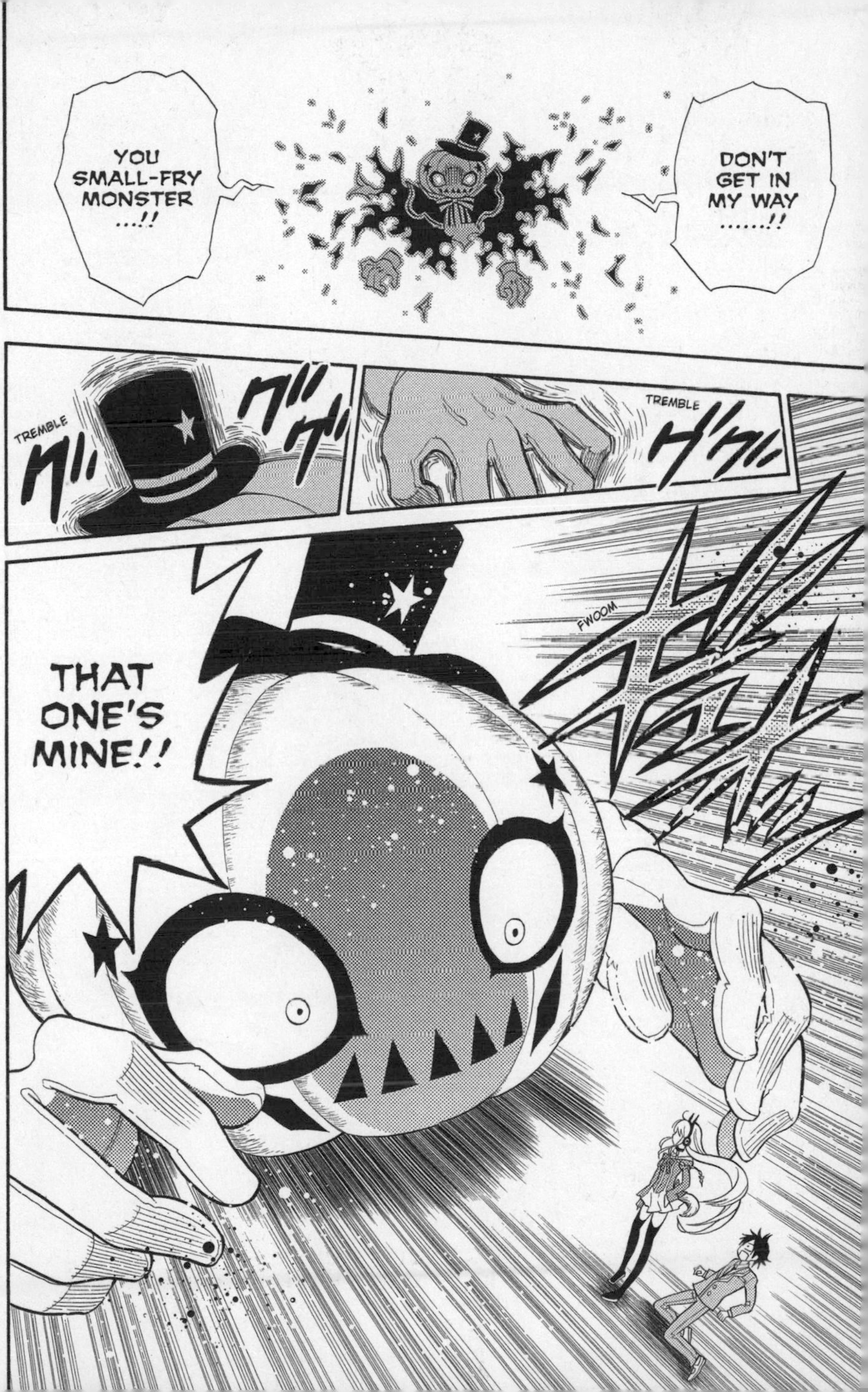
DON'T GET IN MY WAY ......!!
YOU SMALL-FRY MONSTER ....!!
TREMBLE
TREMBLE
FWOOM
THAT ONE'S MINE!!

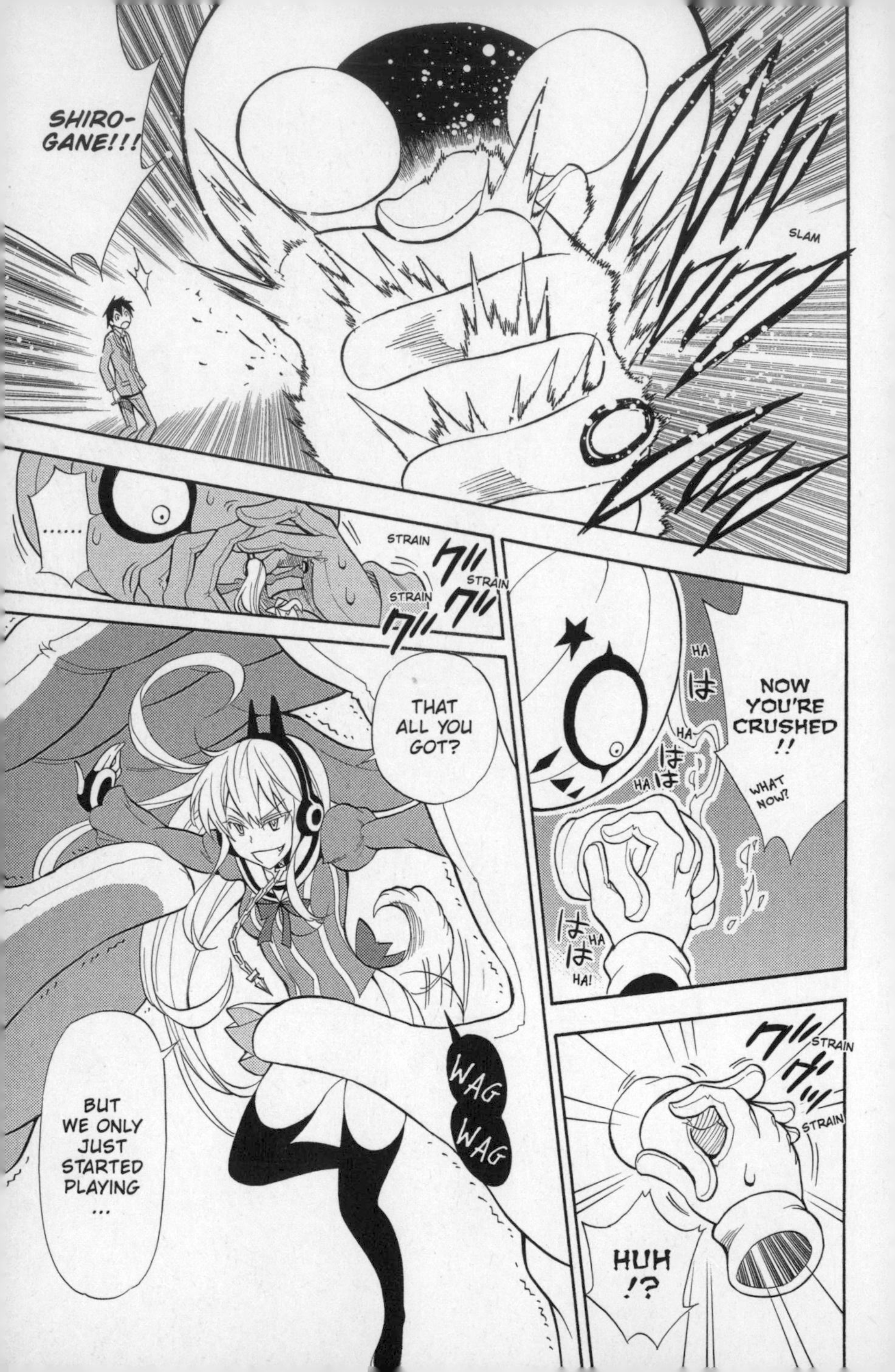
SLAM
SHIRO-GANE!!!
......
STRAIN
STRAIN
STRAIN
HA
HA
HA
NOW YOU'RE CRUSHED!!
WHAT NOW?
HA
HA!
STRAIN
STRAIN
HUH!?
THAT ALL YOU GOT?
WAG WAG
BUT WE ONLY JUST STARTED PLAYING...

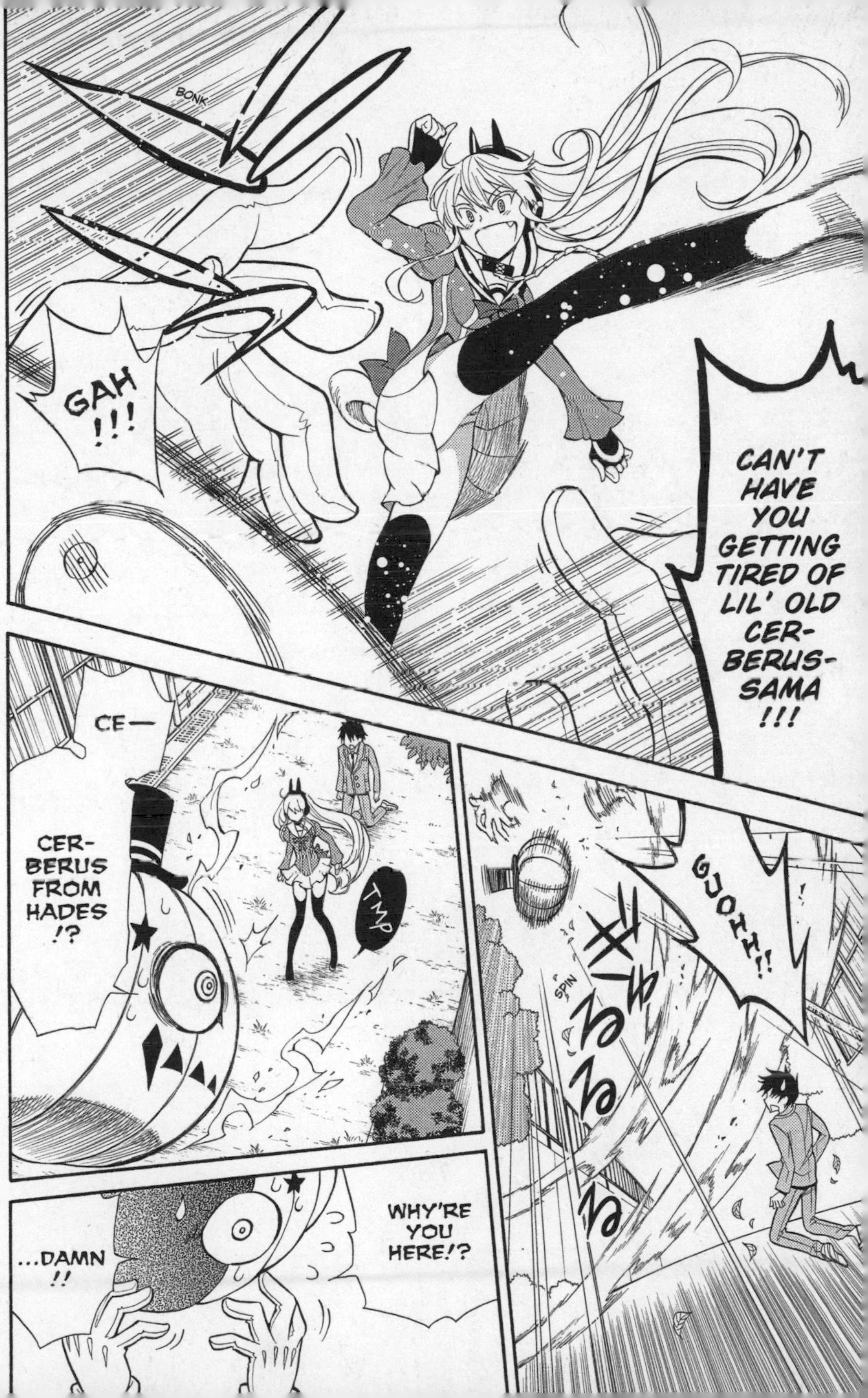

CAN'T HAVE YOU GETTING TIRED OF LIL' OLD CER-BERUS-SAMA!!!
BONK
GAH!!!
GUOHH!!
SPIN
CE—
CER-BERUS FROM HADES!?
TMP
WHY'RE YOU HERE!?
...DAMN!!

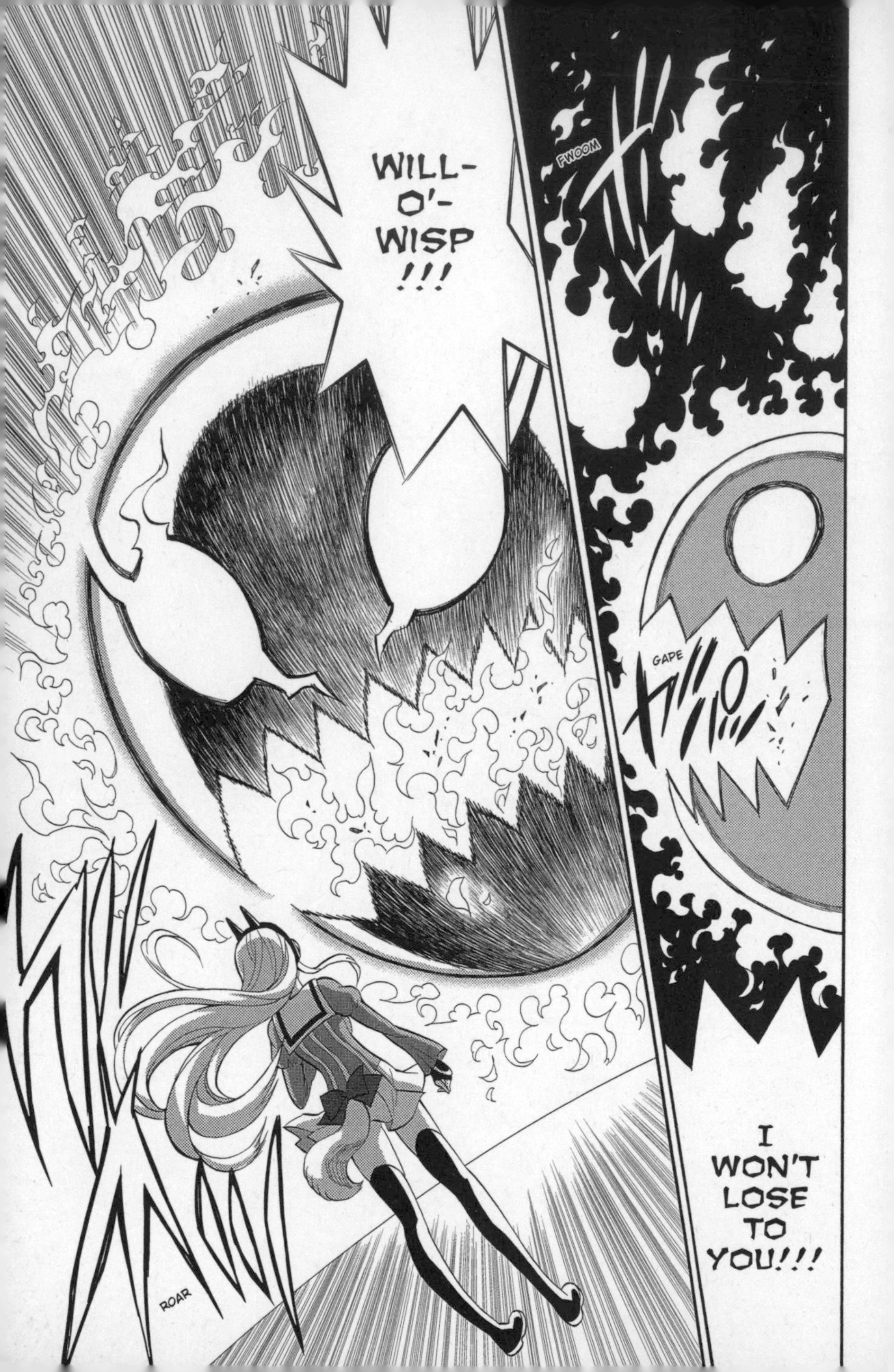
FWOOM
GAPE
I WON'T LOSE TO YOU!!!
WILL-O'-WISP!!!
ROAR

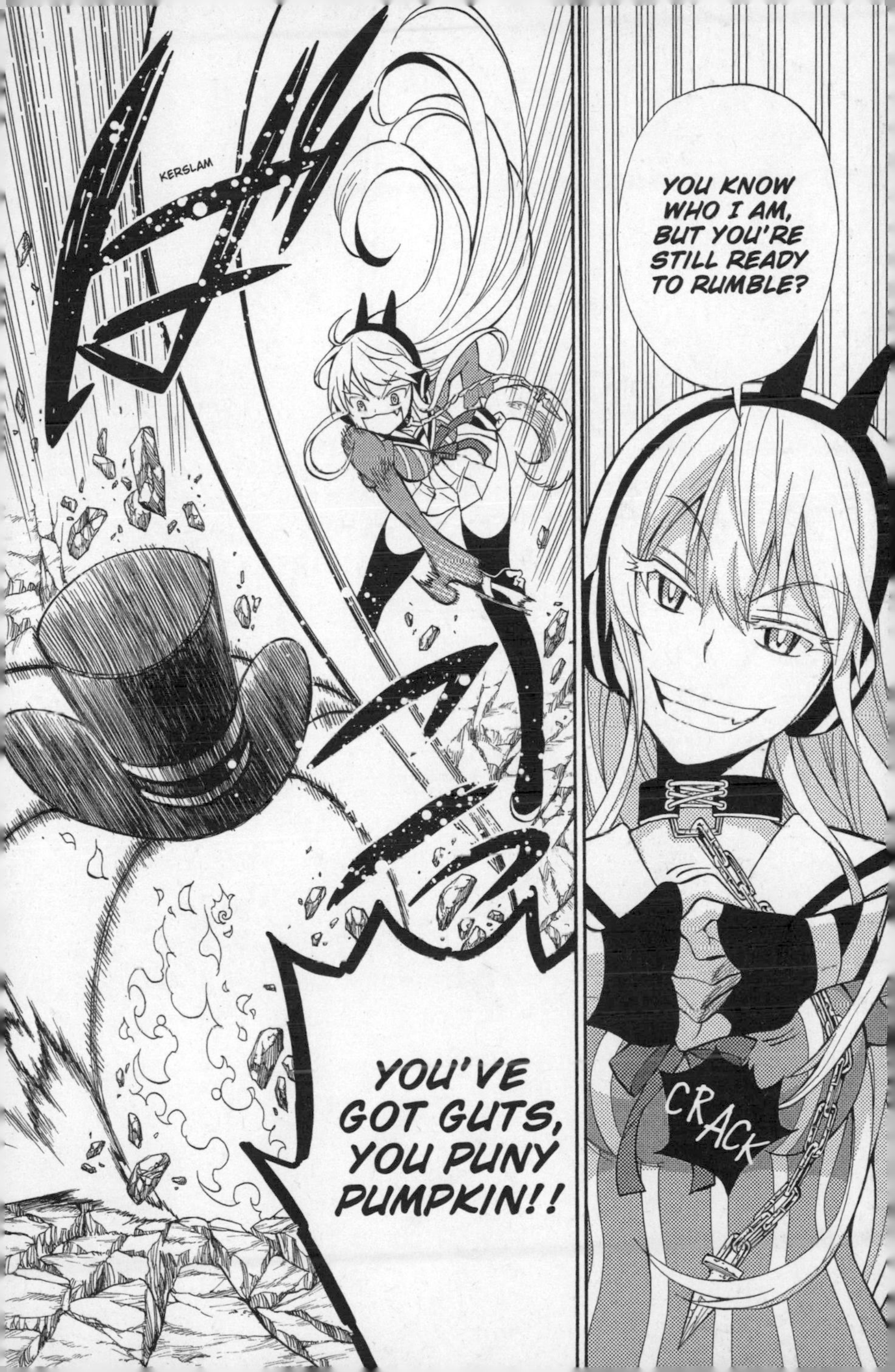
YOU KNOW WHO I AM, BUT YOU'RE STILL READY TO RUMBLE?
CRACK
KERSLAM
YOU'VE GOT GUTS, YOU PUNY PUMPKIN!!

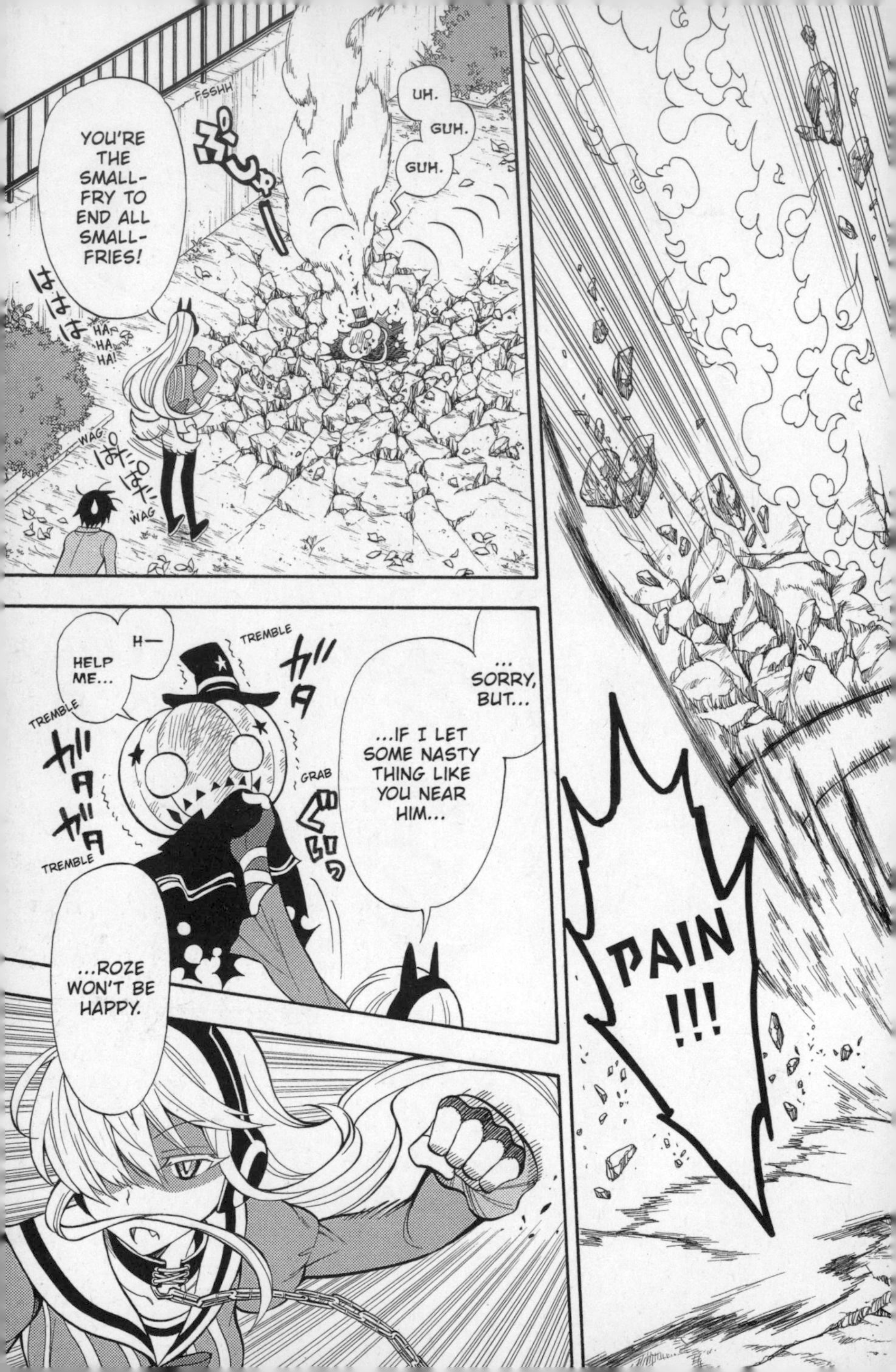
PAIN !!!
UH.
GUH.
GUH.
FSSHH
YOU'RE THE SMALL-FRY TO END ALL SMALL-FRIES!
ははは
HA HA HA!
WAG
WAG
...SORRY, BUT...
...IF I LET SOME NASTY THING LIKE YOU NEAR HIM...
GRAB
TREMBLE
H— HELP ME...
TREMBLE
TREMBLE
...ROZE WON'T BE HAPPY.

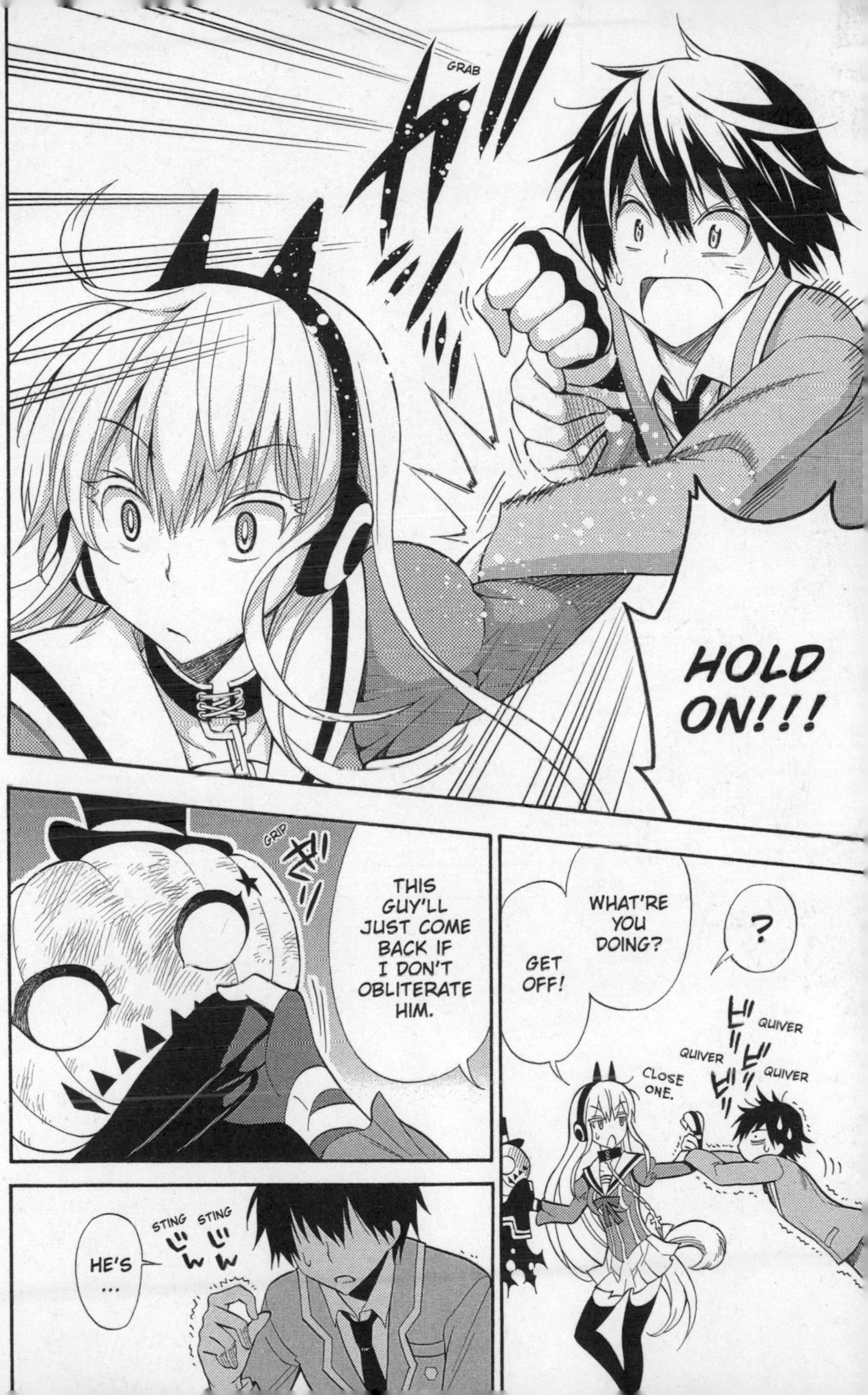
GRAB
HOLD ON!!!
?
WHAT'RE YOU DOING?
GET OFF!
QUIVER
QUIVER
QUIVER
CLOSE ONE.
GRIP
THIS GUY'LL JUST COME BACK IF I DON'T OBLITERATE HIM.
STING STING
HE'S ...

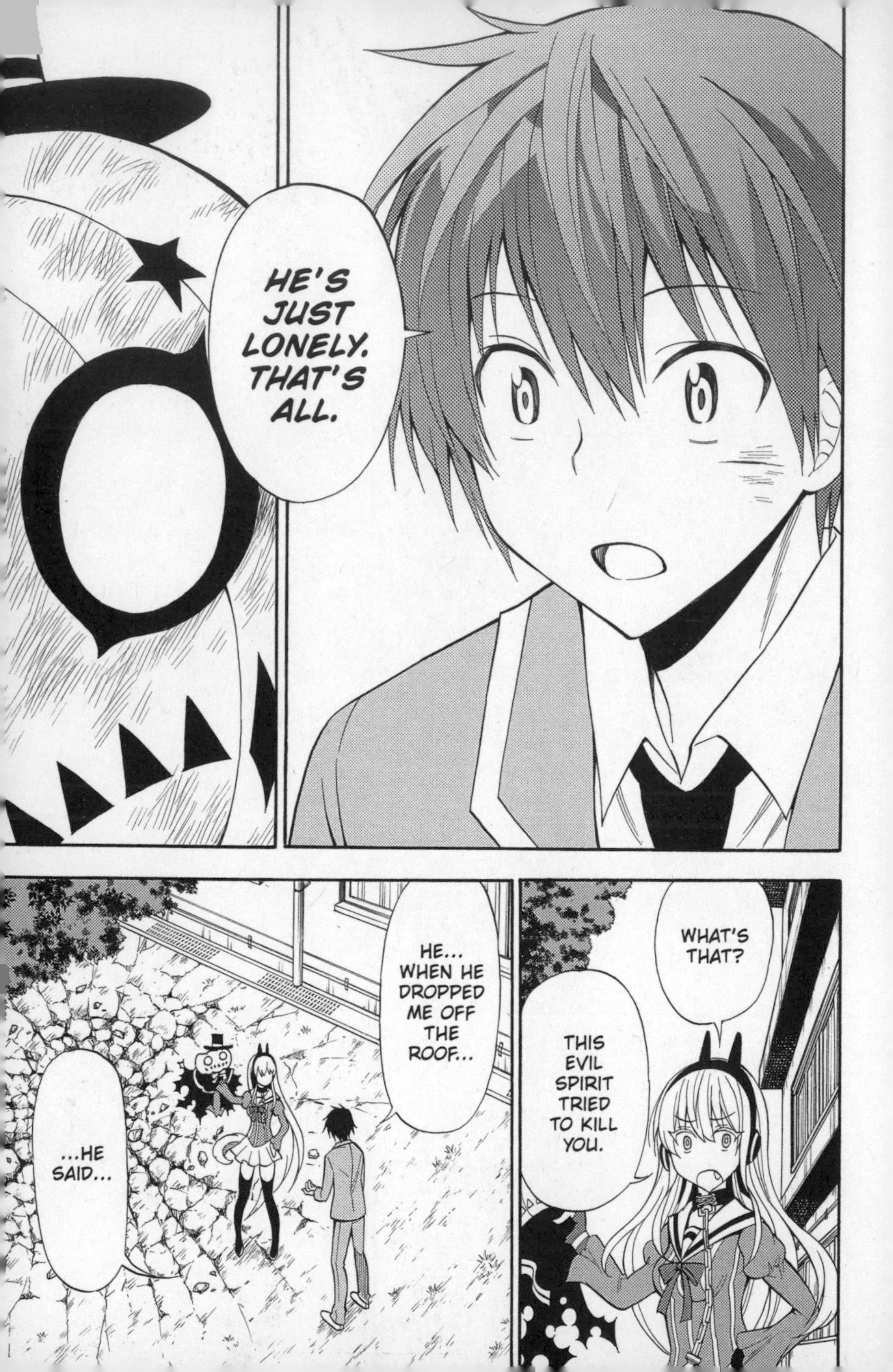
HE'S JUST LONELY. THAT'S ALL.
WHAT'S THAT?
THIS EVIL SPIRIT TRIED TO KILL YOU.
HE... WHEN HE DROPPED ME OFF THE ROOF...
...HE SAID...

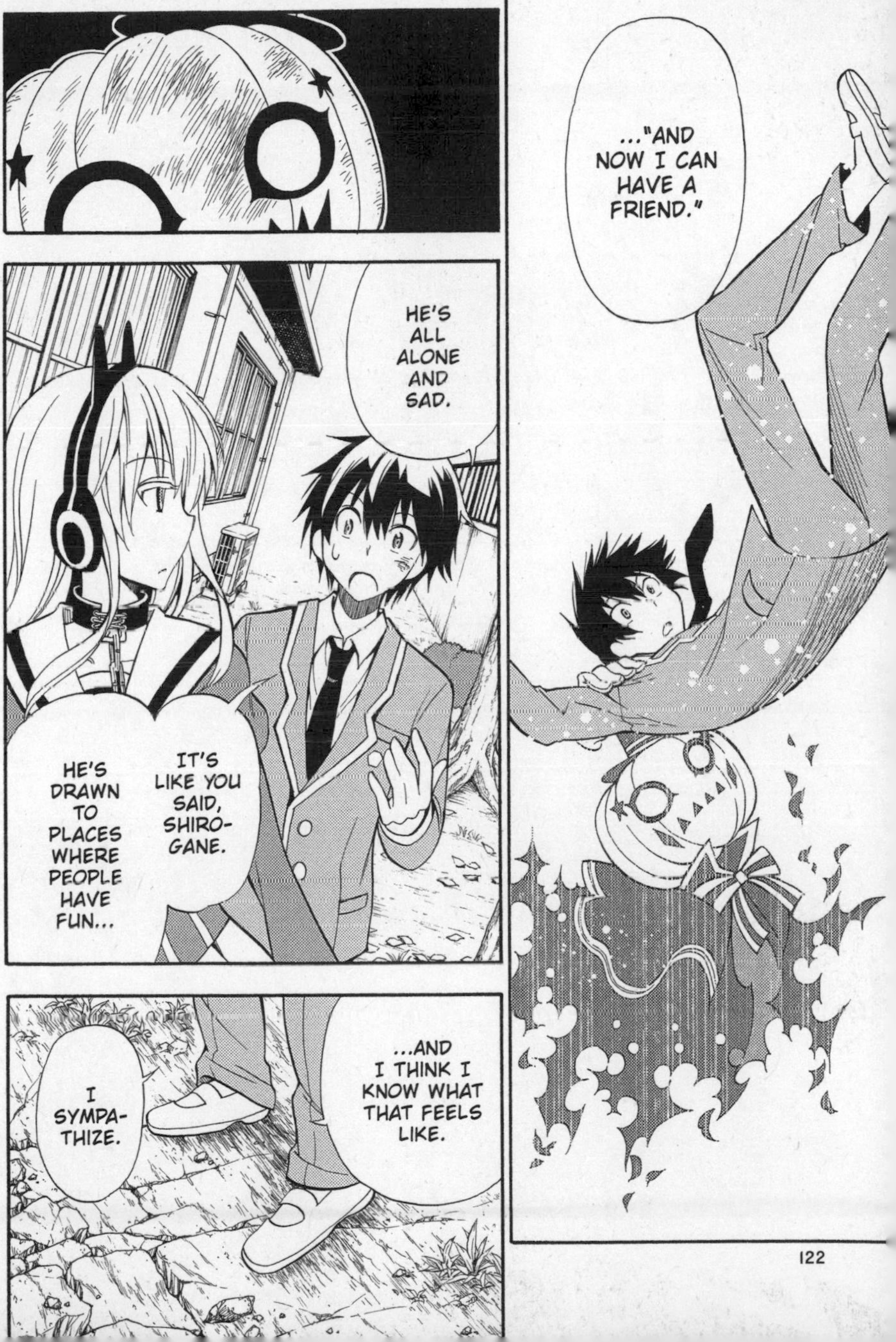
..."AND NOW I CAN HAVE A FRIEND."
HE'S ALL ALONE AND SAD.
IT'S LIKE YOU SAID, SHIROGANE.
HE'S DRAWN TO PLACES WHERE PEOPLE HAVE FUN...
...AND I THINK I KNOW WHAT THAT FEELS LIKE.
I SYMPATHIZE.

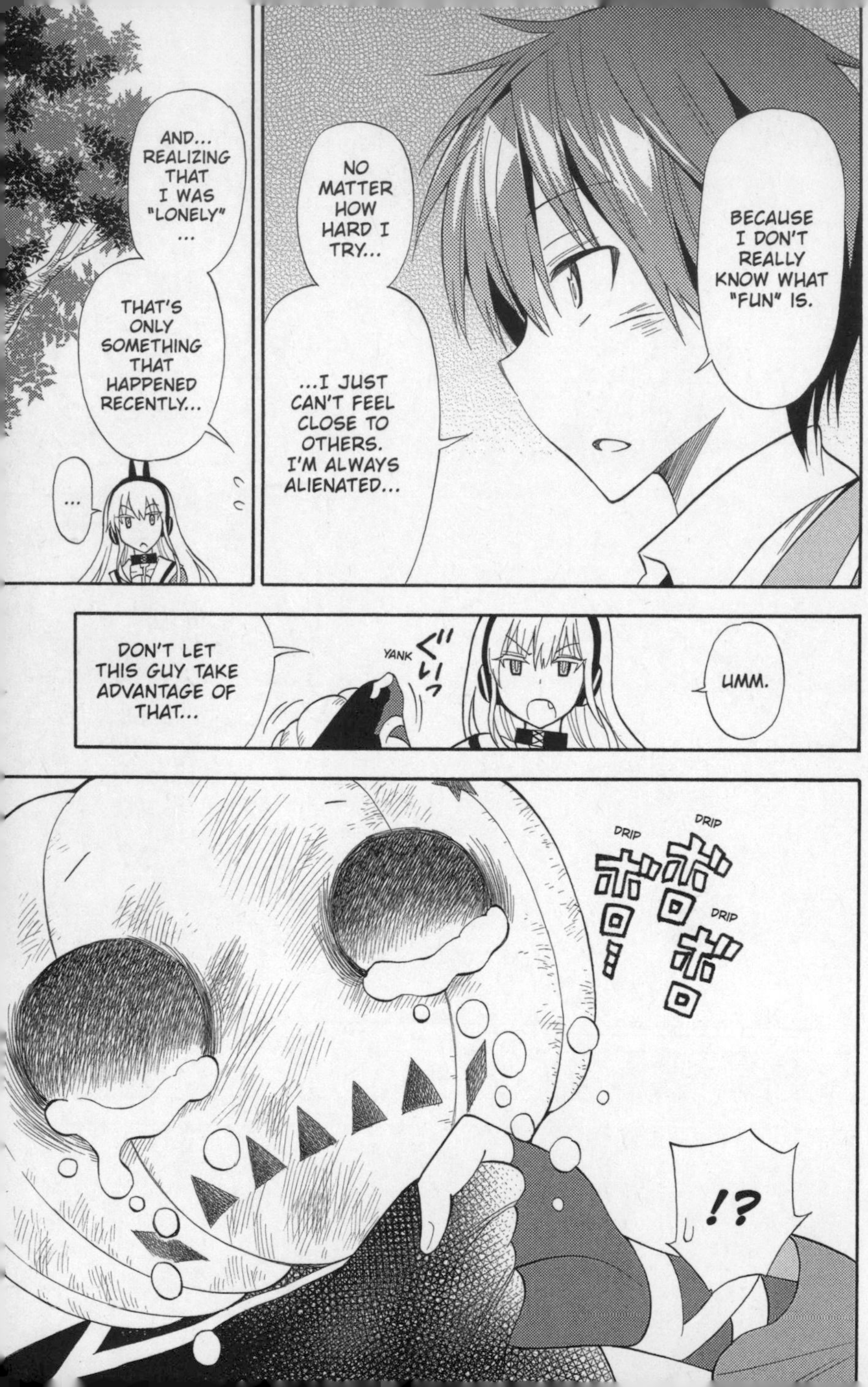
BECAUSE I DON'T REALLY KNOW WHAT "FUN" IS.
NO MATTER HOW HARD I TRY...
...I JUST CAN'T FEEL CLOSE TO OTHERS. I'M ALWAYS ALIENATED...
AND... REALIZING THAT I WAS "LONELY" ...
THAT'S ONLY SOMETHING THAT HAPPENED RECENTLY...
...
UMM.
YANK ぐいっ
DON'T LET THIS GUY TAKE ADVANTAGE OF THAT...
DRIP
DRIP
DRIP
!?

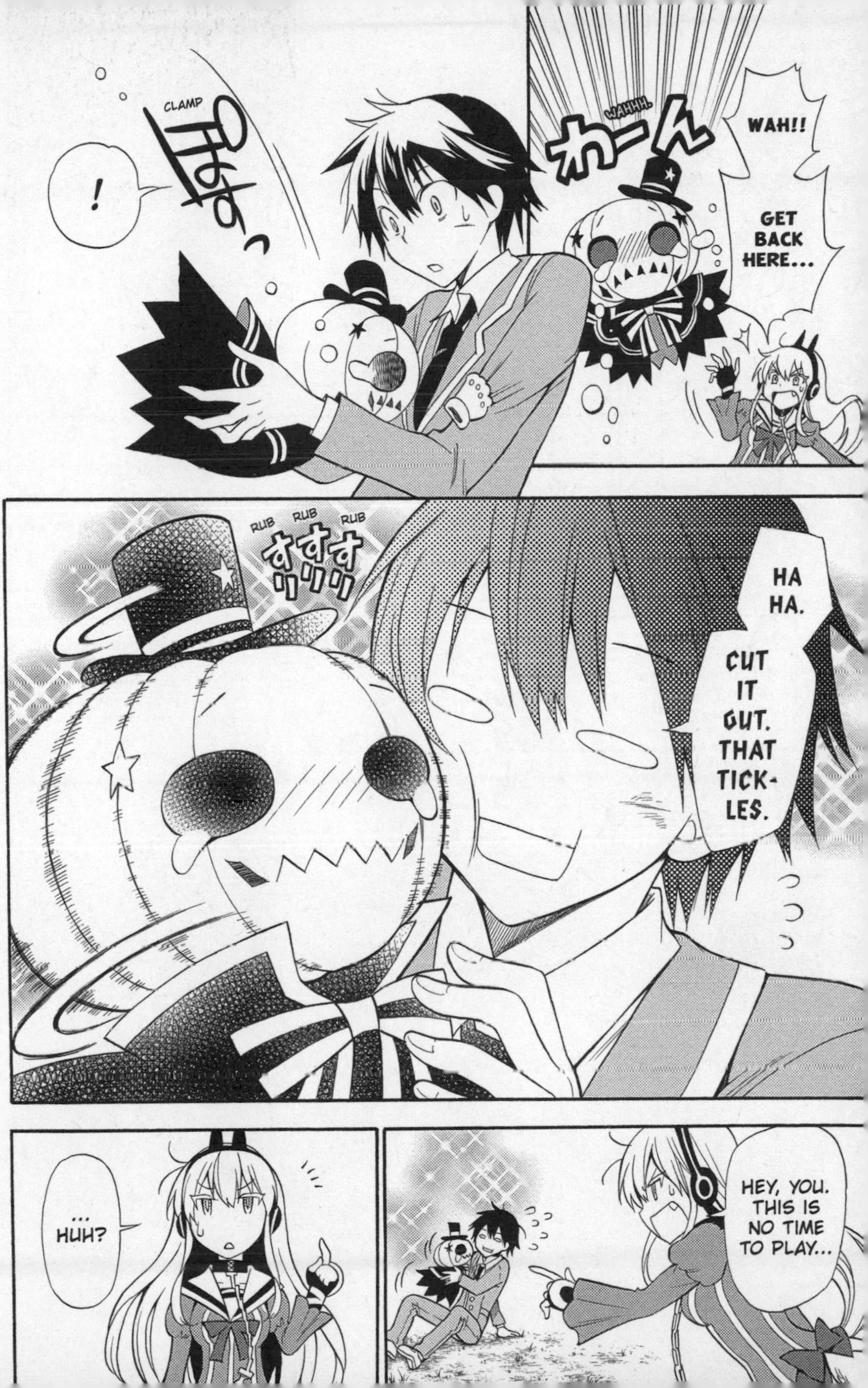
WAHHH.
わーん
WAH!!
GET BACK HERE...
CLAMP
ぽすっ
!
RUB RUB RUB
すすす
HA HA.
CUT IT OUT. THAT TICKLES.
HEY, YOU. THIS IS NO TIME TO PLAY...
... HUH?

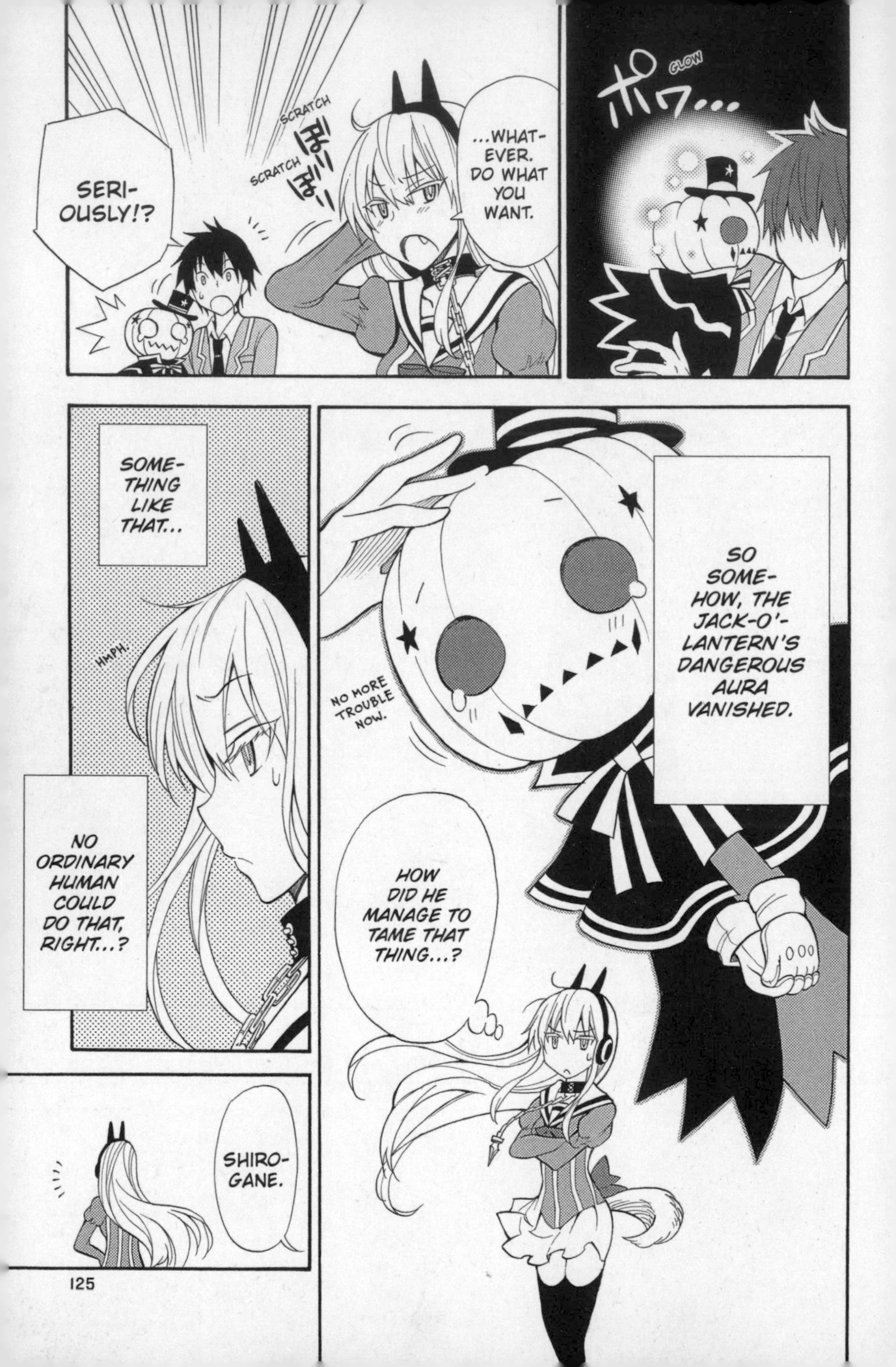
GLOW
ポワ…
...WHAT-EVER. DO WHAT YOU WANT.
SCRATCH
SCRATCH
SERI-OUSLY!?
SO SOME-HOW, THE JACK-O'-LANTERN'S DANGEROUS AURA VANISHED.
NO MORE TROUBLE NOW.
HOW DID HE MANAGE TO TAME THAT THING...?
SOME-THING LIKE THAT...
HMPH.
NO ORDINARY HUMAN COULD DO THAT, RIGHT...?
SHIRO-GANE.

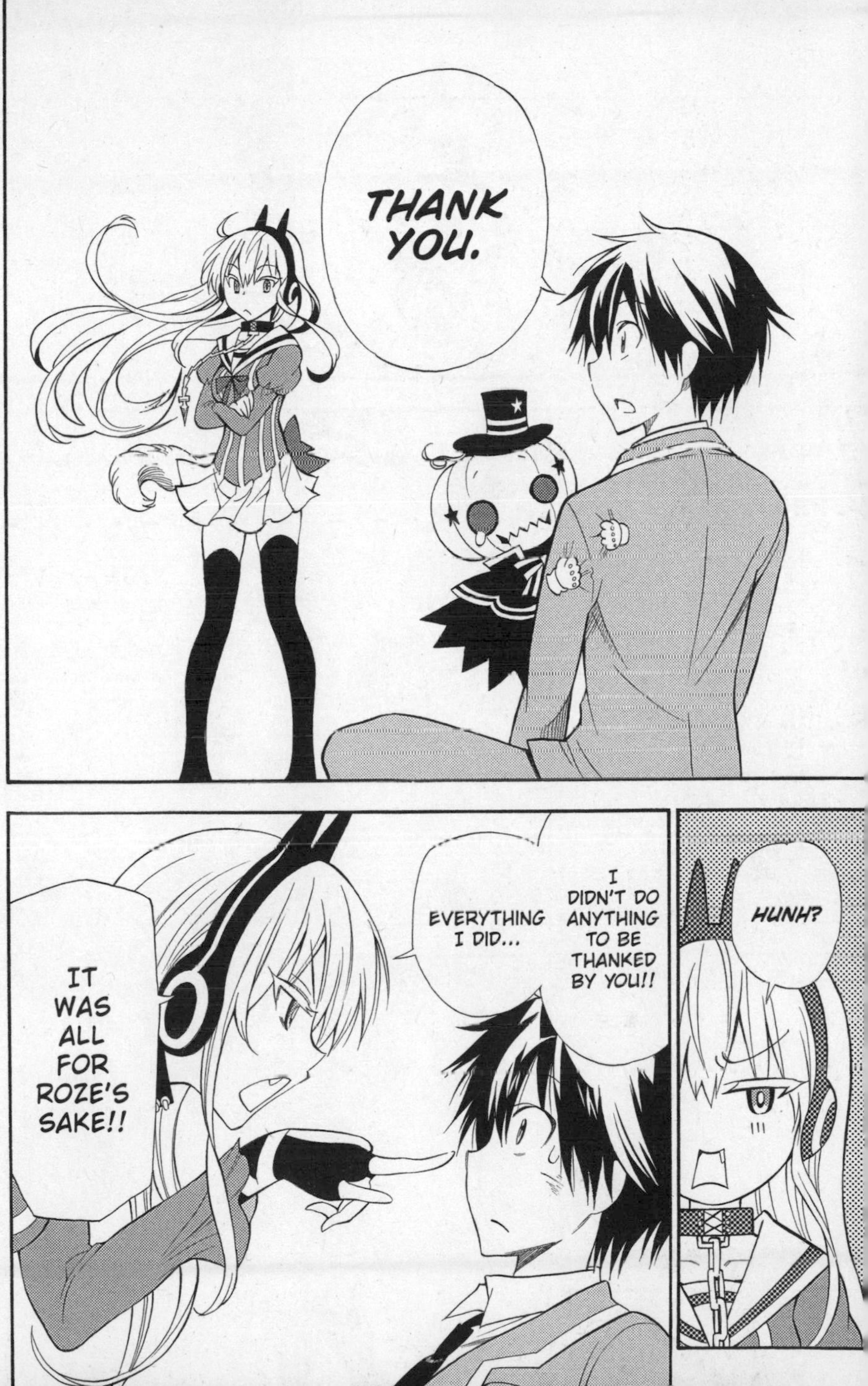
THANK YOU.
HUNH?
I DIDN'T DO ANYTHING TO BE THANKED BY YOU!!
EVERYTHING I DID...
IT WAS ALL FOR ROZE'S SAKE!!

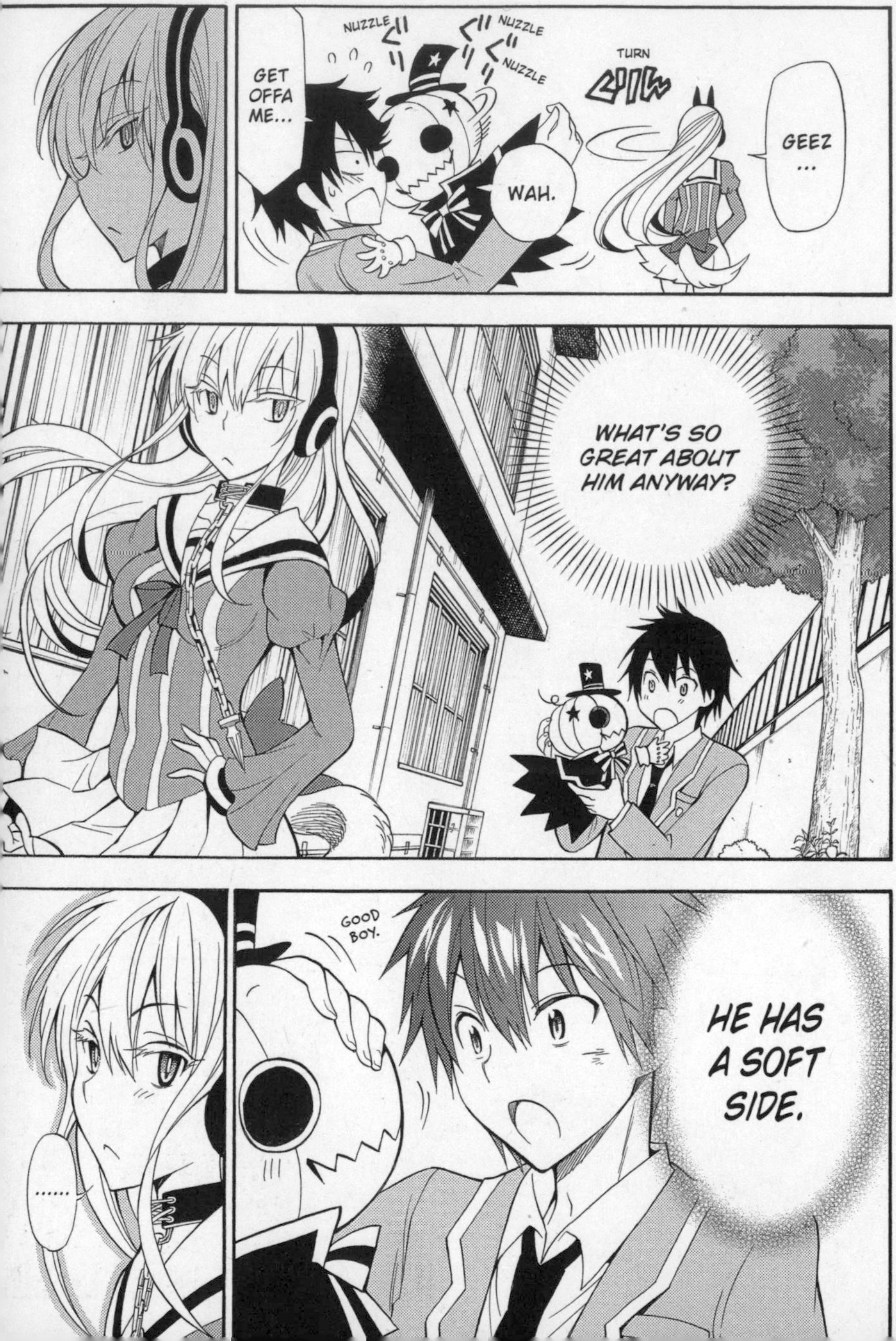
GEEZ ...
TURN
NUZZLE
NUZZLE
NUZZLE
GET OFFA ME...
WAH.
WHAT'S SO GREAT ABOUT HIM ANYWAY?
GOOD BOY.
HE HAS A SOFT SIDE.
......

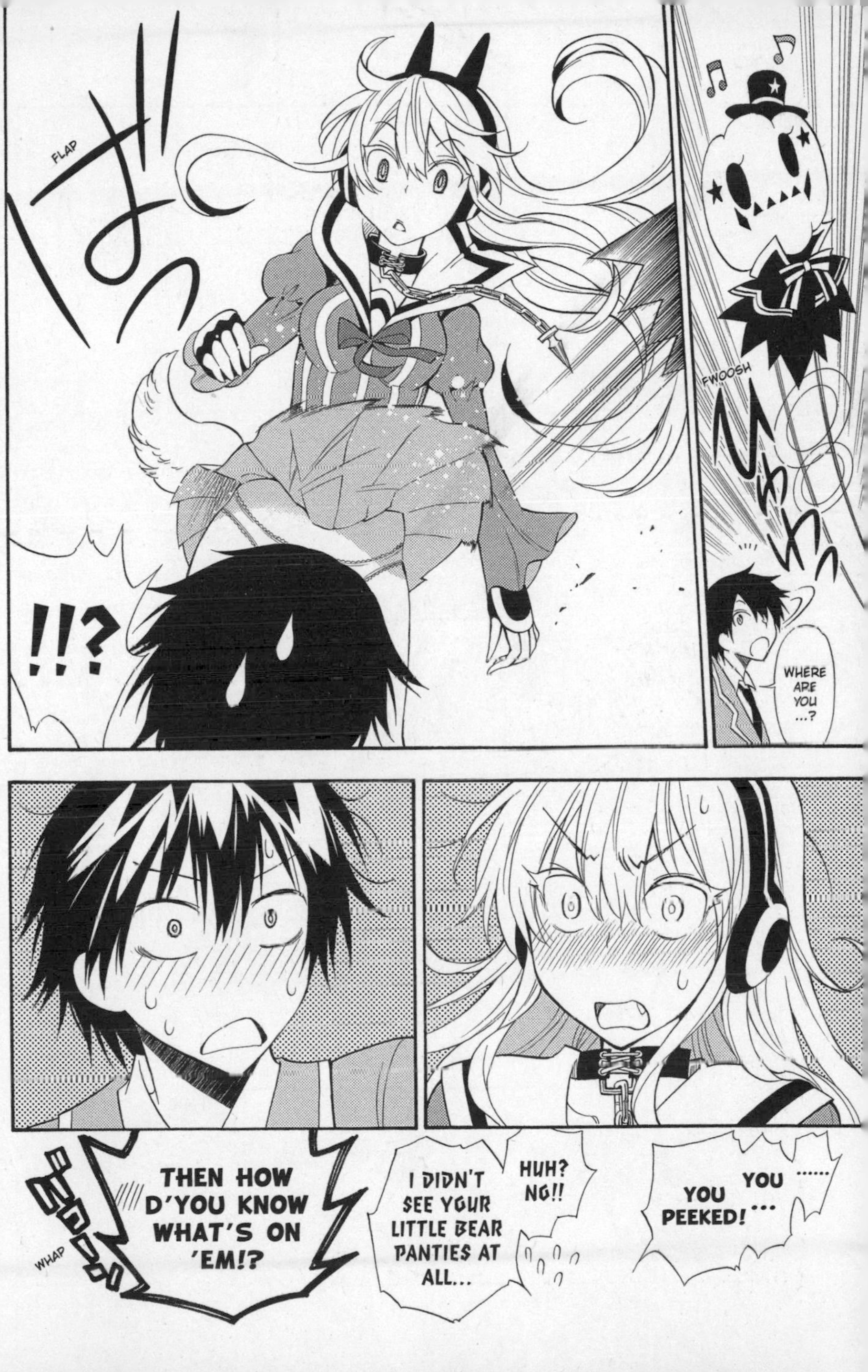
FWOOSH
WHERE ARE YOU ...?
FLAP
!!?
...... YOU ... YOU PEEKED!
HUH? NO!!
I DIDN'T SEE YOUR LITTLE BEAR PANTIES AT ALL...
THEN HOW D'YOU KNOW WHAT'S ON 'EM!?
WHAP

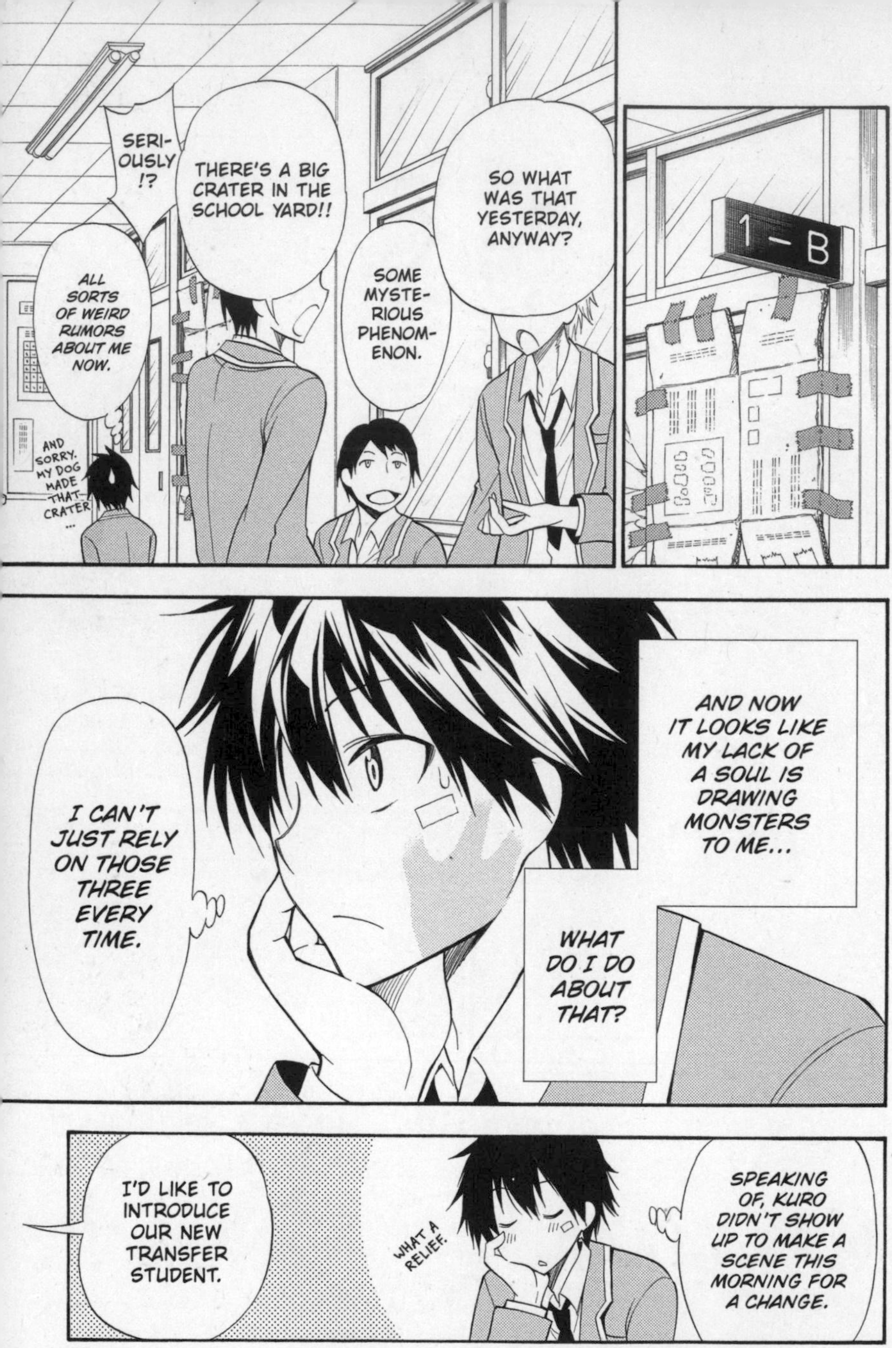
SO WHAT WAS THAT YESTERDAY, ANYWAY?
THERE'S A BIG CRATER IN THE SCHOOL YARD!!
SERI-OUSLY!?
SOME MYSTE-RIOUS PHENOM-ENON.
ALL SORTS OF WEIRD RUMORS ABOUT ME NOW.
AND SORRY. MY DOG MADE THAT CRATER...
AND NOW IT LOOKS LIKE MY LACK OF A SOUL IS DRAWING MONSTERS TO ME...
WHAT DO I DO ABOUT THAT?
I CAN'T JUST RELY ON THOSE THREE EVERY TIME.
SPEAKING OF, KURO DIDN'T SHOW UP TO MAKE A SCENE THIS MORNING FOR A CHANGE.
WHAT A RELIEF.
I'D LIKE TO INTRODUCE OUR NEW TRANSFER STUDENT.

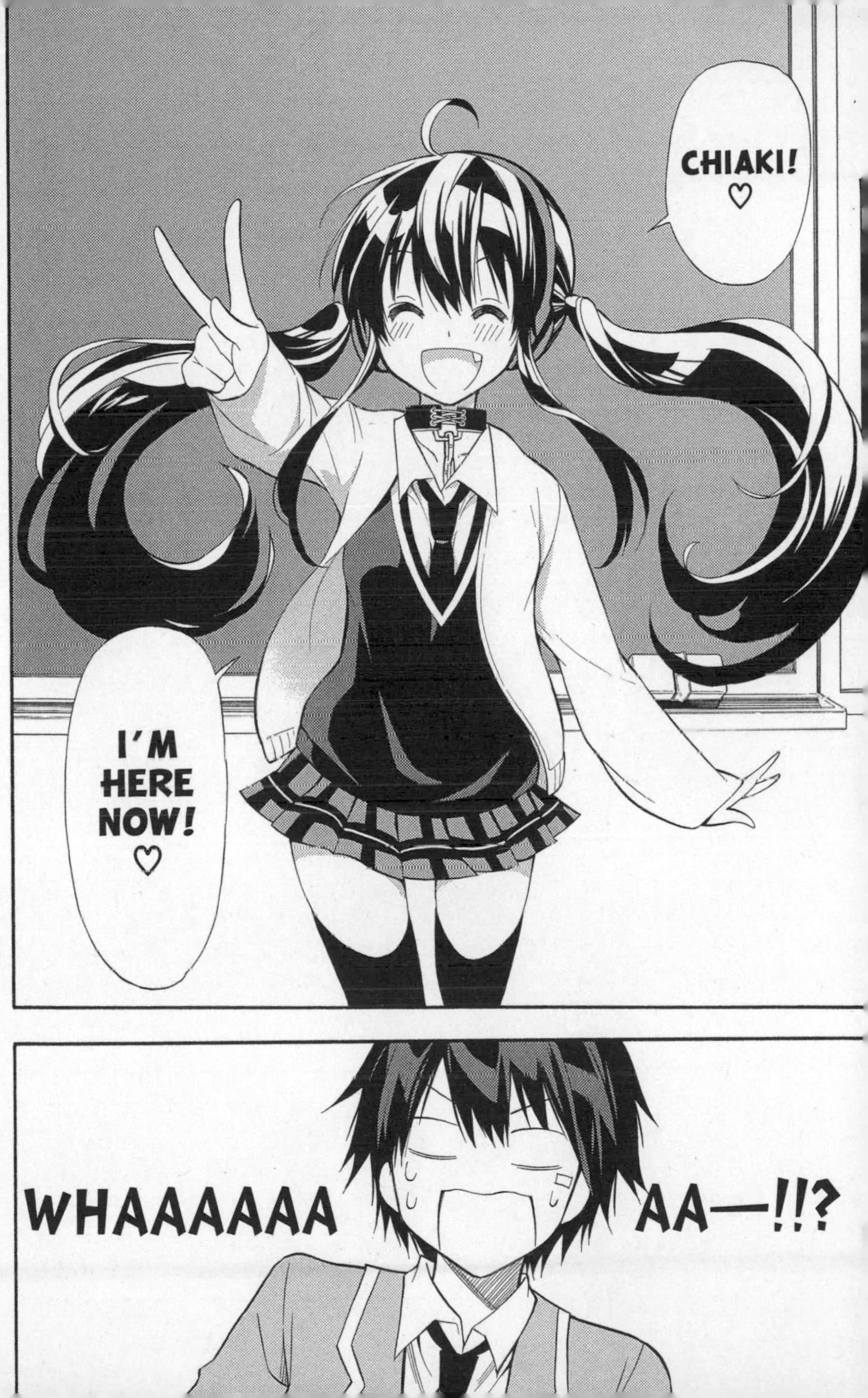
CHIAKI! ♡
I'M HERE NOW! ♡
WHAAAAAA AA—!!?

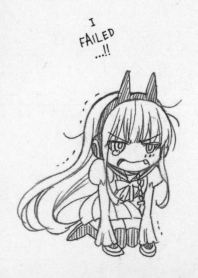

TODAY'S CERBERUS

I FAILED ...!!

TODAY'S CERBERUS

GROW
UP BIG,
NOW.

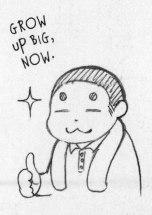

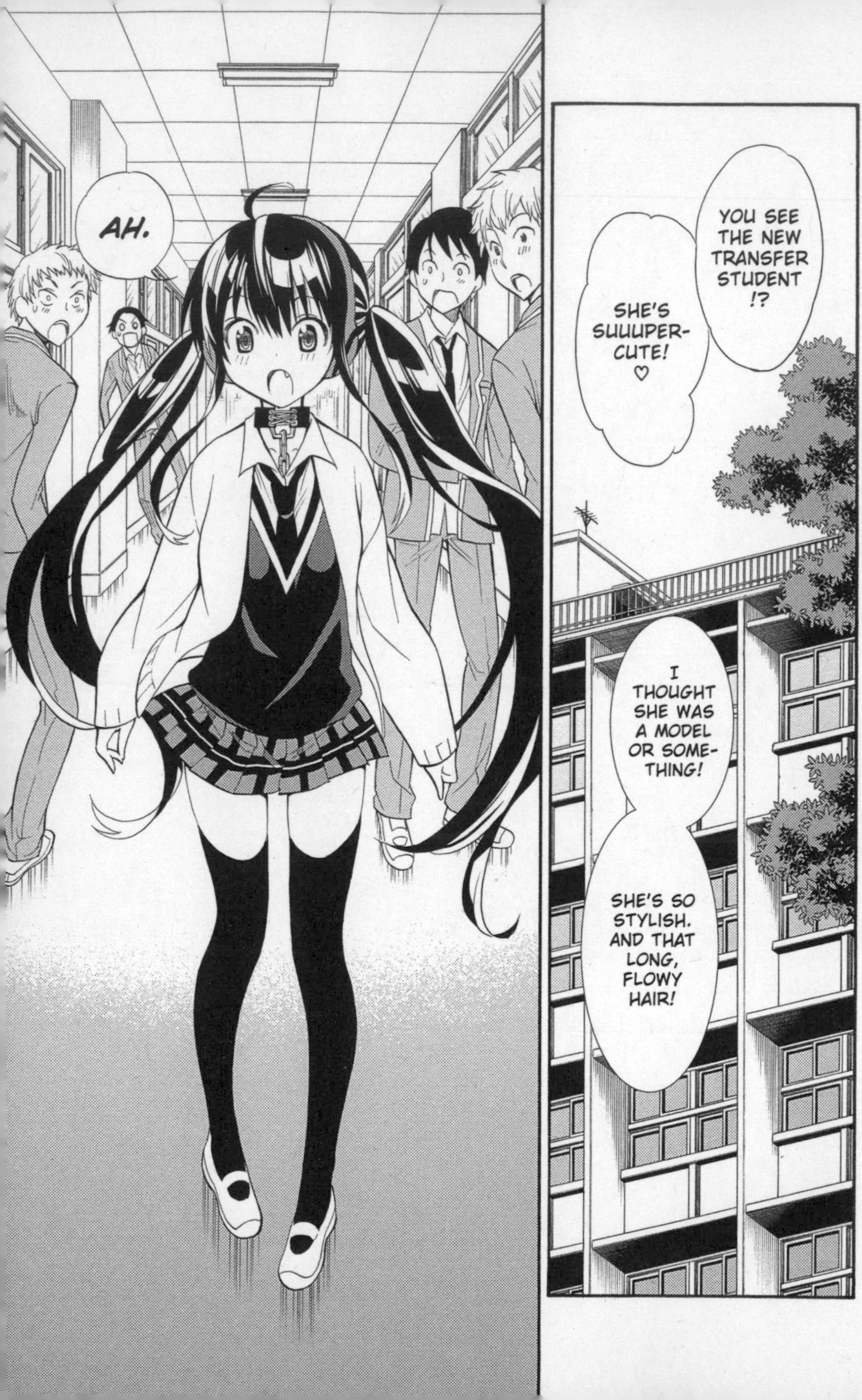
YOU SEE THE NEW TRANSFER STUDENT!?
SHE'S SUUUPER-CUTE! ♡
I THOUGHT SHE WAS A MODEL OR SOME-THING!
SHE'S SO STYLISH. AND THAT LONG, FLOWY HAIR!
AH.

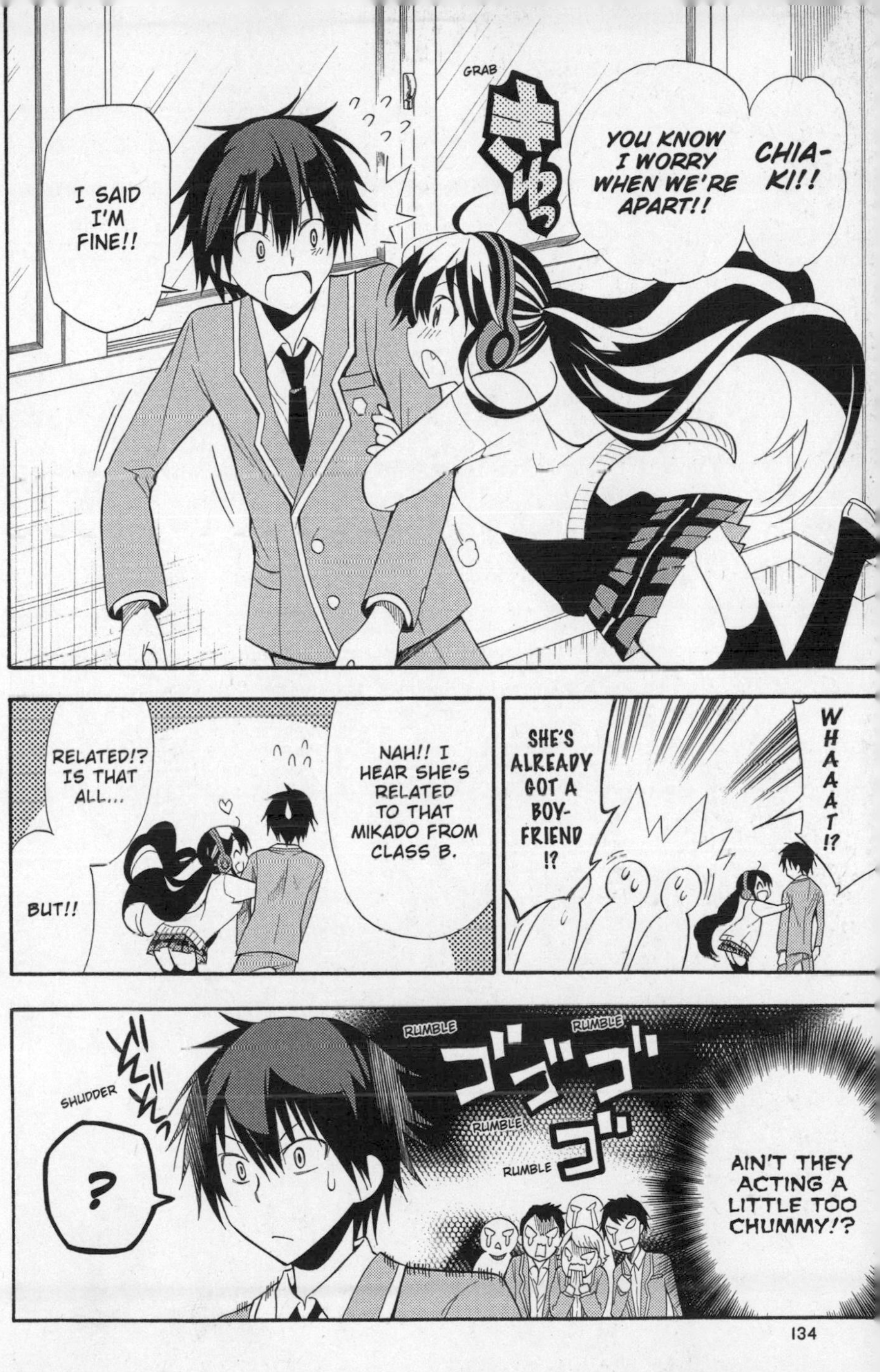
CHIA-KI!!
YOU KNOW I WORRY WHEN WE'RE APART!!
GRAB
I SAID I'M FINE!!
WHAAAAT!?
SHE'S ALREADY GOT A BOY-FRIEND!?
NAH!! I HEAR SHE'S RELATED TO THAT MIKADO FROM CLASS B.
RELATED!? IS THAT ALL...
BUT!!
AIN'T THEY ACTING A LITTLE TOO CHUMMY!?
RUMBLE
RUMBLE
RUMBLE
RUMBLE
SHUDDER
?

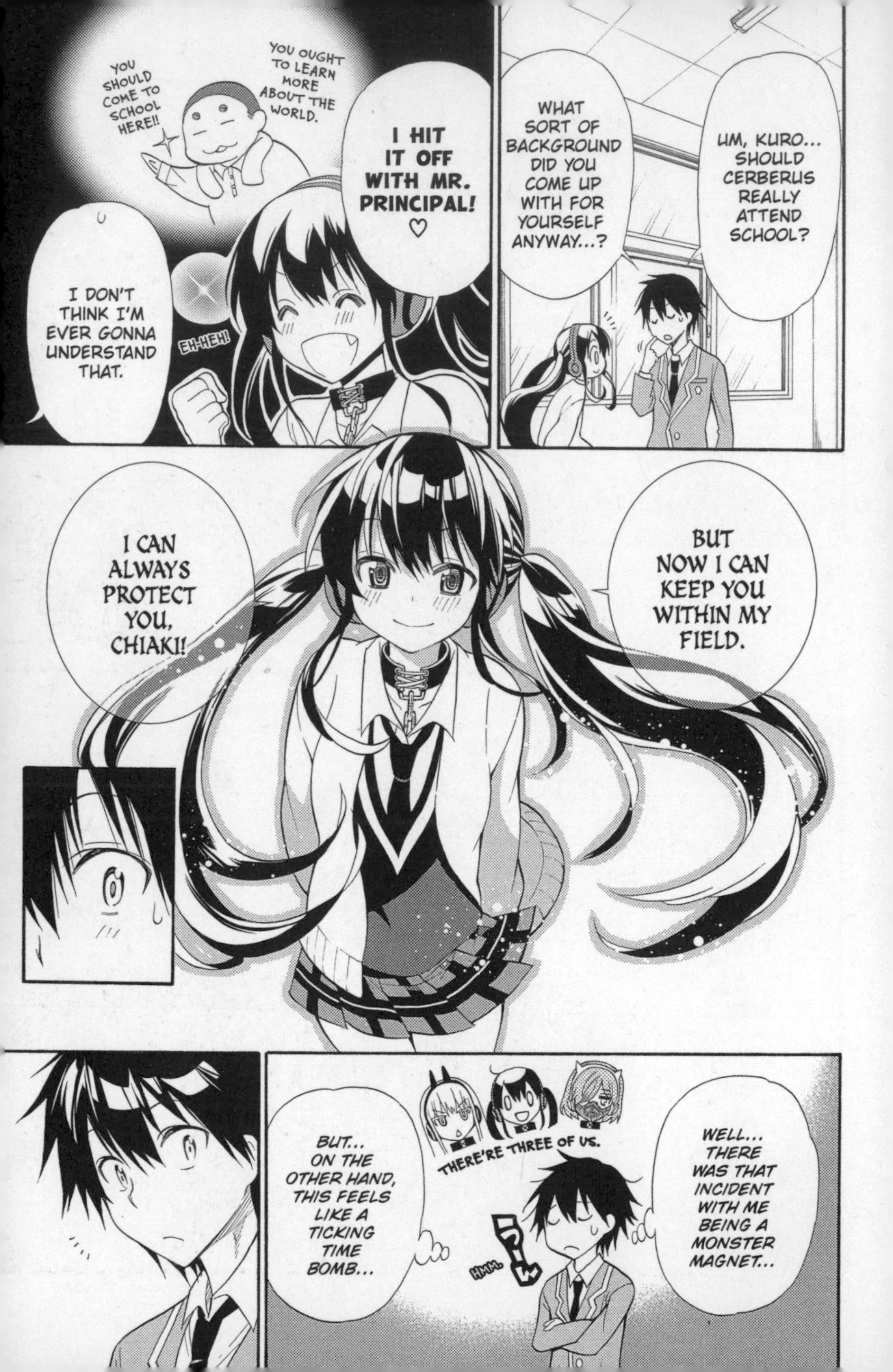
UM, KURO... SHOULD CERBERUS REALLY ATTEND SCHOOL?
WHAT SORT OF BACKGROUND DID YOU COME UP WITH FOR YOURSELF ANYWAY...?
I HIT IT OFF WITH MR. PRINCIPAL! ♡
YOU OUGHT TO LEARN MORE ABOUT THE WORLD.
YOU SHOULD COME TO SCHOOL HERE!!
EH-HEH!
I DON'T THINK I'M EVER GONNA UNDERSTAND THAT.
BUT NOW I CAN KEEP YOU WITHIN MY FIELD.
I CAN ALWAYS PROTECT YOU, CHIAKI!
WELL... THERE WAS THAT INCIDENT WITH ME BEING A MONSTER MAGNET...
HMM.
THERE'RE THREE OF US.
BUT... ON THE OTHER HAND, THIS FEELS LIKE A TICKING TIME BOMB...

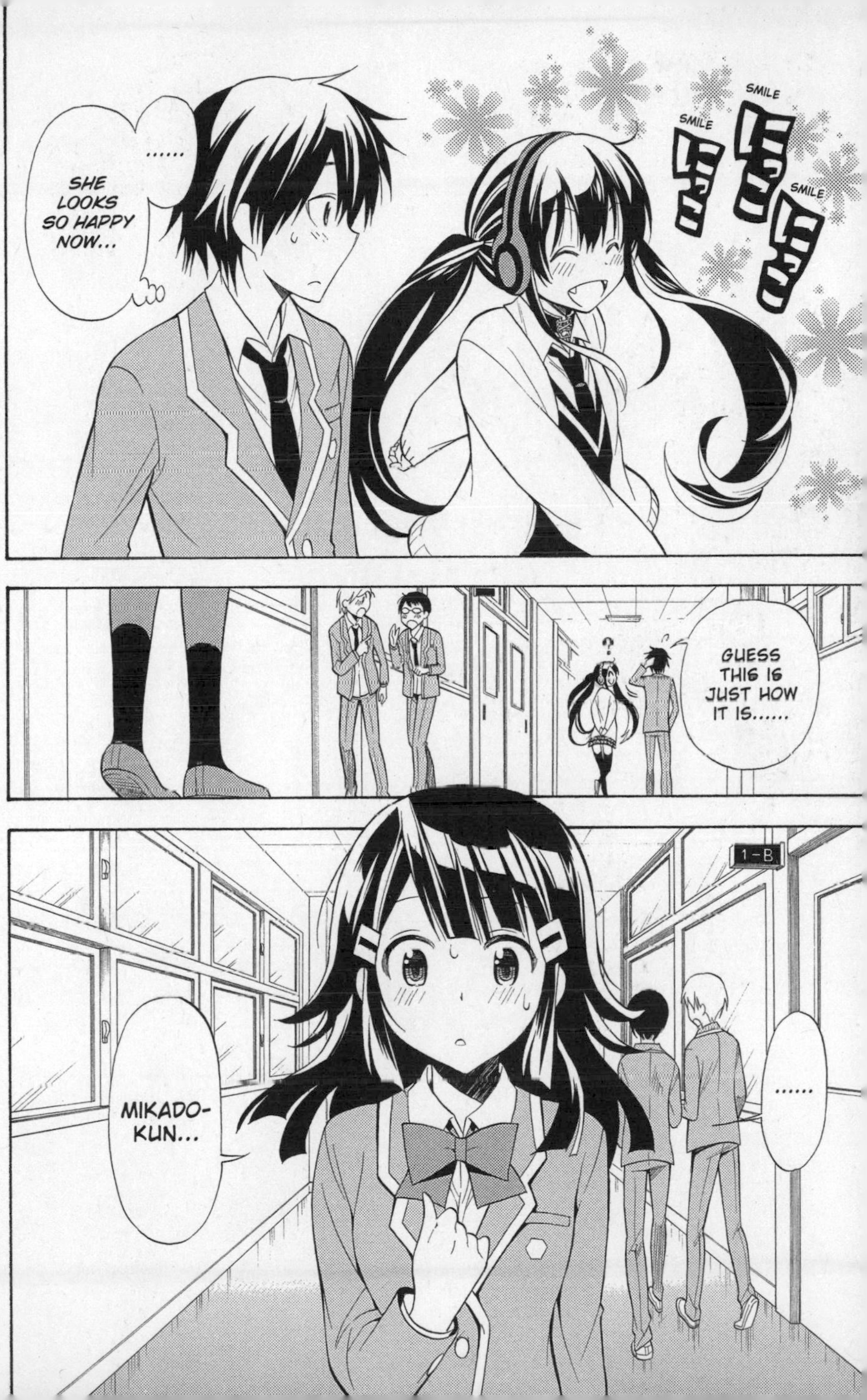
SMILE
SMILE
SMILE
......
SHE LOOKS SO HAPPY NOW...
GUESS THIS IS JUST HOW IT IS......
1-B
......
MIKADO-KUN...

CHAPTER 3
HINATA KOMONE

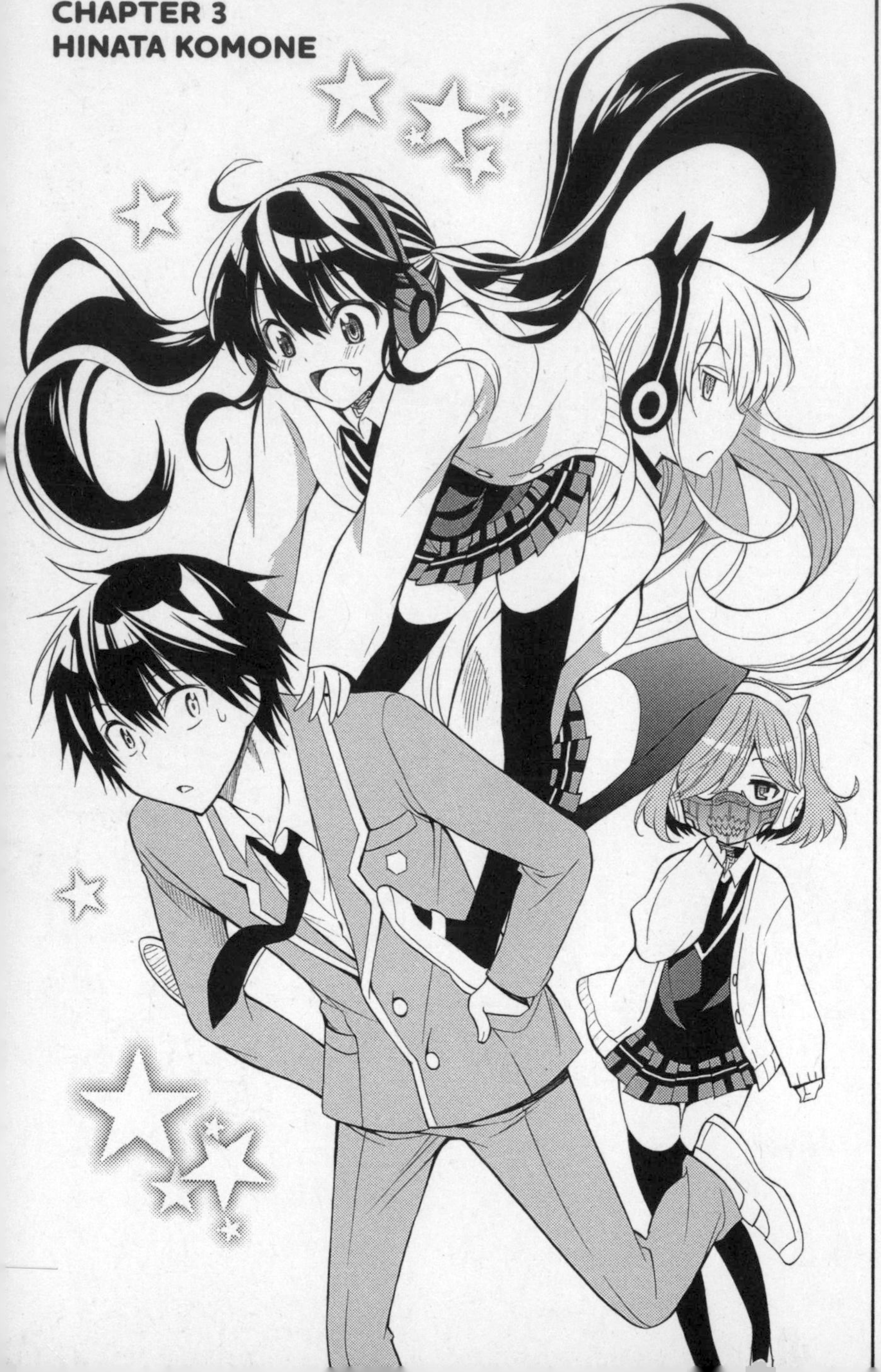

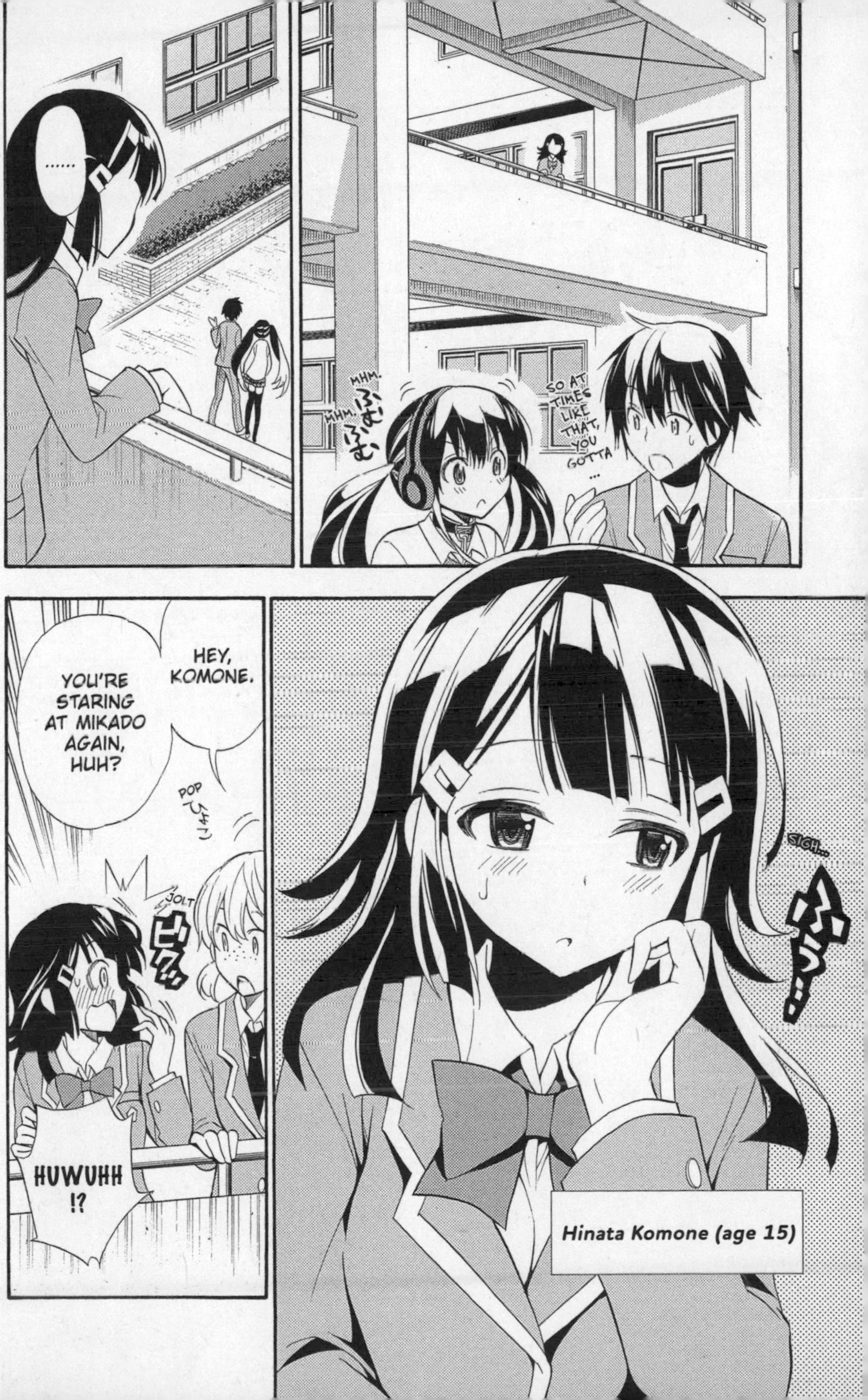
SO AT TIMES LIKE THAT, YOU GOTTA ...
MHM. MHM.
ふむふむ
......
SIGH...
Hinata Komone (age 15)
HEY, KOMONE.
YOU'RE STARING AT MIKADO AGAIN, HUH?
POP
JOLT
HUWUHH !?

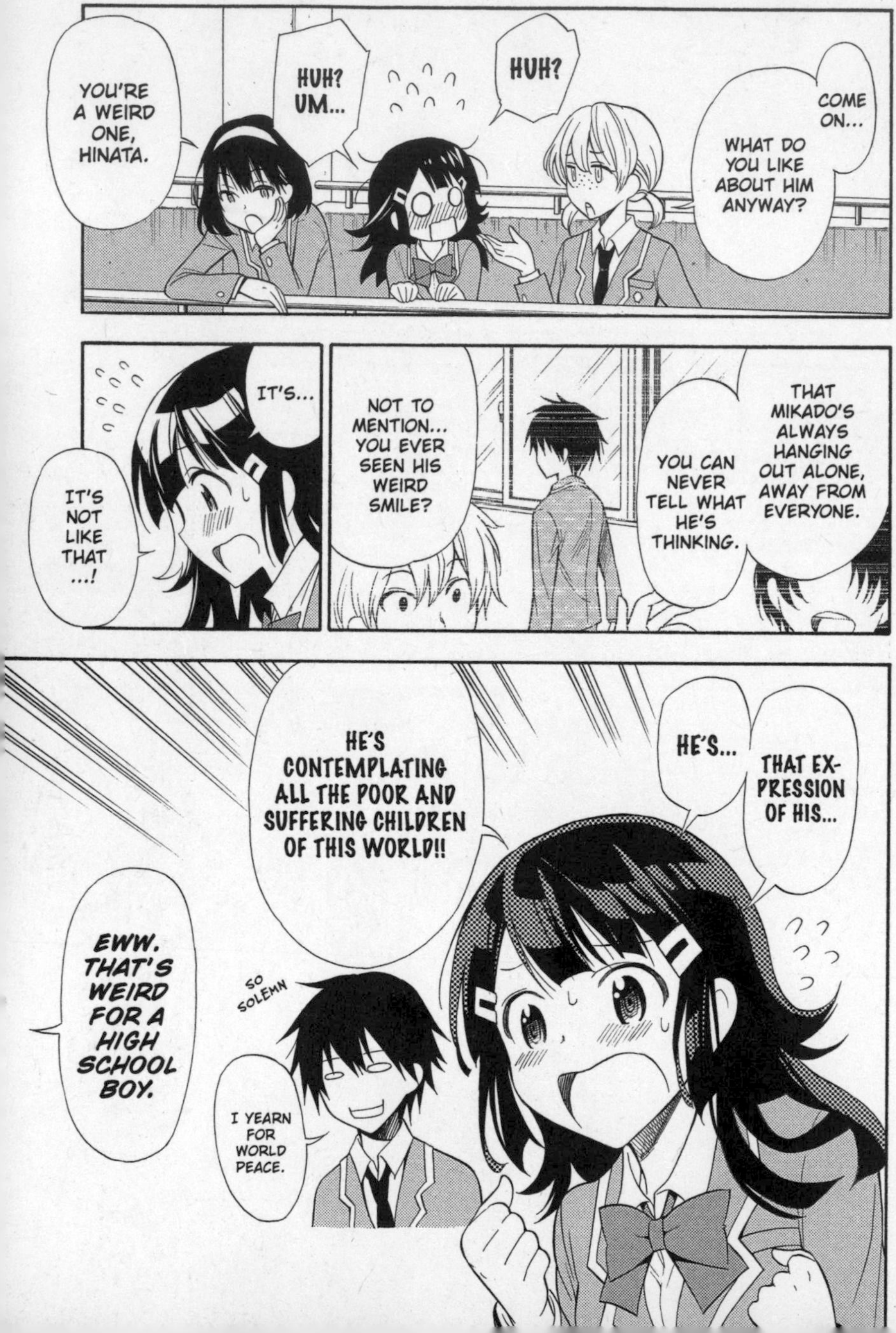
COME ON...
WHAT DO YOU LIKE ABOUT HIM ANYWAY?
HUH?
HUH? UM...
YOU'RE A WEIRD ONE, HINATA.
THAT MIKADO'S ALWAYS HANGING OUT ALONE, AWAY FROM EVERYONE.
YOU CAN NEVER TELL WHAT HE'S THINKING.
NOT TO MENTION... YOU EVER SEEN HIS WEIRD SMILE?
IT'S...
IT'S NOT LIKE THAT ...!
THAT EX-PRESSION OF HIS...
HE'S...
HE'S CONTEMPLATING ALL THE POOR AND SUFFERING CHILDREN OF THIS WORLD!!
SO SOLEMN
I YEARN FOR WORLD PEACE.
EWW. THAT'S WEIRD FOR A HIGH SCHOOL BOY.

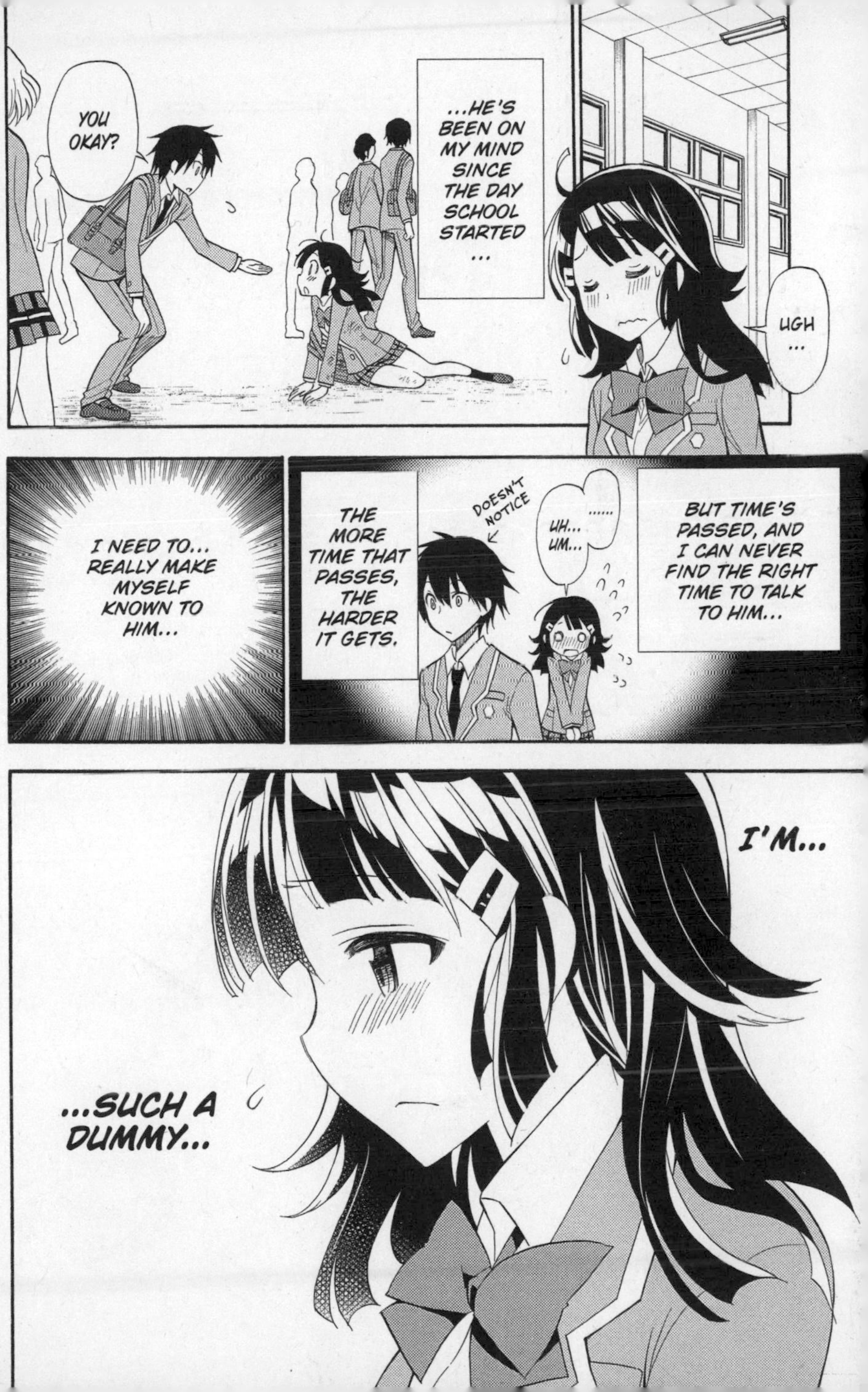
...HE'S BEEN ON MY MIND SINCE THE DAY SCHOOL STARTED...
UGH...
YOU OKAY?
BUT TIME'S PASSED, AND I CAN NEVER FIND THE RIGHT TIME TO TALK TO HIM...
......
UH... UM...
DOESN'T NOTICE
THE MORE TIME THAT PASSES, THE HARDER IT GETS.
I NEED TO... REALLY MAKE MYSELF KNOWN TO HIM...
I'M...
...SUCH A DUMMY...

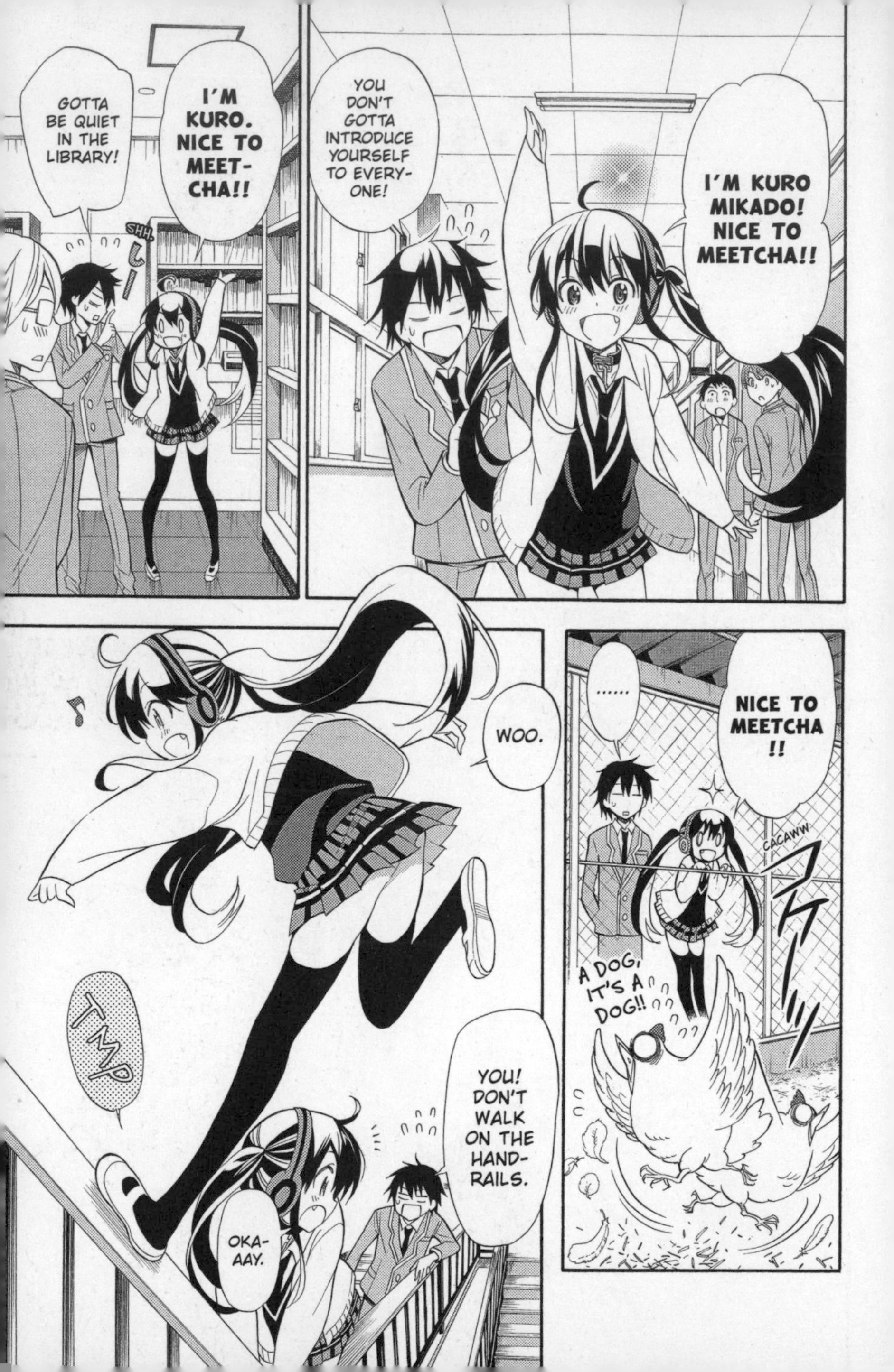
I'M KURO MIKADO! NICE TO MEETCHA!!
YOU DON'T GOTTA INTRODUCE YOURSELF TO EVERY-ONE!
I'M KURO. NICE TO MEET-CHA!!
GOTTA BE QUIET IN THE LIBRARY!
SHH.
NICE TO MEETCHA !!
......
CACAWW
A DOG, IT'S A DOG!!
WOO.
TMP
YOU! DON'T WALK ON THE HAND-RAILS.
OKA-AAY.

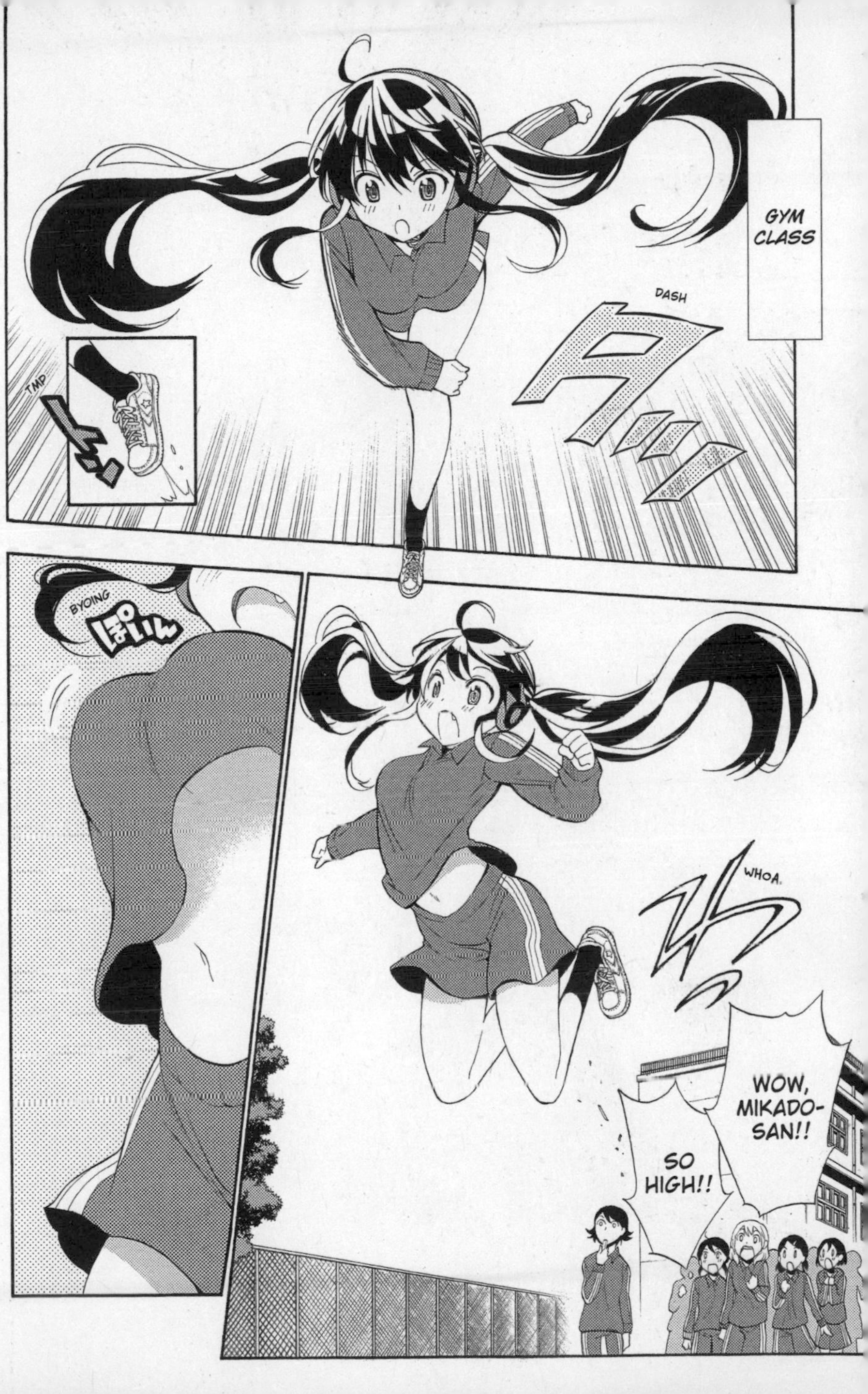
GYM CLASS
DASH
タッ
TMP
WHOA.
WOW, MIKADO-SAN!!
SO HIGH!!
BYOING
ぽいん

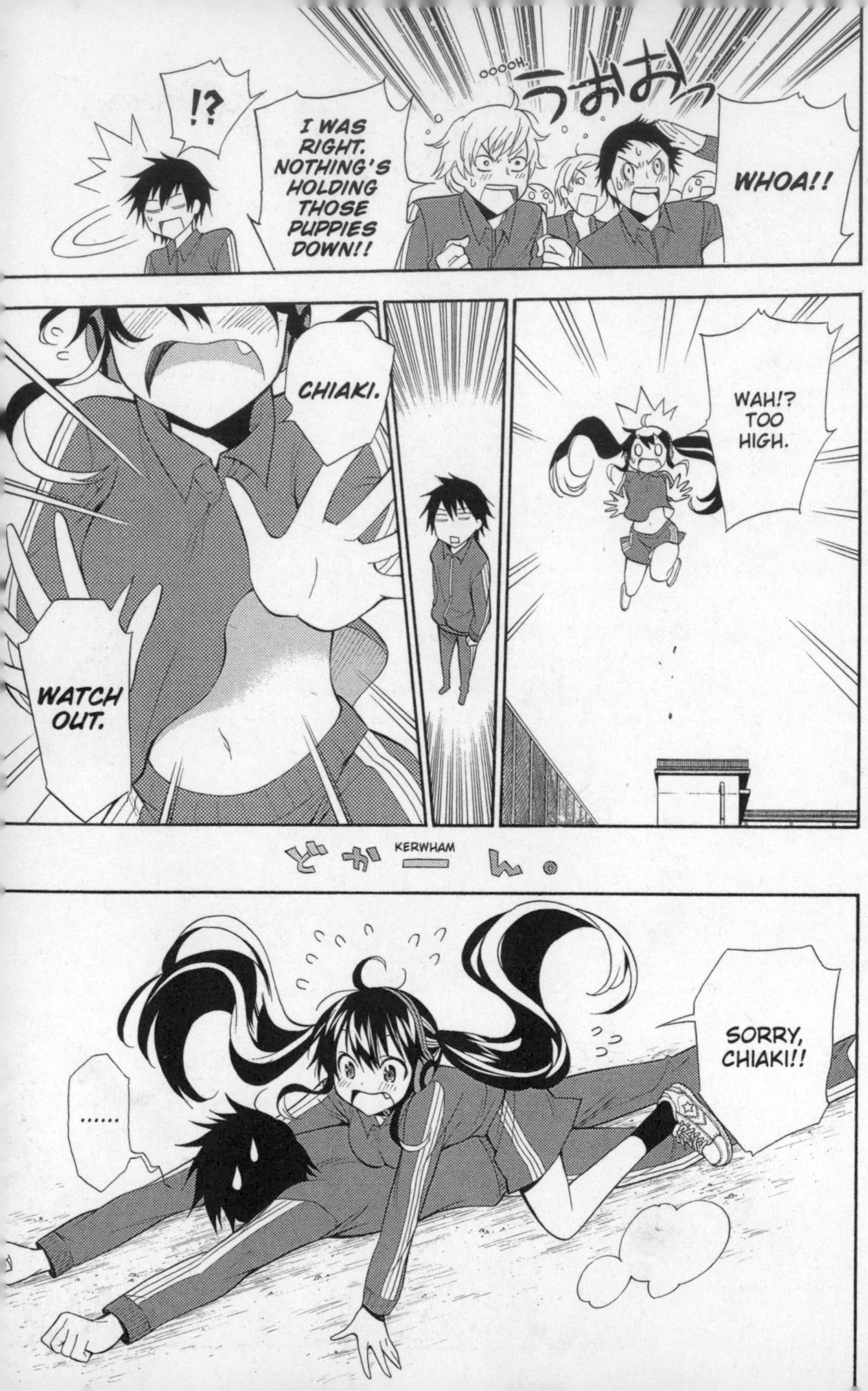
WHOA!!
OOOOH.
うおおっ
I WAS RIGHT. NOTHING'S HOLDING THOSE PUPPIES DOWN!!
!?
WAH!? TOO HIGH.
CHIAKI.
WATCH OUT.
どかーーん。
KERWHAM
SORRY, CHIAKI!!
......

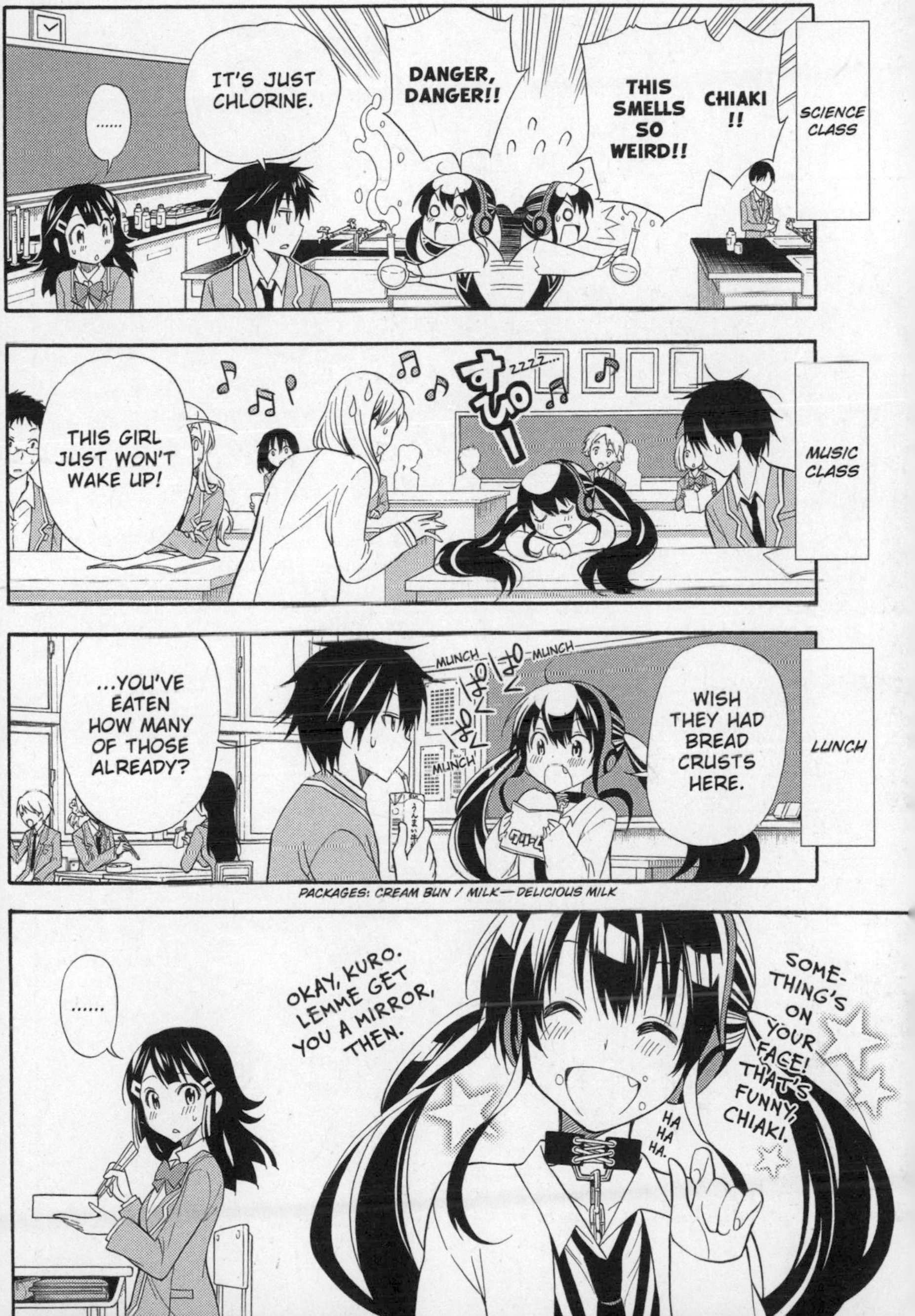
SCIENCE CLASS
CHIAKI !!
THIS SMELLS SO WEIRD!!
DANGER, DANGER!!
IT'S JUST CHLORINE.
......
MUSIC CLASS
ZZZZ...
すぴー
THIS GIRL JUST WON'T WAKE UP!
LUNCH
MUNCH
MUNCH
MUNCH
WISH THEY HAD BREAD CRUSTS HERE.
...YOU'VE EATEN HOW MANY OF THOSE ALREADY?
PACKAGES: CREAM BUN / MILK—DELICIOUS MILK
SOME-THING'S ON YOUR FACE! THAT'S FUNNY, CHIAKI.
HA HA HA.
OKAY, KURO. LEMME GET YOU A MIRROR, THEN.
......

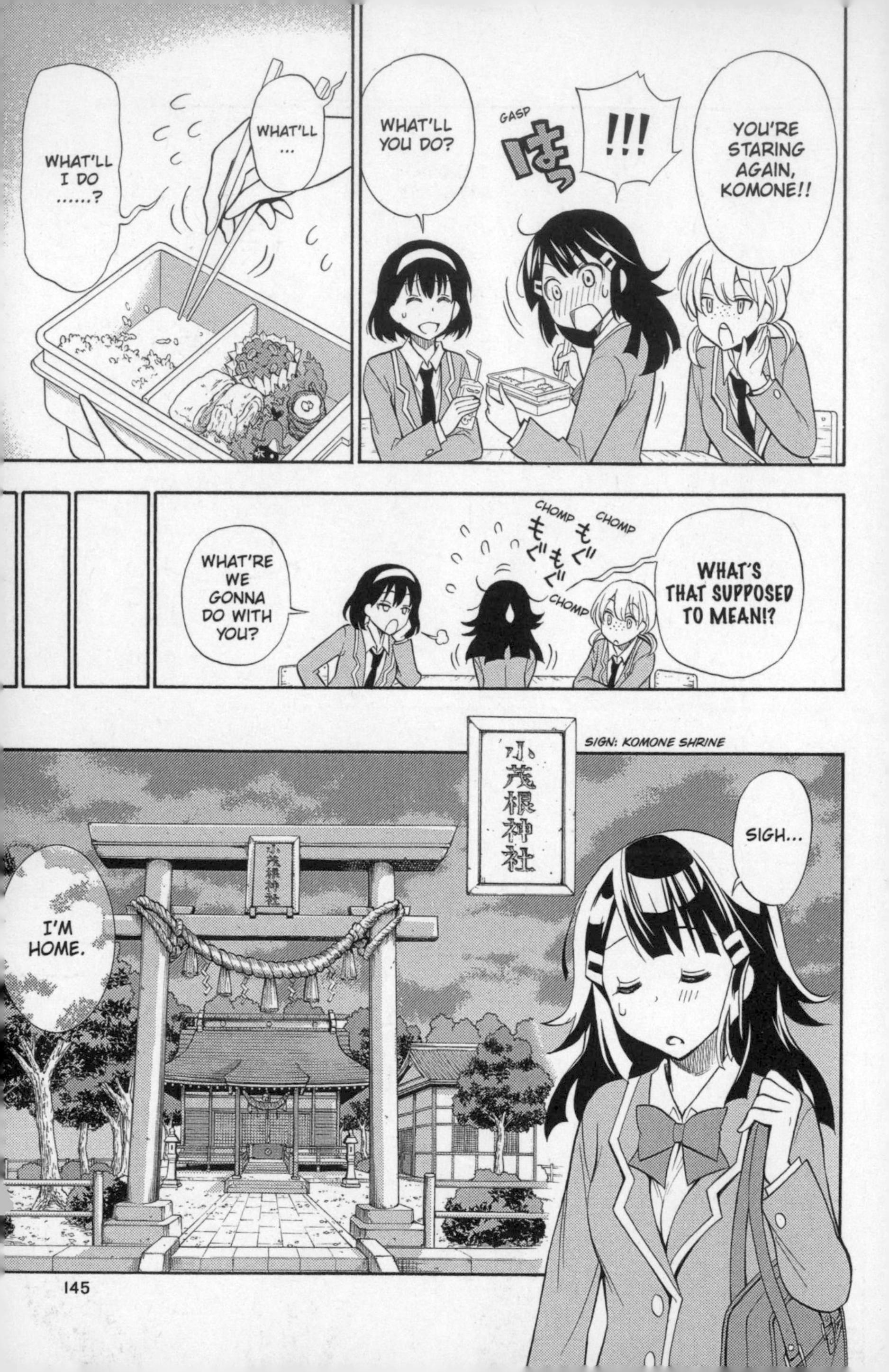
YOU'RE STARING AGAIN, KOMONE!!
!!!
GASP
はっ
WHAT'LL YOU DO?
WHAT'LL ...
WHAT'LL I DO ......?
WHAT'S THAT SUPPOSED TO MEAN!?
CHOMP
CHOMP
CHOMP
もぐもぐもぐ
WHAT'RE WE GONNA DO WITH YOU?
SIGN: KOMONE SHRINE
小茂根神社
SIGH...
小茂根神社
I'M HOME.

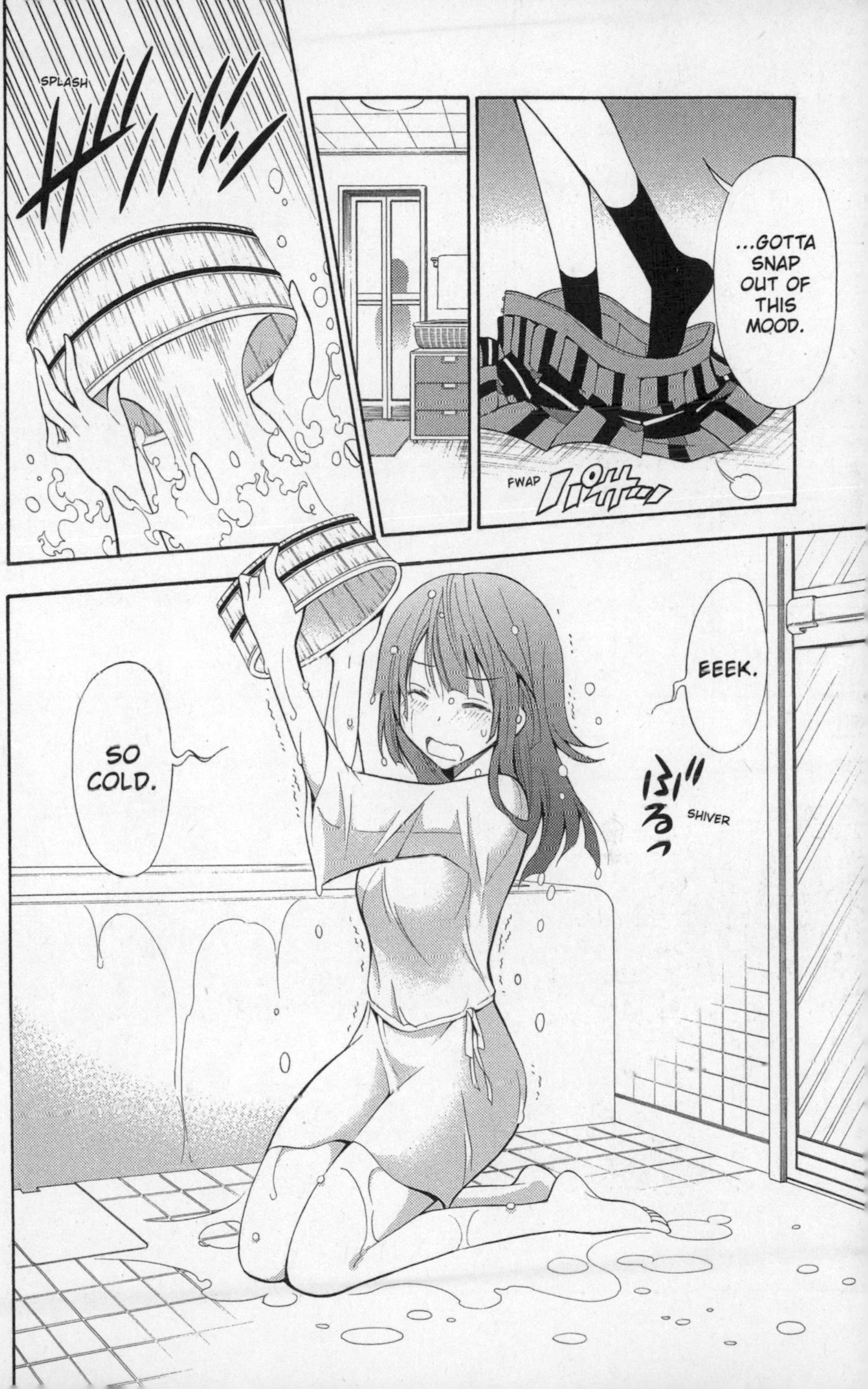
...GOTTA SNAP OUT OF THIS MOOD.
FWAP
SPLASH
EEEK.
SHIVER
SO COLD.

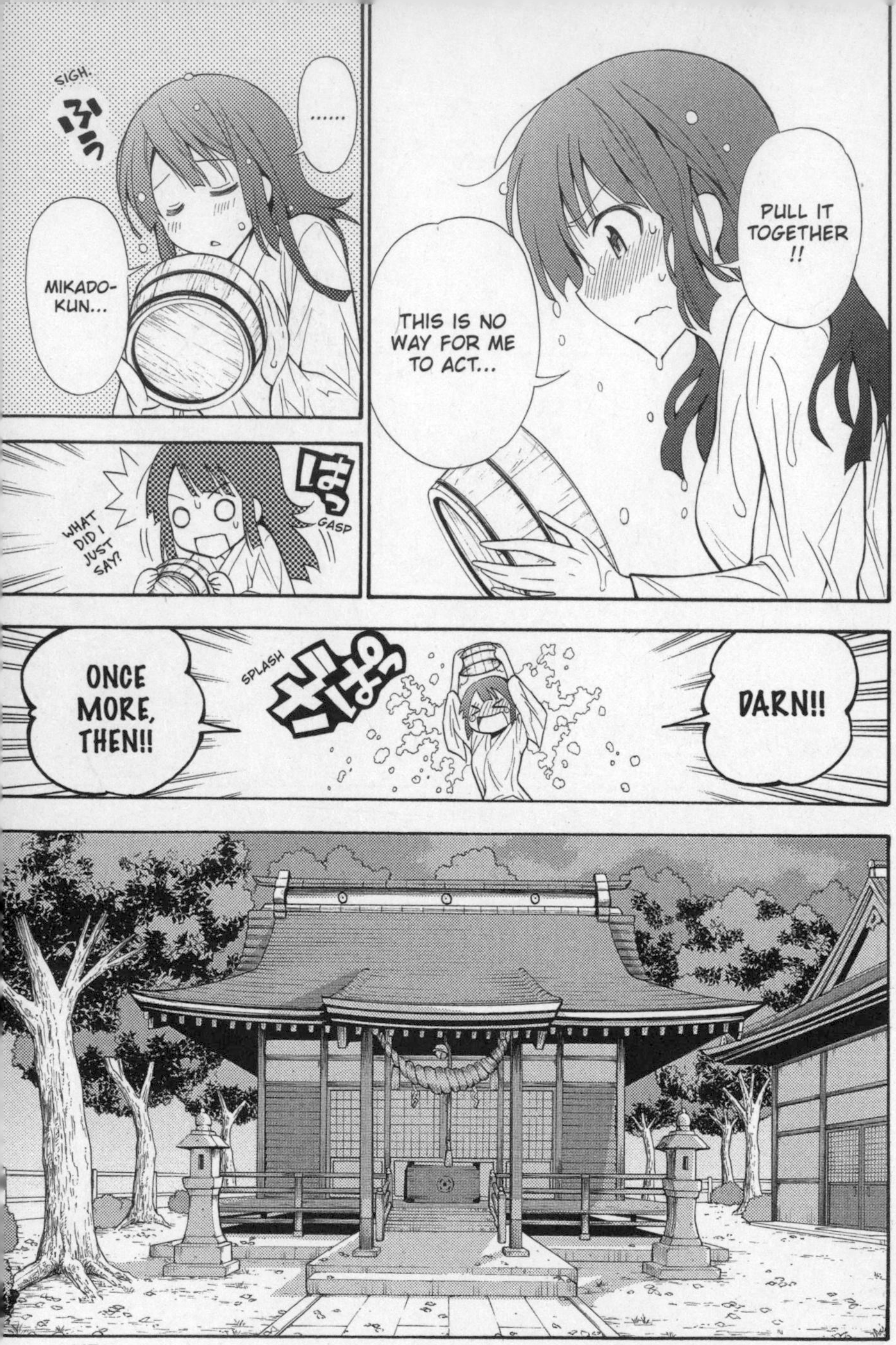
PULL IT TOGETHER!!
THIS IS NO WAY FOR ME TO ACT...
......
ふぅ
SIGH.
MIKADO-KUN...
はっ
GASP
WHAT DID I JUST SAY?
DARN!!
ざぱっ
SPLASH
ONCE MORE, THEN!!

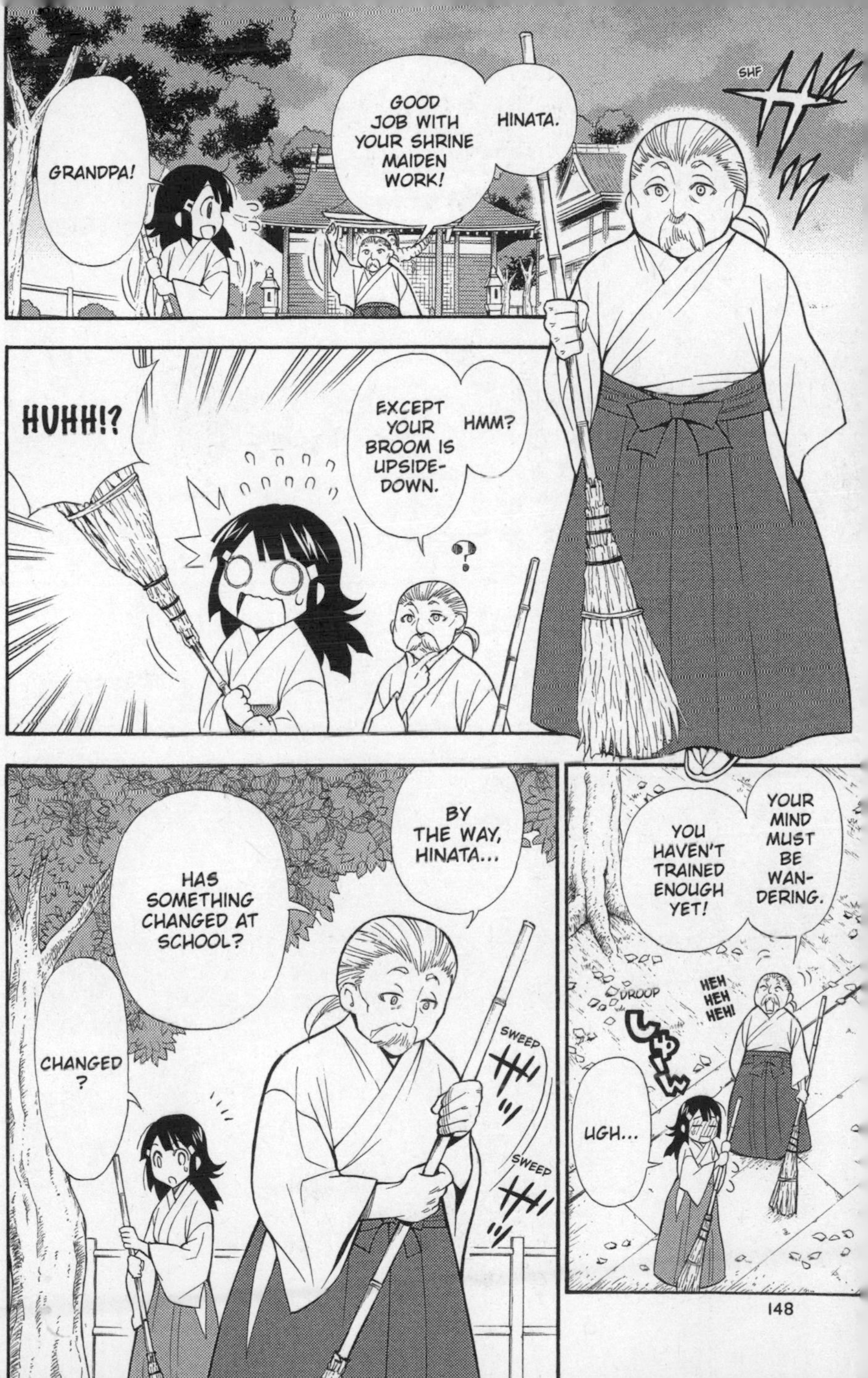
SHF
HINATA.
GOOD JOB WITH YOUR SHRINE MAIDEN WORK!
GRANDPA!
HMM?
EXCEPT YOUR BROOM IS UPSIDE-DOWN.
HUHH!?
YOUR MIND MUST BE WAN-DERING.
YOU HAVEN'T TRAINED ENOUGH YET!
HEH HEH HEH!
DROOP
UGH...
BY THE WAY, HINATA...
HAS SOMETHING CHANGED AT SCHOOL?
SWEEP
SWEEP
CHANGED?

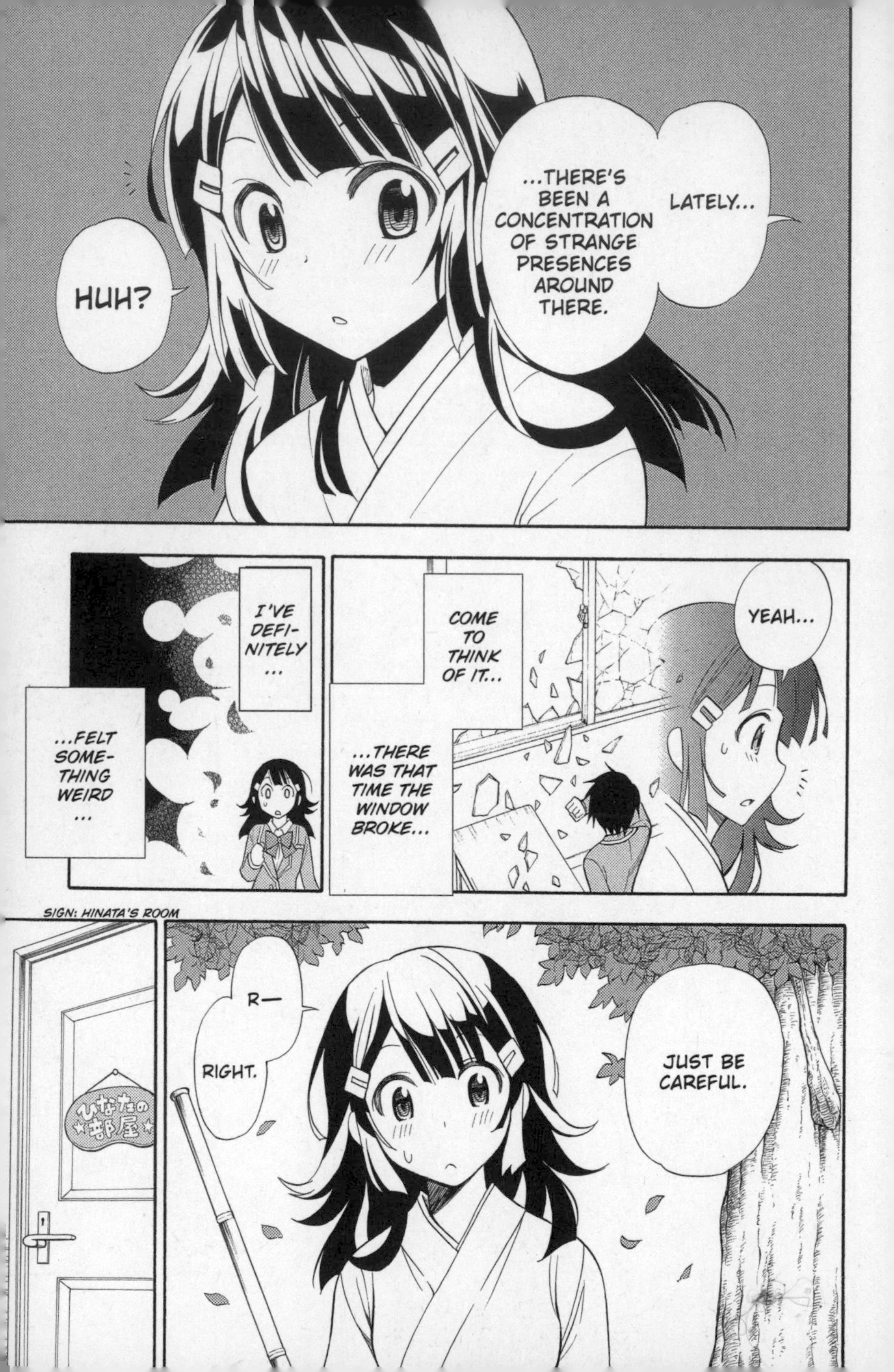
LATELY...
...THERE'S BEEN A CONCENTRATION OF STRANGE PRESENCES AROUND THERE.
HUH?
YEAH...
COME TO THINK OF IT...
...THERE WAS THAT TIME THE WINDOW BROKE...
I'VE DEFINITELY...
...FELT SOMETHING WEIRD...
SIGN: HINATA'S ROOM
JUST BE CAREFUL.
R— RIGHT.
ひなたの部屋

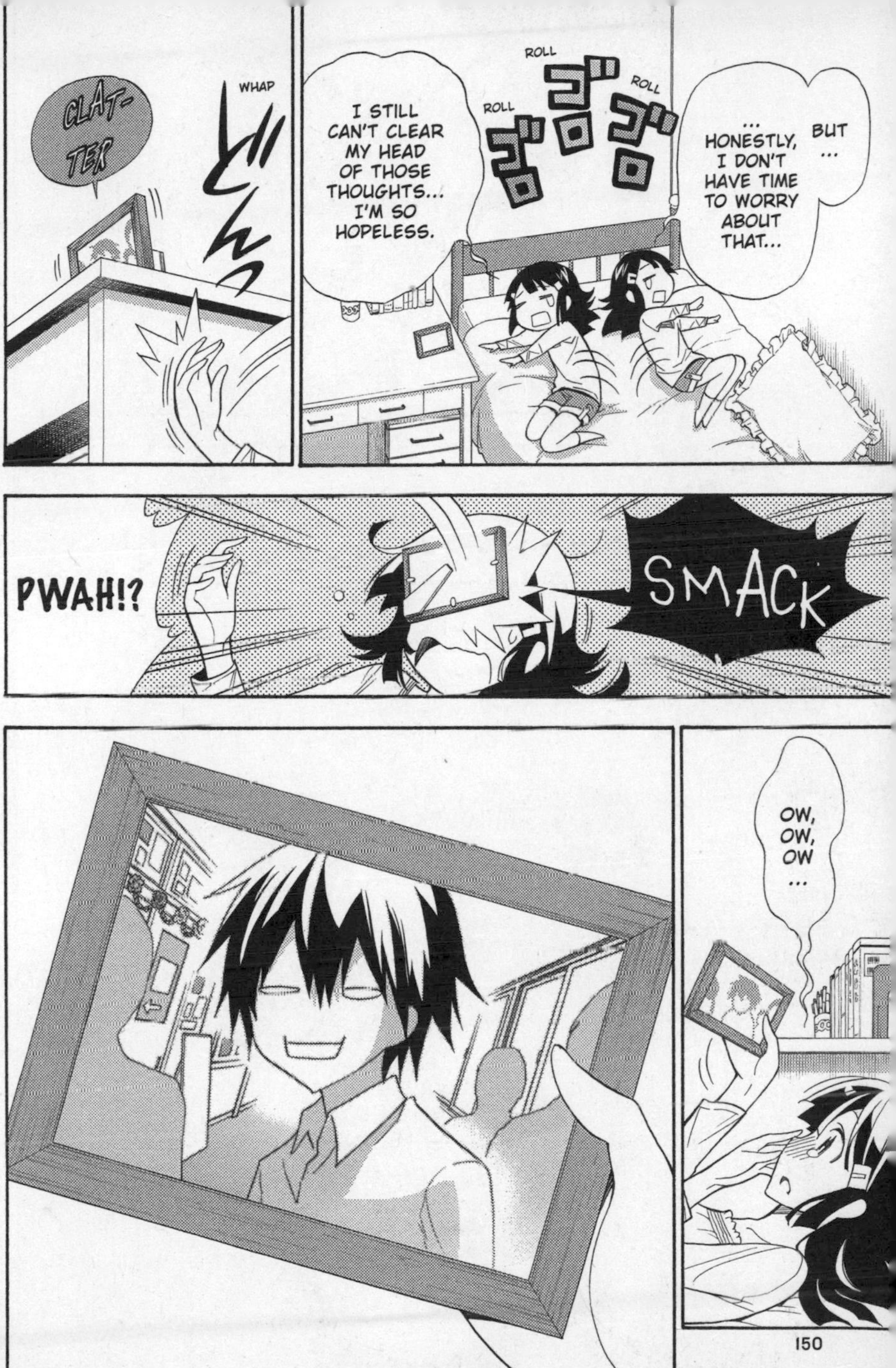
BUT ...
... HONESTLY, I DON'T HAVE TIME TO WORRY ABOUT THAT...
ROLL
ROLL
ROLL
I STILL CAN'T CLEAR MY HEAD OF THOSE THOUGHTS... I'M SO HOPELESS.
WHAP
CLAT-TER
SMACK
PWAH!?
OW, OW, OW ...

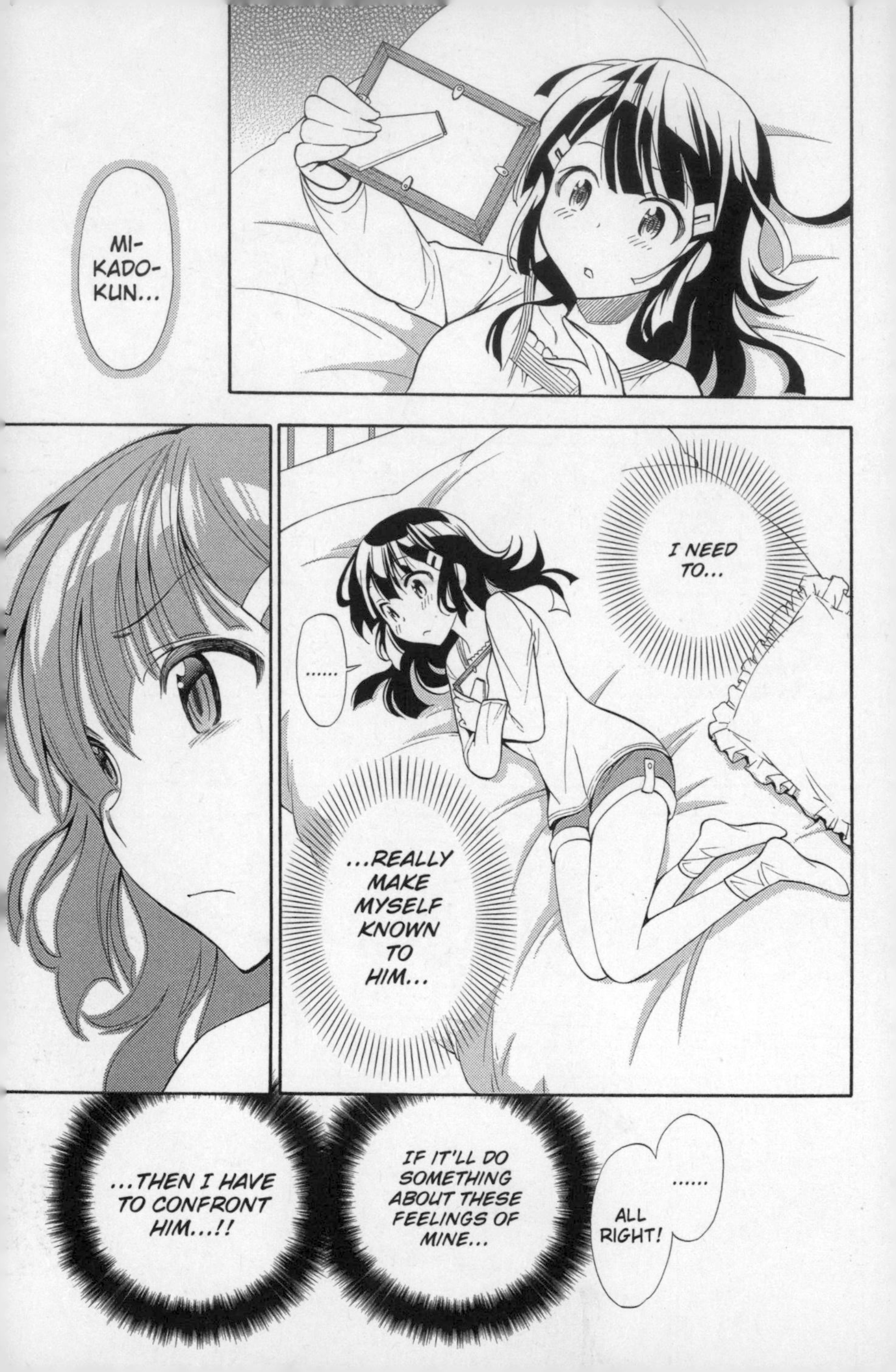
MI-KADO-KUN...
I NEED TO...
......
...REALLY MAKE MYSELF KNOWN TO HIM...
...... ALL RIGHT!
IF IT'LL DO SOMETHING ABOUT THESE FEELINGS OF MINE...
...THEN I HAVE TO CONFRONT HIM...!!

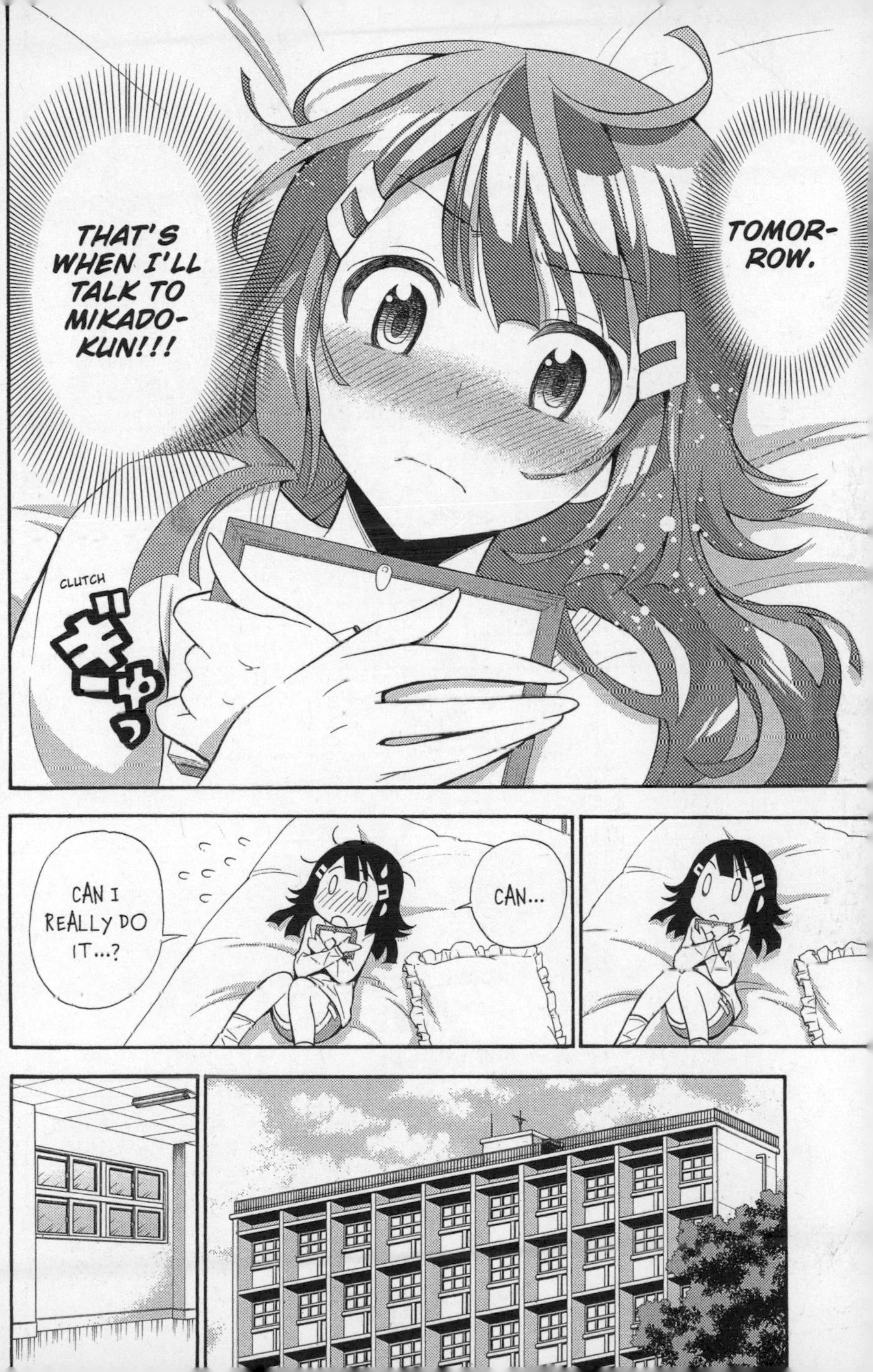

TOMOR-ROW.
THAT'S WHEN I'LL TALK TO MIKADO-KUN!!!
CLUTCH
CAN...
CAN I REALLY DO IT...?

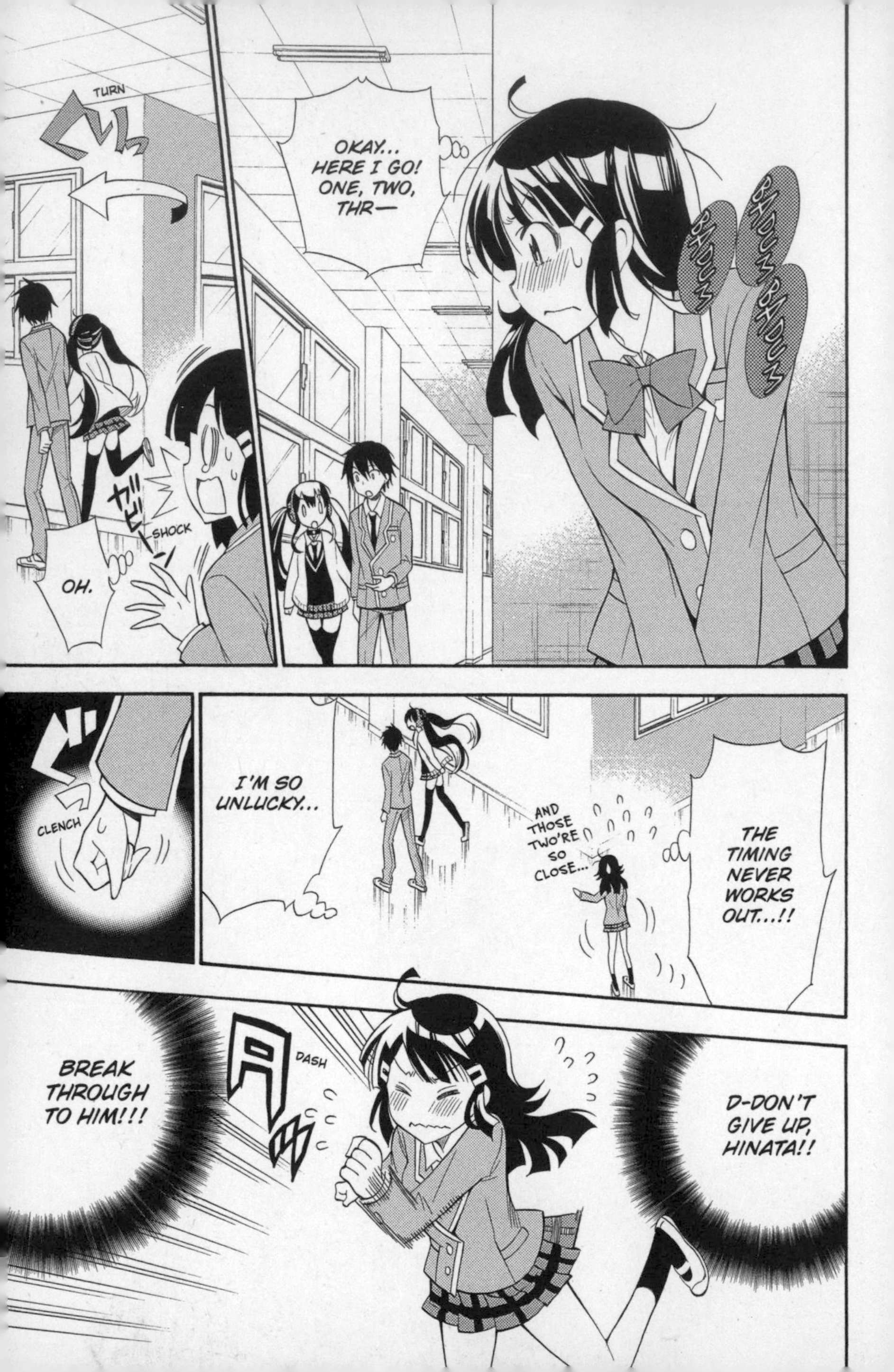
BADUM
BADUM BADUM BADUM
OKAY... HERE I GO! ONE, TWO, THR—
TURN
SHOCK
OH.
THE TIMING NEVER WORKS OUT...!!
AND THOSE TWO'RE SO CLOSE...
I'M SO UNLUCKY...
CLENCH
D-DON'T GIVE UP, HINATA!!
DASH
BREAK THROUGH TO HIM!!!

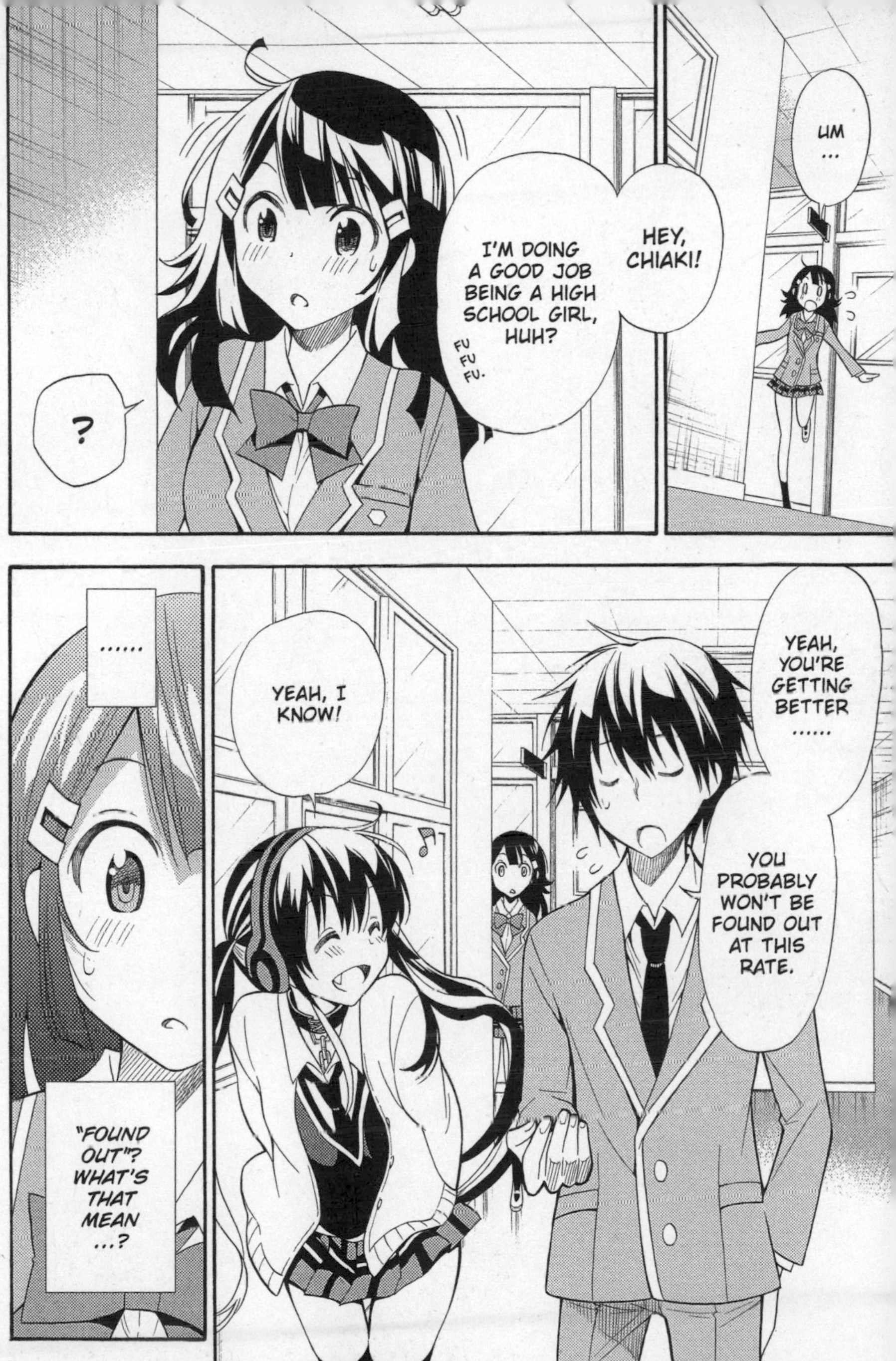
UM ...
HEY, CHIAKI!
I'M DOING A GOOD JOB BEING A HIGH SCHOOL GIRL, HUH?
FU FU FU.
?
YEAH, YOU'RE GETTING BETTER ......
YOU PROBABLY WON'T BE FOUND OUT AT THIS RATE.
YEAH, I KNOW!
......
"FOUND OUT"? WHAT'S THAT MEAN ...?

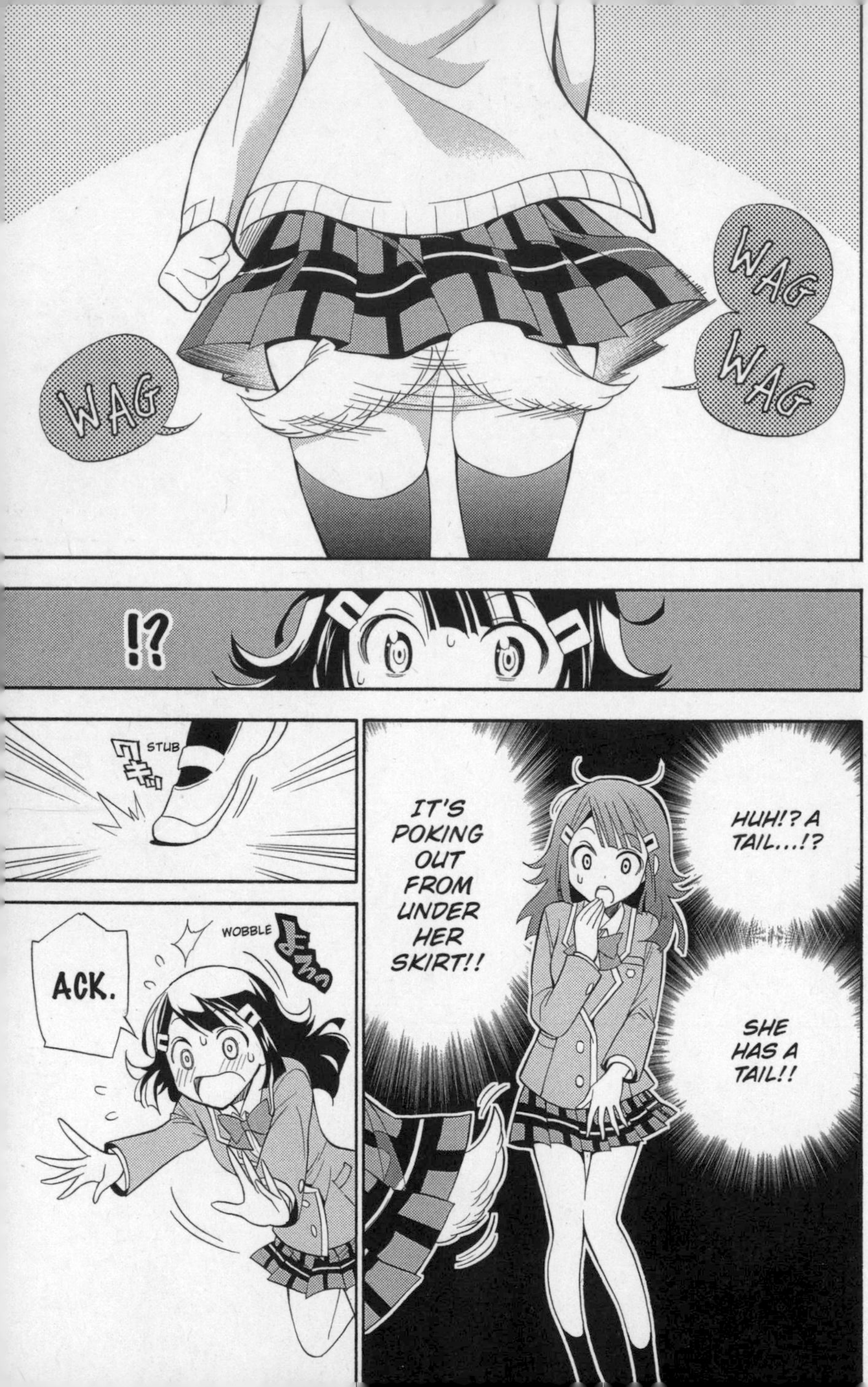
WAG WAG
WAG
!?
HUH!? A TAIL...!?
SHE HAS A TAIL!!
IT'S POKING OUT FROM UNDER HER SKIRT!!
STUB
WOBBLE
ACK.

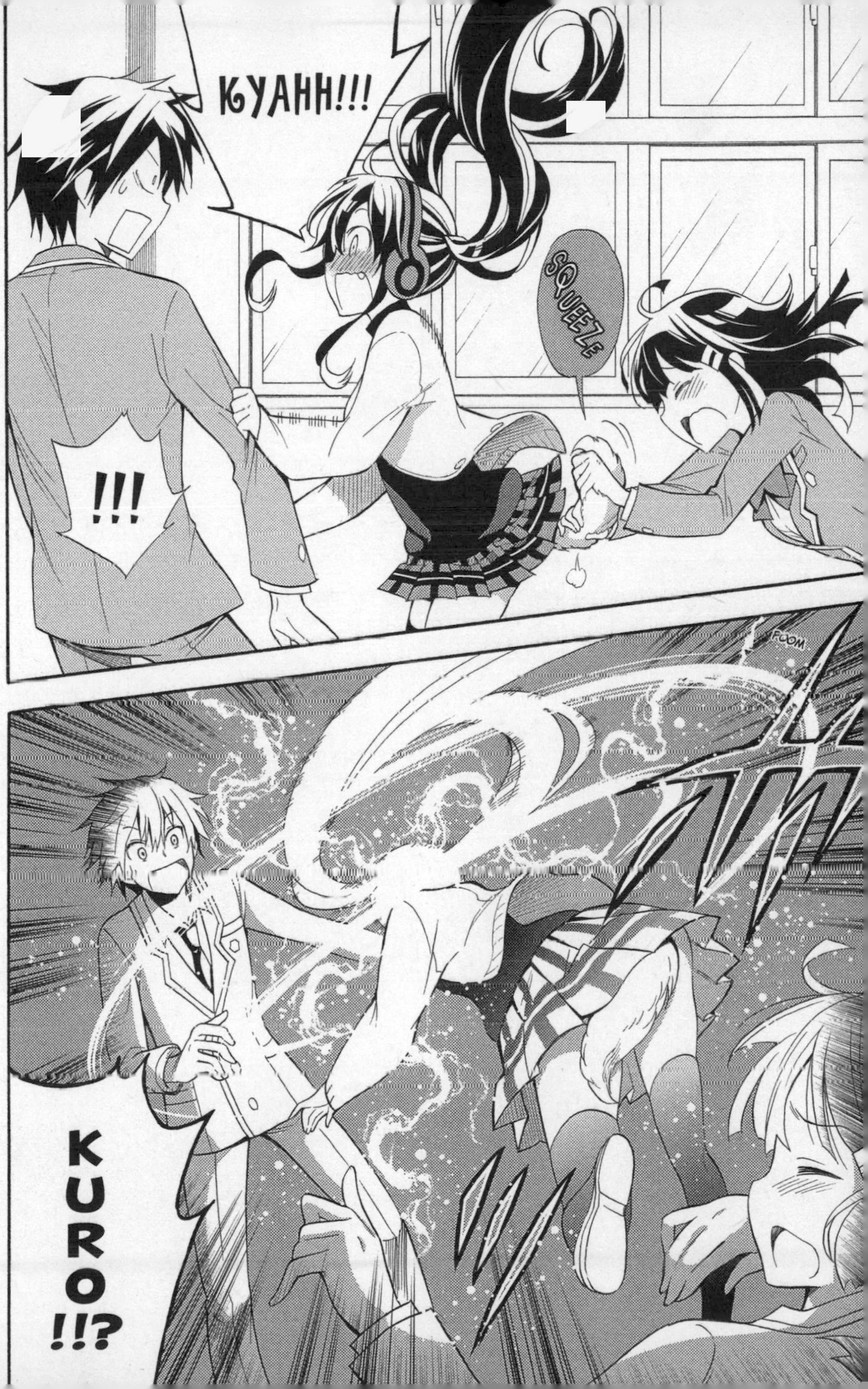
KYAHH!!!
SQUEEZE
!!!
POOM
KURO!!?

TODAY'S CERBERUS

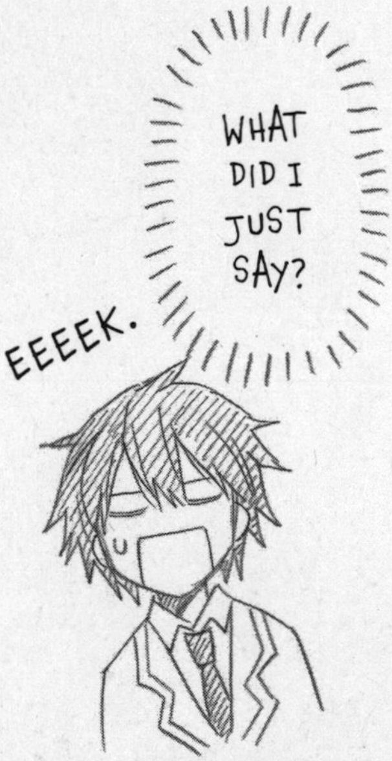
WHAT DID I JUST SAY?
EEEEK.

TODAY'S CERBERUS

MY
EYES!!

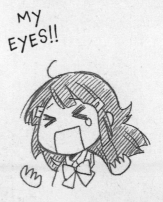

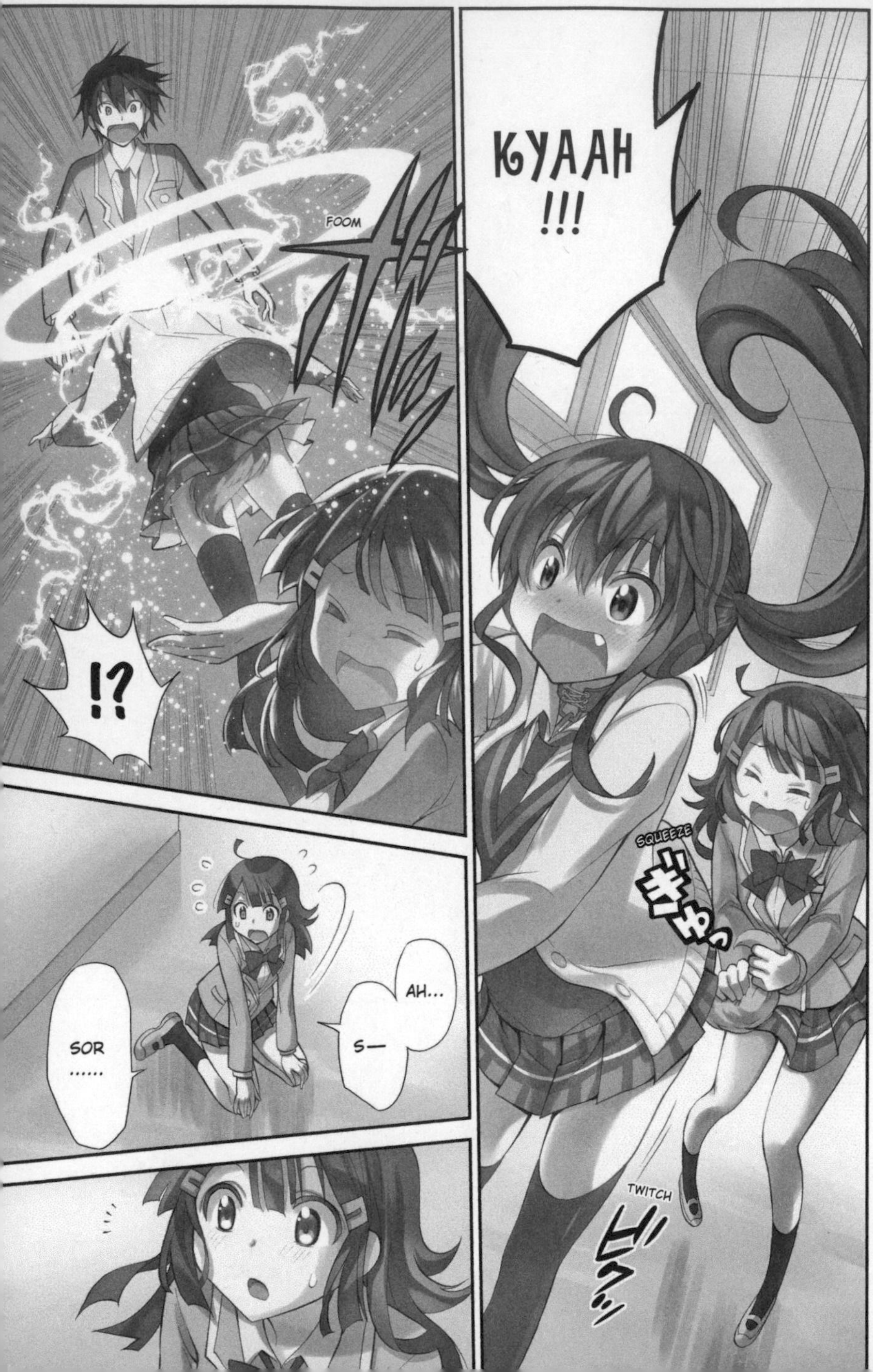
KYAAH !!!
SQUEEZE
ぎゅっ
TWITCH
ビクッ
FOOM
!?
AH...
S—
SOR ......

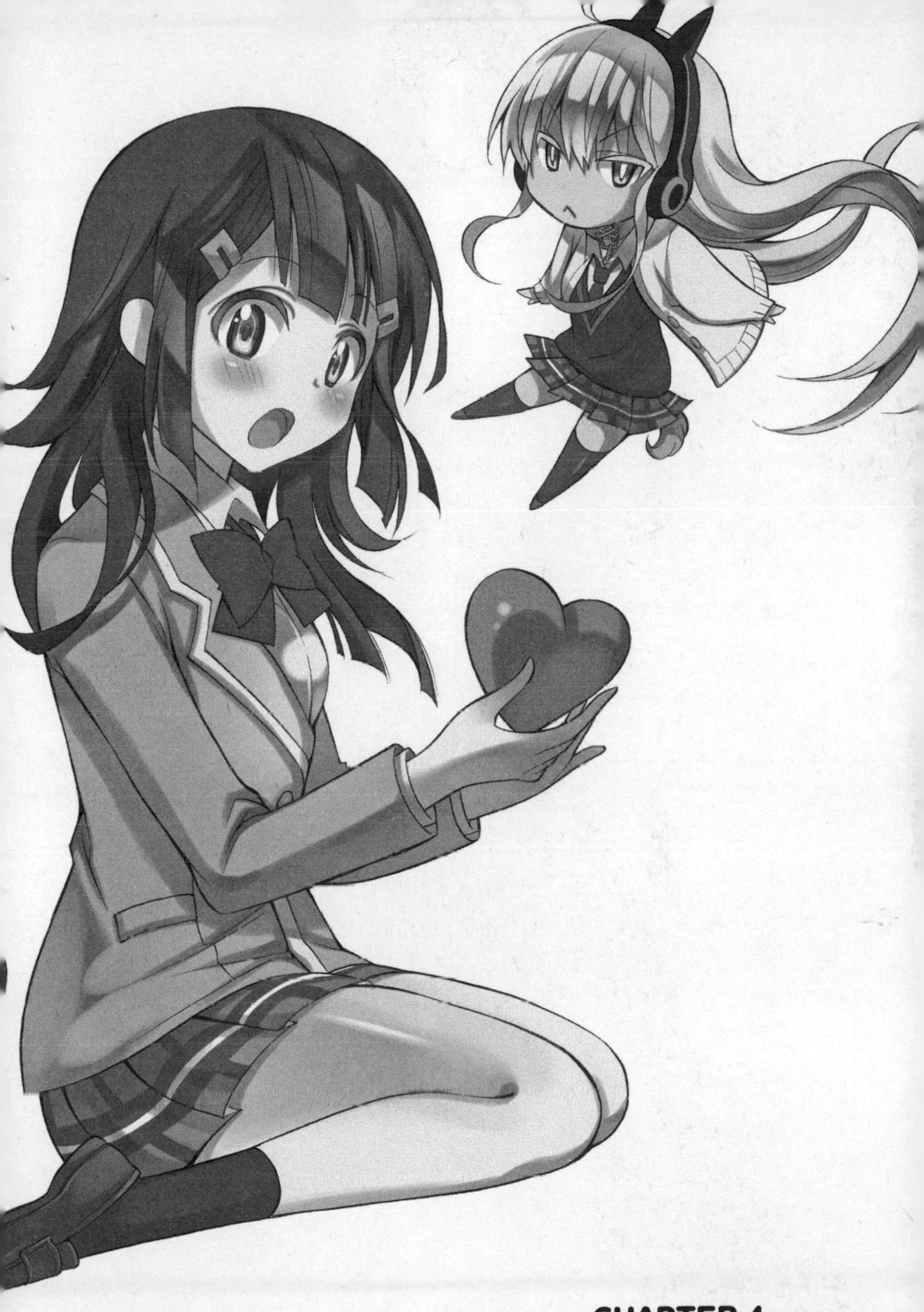

CHAPTER 4
FIGHT ON, GIRLS!

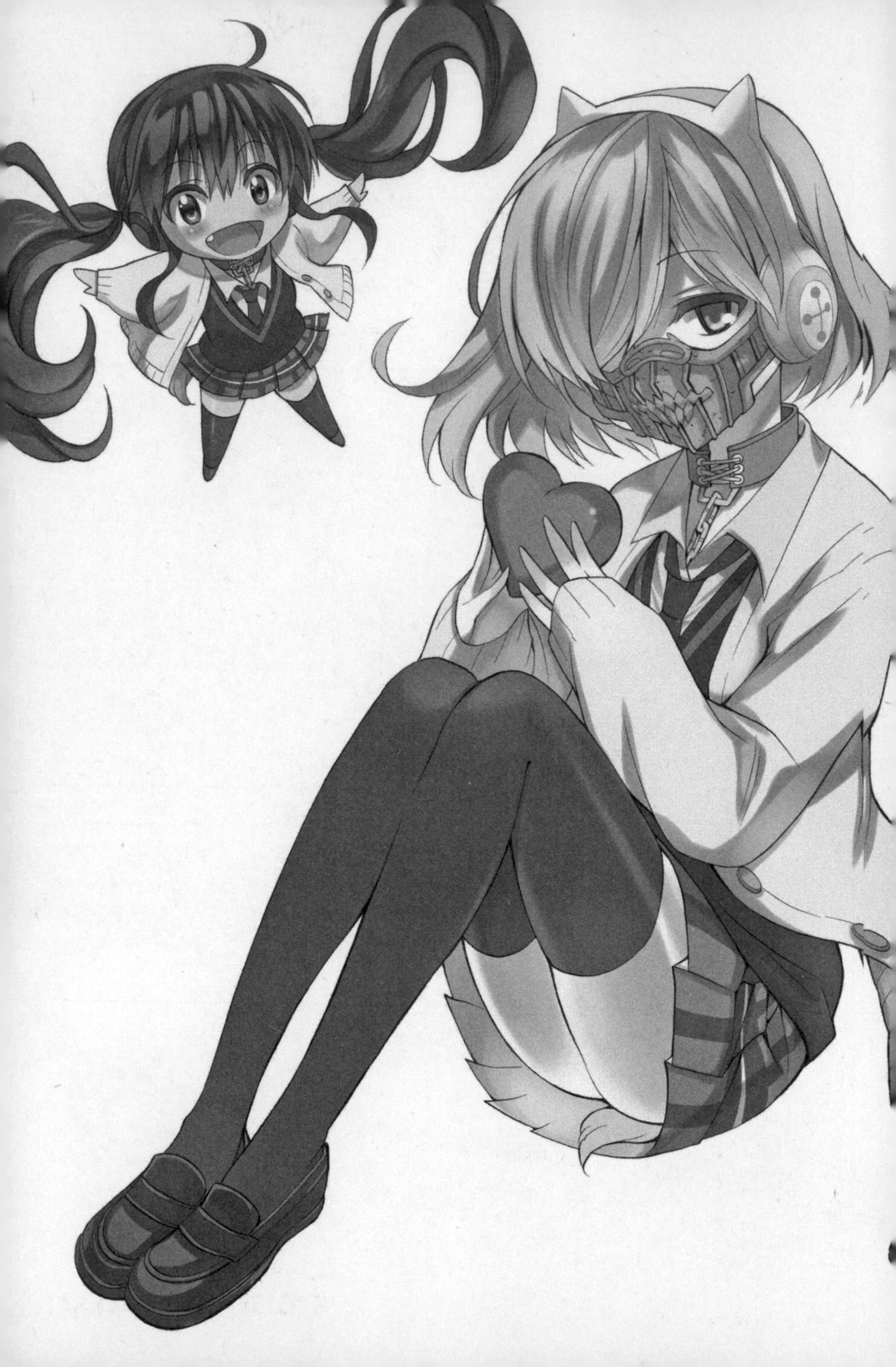

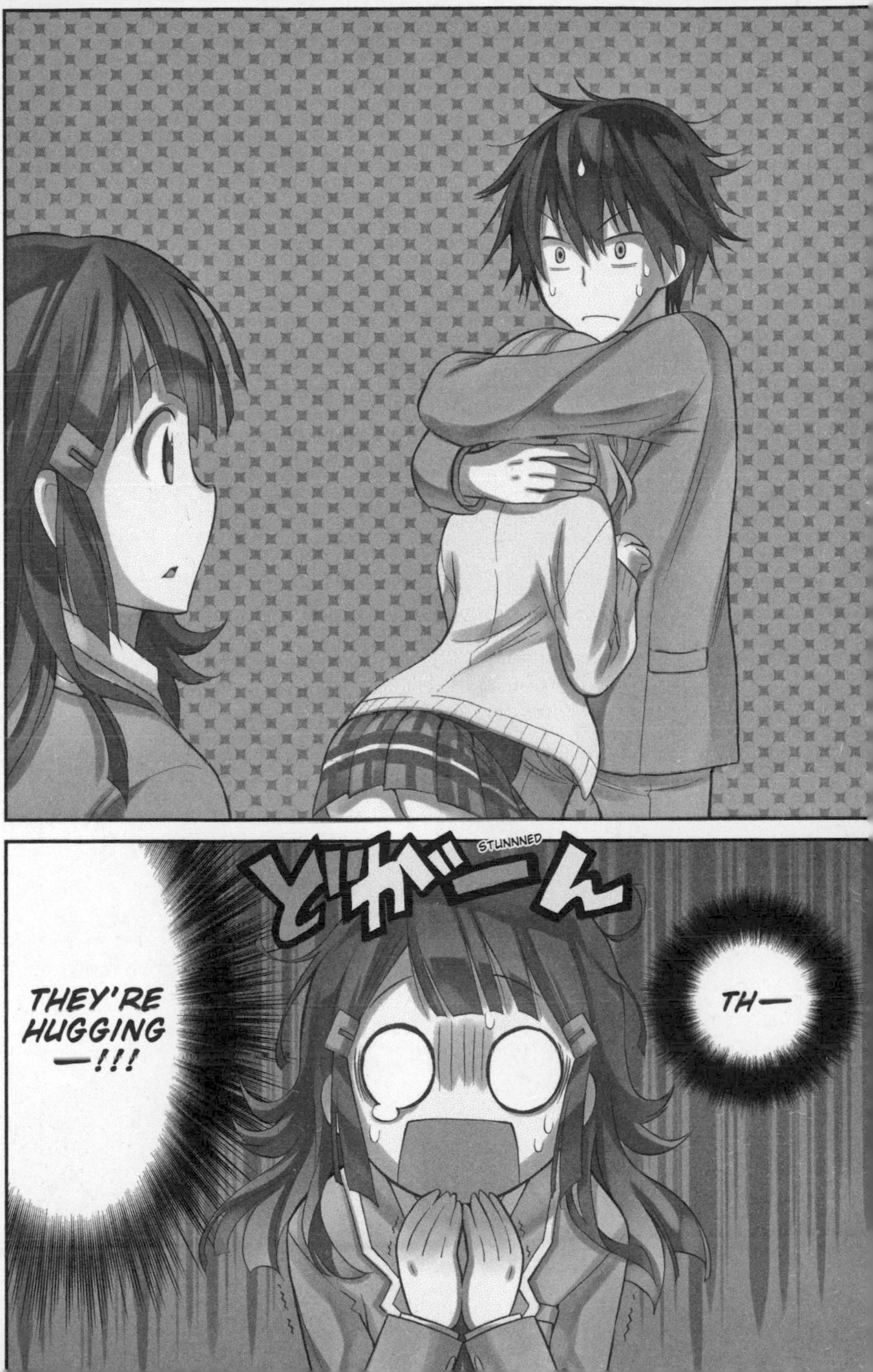
どがーん
STUNNNED
TH—
THEY'RE HUGGING—!!!

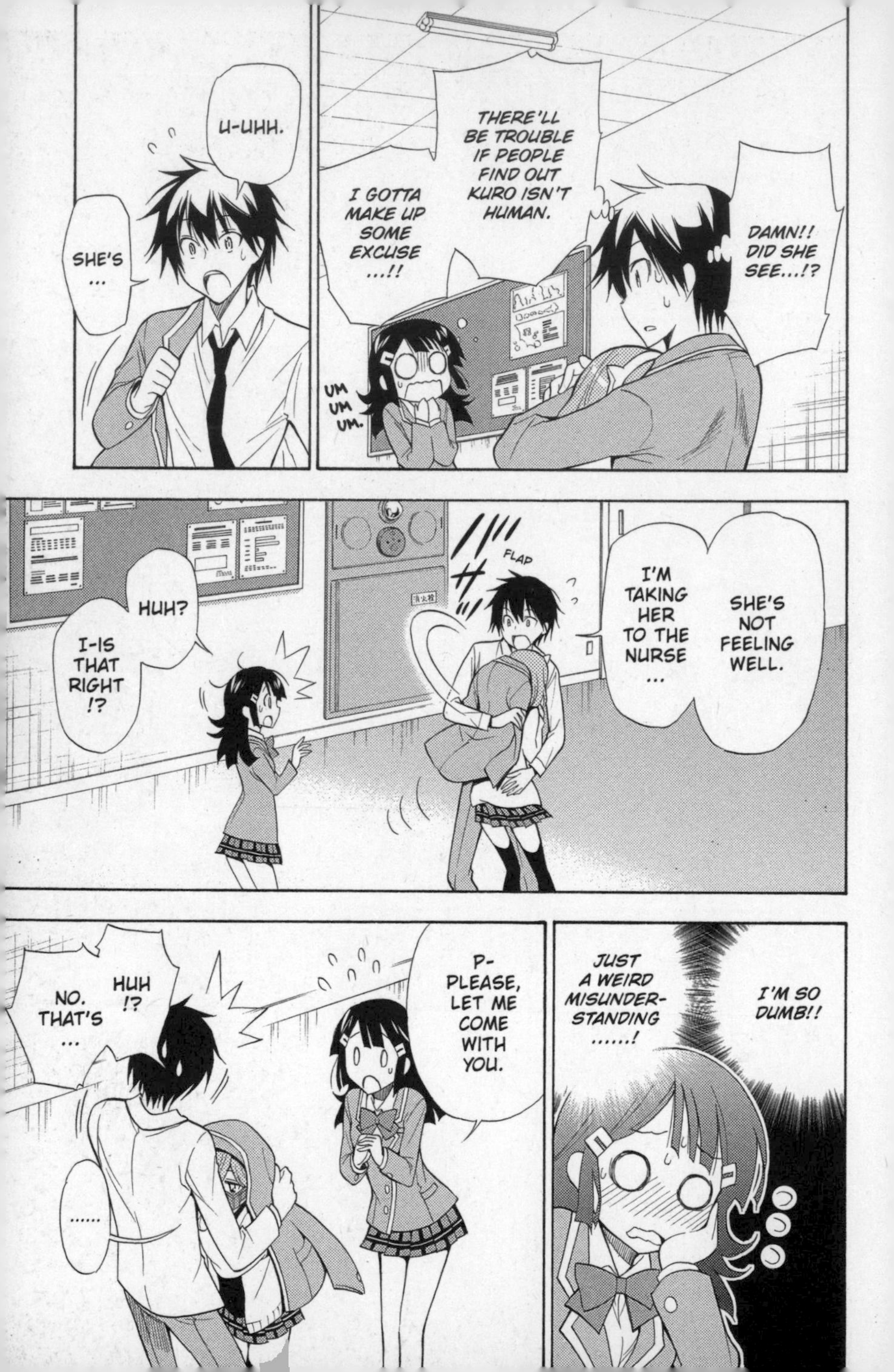
DAMN!! DID SHE SEE...!?
THERE'LL BE TROUBLE IF PEOPLE FIND OUT KURO ISN'T HUMAN.
I GOTTA MAKE UP SOME EXCUSE ...!!
UM UM UM.
U-UHH.
SHE'S ...
SHE'S NOT FEELING WELL.
I'M TAKING HER TO THE NURSE ...
FLAP
HUH?
I-IS THAT RIGHT !?
I'M SO DUMB!!
JUST A WEIRD MISUNDER-STANDING ......!
P-PLEASE, LET ME COME WITH YOU.
HUH !?
NO. THAT'S ...
......

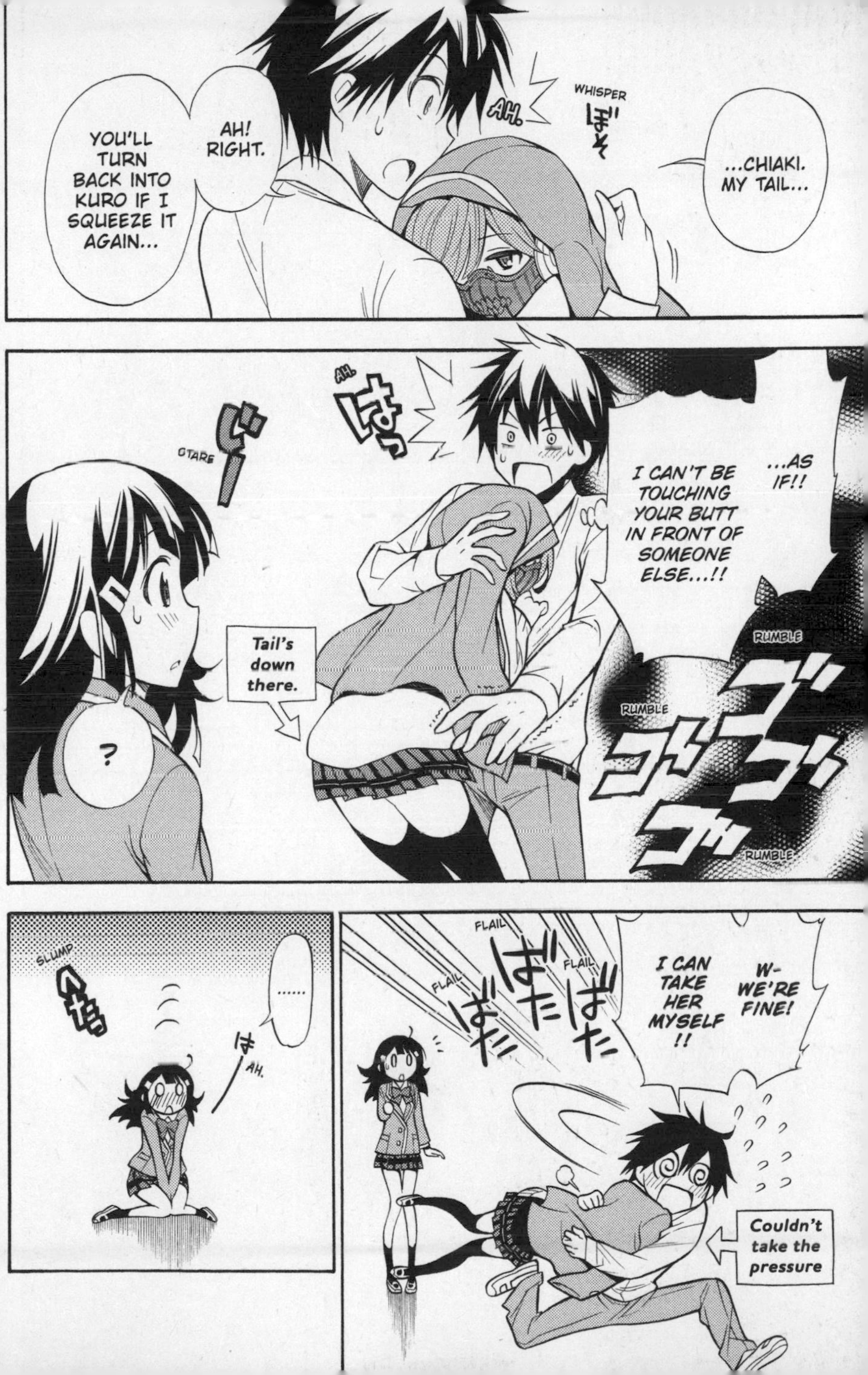
WHISPER
...CHIAKI. MY TAIL...
AH.
AH! RIGHT.
YOU'LL TURN BACK INTO KURO IF I SQUEEZE IT AGAIN...
...AS IF!!
I CAN'T BE TOUCHING YOUR BUTT IN FRONT OF SOMEONE ELSE...!!
RUMBLE
RUMBLE
RUMBLE
AH.
STARE
Tail's down there.
?
W-WE'RE FINE!
I CAN TAKE HER MYSELF!!
FLAIL
FLAIL
FLAIL
Couldn't take the pressure
......
AH.
SLUMP

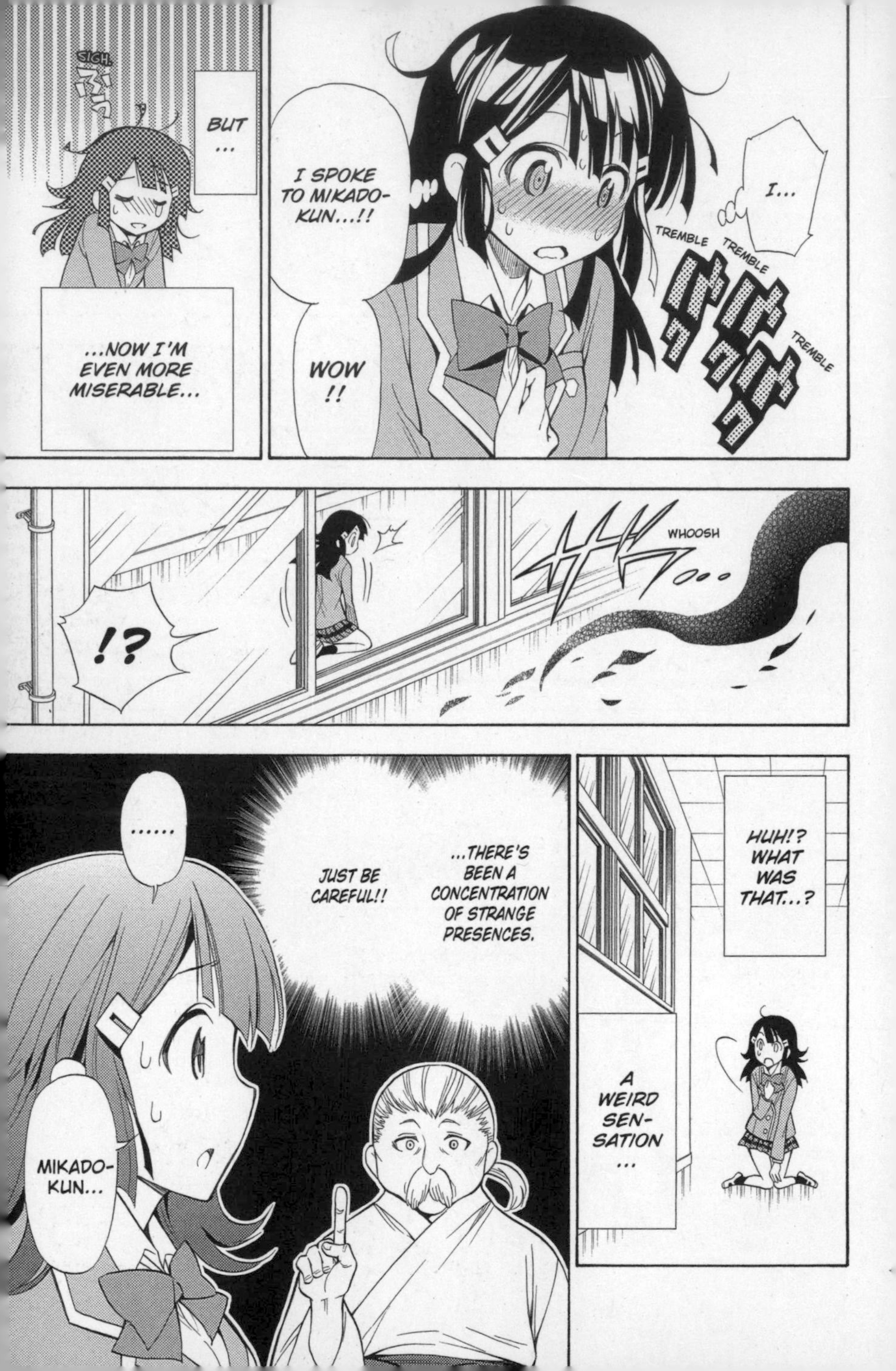
I...
TREMBLE TREMBLE TREMBLE
I SPOKE TO MIKADO-KUN...!!
WOW !!
BUT ...
SIGH.
...NOW I'M EVEN MORE MISERABLE...
WHOOSH
!?
HUH!? WHAT WAS THAT...?
A WEIRD SENSATION ...
......
...THERE'S BEEN A CONCENTRATION OF STRANGE PRESENCES.
JUST BE CAREFUL!!
MIKADO-KUN...

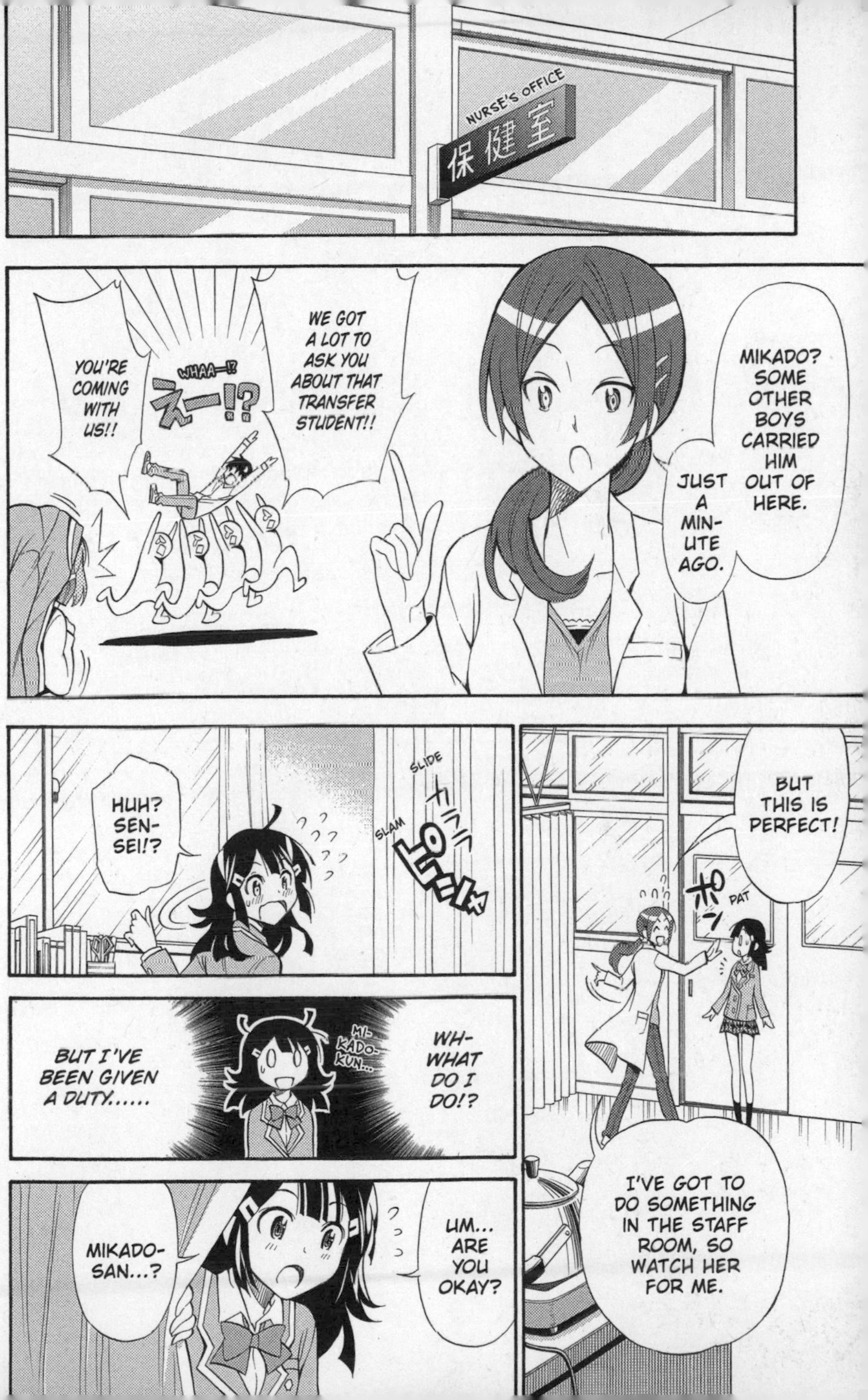
NURSE'S OFFICE
保健室
MIKADO? SOME OTHER BOYS CARRIED HIM OUT OF HERE.
JUST A MIN-UTE AGO.
WE GOT A LOT TO ASK YOU ABOUT THAT TRANSFER STUDENT!!
WHAA—!?
えー!?
YOU'RE COMING WITH US!!
BUT THIS IS PERFECT!
PAT
I'VE GOT TO DO SOMETHING IN THE STAFF ROOM, SO WATCH HER FOR ME.
SLIDE
SLAM
HUH? SEN-SEI!?
WH-WHAT DO I DO!?
MI-KADO-KUN...
BUT I'VE BEEN GIVEN A DUTY......
UM... ARE YOU OKAY?
MIKADO-SAN...?

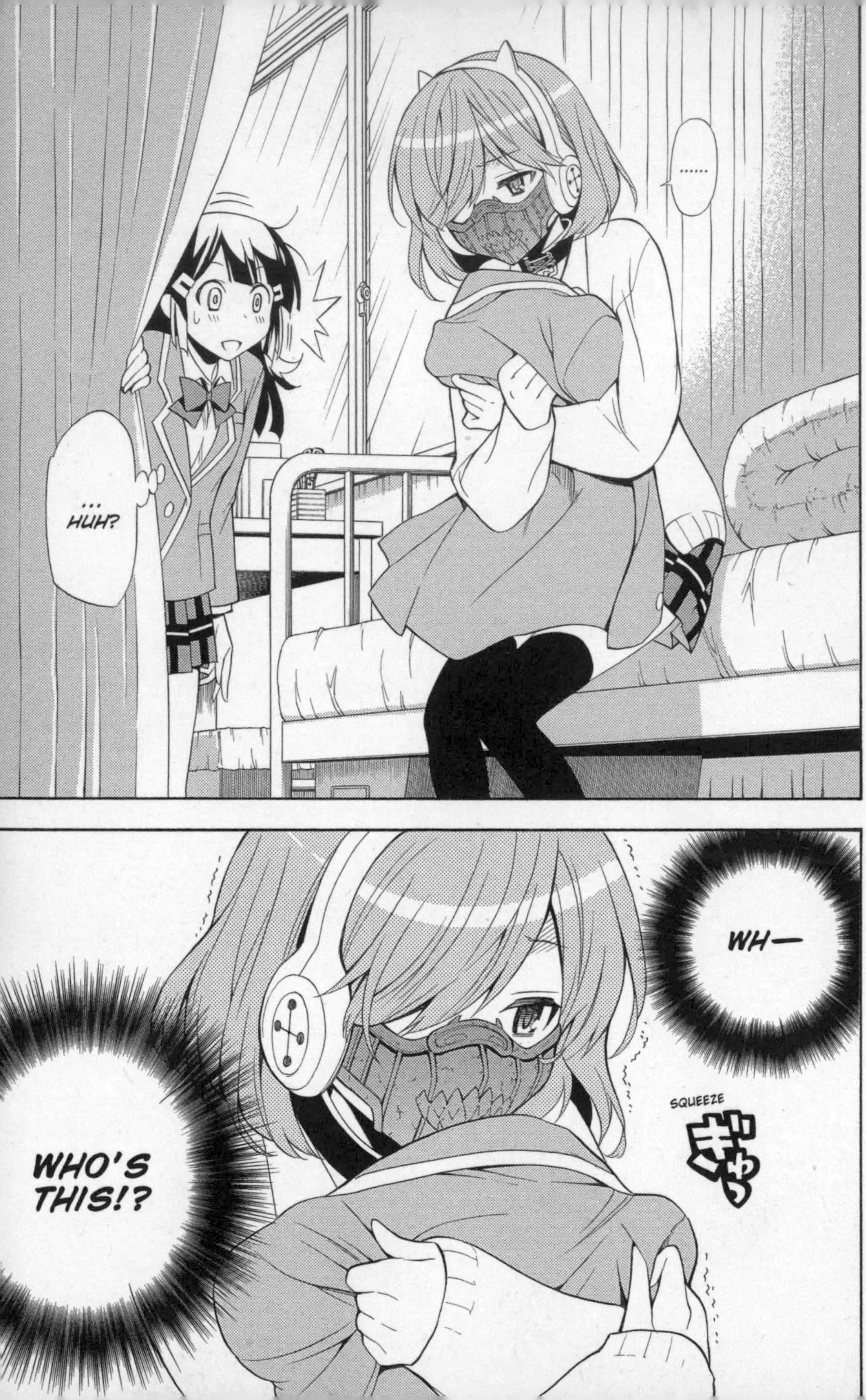
......
... HUH?
WH—
SQUEEZE
ぎゅっ
WHO'S THIS!?

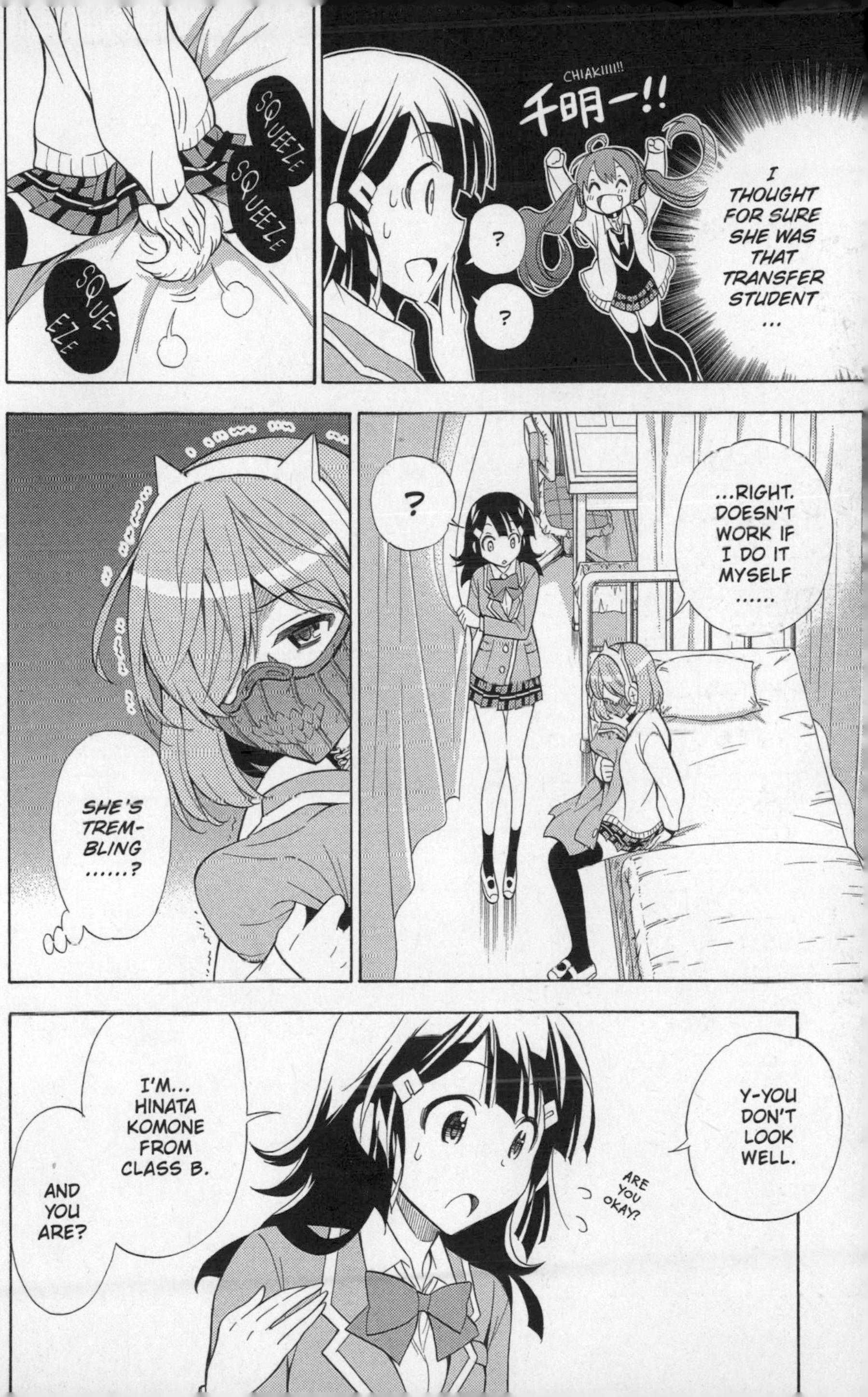
CHIAKIIII!!
千明ー!!
I THOUGHT FOR SURE SHE WAS THAT TRANSFER STUDENT ...
?
?
SQUEEZE
SQUEEZE
SQUE-EZE
...RIGHT. DOESN'T WORK IF I DO IT MYSELF ......
?
SHE'S TREM-BLING ......?
Y-YOU DON'T LOOK WELL.
ARE YOU OKAY?
I'M... HINATA KOMONE FROM CLASS B.
AND YOU ARE?

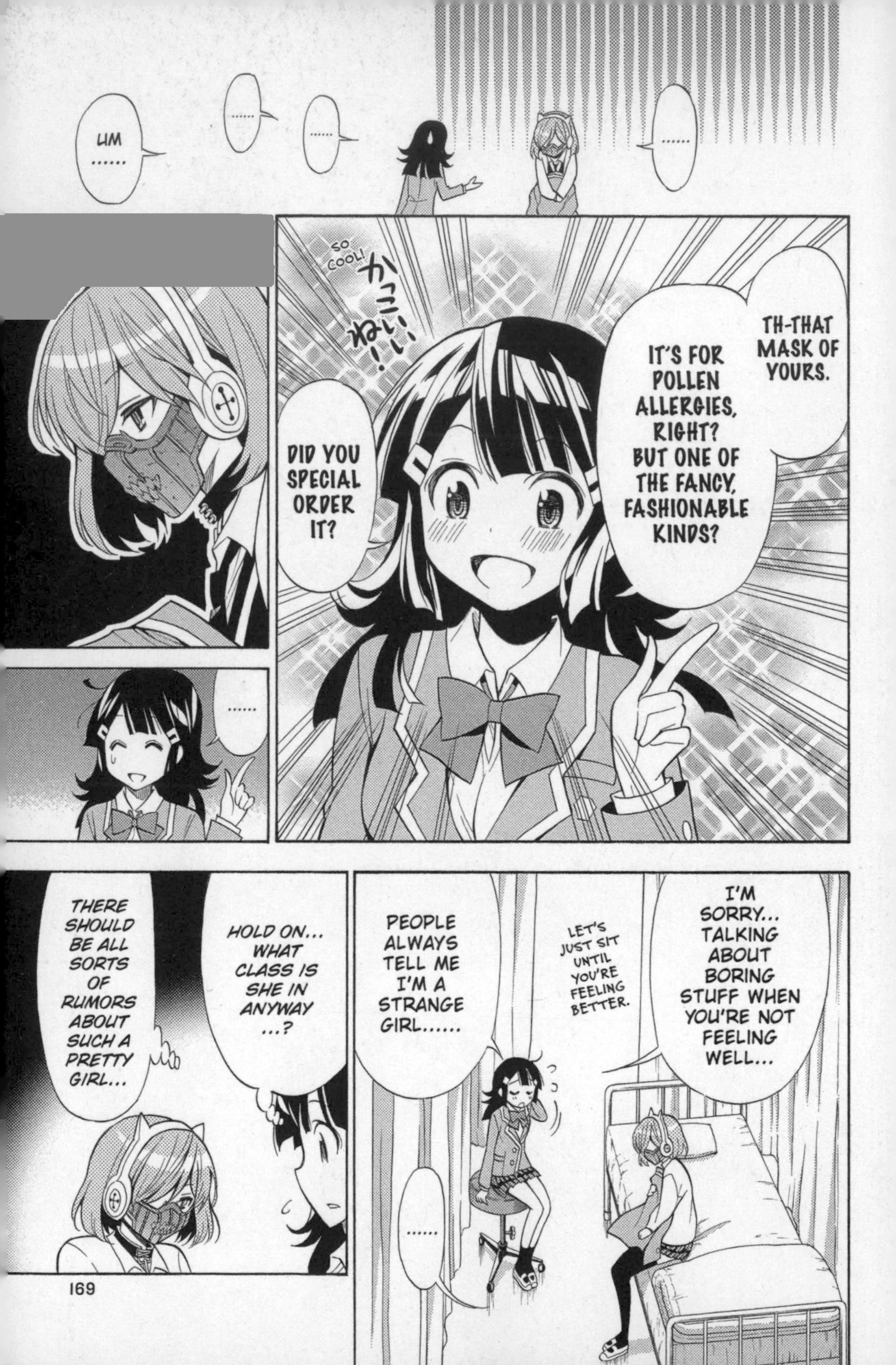
......
......
......
UM ......
TH-THAT MASK OF YOURS.
IT'S FOR POLLEN ALLERGIES, RIGHT? BUT ONE OF THE FANCY, FASHIONABLE KINDS?
DID YOU SPECIAL ORDER IT?
SO COOL!
......
I'M SORRY... TALKING ABOUT BORING STUFF WHEN YOU'RE NOT FEELING WELL...
LET'S JUST SIT UNTIL YOU'RE FEELING BETTER.
PEOPLE ALWAYS TELL ME I'M A STRANGE GIRL......
......
HOLD ON... WHAT CLASS IS SHE IN ANYWAY ...?
THERE SHOULD BE ALL SORTS OF RUMORS ABOUT SUCH A PRETTY GIRL...

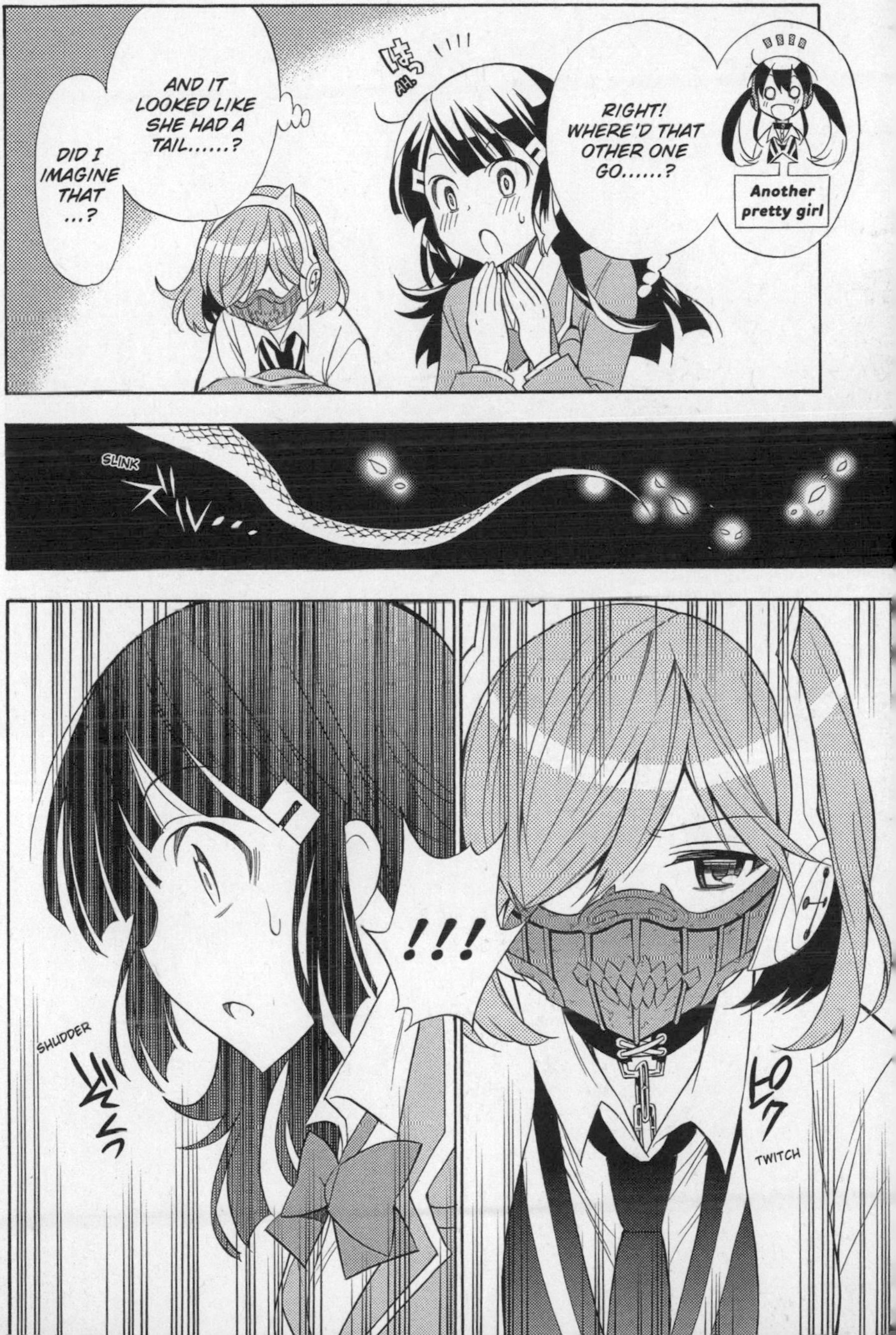
RIGHT! WHERE'D THAT OTHER ONE GO......?
Another pretty girl
AH
AND IT LOOKED LIKE SHE HAD A TAIL......?
DID I IMAGINE THAT ...?
SLINK
TWITCH
!!!
SHUDDER

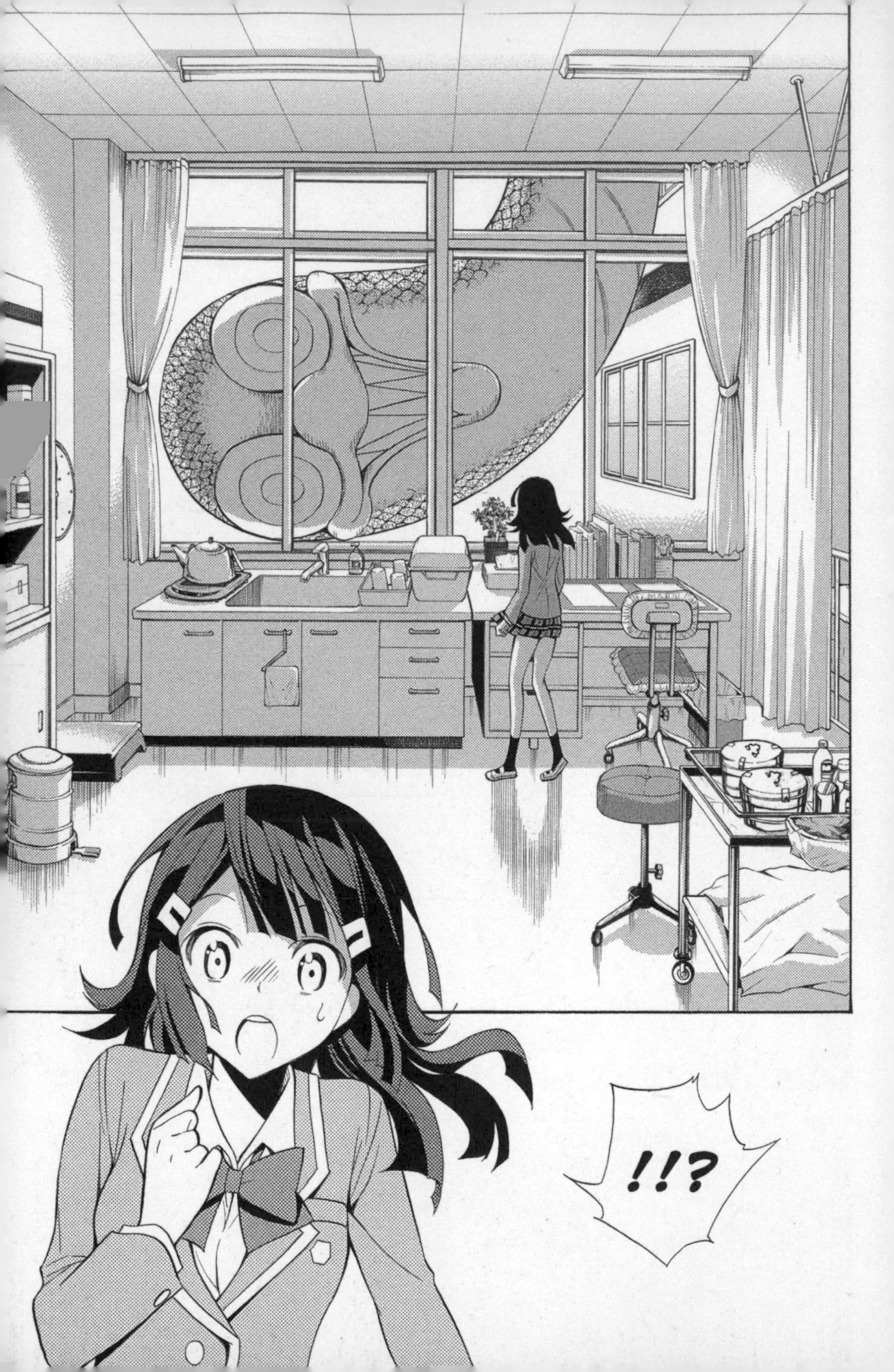
!!?

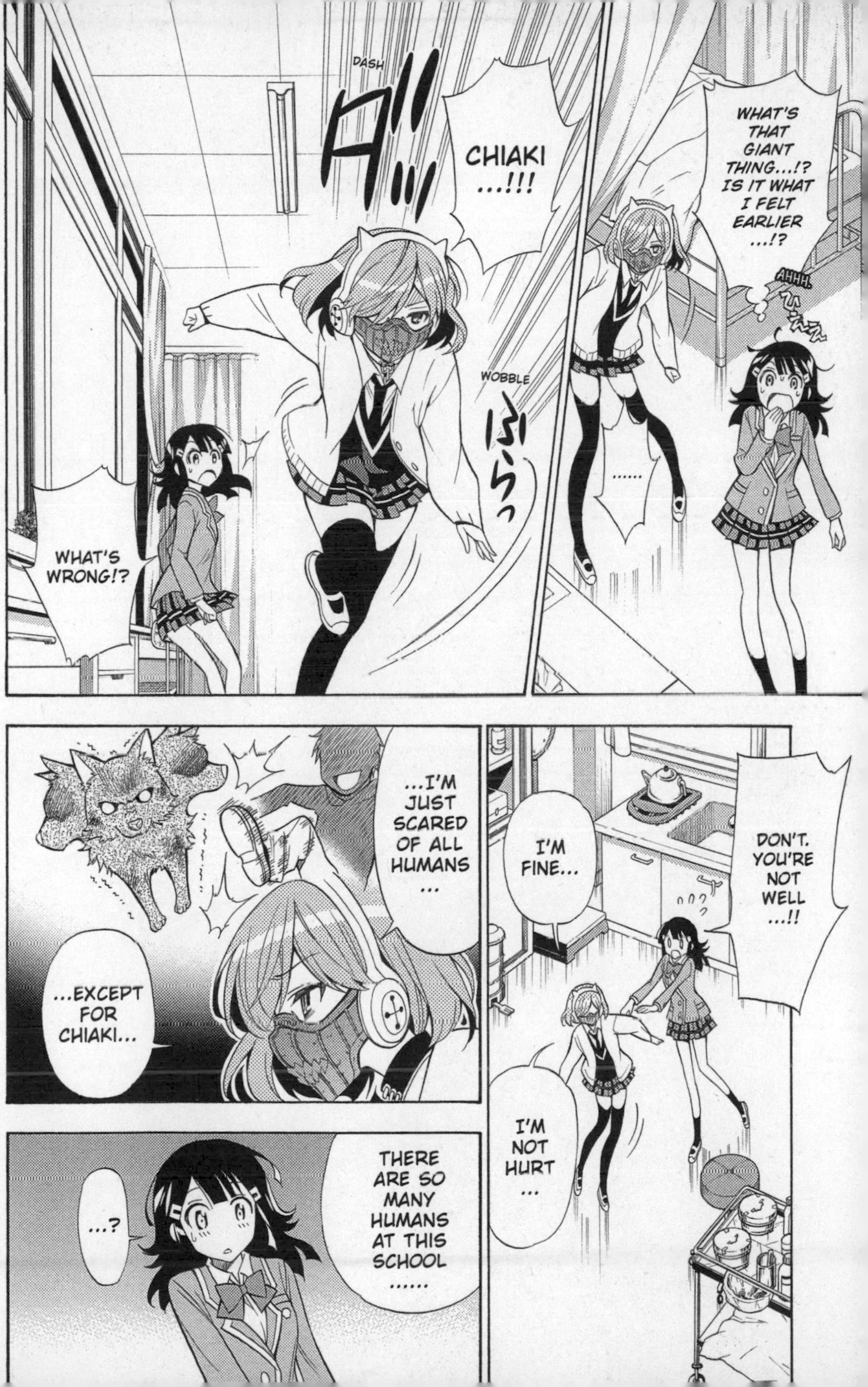
WHAT'S THAT GIANT THING...!? IS IT WHAT I FELT EARLIER ...!?
AHHH
......
DASH
CHIAKI ...!!!
WOBBLE
WHAT'S WRONG!?
DON'T. YOU'RE NOT WELL ...!!
I'M FINE...
I'M NOT HURT ...
...I'M JUST SCARED OF ALL HUMANS ...
...EXCEPT FOR CHIAKI...
THERE ARE SO MANY HUMANS AT THIS SCHOOL ......
...?

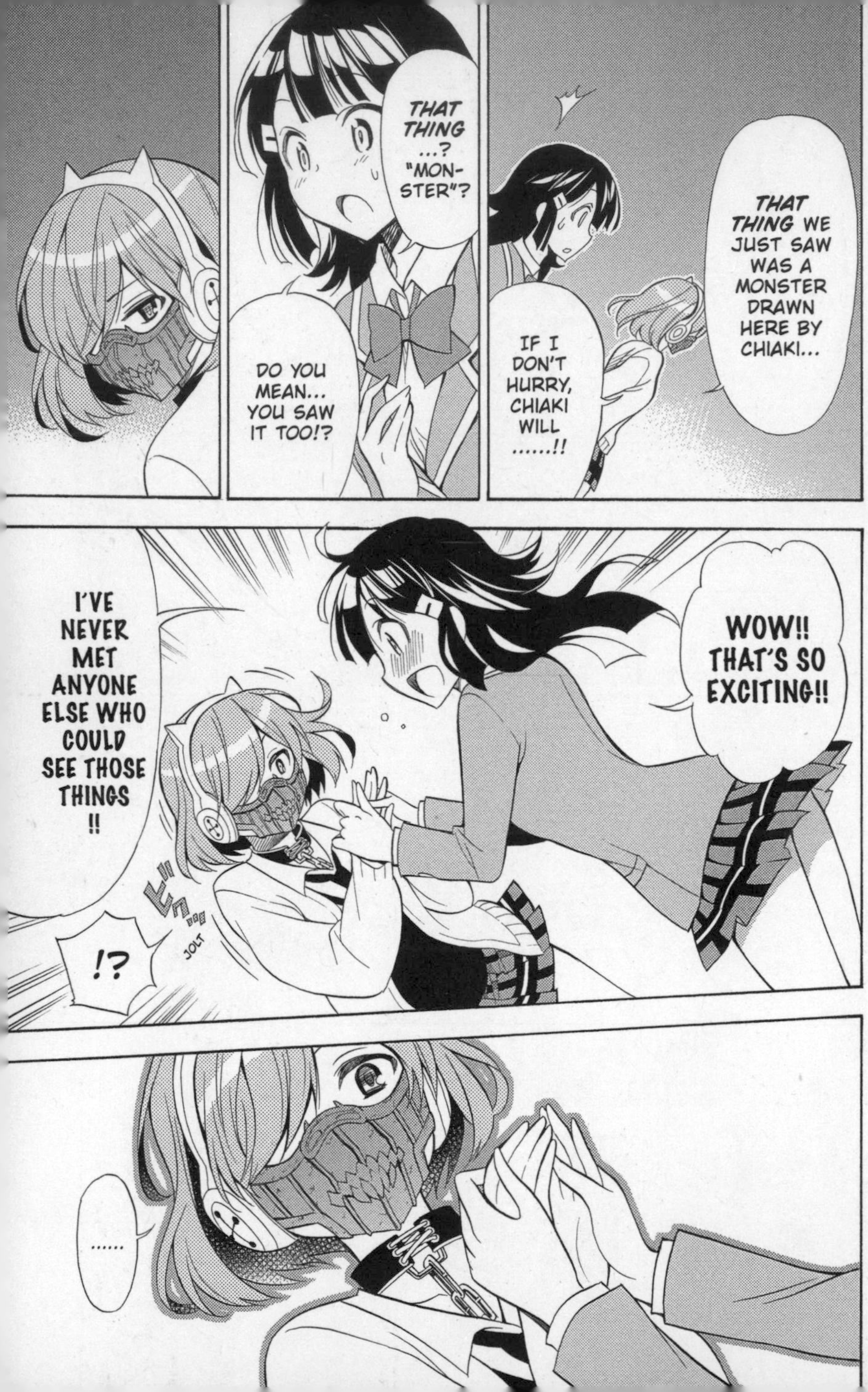
THAT THING WE JUST SAW WAS A MONSTER DRAWN HERE BY CHIAKI...
IF I DON'T HURRY, CHIAKI WILL ......!!
THAT THING ...? "MON-STER"?
DO YOU MEAN... YOU SAW IT TOO!?
WOW!! THAT'S SO EXCITING!!
I'VE NEVER MET ANYONE ELSE WHO COULD SEE THOSE THINGS !!
JOLT
!?
......

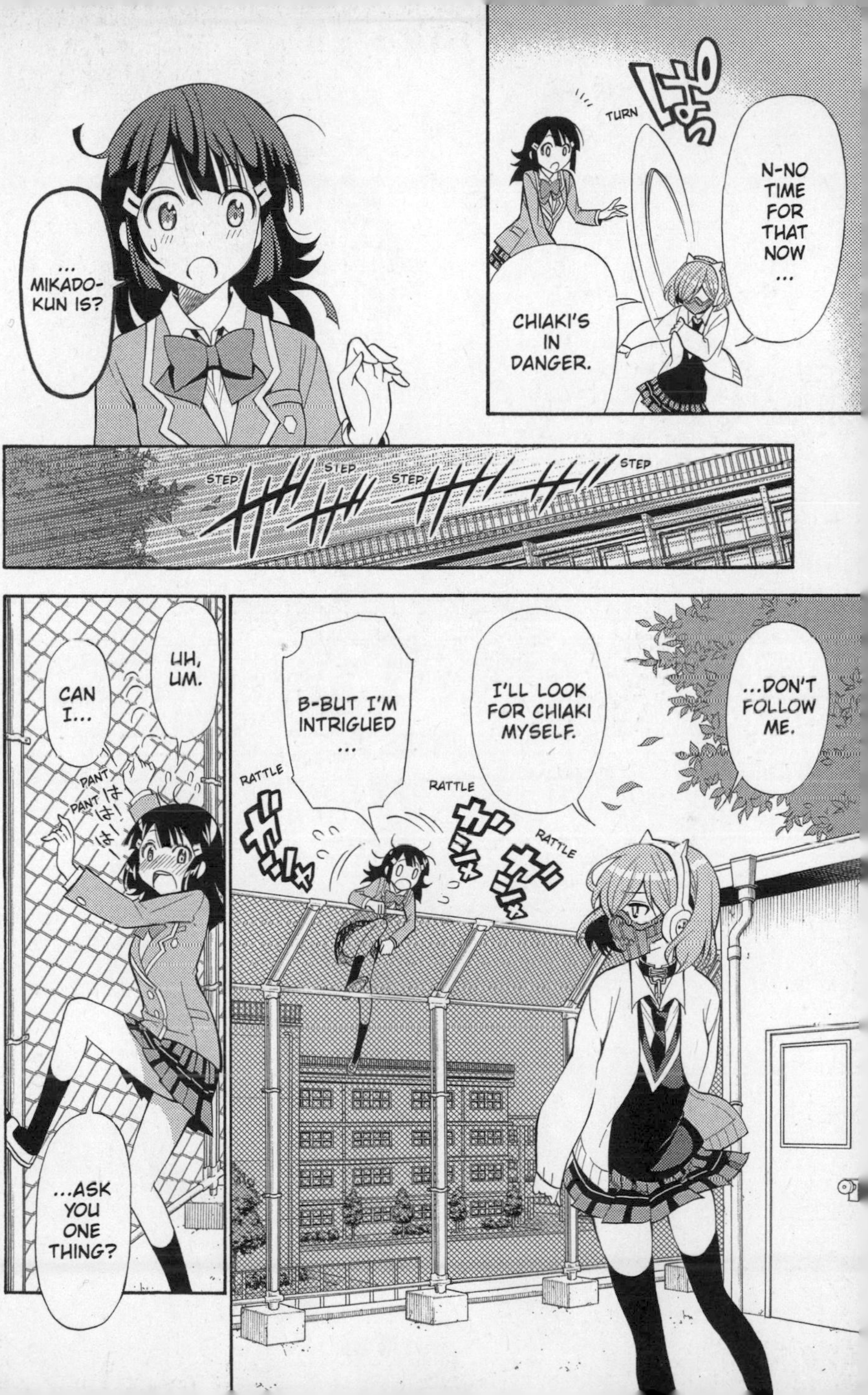

TURN
N-NO TIME FOR THAT NOW ...
CHIAKI'S IN DANGER.
... MIKADO-KUN IS?
STEP
STEP
STEP
STEP
...DON'T FOLLOW ME.
I'LL LOOK FOR CHIAKI MYSELF.
RATTLE
RATTLE
B-BUT I'M INTRIGUED ...
RATTLE
UH, UM.
CAN I...
PANT PANT
はっ！はっ！
...ASK YOU ONE THING?

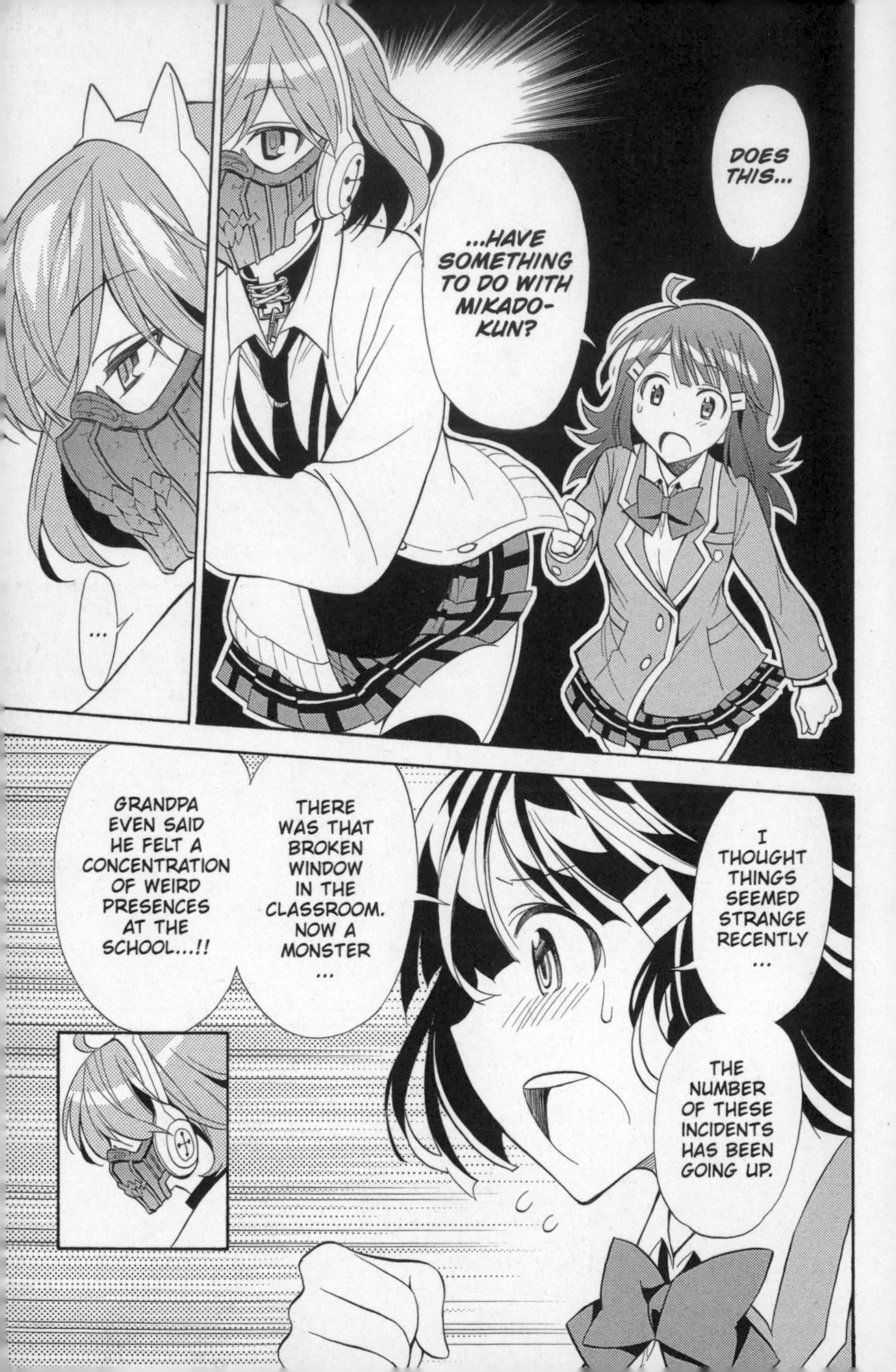
DOES THIS...
...HAVE SOMETHING TO DO WITH MIKADO-KUN?
...
I THOUGHT THINGS SEEMED STRANGE RECENTLY...
THE NUMBER OF THESE INCIDENTS HAS BEEN GOING UP.
THERE WAS THAT BROKEN WINDOW IN THE CLASSROOM. NOW A MONSTER...
GRANDPA EVEN SAID HE FELT A CONCENTRATION OF WEIRD PRESENCES AT THE SCHOOL...!!

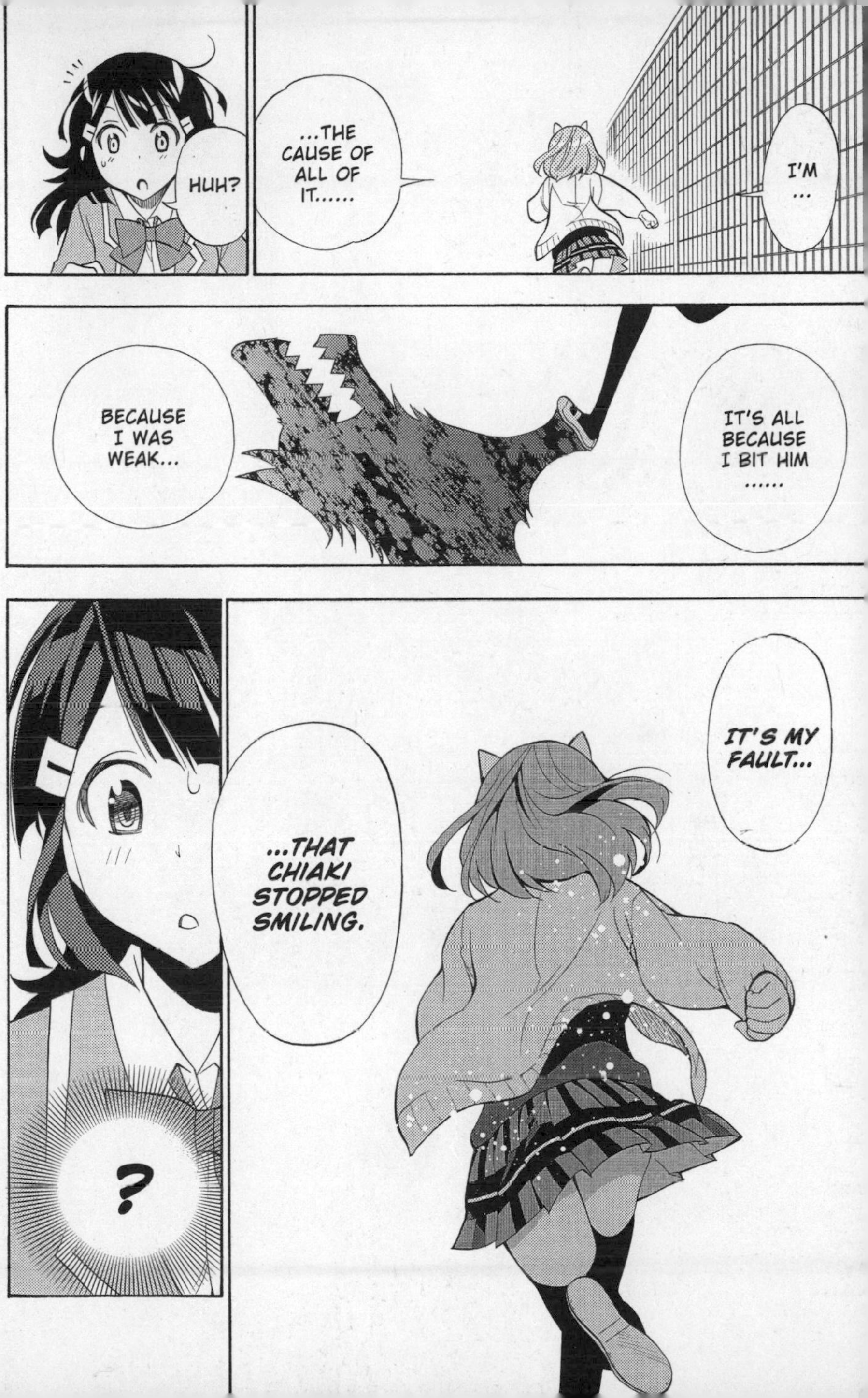
I'M ...
...THE CAUSE OF ALL OF IT......
HUH?
IT'S ALL BECAUSE I BIT HIM ......
BECAUSE I WAS WEAK...
IT'S MY FAULT...
...THAT CHIAKI STOPPED SMILING.
?

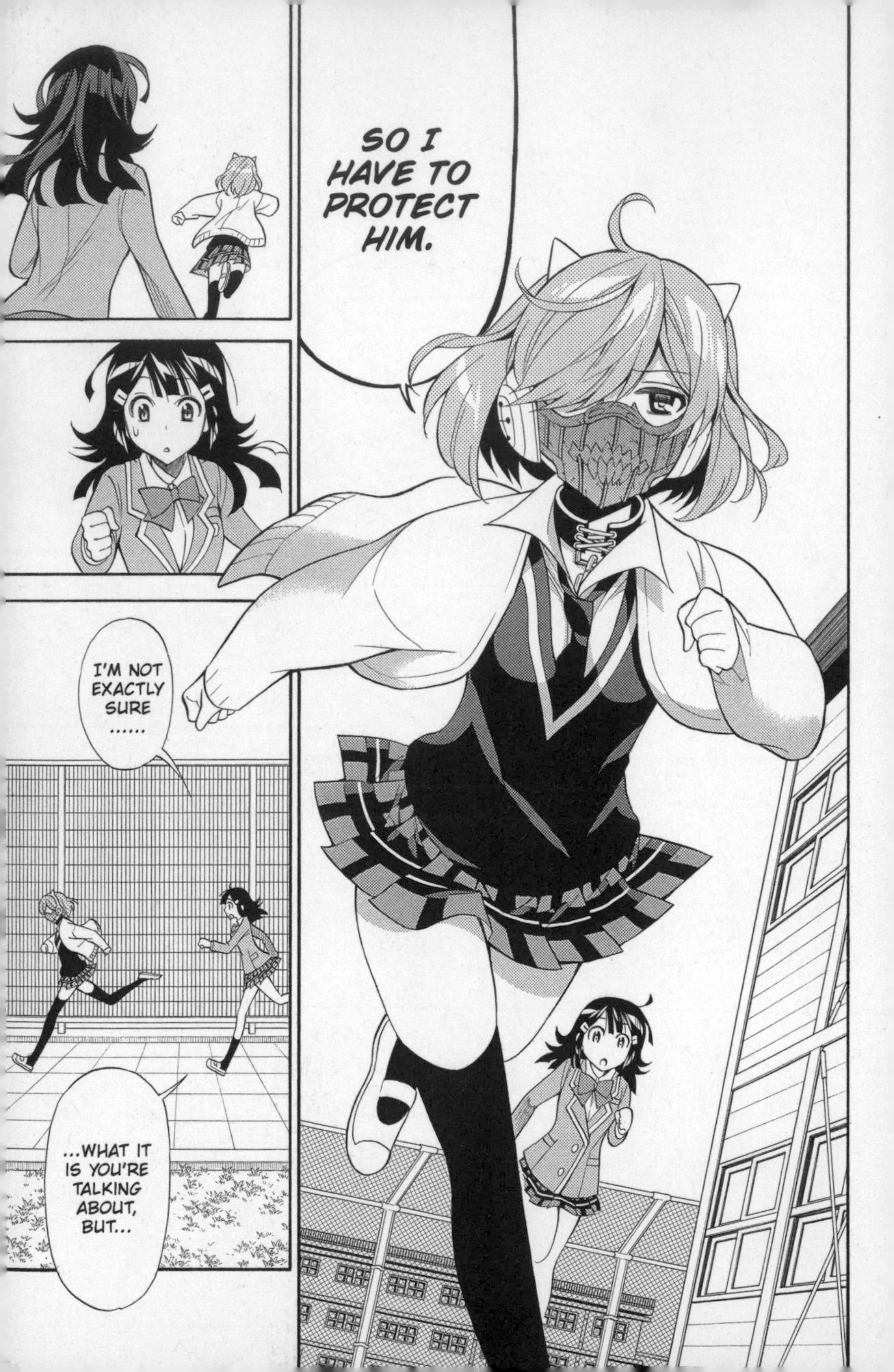
SO I HAVE TO PROTECT HIM.
I'M NOT EXACTLY SURE ......
...WHAT IT IS YOU'RE TALKING ABOUT, BUT...

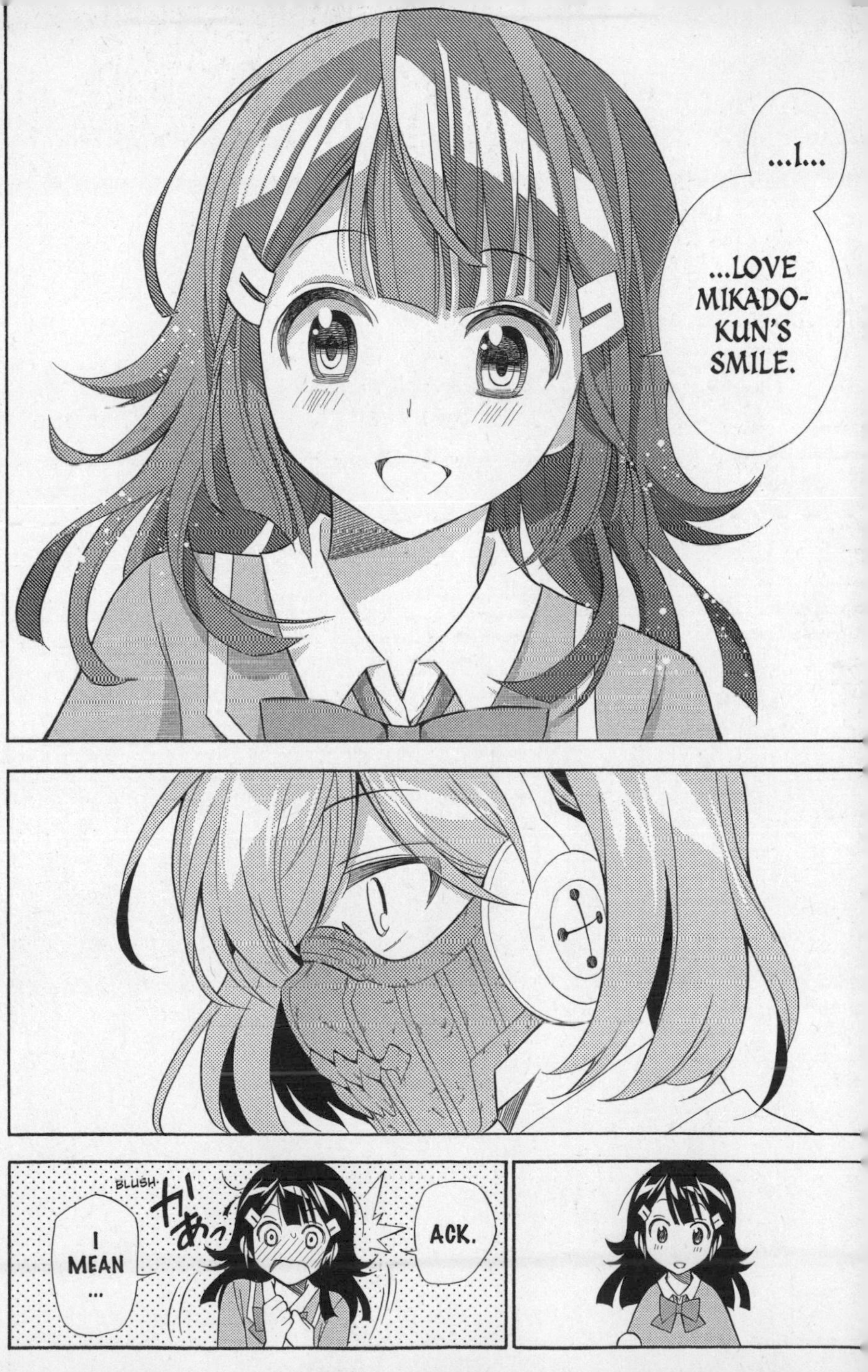
...I...
...LOVE MIKADO-KUN'S SMILE.
ACK.
かあっ
BLUSH
I MEAN ...

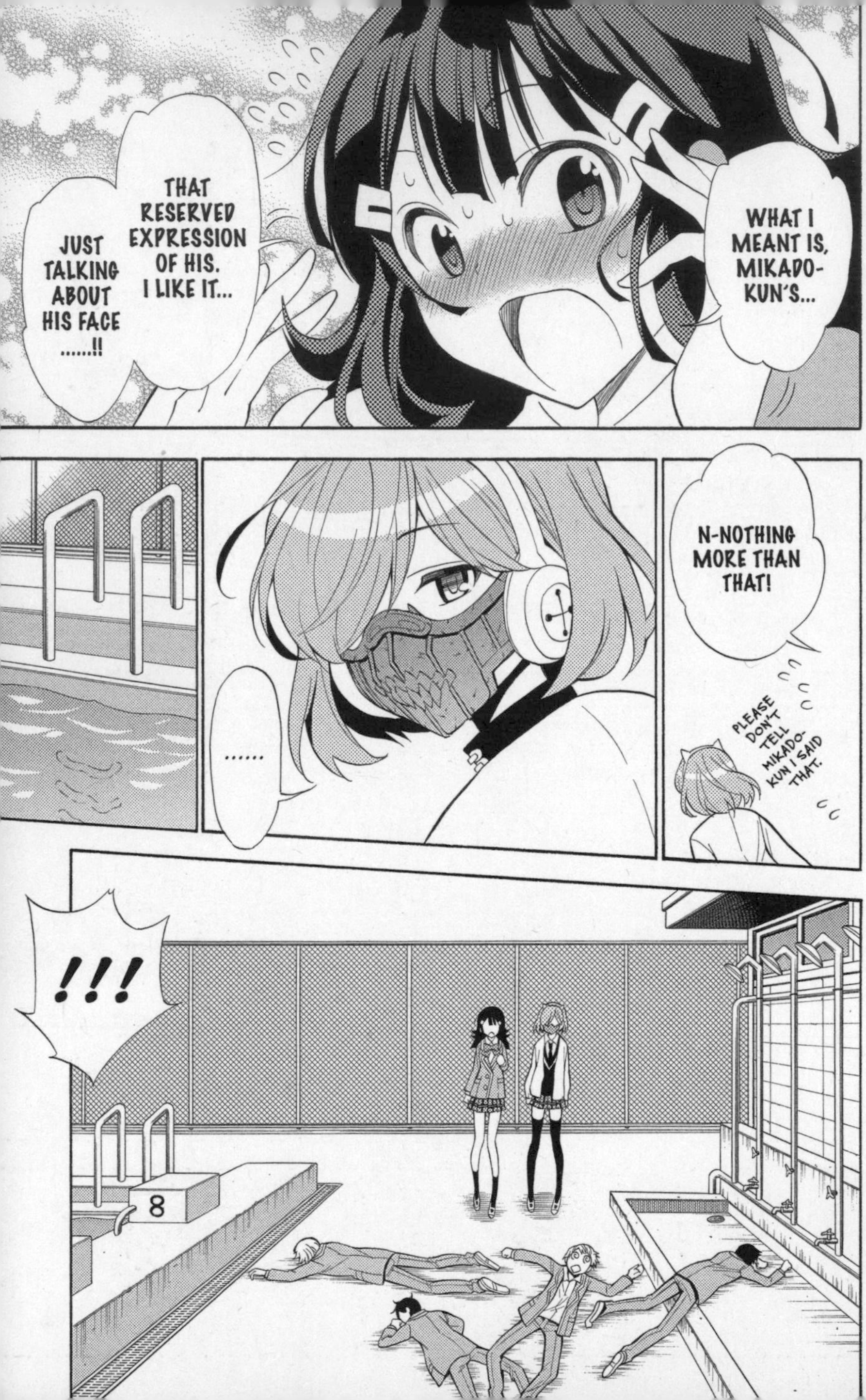
WHAT I MEANT IS, MIKADO-KUN'S...
THAT RESERVED EXPRESSION OF HIS. I LIKE IT...
JUST TALKING ABOUT HIS FACE ......!!
N-NOTHING MORE THAN THAT!
PLEASE DON'T TELL MIKADO-KUN I SAID THAT.
......
!!!

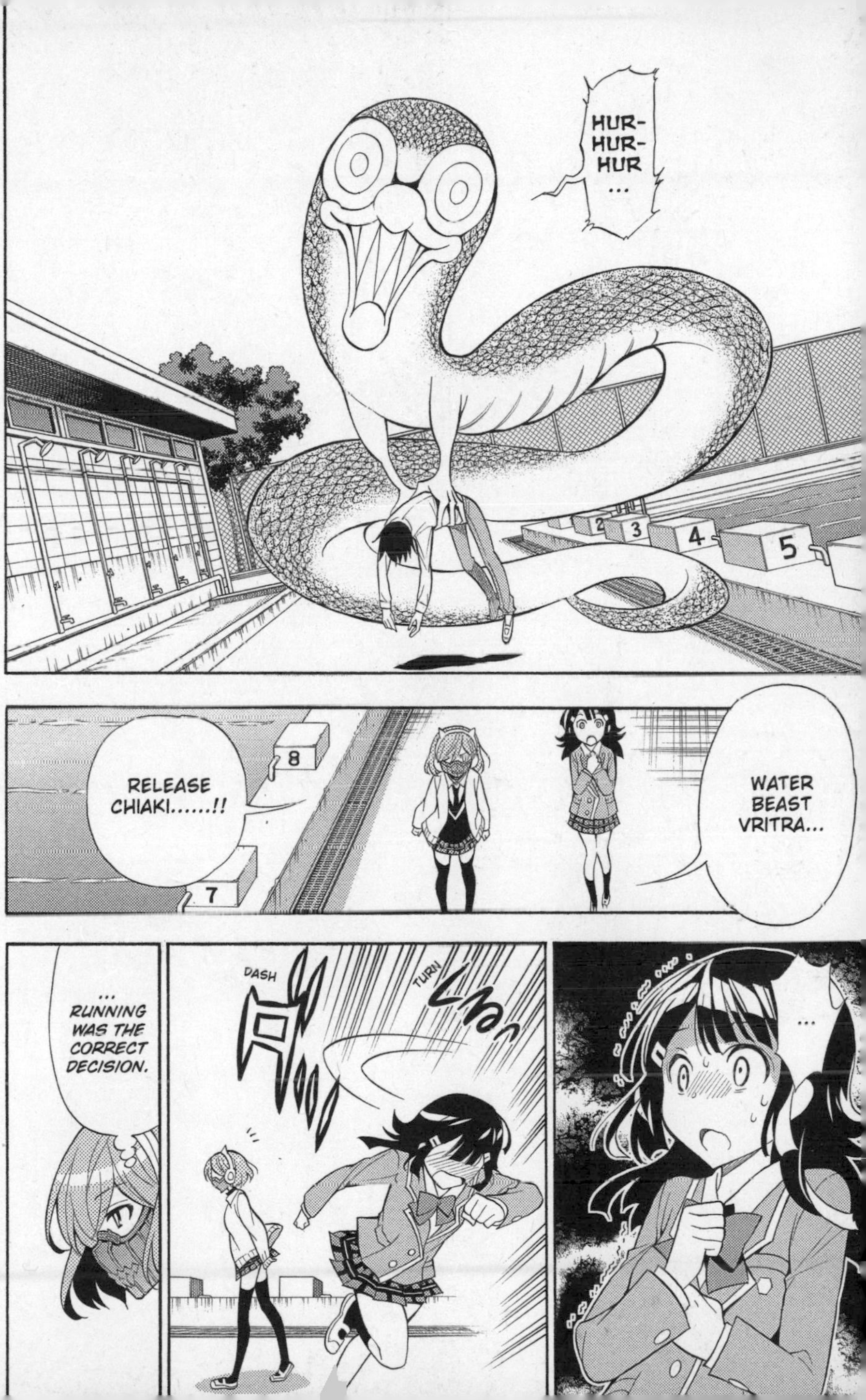
HUR-HUR-HUR...
WATER BEAST VRITRA...
RELEASE CHIAKI......!!
...
TURN
DASH
... RUNNING WAS THE CORRECT DECISION.

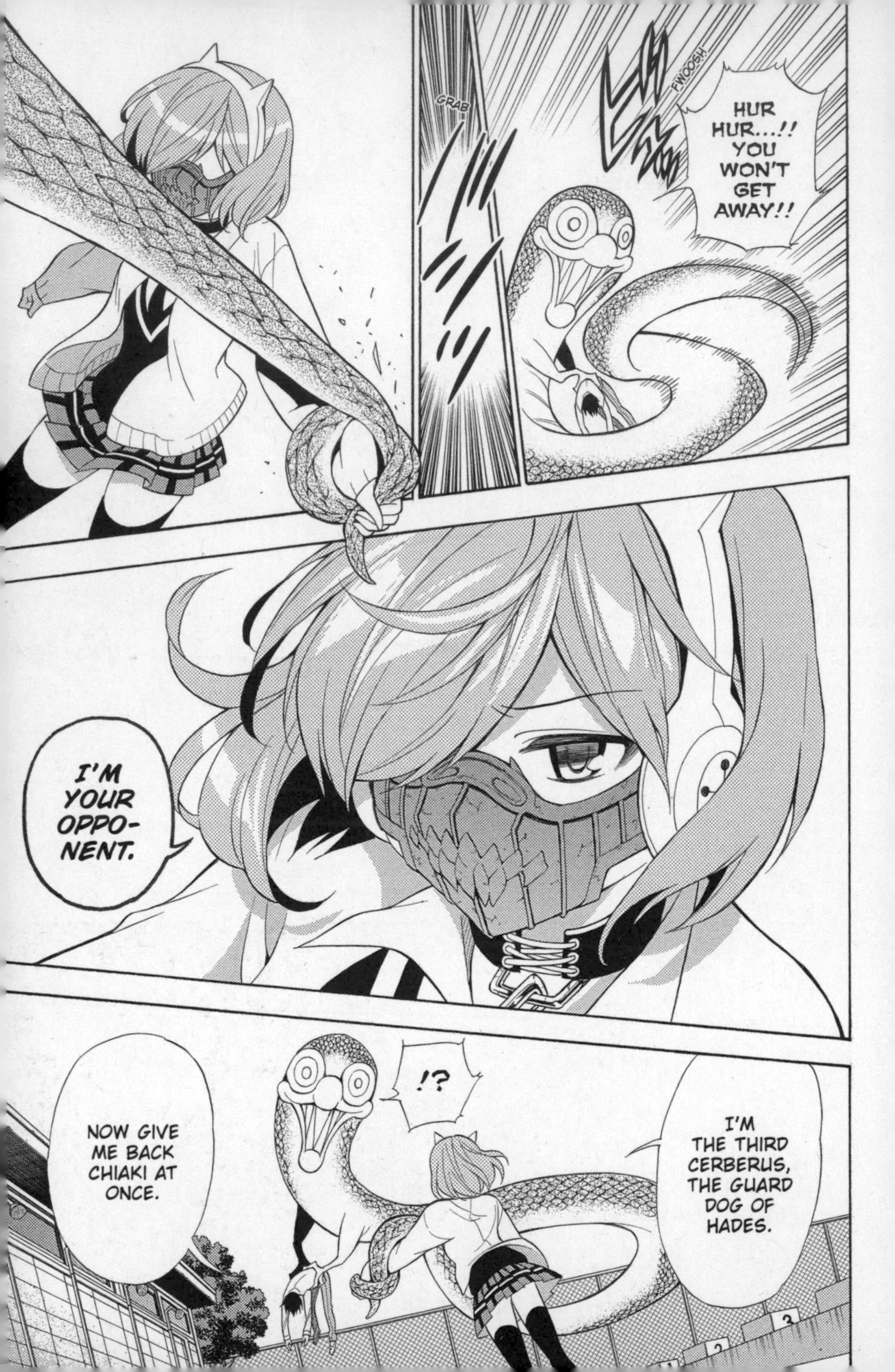
FWOOSH
HUR HUR...!! YOU WON'T GET AWAY!!
GRAB
I'M YOUR OPPO-NENT.
I'M THE THIRD CERBERUS, THE GUARD DOG OF HADES.
!?
NOW GIVE ME BACK CHIAKI AT ONCE.

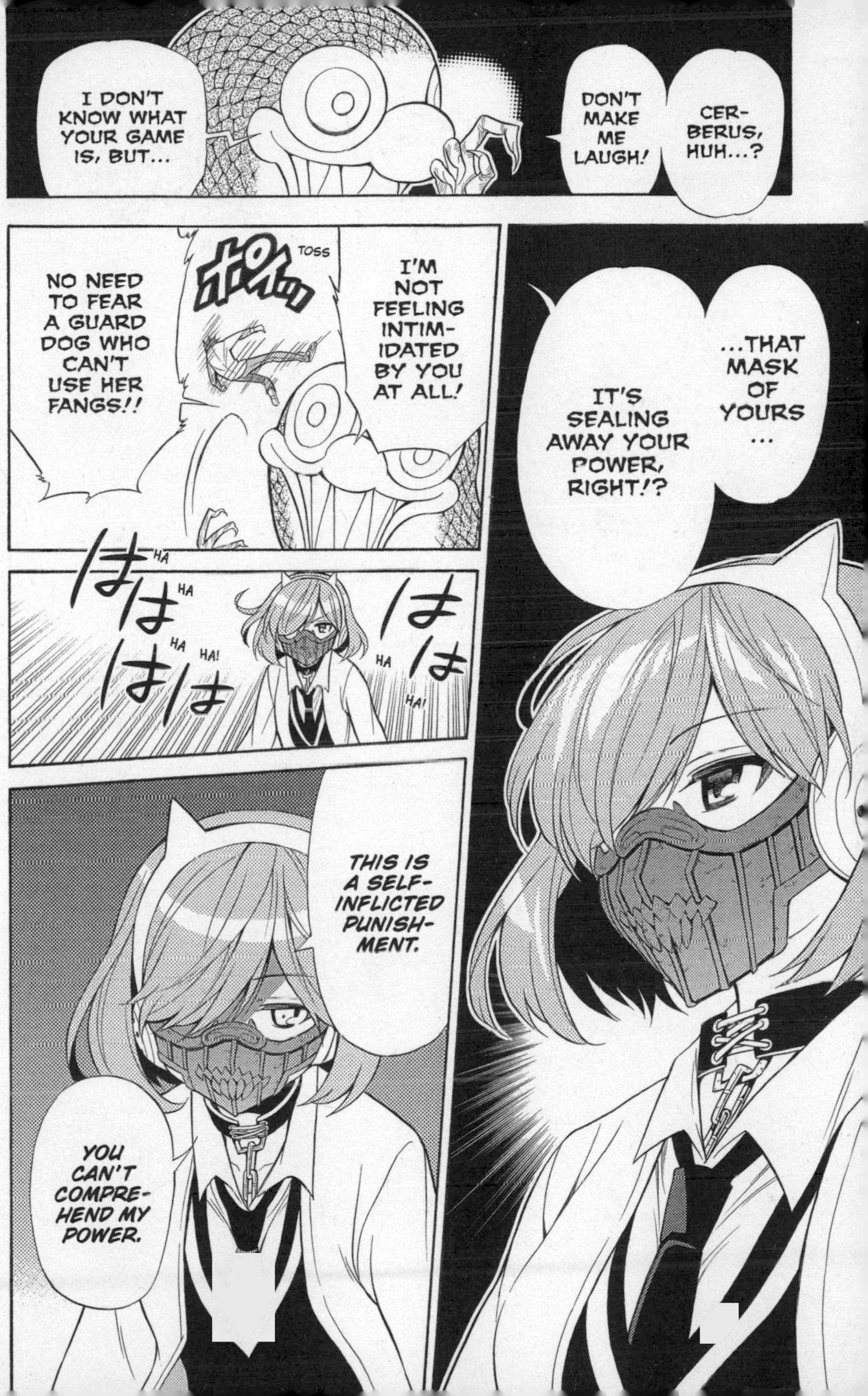
CER-BERUS, HUH...?
DON'T MAKE ME LAUGH!
I DON'T KNOW WHAT YOUR GAME IS, BUT...
...THAT MASK OF YOURS...
IT'S SEALING AWAY YOUR POWER, RIGHT!?
I'M NOT FEELING INTIM-IDATED BY YOU AT ALL!
ポイッ TOSS
NO NEED TO FEAR A GUARD DOG WHO CAN'T USE HER FANGS!!
はは HA HA!
はははは HA HA HA HA!
THIS IS A SELF-INFLICTED PUNISH-MENT.
YOU CAN'T COMPRE-HEND MY POWER.

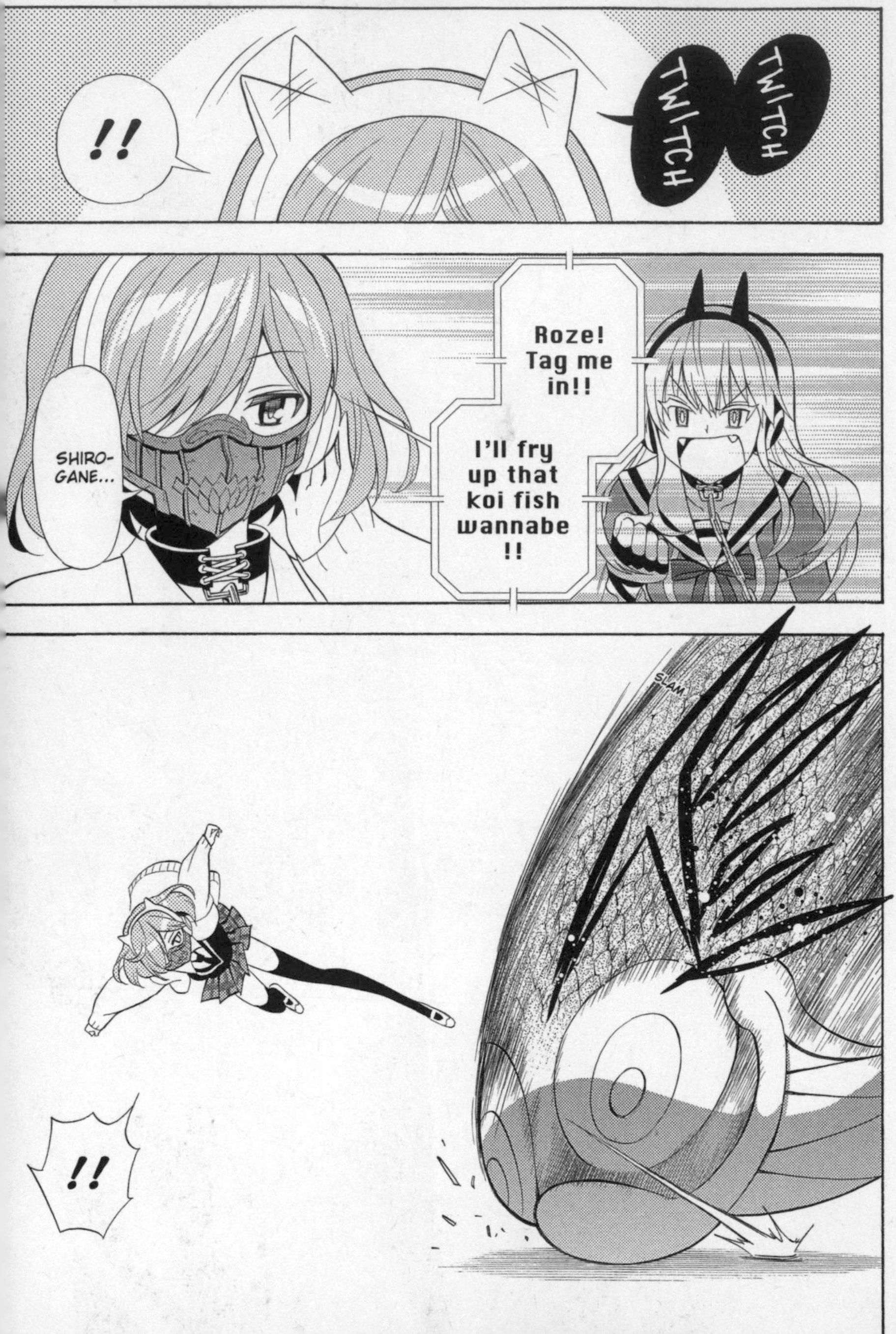
TWITCH TWITCH
!!
Roze! Tag me in!!
I'll fry up that koi fish wannabe !!
SHIRO-GANE...
SLAM
!!

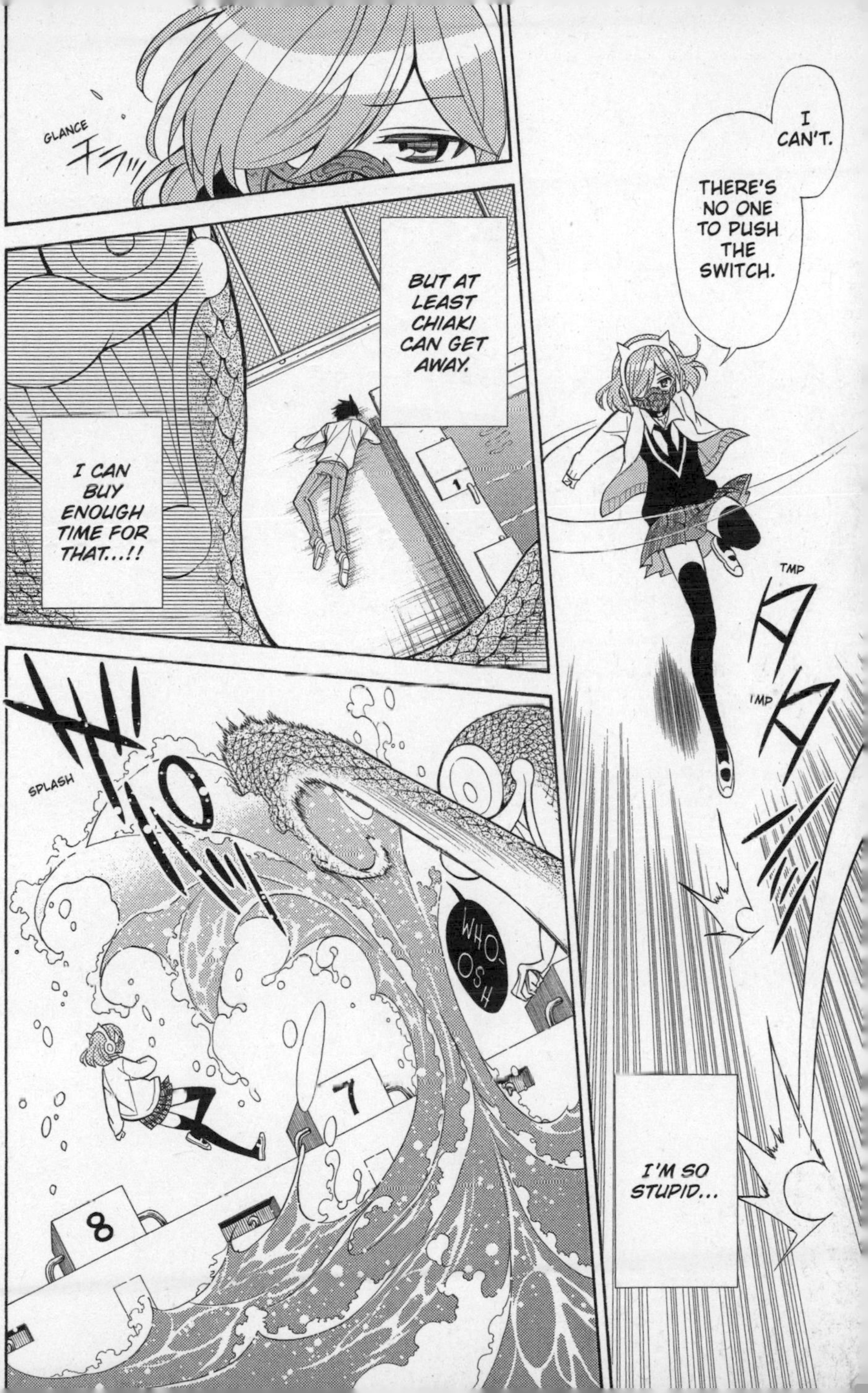
I CAN'T.
THERE'S NO ONE TO PUSH THE SWITCH.
TMP
TMP
I'M SO STUPID...
GLANCE
BUT AT LEAST CHIAKI CAN GET AWAY.
I CAN BUY ENOUGH TIME FOR THAT...!!
SPLASH
WHO-OSH

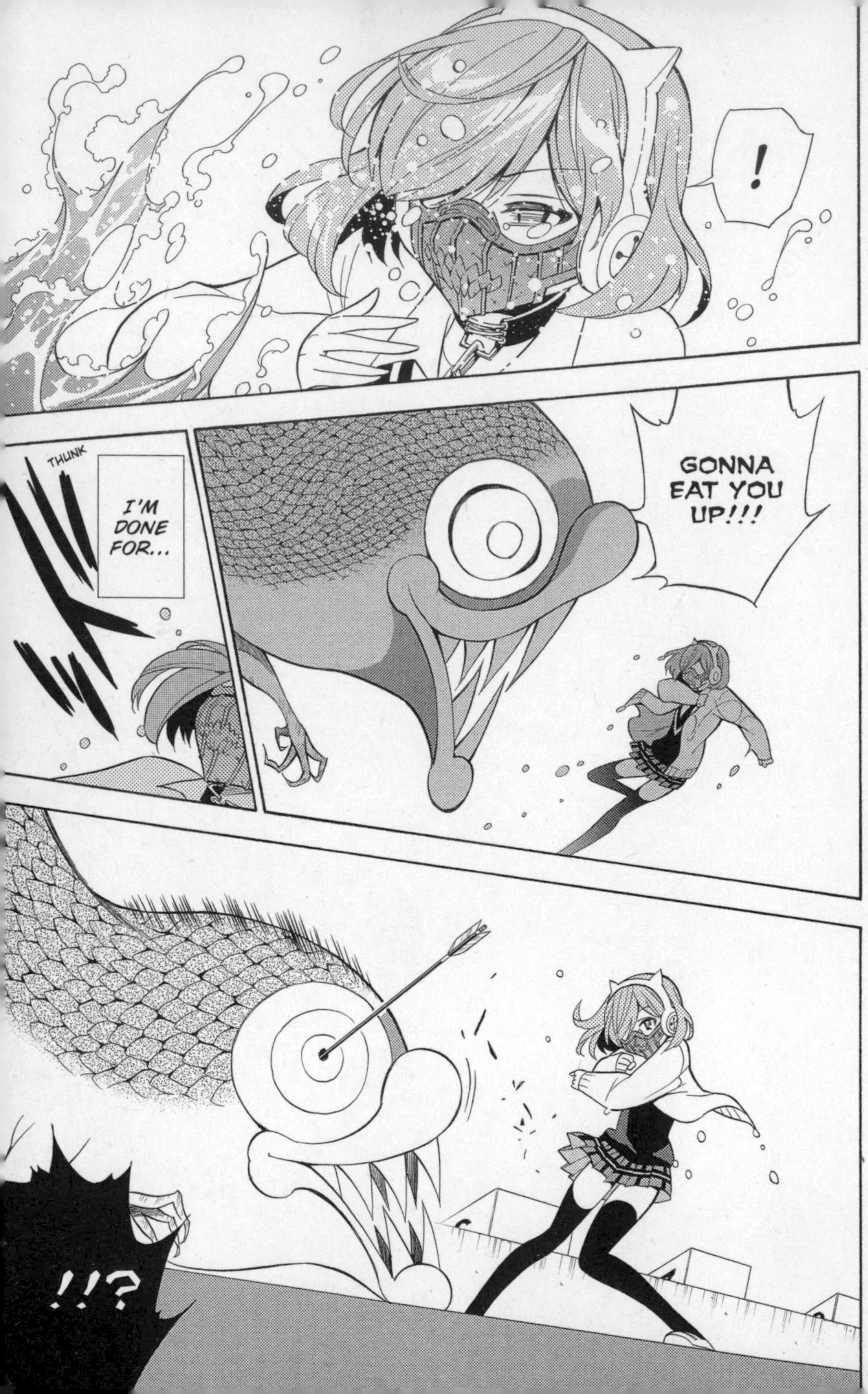
!
GONNA EAT YOU UP!!!
I'M DONE FOR...
THUNK
!!?

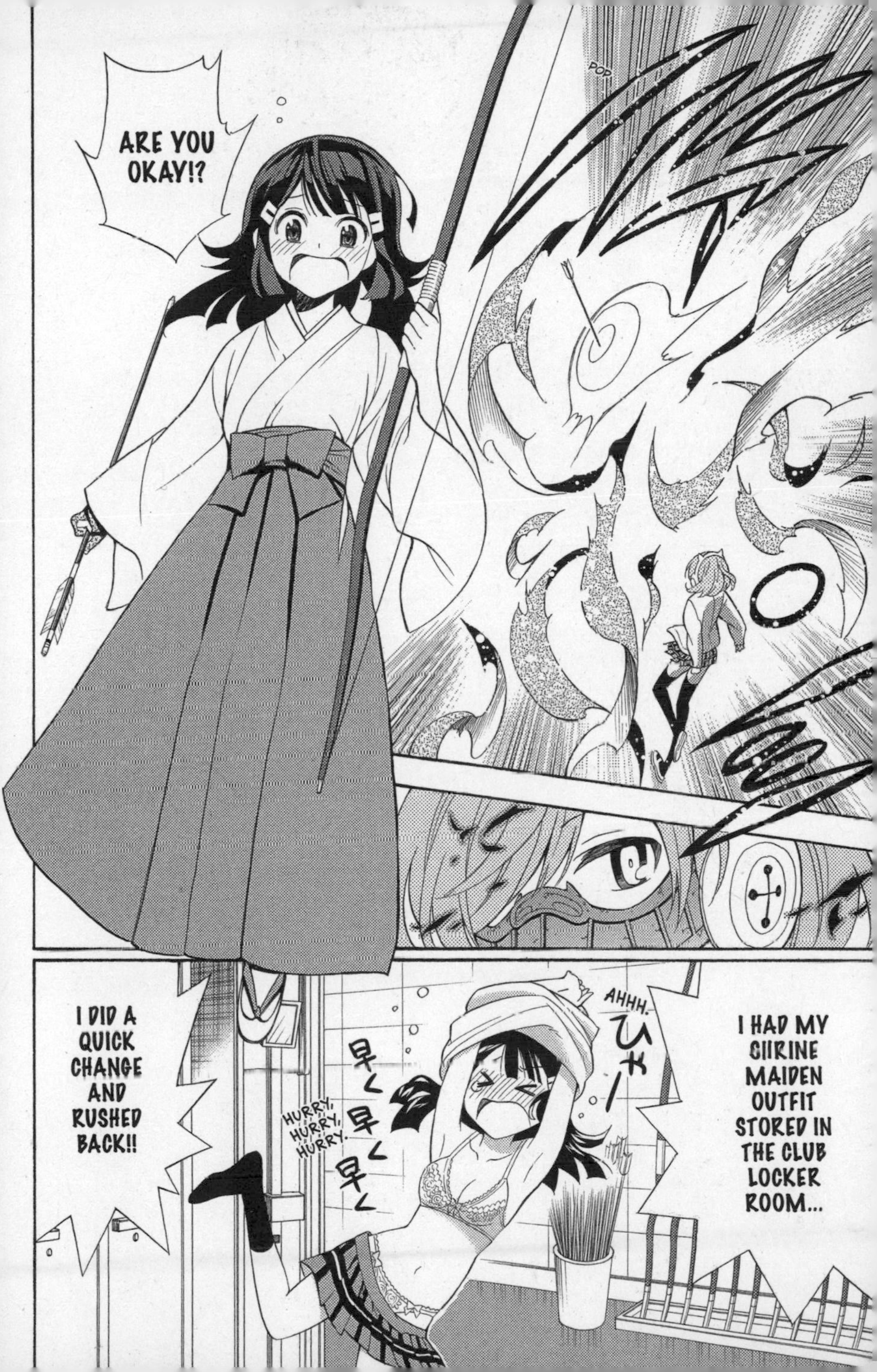
POP
ARE YOU OKAY!?
I HAD MY SHRINE MAIDEN OUTFIT STORED IN THE CLUB LOCKER ROOM...
ひゃー
AHHH.
早く早く早く
HURRY, HURRY, HURRY.
I DID A QUICK CHANGE AND RUSHED BACK!!

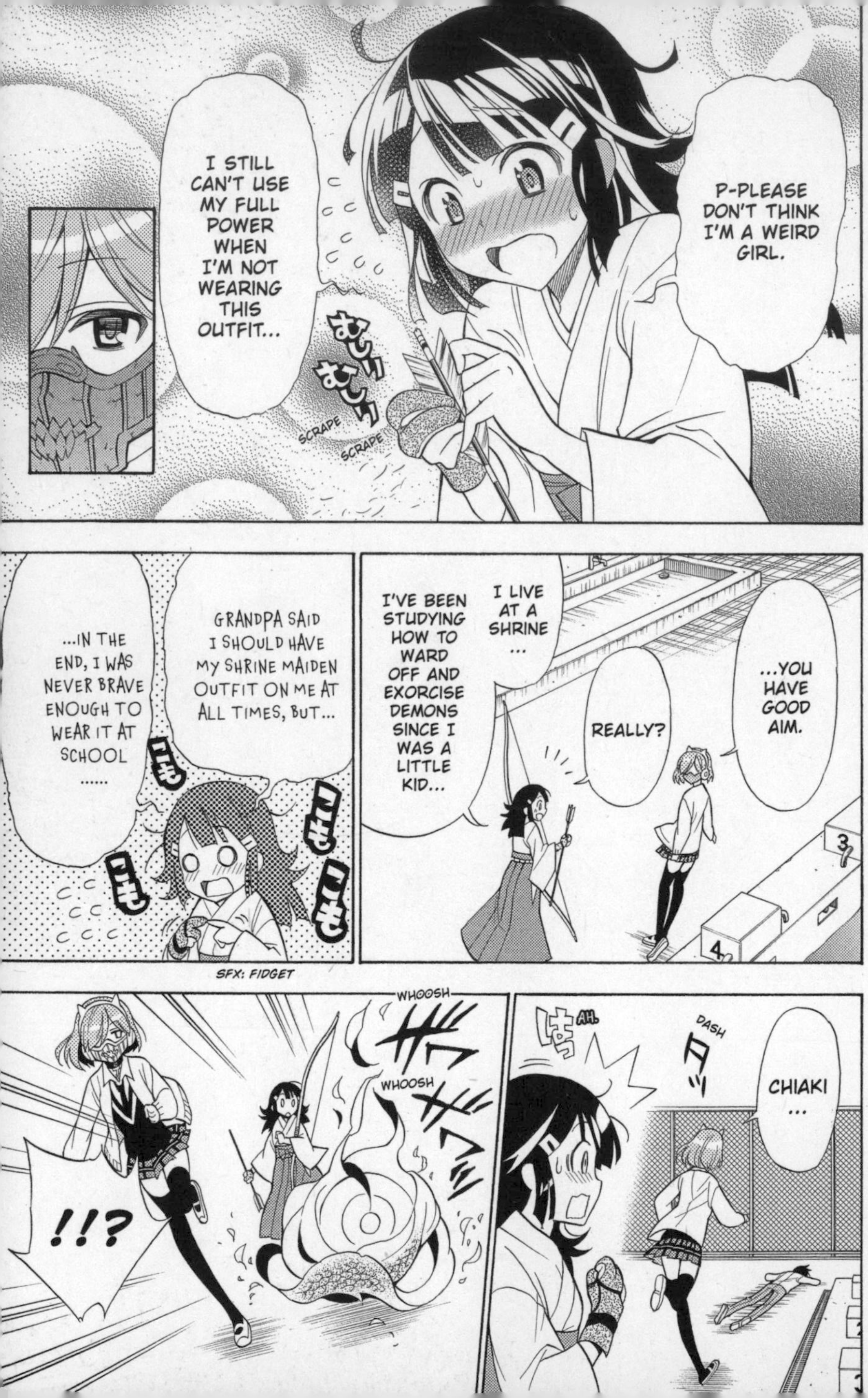
P-PLEASE DON'T THINK I'M A WEIRD GIRL.
I STILL CAN'T USE MY FULL POWER WHEN I'M NOT WEARING THIS OUTFIT...
SCRAPE
SCRAPE
...YOU HAVE GOOD AIM.
REALLY?
I LIVE AT A SHRINE ...
I'VE BEEN STUDYING HOW TO WARD OFF AND EXORCISE DEMONS SINCE I WAS A LITTLE KID...
GRANDPA SAID I SHOULD HAVE MY SHRINE MAIDEN OUTFIT ON ME AT ALL TIMES, BUT...
...IN THE END, I WAS NEVER BRAVE ENOUGH TO WEAR IT AT SCHOOL ......
SFX: FIDGET
CHIAKI ...
DASH
AH.
WHOOSH
WHOOSH
!!?

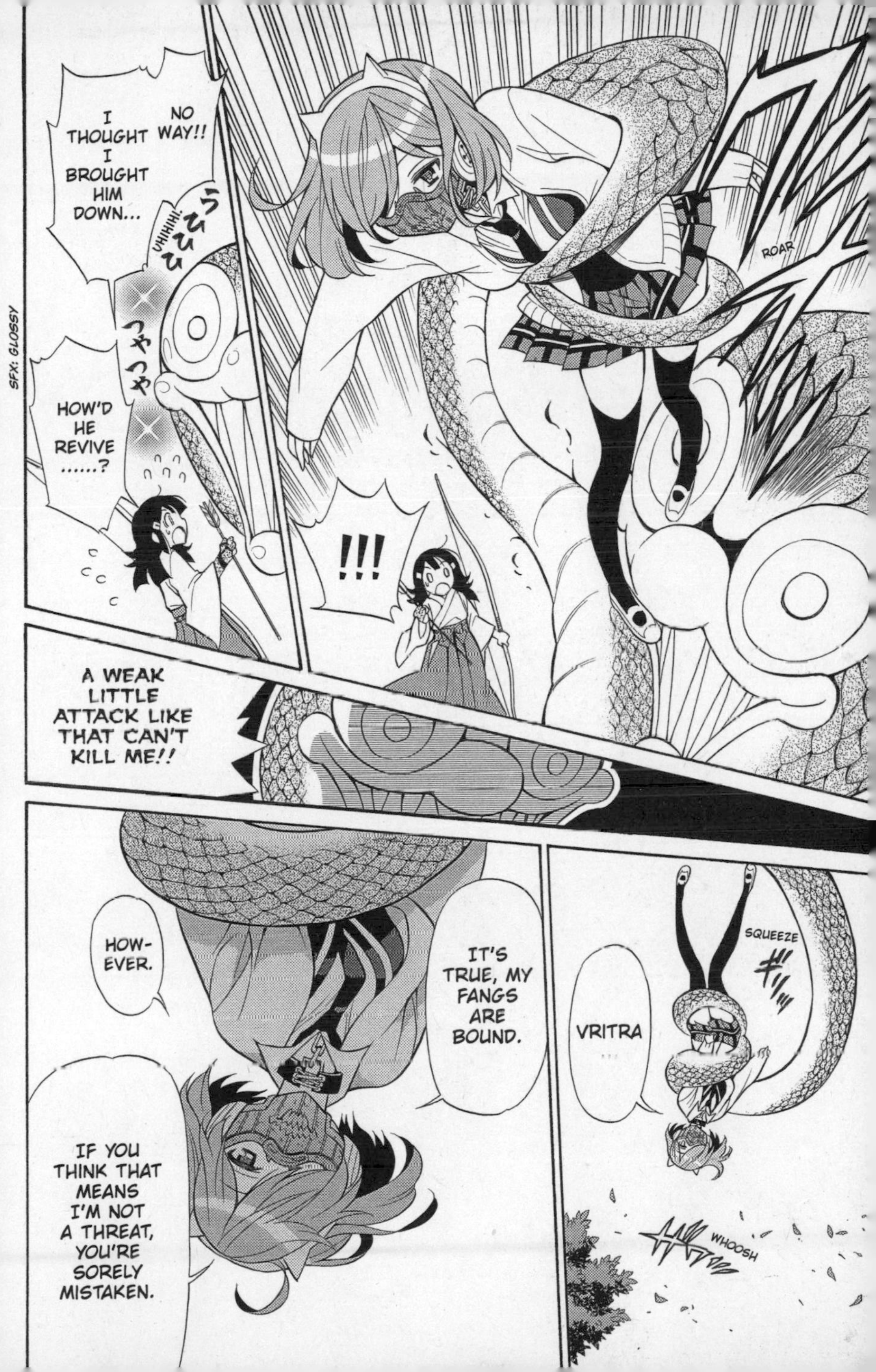
ROAR
NO WAY!!
I THOUGHT I BROUGHT HIM DOWN...
UHIHIHI
SFX: GLOSSY
HOW'D HE REVIVE ......?
!!!
A WEAK LITTLE ATTACK LIKE THAT CAN'T KILL ME!!
SQUEEZE
VRITRA ...
WHOOSH
IT'S TRUE, MY FANGS ARE BOUND.
HOW-EVER.
IF YOU THINK THAT MEANS I'M NOT A THREAT, YOU'RE SORELY MISTAKEN.

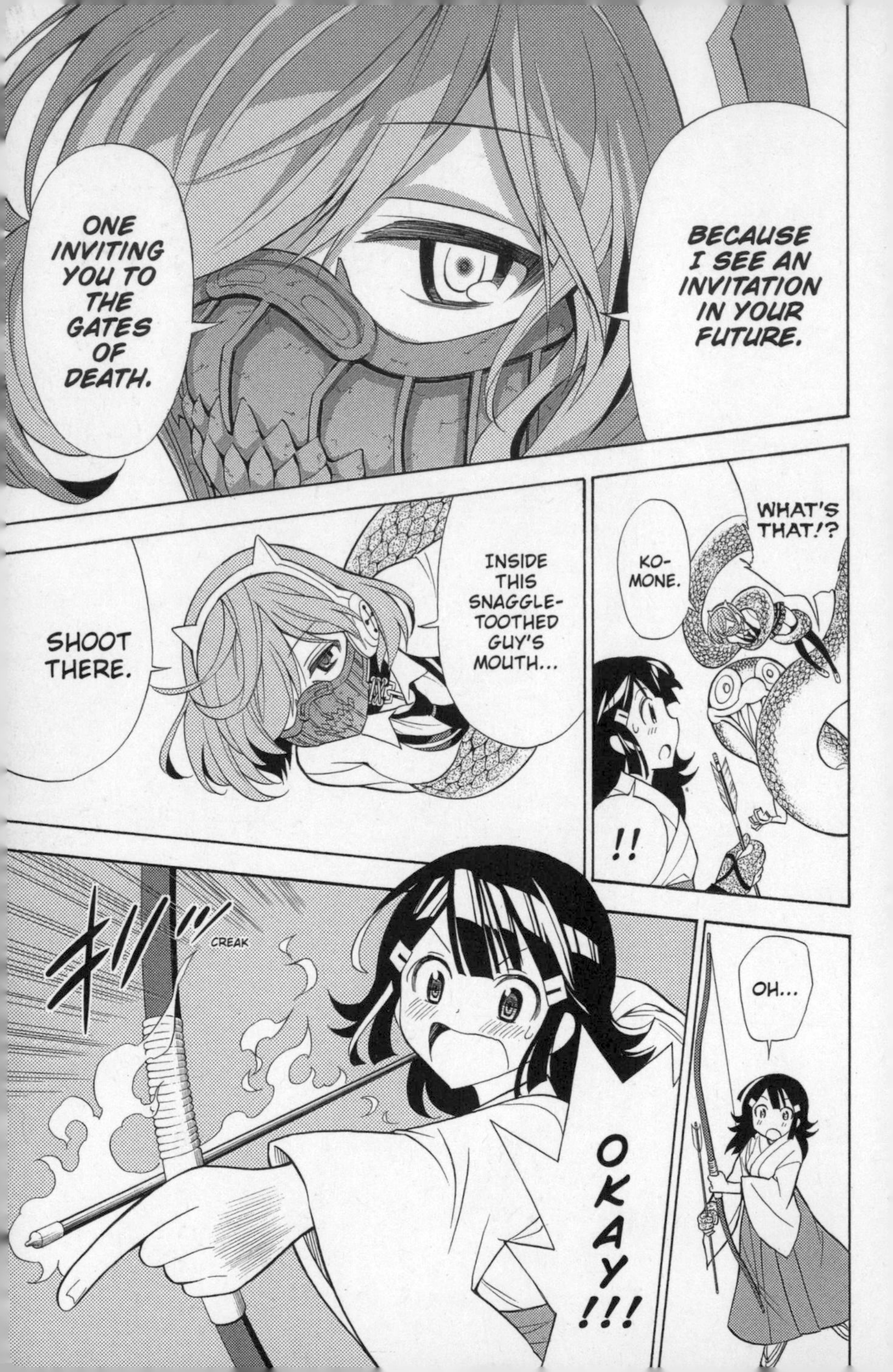
BECAUSE I SEE AN INVITATION IN YOUR FUTURE.
ONE INVITING YOU TO THE GATES OF DEATH.
WHAT'S THAT!?
KO-MONE.
!!
INSIDE THIS SNAGGLE-TOOTHED GUY'S MOUTH...
SHOOT THERE.
OH...
OKAY!!!
CREAK

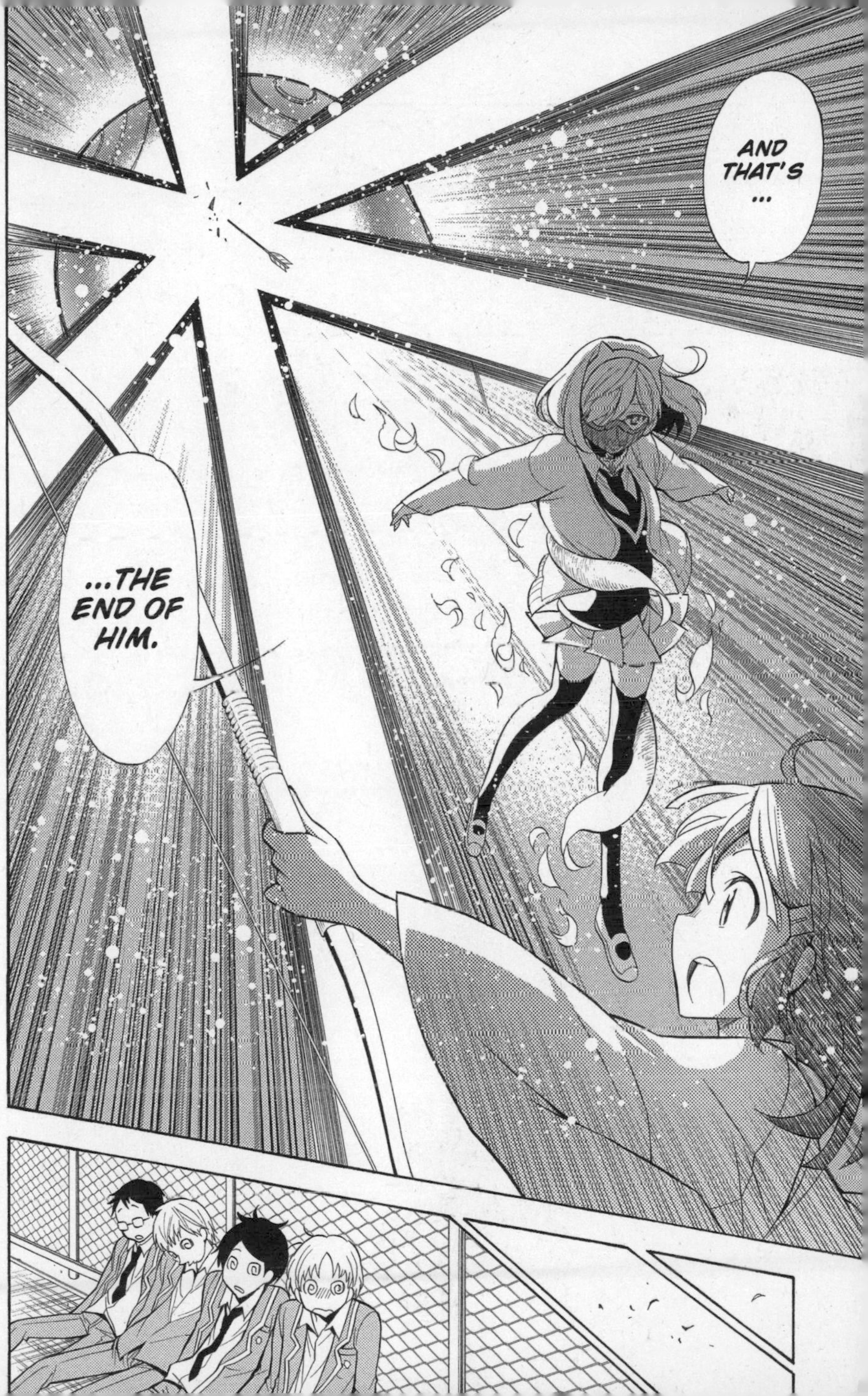
AND THAT'S ...
...THE END OF HIM.

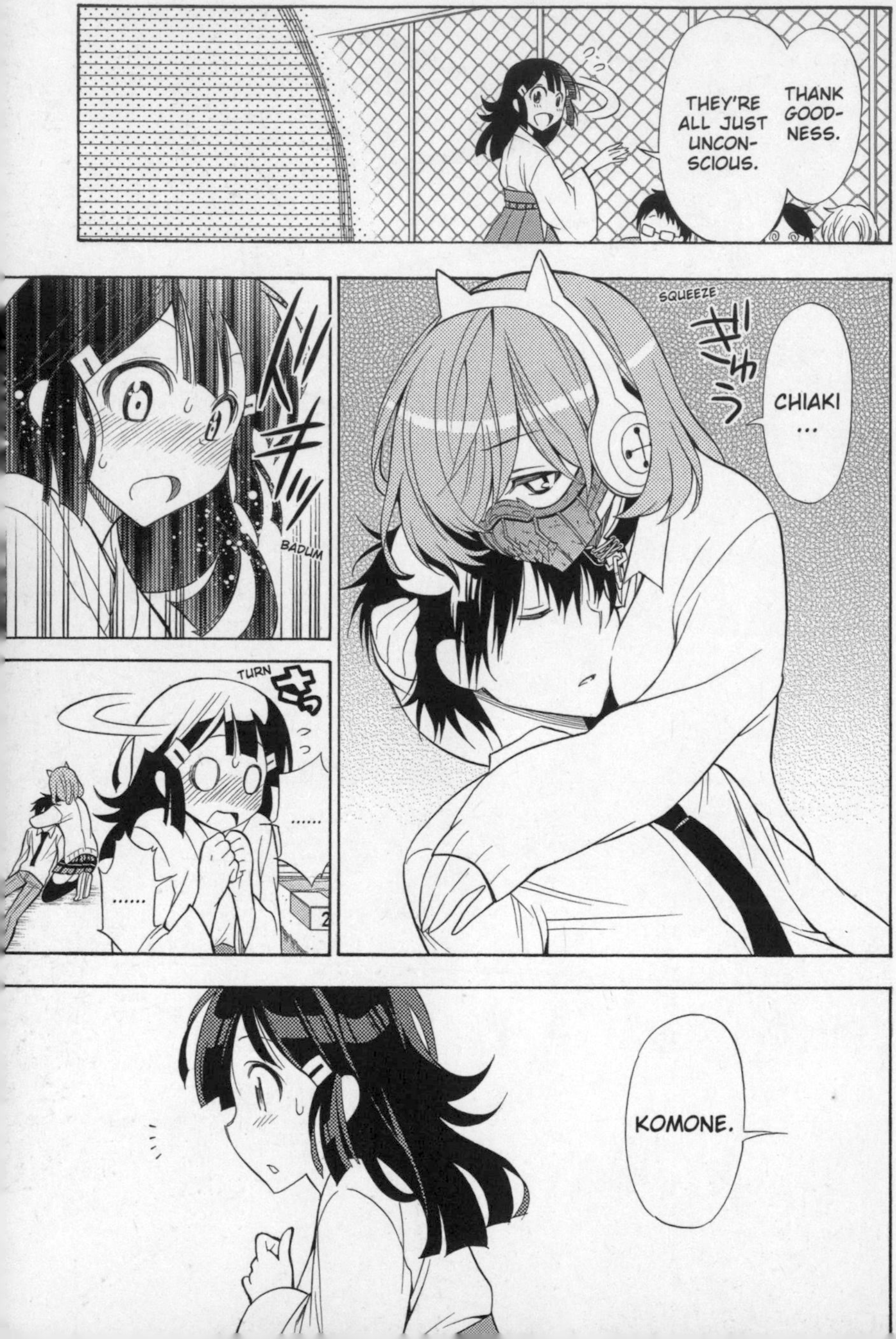
THANK GOODNESS.
THEY'RE ALL JUST UNCONSCIOUS.
SQUEEZE
CHIAKI...
BADUM
TURN
......
......
KOMONE.

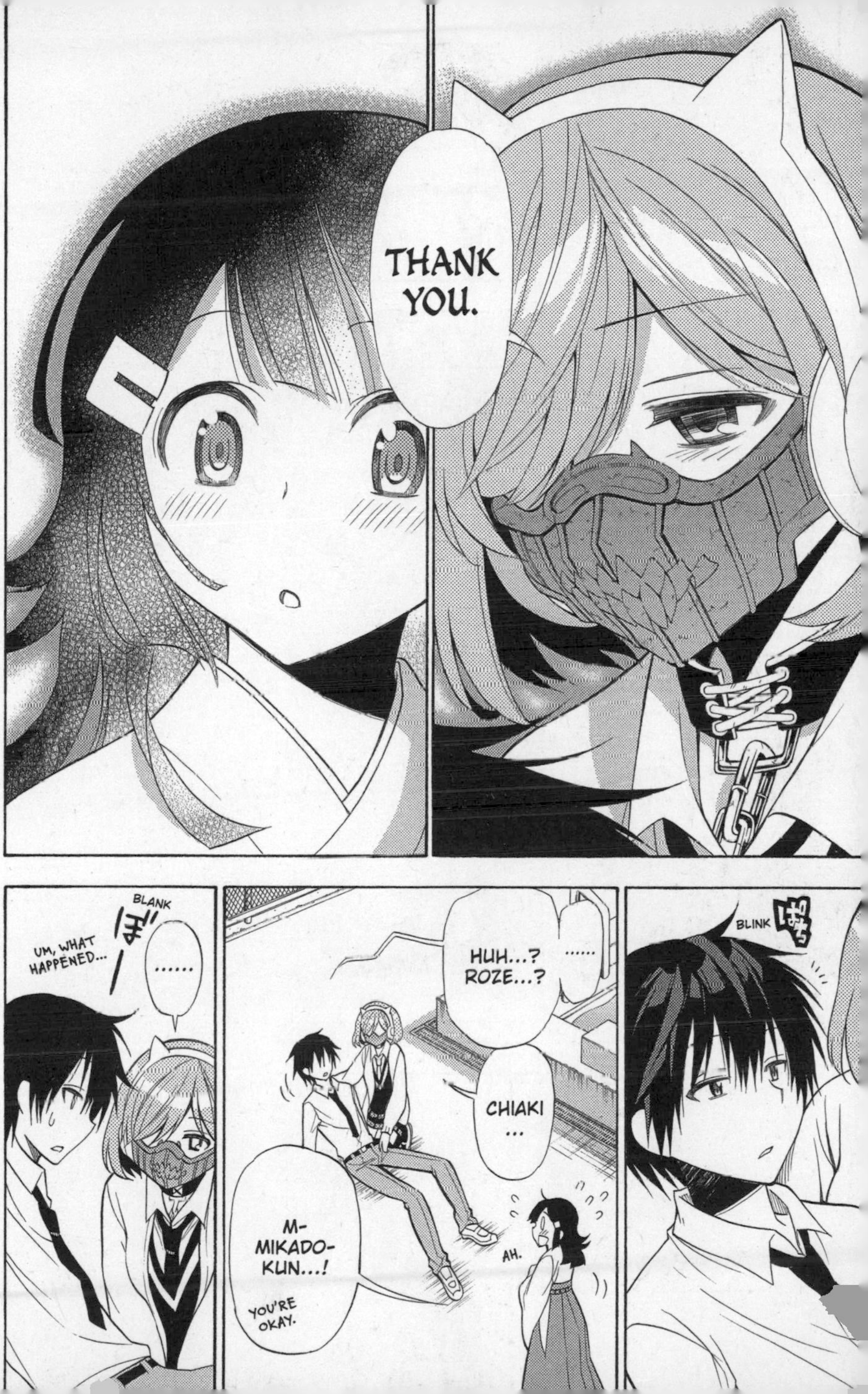
THANK YOU.
BLINK
......
HUH...? ROZE...?
CHIAKI ...
AH.
M-MIKADO-KUN...!
YOU'RE OKAY.
......
BLANK
UM, WHAT HAPPENED...

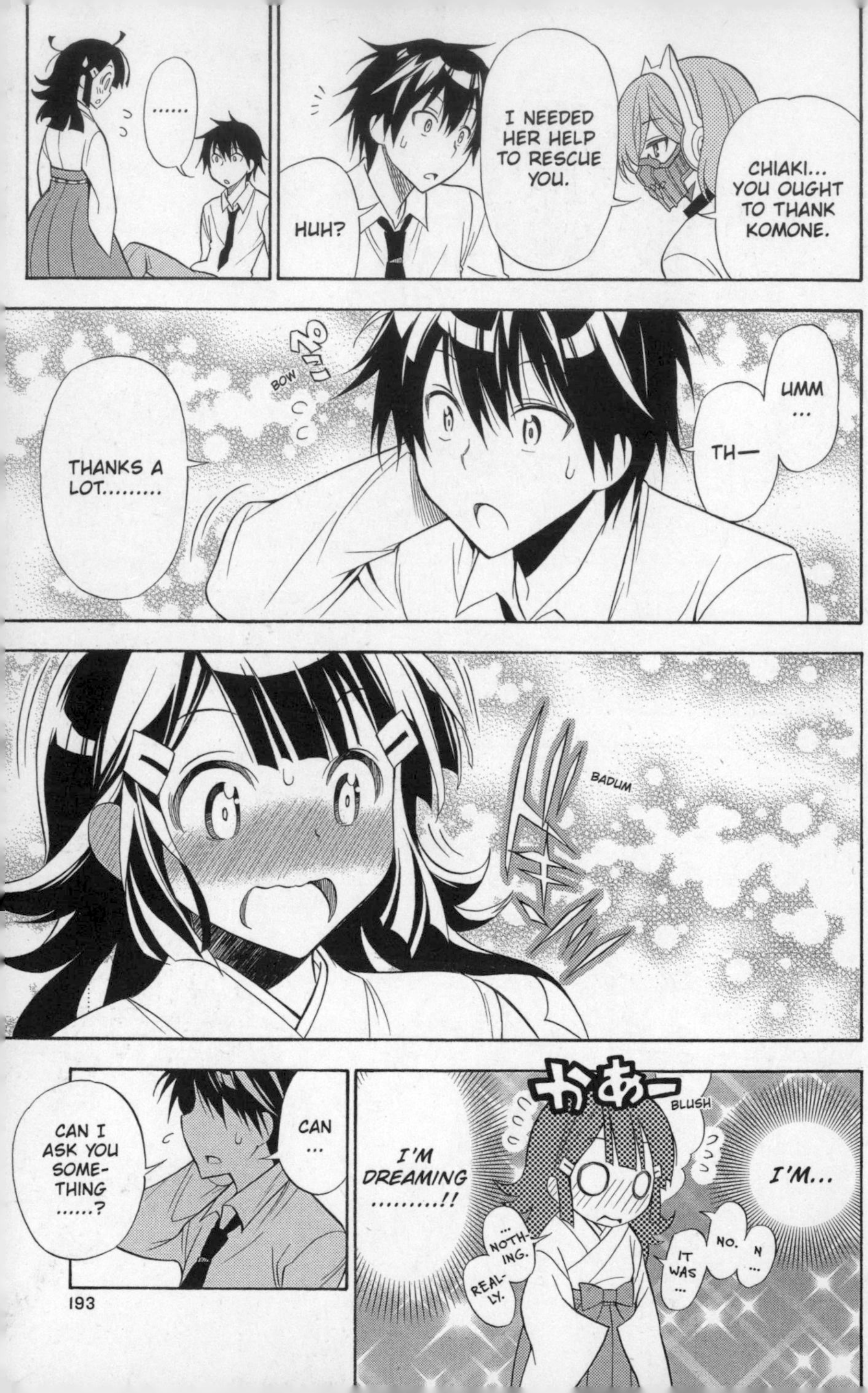
CHIAKI... YOU OUGHT TO THANK KOMONE.
I NEEDED HER HELP TO RESCUE YOU.
HUH?
......
UMM ...
TH—
BOW
THANKS A LOT.........
BADUM
I'M...
NO. N ...
IT WAS ...
... NOTHING. REALLY.
I'M DREAMING ....!!
かあー
BLUSH
CAN ...
CAN I ASK YOU SOMETHING ......?

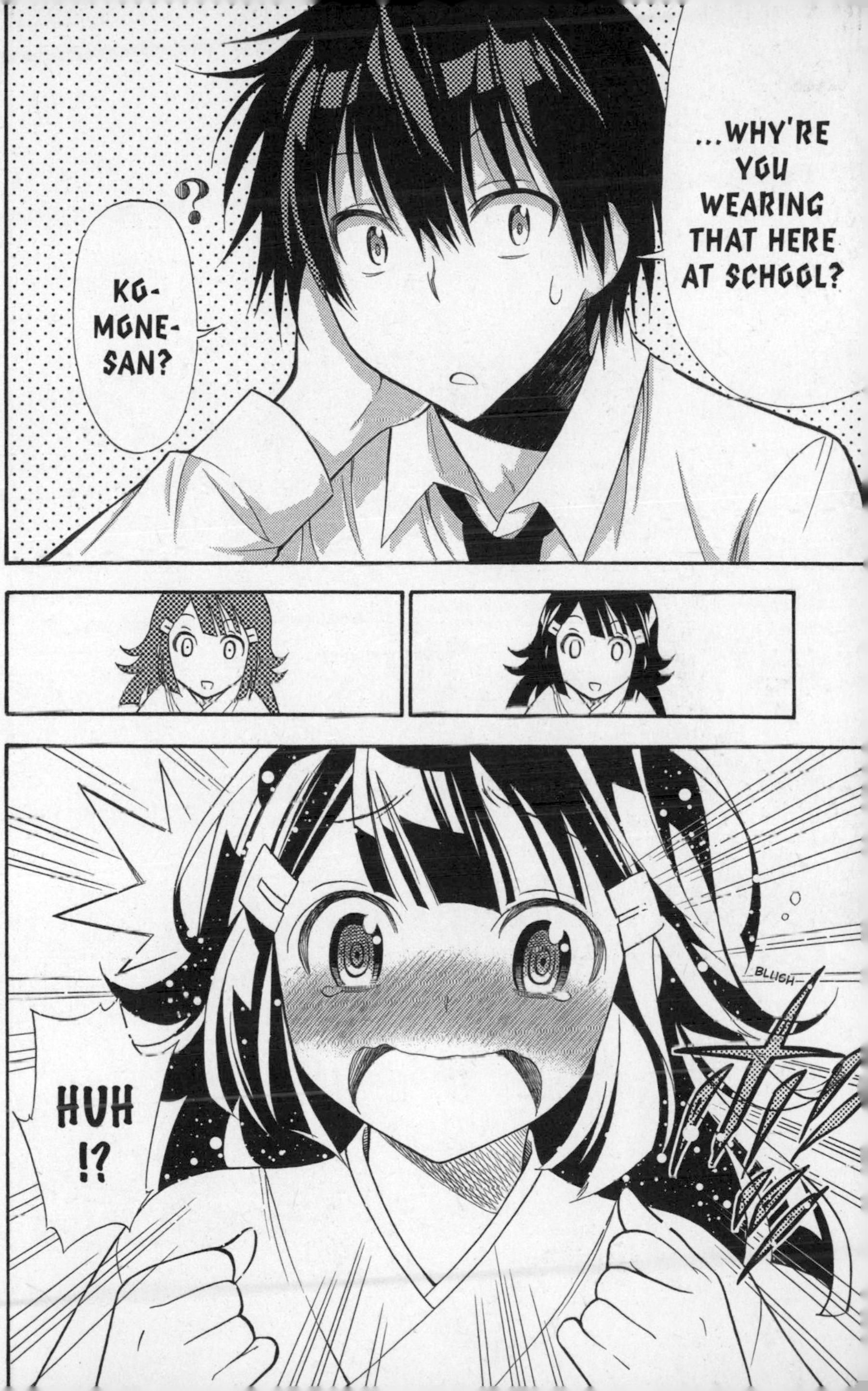
...WHY'RE YOU WEARING THAT HERE AT SCHOOL?
KO-MONE-SAN?
BLUSH
HUH!?

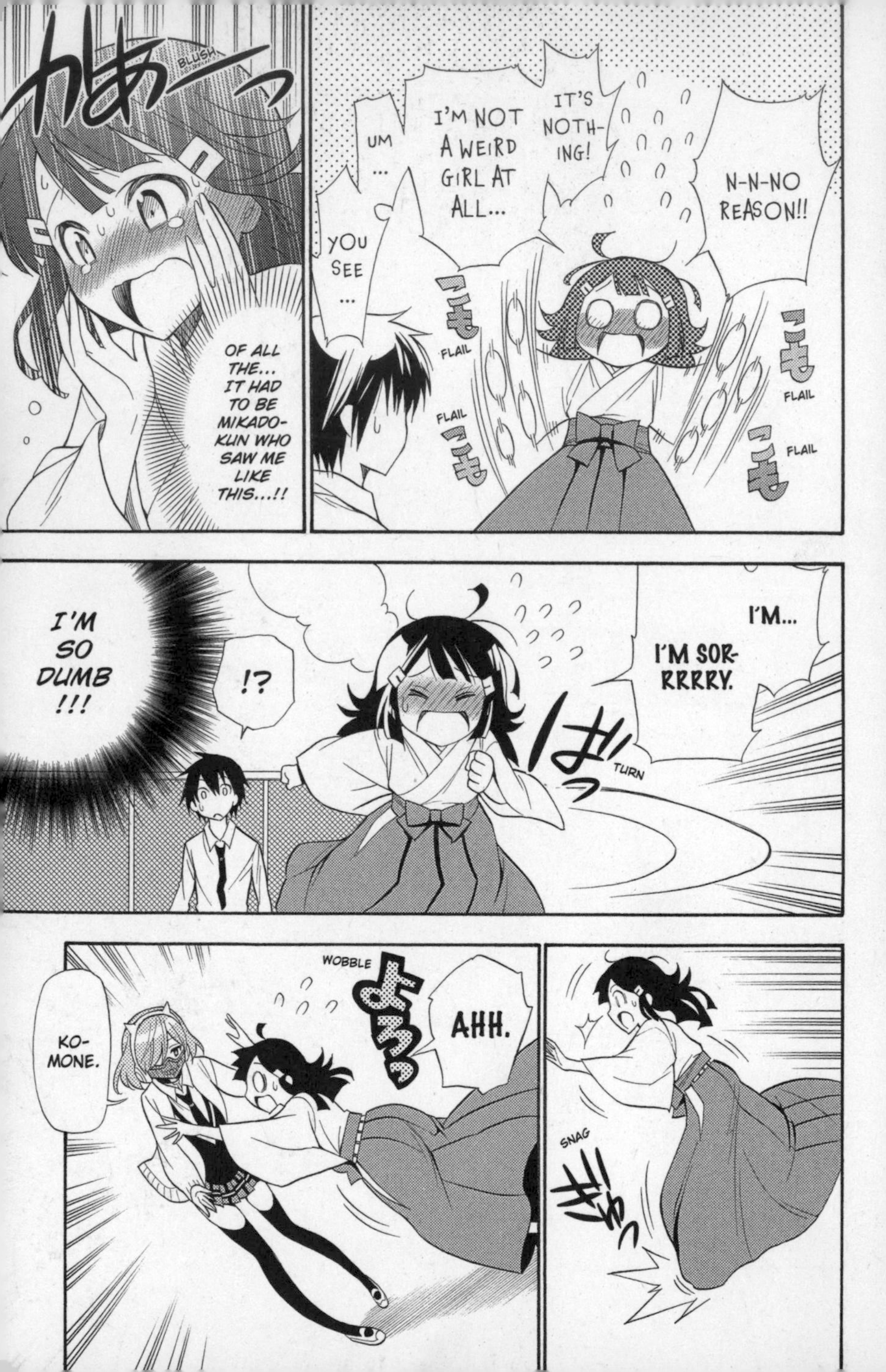

UM ... YOU SEE ...
I'M NOT A WEIRD GIRL AT ALL...
IT'S NOTH-ING!
N-N-NO REASON!!
FLAIL
FLAIL
FLAIL
FLAIL
BLUSH
OF ALL THE... IT HAD TO BE MIKADO-KUN WHO SAW ME LIKE THIS...!!
I'M...
I'M SOR-RRRRY.
TURN
!?
I'M SO DUMB!!!
SNAG
WOBBLE
AHH.
KO-MONE.

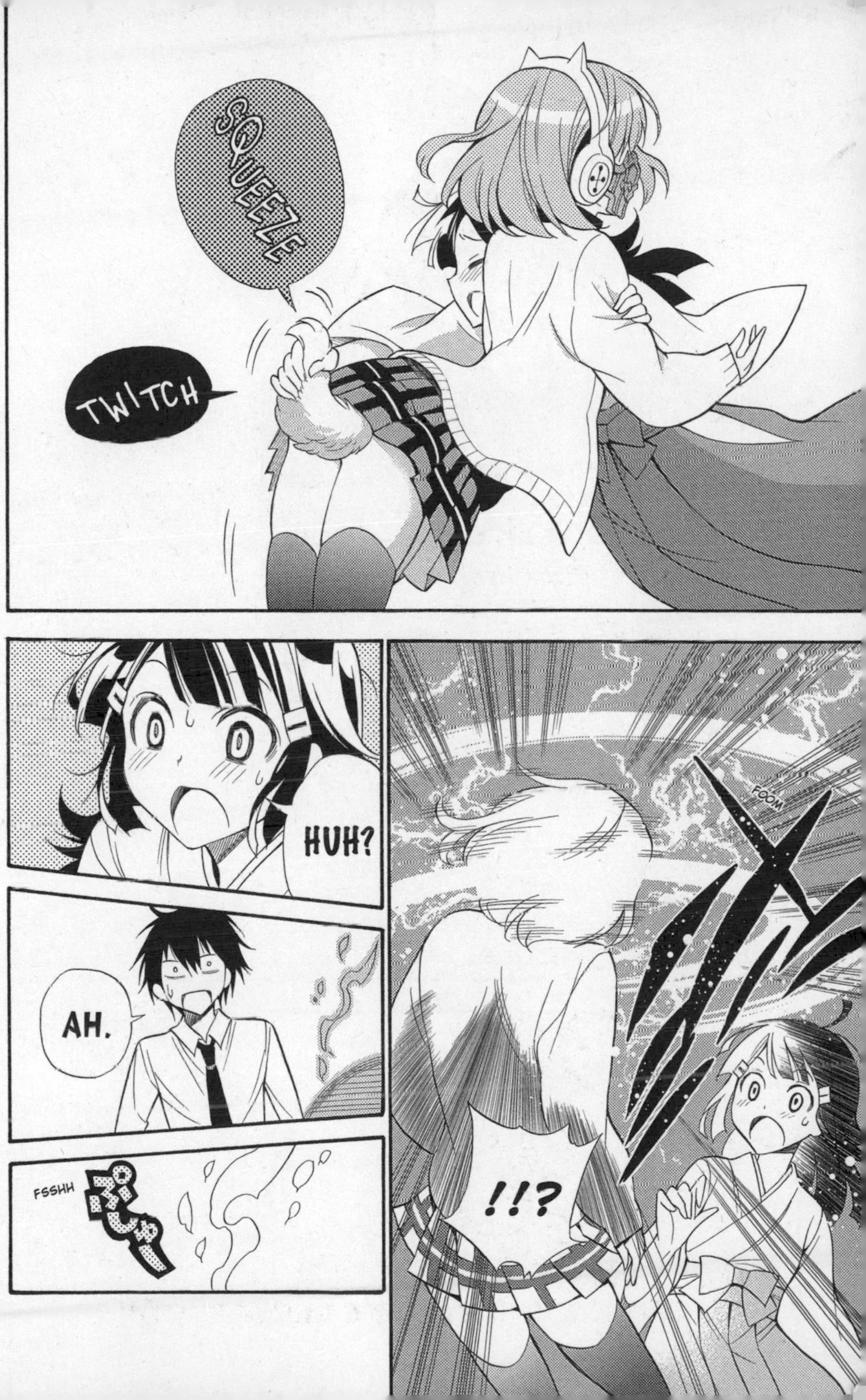
SQUEEZE
TWITCH
FOOM
!!?
HUH?
AH.
FSSHH

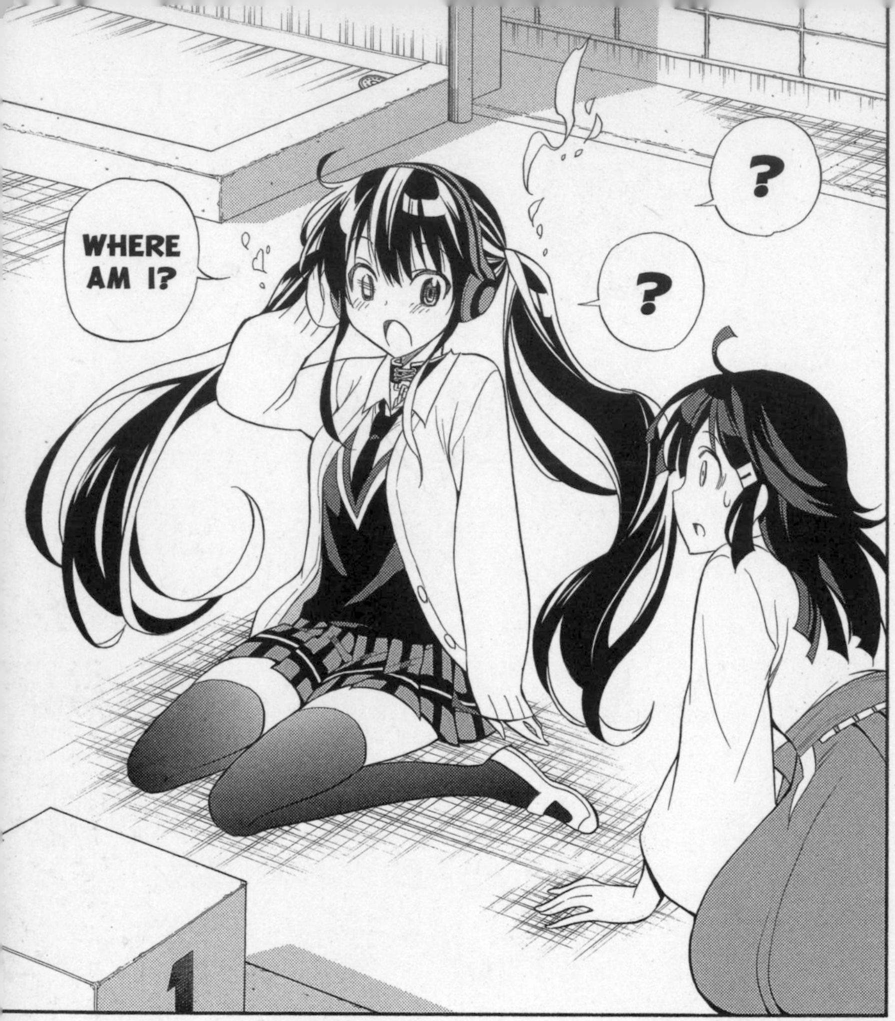
?
?
WHERE AM I?

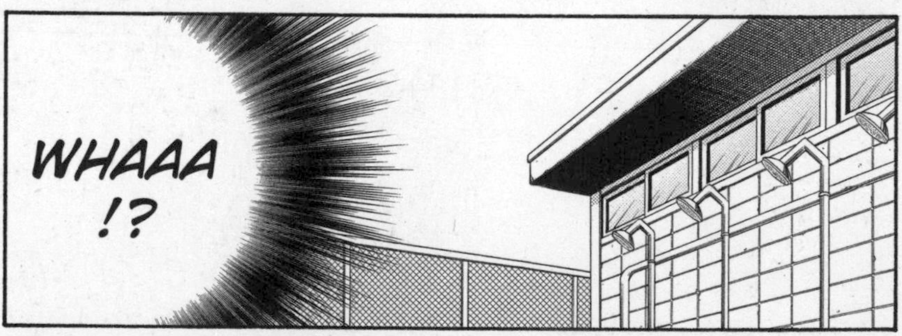
WHAAA !?

TO BE CONTINUED IN **TODAY'S CERBERUS ②**!

TODAY'S CERBERUS

MENTAL
IMAGE

KOMONE A FEW
HOURS LATER

MIKADO-KUN
CALLED ME BY
MY NAME... ♥

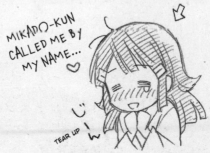

TEAR UP

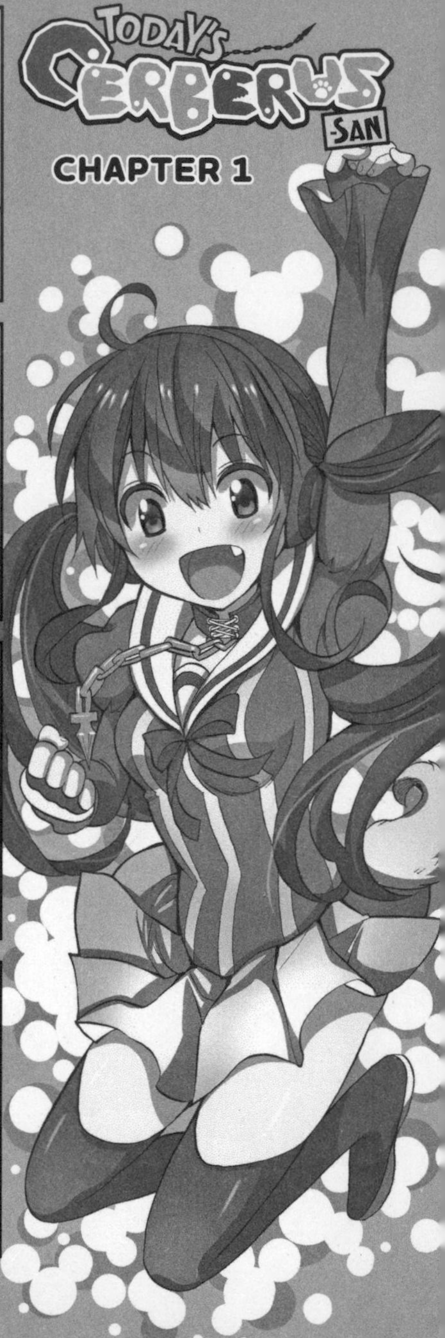
TODAY'S CERBERUS -SAN
CHAPTER 1

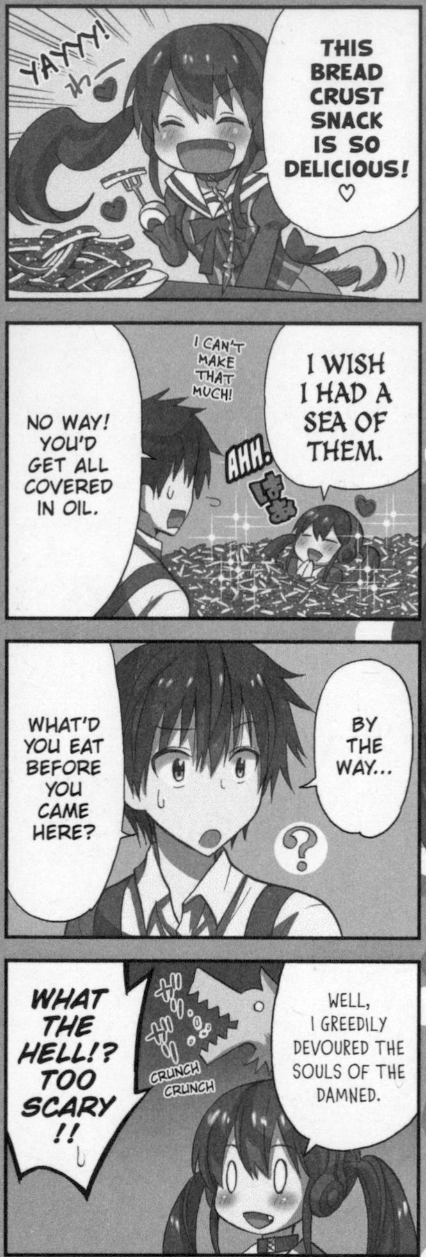
THIS BREAD CRUST SNACK IS SO DELICIOUS! ♡
YAYYY!
I WISH I HAD A SEA OF THEM.
I CAN'T MAKE THAT MUCH!
AHH.
NO WAY! YOU'D GET ALL COVERED IN OIL.
BY THE WAY...
WHAT'D YOU EAT BEFORE YOU CAME HERE?
WELL, I GREEDILY DEVOURED THE SOULS OF THE DAMNED.
CRUNCH CRUNCH
WHAT THE HELL!? TOO SCARY!!

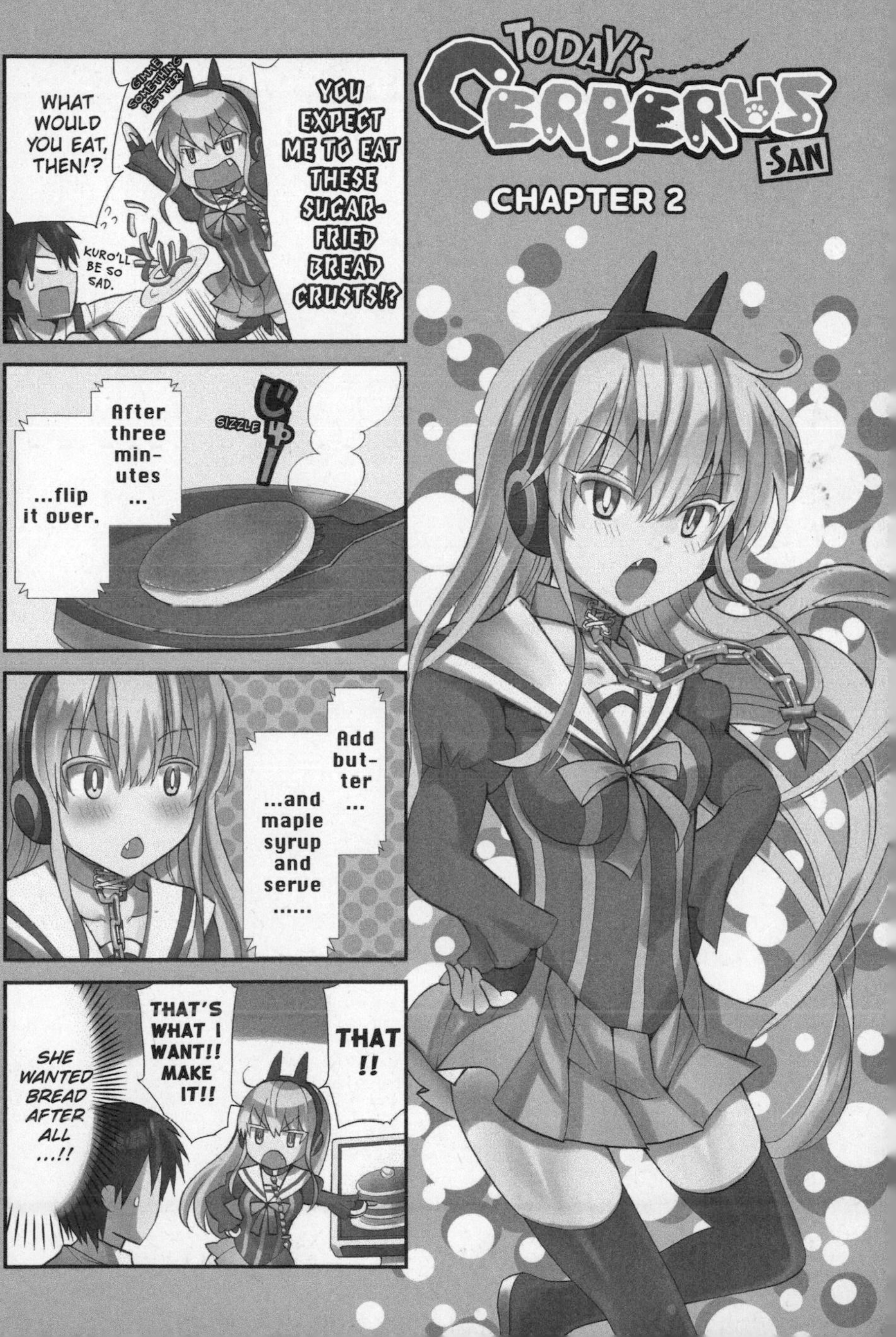
TODAY'S CERBERUS -SAN
CHAPTER 2
YOU EXPECT ME TO EAT THESE SUGAR-FRIED BREAD CRUSTS!?
GIMME SOMETHING BETTER!
WHAT WOULD YOU EAT, THEN!?
KURO'LL BE SO SAD.
After three min-utes ...
...flip it over.
SIZZLE
Add but-ter ...
...and maple syrup and serve ......
THAT !!
THAT'S WHAT I WANT!! MAKE IT!!
SHE WANTED BREAD AFTER ALL ...!!

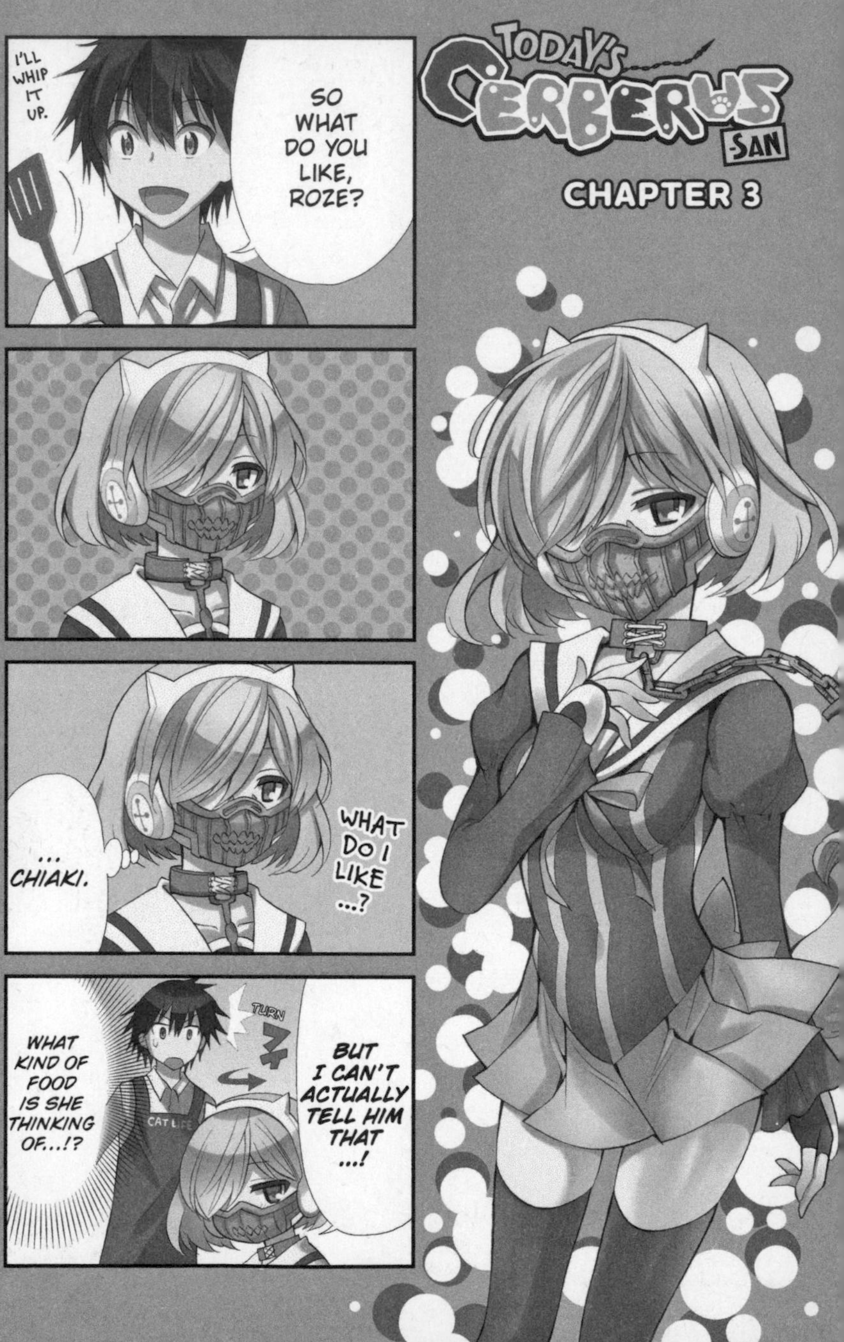
TODAY'S CERBERUS -SAN
CHAPTER 3
SO WHAT DO YOU LIKE, ROZE?
I'LL WHIP IT UP.
WHAT DO I LIKE ...?
... CHIAKI.
BUT I CAN'T ACTUALLY TELL HIM THAT ...!
TURN
WHAT KIND OF FOOD IS SHE THINKING OF...!?
CAT LIFE

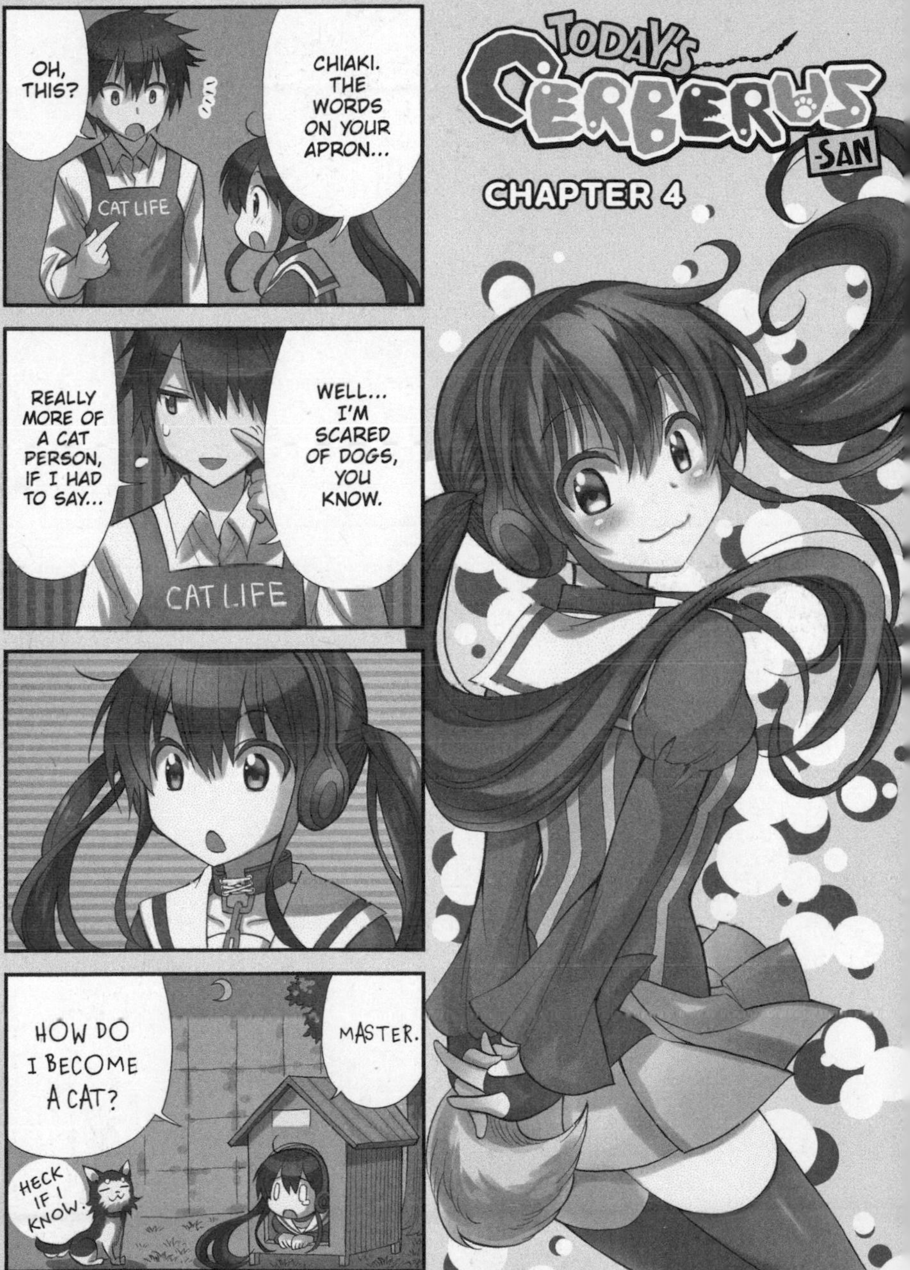
TODAY'S CERBERUS -SAN
CHAPTER 4
CHIAKI. THE WORDS ON YOUR APRON...
OH, THIS?
CAT LIFE
WELL... I'M SCARED OF DOGS, YOU KNOW.
REALLY MORE OF A CAT PERSON, IF I HAD TO SAY...
CAT LIFE
MASTER.
HOW DO I BECOME A CAT?
HECK IF I KNOW.

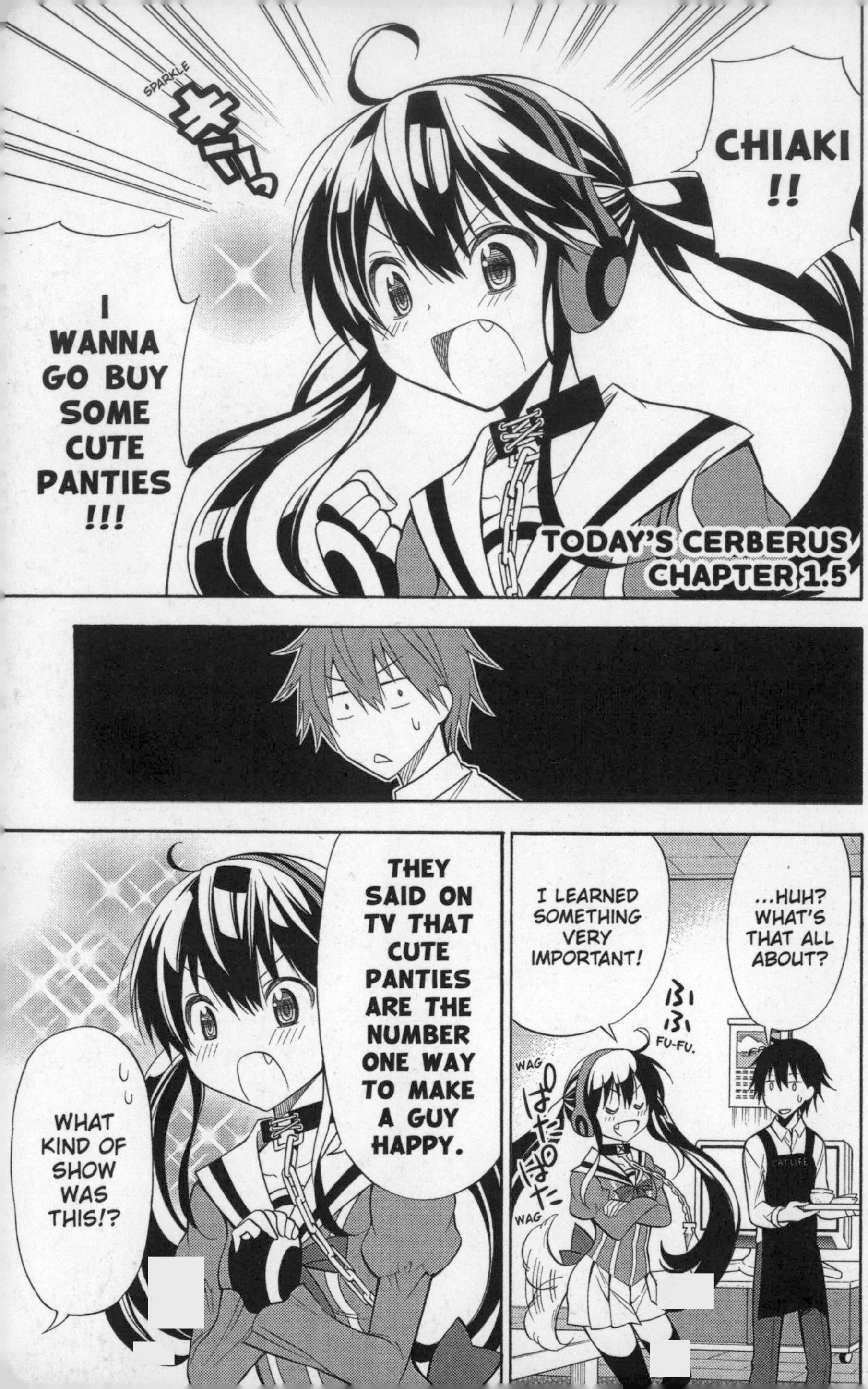
CHIAKI !!
SPARKLE
I WANNA GO BUY SOME CUTE PANTIES !!!
TODAY'S CERBERUS CHAPTER 1.5
...HUH? WHAT'S THAT ALL ABOUT?
I LEARNED SOMETHING VERY IMPORTANT!
ふふ
FU-FU.
WAG
WAG
THEY SAID ON TV THAT CUTE PANTIES ARE THE NUMBER ONE WAY TO MAKE A GUY HAPPY.
WHAT KIND OF SHOW WAS THIS!?

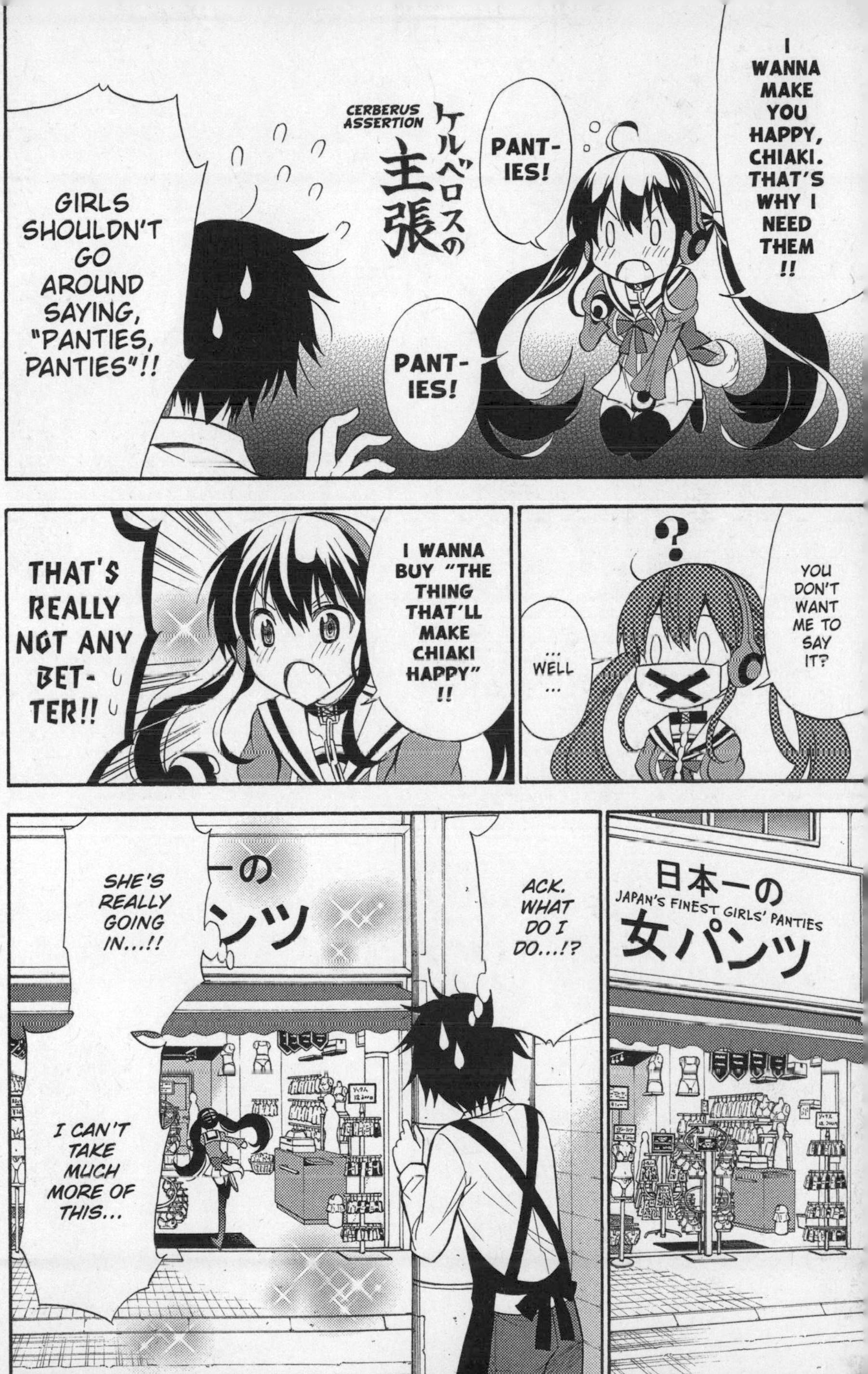
I WANNA MAKE YOU HAPPY, CHIAKI. THAT'S WHY I NEED THEM!!
PANTIES!
ケルベロスの主張
CERBERUS ASSERTION
PANTIES!
GIRLS SHOULDN'T GO AROUND SAYING, "PANTIES, PANTIES"!!
YOU DON'T WANT ME TO SAY IT?
...WELL...
I WANNA BUY "THE THING THAT'LL MAKE CHIAKI HAPPY"!!
THAT'S REALLY NOT ANY BETTER!!
日本一の女パンツ
JAPAN'S FINEST GIRLS' PANTIES
ACK. WHAT DO I DO...!?
SHE'S REALLY GOING IN...!!
I CAN'T TAKE MUCH MORE OF THIS...

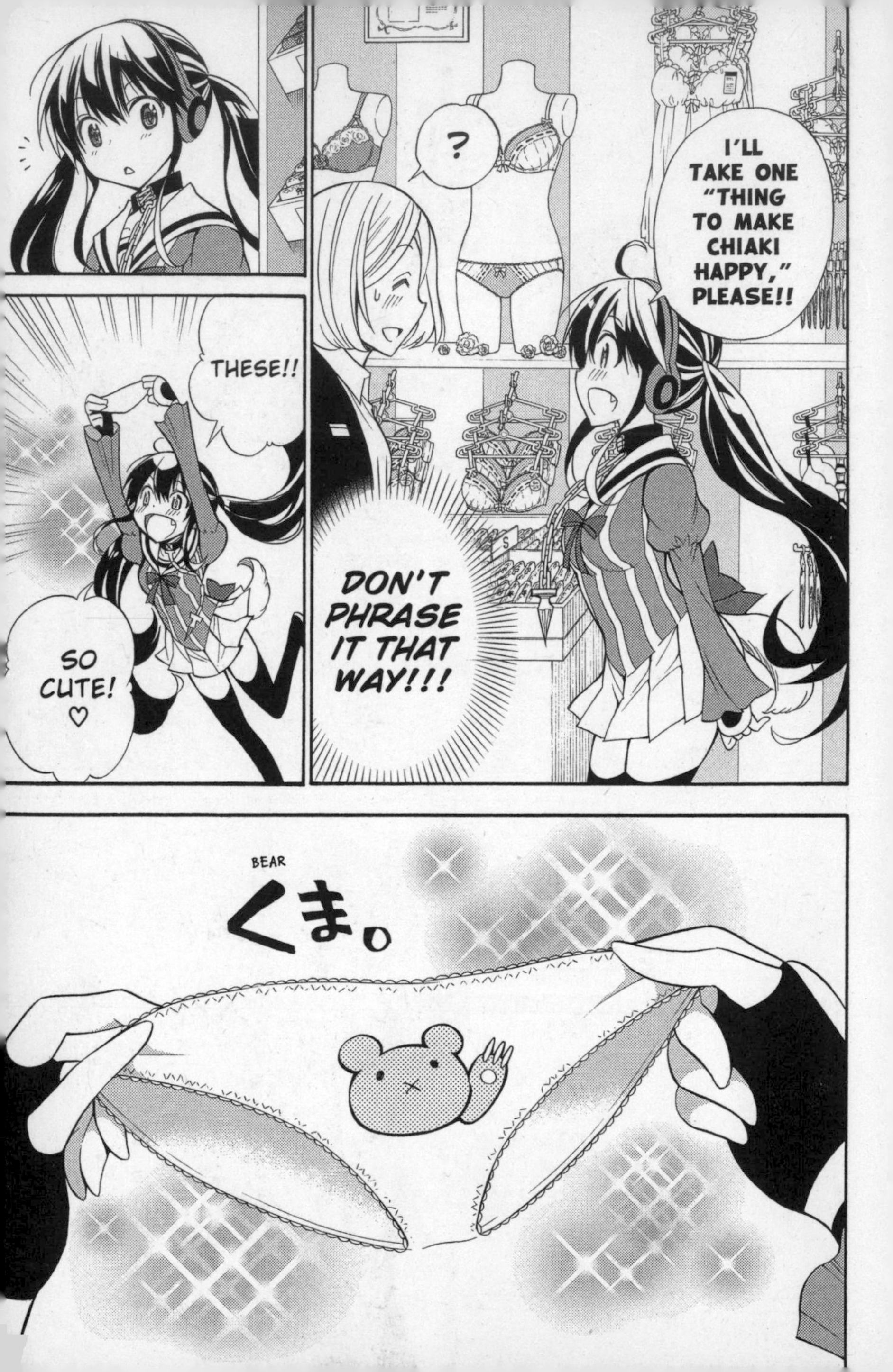
I'LL TAKE ONE "THING TO MAKE CHIAKI HAPPY," PLEASE!!
?
DON'T PHRASE IT THAT WAY!!!
THESE!!
SO CUTE! ♡
BEAR
くま。

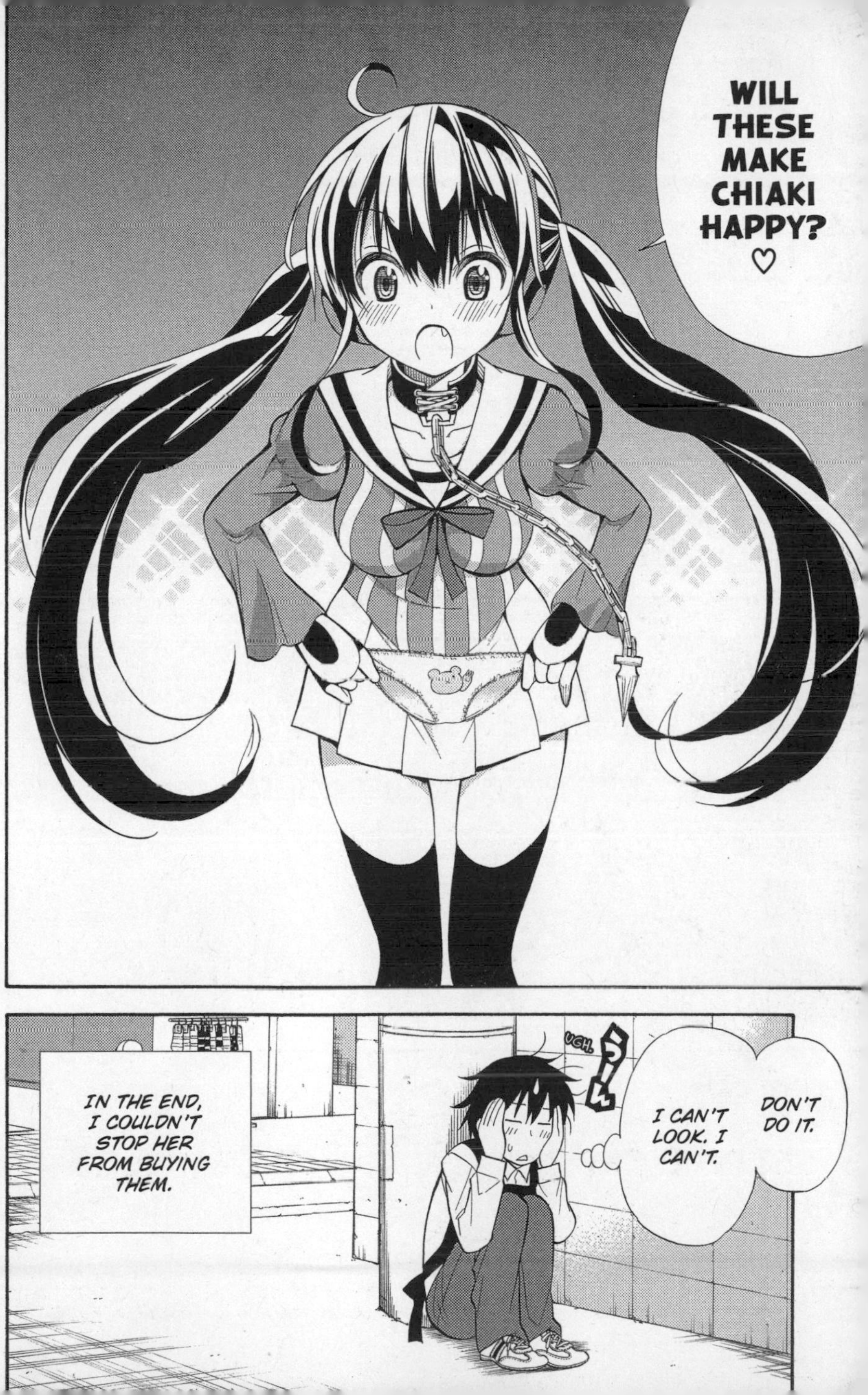
WILL THESE MAKE CHIAKI HAPPY? ♡
UCH.
I CAN'T LOOK. I CAN'T. DON'T DO IT.
IN THE END, I COULDN'T STOP HER FROM BUYING THEM.

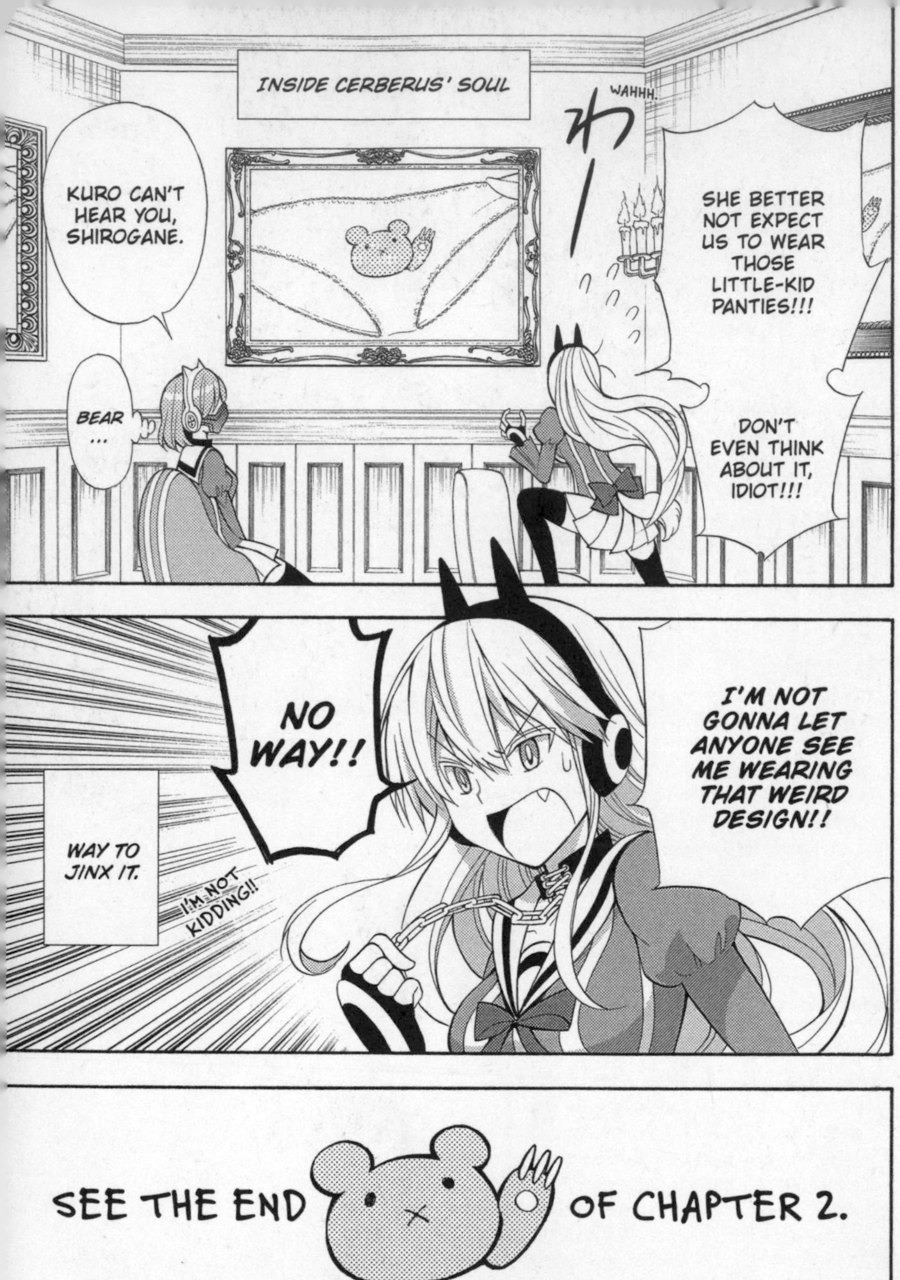
INSIDE CERBERUS' SOUL
WAHHH.
SHE BETTER NOT EXPECT US TO WEAR THOSE LITTLE-KID PANTIES!!!
DON'T EVEN THINK ABOUT IT, IDIOT!!!
KURO CAN'T HEAR YOU, SHIROGANE.
BEAR ...
I'M NOT GONNA LET ANYONE SEE ME WEARING THAT WEIRD DESIGN!!
NO WAY!!
I'M NOT KIDDING!!
WAY TO JINX IT.
SEE THE END OF CHAPTER 2.

STAFF-> MORI · GARAKUTA IMAYAMA · FUJIKO DOSEI · YUU JUNA · WATARINI FUNE

NOTES

COMMON HONORIFICS

no honorific: Indicates familiarity or closeness; if used without permission or reason, addressing someone in this manner would constitute an insult.

-san: The Japanese equivalent of Mr./Mrs./Miss. If a situation calls for politeness, this is the fail-safe honorific.

-kun: Used most often when referring to boys, this indicates affection or familiarity. Occasionally used by older men among their peers, but it may also be used by anyone referring to a person of lower standing.

-chan: An affectionate honorific indicating familiarity used mostly in reference to girls; also used in reference to cute persons or animals of either gender.

-sensei: A respectful term for teachers, artists, or high-level professionals.

PAGE 20

Taizo is a parody of "Daiso," which is one of Japan's prominent one-hundred yen shops (basically like a dollar store in the United States).

PAGE 22

In Greek mythology, Orthros is a two-headed, serpent-tailed monster dog and kin to Cerberus. As the myths go, he fathered the Sphinx and the Nemean Lion.

PAGE 63

Chiaki's comment is more on the nose than he apparently realizes, because his last name (Mikado) actually means "imperial gate." Cerberus couldn't have picked a more fitting person to guard!

PAGE 89

Chiaki's three-course egg meal is a what's what of Japanese egg dishes. First, we have his traditional Japanese omelet. Apart from the oval shape, ketchup topping, and tendency to be filled with rice, its consistency isn't that different from that of omelets in the West. Then, there's the egg custard (*chanwanmushi* in Japanese), which is steamed in a teacup and usually filled with other ingredients like mushrooms and shrimp. Finally, there's the rolled egg omelet with dashi broth (*dashi maki tamago*). Unlike the ones often served as sushi, this one tends to be not sweet, and the broth softens the texture of the egg.

TODAY'S CERBERUS

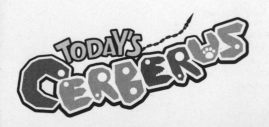

TODAY'S CERBERUS ❶

Ato Sakurai

Translation: Caleb Cook • **Lettering: Bianca Pistillo**

TODAY'S KERBEROS Vol. 1 ©2014 Ato Sakurai/SQUARE ENIX CO., LTD. First published in Japan in 2014 by SQUARE ENIX CO., LTD. English translation rights arranged with SQUARE ENIX CO., LTD. and Yen Press, LLC through Tuttle-Mori Agency, Inc.

English Translation ©2015 by SQUARE ENIX CO., LTD.

Yen Press
1290 Avenue of the Americas
New York, NY 10104

Visit us at yenpress.com
facebook.com/yenpress
twitter.com/yenpress
yenpress.tumblr.com
instagram.com/yenpress

First Yen Press Print Edition: October 2015

Yen Press is an imprint of Yen Press, LLC.
The Yen Press name and logo are trademarks of Yen Press, LLC.

Library of Congress Control Number: 2016946072

ISBNs: 978-0-316-54545-7 (paperback)
       978-0-316-30801-4 (ebook)
       978-0-316-30802-1 (app)

10 9 8 7 6 5 4 3 2 1

BVG

Printed in the United States of America

D0200191